Beyond Binary Histories

Beyond Binary Histories

Re-imagining Eurasia to c. 1830

Victor Lieberman, Editor

Ann Arbor

The University of Michigan Press

First published by the University of Michigan Press 1999

Published in the United States of America by
The University of Michigan Press
Manufactured in the United States of America
♾ Printed on acid-free paper

2002 2001 2000 1999 4 3 2 1

A CIP catalog record for this book is available from the British Library.

Essays reprinted from *Modern Asian Studies,* 31, 3 (1997), pp. 449–762.

Library of Congress Cataloging-in-Publication Data

Beyond binary histories : re-imagining Eurasia to c. 1830 / Victor Lieberman, editor.
p. cm.
All but one were papers originally presented at a workshop entitled The Eurasian context of the early modern history of mainland South East Asia, 1400–1800, held June 22–24, 1995, University of London.
Includes bibliographical references (p.) and index.
Contents : Transcending East-West dichotomies : state and culture formation in six ostensibly disparate areas / Victor Lieberman — Was early modern Japan culturally integrated? / Mary Elizabeth Berry — The birth of Europe as a Eurasian phenomenon / R.I. Moore — State building in early modern Europe : the case of France / James B. Collins — Merciful father, impersonal state : Russian autocracy in comparative perspective / Valerie Kivelson — Literati culture and integration in Dai Viet, c.1430–c.1840 / John K. Whitmore — Southeast Asia "inside out," 1300–1800 / David K. Wyatt — Civilization on loan : the making of an upstart polity : Mataram and its successors, 1600–1830 / Peter Carey — Connected histories : notes towards a reconfiguration of early modern Eurasia / Sanjay Subrahmanyam.
ISBN 0-472-08633-2 (alk. paper)
1. Asia, Southeastern—History Congresses. 2. Eurasia—History Congresses. I. Lieberman, Victor B., 1945– .
DS526.3.B49 1999
959—dc21

99-29479
CIP

Acknowledgements

The contribution to this volume by Professor James B. Collins was specially commissioned. Initial drafts of the other essays were first presented at a workshop on "The Eurasian Context of the Early Modern History of Mainland South East Asia, 1400–1800," which was held at the School of Oriental and African Studies (SOAS) of the University of London, June 22–24, 1995. That gathering was organized thanks to the imagination and enthusiasm of Professor Ian Brown, then Director of the Centre of South East Asian Studies at SOAS, and was funded with grants from SOAS, *Modern Asian Studies* and Cambridge University Press, and the British Academy.

Publication of the present volume has been aided by grants from three University of Michigan bodies: the Department of History, the Center for South and Southeast Asian Studies, and especially the Office of the Vice President for Research. I am grateful as well to Ms. Ingrid Erickson, Assistant Editor at the University of Michigan Press, for her patient support and to Professor Marvin Becker, adviser to the Michigan series Studies in Medieval and Early Modern Civilization, for his friendship and intellectual generosity.

Contents

Introduction: Eurasian Variants

VICTOR LIEBERMAN

This collection of essays grew out of a workshop at the School of Oriental and African Studies of the University of London that sought to rethink both the relation of Southeast Asia to Eurasia and the history of Eurasia itself during much of the second millennium.

Until recently historians and anthropologists of Southeast Asia tended to see indigenous civilization as intensely conservative, if not static. They recognized, of course, that before 1800 India, China, and Europe had impinged on the region continuously. Indeed, such inputs were critical to whatever dynamism Southeast Asian high culture possessed. But such influences were decidedly limited, either because Indian and Chinese stimuli had waned after initial contact or because the massive body of Southeast Asian civilization had absorbed and neutralized alien features. Underneath superficial changes in form and nomenclature, the essential rhythms of indigenous life remained unchanged. In the famous dictum of B. Schrieke, "the Java of around 1700 A.D. was in reality the same as the Java of around 700 A.D."[1] Southeast Asian societies thus existed in space but not in time. By implication, an existential chasm separated indigenous mentalities from those of Europe. In the hands of Clifford Geertz and other devotees of self-sufficient cultural worlds, Southeast Asian actors, obsessed with ritual but indifferent to problems of hard economic power, were fundamentally unlike Western historical figures.[2]

In the last few years an "early modern" school has begun to challenge these assumptions. Implicitly or explicitly, historians have begun to ask why a region so obviously responsive to global economic currents in their own day would have remained inert in earlier eras. The new historiography has in fact marshalled a substantial amount of evidence to argue that between

1. B. Schrieke, *Indonesian Sociological Studies*, 2 vols. (The Hague, 1955, 1957), 2: 100. For comparable emphases, see G. E. Harvey, *A History of Burma* (London, rpt. 1967), 249; Soemarsaid Moertono, *State and Statecraft in Old Java* (Ithaca, 1981); Michael Aung-Thwin, "The 'Classical' in Southeast Asia: The Present in the Past," *Journal of Southeast Asian Studies* 26 (1995): 75–91.

2. Clifford Geertz, *Negara: The Theatre State in Nineteenth-Century Bali* (Princeton, 1980), and note 1.

c. 1450 and 1670 societies across Southeast Asia experienced a commercial and urban vigor, a trend towards political absolutism, and an emphasis on orthodox, textual religions that in combination gave birth to an "Age of Commerce," also termed the "early modern period." Stimuli still derived primarily from outside the region, in the form of intensifying Indian Ocean and Chinese commercial demand and European firearms, but in this paradigm for the first time, local structures of all sorts were continuously and profoundly transformed by global pressures.[3]

Thus Orientalist encapsulation has been breached, and this breach bespeaks a willingness to engage with historians from other parts of the world. Yet this engagement remains tentative, its terms undefined. The phrase *early modern* has been borrowed openly and self-consciously from European usage and, as such, implies a degree of comparability to Europe.[4] But what defines that comparability? Is it simply a transitional concept, a chronological filler, in the sense that something important seems to have happened in both Europe and Southeast Asia c. 1450–1670, and therefore in each case deserves a separate periodization? But then why use the common term *early modern,* with the implication not only that the substance of pre-1670 change in both Southeast Asia and Europe was similar, but also that the trajectories of both regions were somehow comparable, that both were en route to an unspecified "modernity"? Some historians, it is true, have suggested that commercial growth, urbanization, and "absolutist states" in Southeast Asia recall developments in Europe itself between c. 1450 and 1670. Yet these same writers immediately assert that Southeast Asian political and urban structures diverged in basic respects from those of Europe and that Southeast Asia was consistently hostile to European-style capitalism. They claim furthermore that whatever limited progress the region had made towards a more competitive position in world trade aborted in the late seventeenth century, and that thereafter European and Southeast Asian political trajectories, already idiosyncratic, diverged ever more sharply.[5]

3. For the interrelated terms *early modern* and *Age of Commerce,* see Anthony Reid, *Southeast Asia in the Age of Commerce,* 1450–1680, 2 vols. (New Haven, 1988, 1993); and the collection of essays in idem, ed., *Southeast Asia in the Early Modern Era* (Ithaca, 1993). Cf. the mix of stimuli and the later chronological focus in Victor Lieberman, "Local Integration and Eurasian Analogies: Structuring Southeast Asian History, c. 1350-c. 1830," *Modern Asian Studies* 27 (1993): 475–572; idem, "Wallerstein's System and the International Context of Eary Modern Southeast Asian History, " *Journal of Asian History* 24 (1990): 70–90.

4. See note 3, esp. Reid, "Introduction: A Time and a Place," in *Southeast Asia in the Early Modern Era,* 6–11; idem, *Age of Commerce,* 1: 235.

5. Reid, "Introduction: A Time and a Place"; idem, "The Structure of Cities in Southeast Asia: Fifteenth to Seventeenth Centuries," *Journal of Southeast Asian Studies* 11 (1980): 225–50; idem, *Age of Commerce,* 2: 267–330; Jeyamalar Kathirithamby-Wells, "Restraints on the Development of Merchant Capitalism in Southeast Asia before c. 1800," in Reid, *Southeast Asia in the Early Modern Era,* 123–48.

In sum, both because comparability has been framed in terms of specific European norms, and because all of Southeast Asia after c. 1670 is said suddenly to have entered an era of impoverishment and isolation, the ways in which Southeast Asia and Europe may have fit some overarching "early modern" transition remain deeply problematic.

Not surprisingly, trends in Southeast Asian studies have paralleled broader Eurasian historiography. Schrieke's vision of Asian immobility found echoes until recently in Chinese, Japanese, and South Asian historiography, which provided empirical justification for the "European exceptionalist" view of world history. Or more accurately, European assumptions of East-West incomparability set the research agenda for Asianists. As enunciated by generations of scholars whose work constituted a central pillar of Western intellectual tradition—and as reproduced unapologetically only last year by the noted economic historian David S. Landes—"European exceptionalism" makes three broad, surprisingly durable claims: *(a)* The institutionalized diffusion of political authority in the West contrasted with the systemic concentration of political authority in Asia. *(b)* Diffuse power in turn permitted a higher degree of market autonomy and economic innovation in Europe than in Asia. *(c)* In both Europe and Asia political and economic structures were embedded in holistic, self-replicating cultures. The disparity between European dynamism and Asian stasis that culminated in the Industrial Revolution therefore also appeared in earlier periods, starting as early as the European Middle Ages.[6]

Even more vigorously than in Southeast Asian studies, however, scholars have begun to question these assumptions of incomparability. Here too revisionism draws strength from an unstated, perhaps unconscious conviction that the growing contemporary equivalence and interdependence be-

6. David S. Landes, *The Wealth and Poverty of Nations* (New York, 1998). The warm reception given to Landes' book, and to the yet more extravagantly Eurocentric history "of the world" by David Fromkin, *The Way of the World* (New York, 1999), leaves little doubt that European exceptionalism remains a dominant trope among professional historians, not to mention the educated public. On the Orientalist bases of nineteenth–twentieth century global historiography, see Edward Said, *Orientalism* (New York, 1978): Perry Anderson, *Lineages of the Absolutist State* (London, 1974), 435–549; Victor Lieberman, "Transcending East-West Dichotomies," in this volume; Andre Gunder Frank, *ReOrient: Global Economy in the Asian Age* (Berkeley, 1998), ch. 1; Linda Darling, "Rethinking Europe and the Islamic World in the Age of Exploration," *Journal of Early Modern History* 2 (1998): 221–46; Paul Cohen, *Discovering History in China* (New York, 1984); Sanjay Subrahmanyam, "Hearing Voices: Vignettes of Early Modernity in South Asia, 1400–1700," *Daedalus* 127, no. 3 (1998): 75–104.

7. See, e.g., *Daedalus* 127, no. 3 (1998) entitled "Early Modernities"; Sanjay Subrahmanyam, ed., *Merchants, Markets and the State in Early Modern India* (Delhi, 1990); Conrad Totman, *Early Modern Japan* (Berkeley, 1993); James McClain, John Merriman, and Ugawa Kaoru, eds., *Edo and Paris: Urban Life and the State in the Early Modern Era* (Ithaca, 1994); and the new *Journal of Early Modern History*.

tween world regions demand historical antecedents. And here too "early modern" often has been invoked as a periodizing rubric.[7] Two revisionist approaches dominate. First, historians have summoned a wealth of empirical evidence from Japan and China to argue that economic change in those countries between c. 1600 and 1800 approached European standards, and that Wesern Europe's solitary departure down the road of industrialization in the early nineteenth century was actually rather fortuitous. E. L. Jones and John Powelson claimed that in Tokugawa Japan the emergence of competitive markets, hence economic innovation, reflected an institutionalized diffusion of power not very different from that of Europe.[8] Yet more recently, historians of China R. Bin Wong and Kenneth Pomeranz have argued that in terms of Smithian growth, proto-industrialization, and living standards, China was not inferior to key sectors of Western Europe until the late 1700s. Thereafter Western Europe's success reflected, above all, its unique access to domestic coal and to New World resources, which together encouraged a peculiar core-periphery specialization favorable to industrial innovation. In other words, contingency and structural opportunity, not cultural advantage or government policy, underlay Europe's surprisingly tardy ascent.[9] In the most polemical revisionist work, which seeks to replace Eurocentrism with an unabashed Sinocentrism, Andre Gunder Frank claims that until the late eighteenth century China's superior productivity ensured that China was the center of a world economy in which Europe was merely a "marginal player."[10]

8. E. L. Jones, *Growth Recurring* (Oxford, 1988), esp. ch. 9; John Powelson, *Centuries of Economic Endeavor* (Ann Arbor, 1994), chs. 1–6. See too sources on Tokugawa economic dynamism in Lieberman, "Transcending," nn. 2, 4, 12.

9. R. Bin Wong, *China Transformed* (Ithaca, 1997); William Laveley and R. Bin Wong, "Revising the Malthusian Narrative: The Comparative Study of Population Dynamics in Late Imperial China," *Journal of Asian Studies* 57 (1998): 714–48; Kenneth Pomeranz, "Re-thinking 18th Century China: A High Standard of Living and Its Implications" (manuscript). On Ming-Qing economic history, see too sources in Lieberman, "Transcending," nn. 3, 4.

10. Frank, *ReOrient*, esp. 75, 100–101, 126–30, 179–97, 270–71. One may well ask how Europe, a region that conducted an extensive internal commerce and that in 1750 dominated the trade of West Africa, the New World, much of coastal India, and maritime Southeast Asia, could have been marginal to the world economy. Frank equates bullion surplus with productive efficiency, whereas many argue that bullion was a commodity whose movement, like that of other commodities, reflected arbitrage profits. By Frank's logic, late eighteenth-century Russia, which ran a consistent surplus with Western Europe, was more efficient than Western Europe, when in fact its agricultural yields and industrial methods were noncompetitive. Frank may err too in emphasizing New World capital accumulation as the key to European industrialization, because in many of the chief Eurasian economies in the sixteenth–eighteenth centuries capital was not the scarce factor. Far more important in China, for example, were land shortages. For revisionist views of European/South Asian economic history, see Subrahmanyam, ed., *Merchants, Markets;* Prasannan Parthasarathi, "Rethinking Wages and Competitiveness in the Eighteenth Century: Britain and South India," *Past and Present* 158 (1998): 79–109.

A second challenge to European exceptionalism examines not economic, but political structures. "Feudalism" was the favored early candidate for those seeking European political institutions in Asia, but outside Japan, this quest stalled when forced to choose between the Scylla of specific incomparability and the Charybdis of ever more elastic, ultimately meaningless redefinition.[11] The search for specific analogues has now shifted to "civil society": Did Asia, like Europe, have a public sphere, located between the official and the private sphere, which was concerned with defining the common good and with issues of policy? Scholars of India and Japan, and less consistently China, have produced qualified support for the notion that expanded recruitment of quasi-official local elites and the growth of academies and urban communications prior to c. 1850 did in fact swell the cohort of men who assumed a public role and, at times, a public voice of dissent, although these arrangements rarely, if ever, enjoyed the legal sanction or political influence of West European civil society.[12] Yet more tentatively, a handful of scholars have begun to compare Asian structures of political collectivity with protonationalist identities in Europe between the seventeenth and early nineteenth centuries.[13]

Precisely because they promise to burst open a constrictive, essentializing paradigm that has dominated comparative historiography for the better part of two centuries, these departures are enormously exciting. But at the same time, not unlike changes in Southeast Asian research, they raise problems stemming in part from their compensatory origins. The indices of comparison—proto-industrial capacity, feudalism, civil society, nationalism—are explicitly Eurocentric and implicitly presentist, that is to say, they assess the potential of various premodern Asian societies to evolve in the direction of the twentieth-century West. To paraphrase Benedict Anderson, they seek to stretch the short, tight skin of Europe over the gigantic body of Asia.[14] In fact, the more subtle and dexterous of these inquiries have proven extremely valuable. But to the degree that they insist on specific European models, such projects face a characteristic tension: they are tempted either to distort Asian institutions to fit European criteria, or to dilute those criteria to the point where genuine comparative insight is lost. This is obvious as

11. Lieberman, "Transcending," n. 2.

12. See Lieberman, "Transcending," n. 5, and more recent essays by Shmuel Eisenstadt and Wolfgang Schluchter, Mary Elizabeth Berry, and Frederic Wakeman, Jr., in *Daedalus* 127, no. 3 (1998), which are rather more supportive of the existence of Asian public spheres.

13. See, e.g., essays by Sheldon Pollock, David Howell, Alexander Woodside, and Bernhard Giesen in *Daedalus* 127, no. 3 (1998); Lieberman, "Local Integration," 521–40; idem, "Ethnic Politics in Eighteenth-Century Burma," *Modern Asian Studies* 12 (1978): 455–82.

14. Benedict Anderson, *Imagined Communities* (rev. ed., London, 1991), 86, referring to the attempt by European dynasts to adapt nationalism to hold together polyglot domains.

regards "feudalism," but I believe it is also true of many "civil society" and "nationalism" inquiries. In the case of Southeast Asia, for example, precolonial evidence of European-style "civil society" is so meager as to torture the concept beyond recognition. Moreover, in so far as we privilege one yardstick (e.g., the potential for industrialization) as an adequate summation of regional differences, we both oversimplify relationships and increase the risk of sterile regional advocacy (*vide* Frank). If we are to reconfigure Eurasia, we must employ generous, abstract criteria that speak without apology to non-European experience and allow us to approach Western Europe as a variation on more general themes. We also must consider a variety of measures in the expectation that pre-1830 Eurasian societies that appear similar in some respects may have diverged significantly in others.

Finally, comparative history must go hand in hand with connective history. The former may be defined as a search for recognizable patterns according to unified criteria without particular regard for chronology, whereas the latter seeks to establish linkages among contemporary societies without necessarily examining internal forms.[15] In fact, there is a growing literature on climatic, biological, and mercantile linkages between c. 1200 and 1800.[16] But with a few exceptions, among whom Jack Goldstone is perhaps most prominent, scholars have been reluctant to use such linkages to explain domestic developments in distant sectors of Eurasia.[17]

By bringing together historians of Southeast Asia and other widely separated regions, the London conference sought to address these problems. Accordingly, the present collection considers four broad sets of questions. First, within each Eurasian region what political, cultural, or socioeconomic transformations, broadly conceived, distinguished all or part of the period c. 1200 to 1830 from antecedent and succeeding eras? In interpreting these changes, how shall we synthesize changes in structure with the psychological meaning such changes may have had for local actors? Second, assuming that we can find appropriately expansive measures, to what extent were transformations in widely separated Eurasian areas truly comparable? Third, in each region what were the principal factors stimulating change and governing its direction? In particular, how did nominally endogenous factors—

15. Cf. Karen Wigen, "Bringing the World Back In: Meditations on the Space-Time of Japanese Early Modernity," paper presented for a SSRC workshop on "What's 'Early Modern' and What's 'Japanese' about 'Early Modern Japan'?", Dec. 1995.

16. See Lieberman, "Transcending," nn. 17–21 and passim.

17. Goldstone, *Revolution and Rebellion in the Early Modern World* (Berkeley, 1991). See too his "The Problem of the 'Early Modern' World," *Journal of the Economic and Social History of the Orient* 41 (1998): 249–84. For a more chronologically limited inquiry testing in Asia the European notion of a seventeenth-century crisis, see *Modern Asian Studies* 24, no. 4 (1990).

institutional, demographic, agricultural—intersect with such exogenous forces as foreign trade and military threats? Fourth, in interpreting synchronized change across Eurasia, what linkages shall we emphasize? That is, in seeking to explain why culturally and physically distant areas experienced comparable changes at roughly the same time, how much weight should we attach to climate, coordinated bullion flows, the dissemination of firearms and New World crops, global epidemics, nomad pressures—and to sheer coincidence? And which elements were most critical in which contexts?

To be sure, parallel inquiries by scholars with different interests and methodologies are likely to produce very imperfect comparisons in the best of circumstances; and here the problem is aggravated by the exceedingly ambitious questions, the vast time span, the large number of potential variables often supported by a weak evidential base. Nor are a handful of case studies that elide vast cultural zones—China, most obviously—going to produce results applicable to all of Eurasia. Nonetheless, we were convinced that our pooled expertise could yield general insights, provided that we operated in a broadly similar framework and considered the same set of initial hypotheses.

To that end, the opening essay "Transcending East-West Dichotomies: State and Culture Formation in Six Ostensibly Disparate Areas" presents a schema of early modern Eurasian history that the other contributors were invited to test and to critique. I attempt in this essay, first, to develop more neutral, less place-specific criteria that allow us to perceive hitherto ignored Eurasian commonalities, and second, to explain those commonalities. Specifically, the essay describes sustained, broadly synchronized movements between c. 1400 and 1830 towards territorial consolidation, administrative centralization, cultural/ethnic integration, and commercial intensification in six regions (modern-day Burma, Thailand, Vietnam, France, Tsarist Russia, and Japan) scattered across the Eurasian rimlands. In economics and politics, and with certain peculiar variations also in the cultural realm, vertical, self-sufficient local networks eroded in favor of denser national/imperial networks. Of necessity, these networks were also more complex and horizontally variegated. In each of the six regions, integrative trends accelerated markedly during the late fifteenth and sixteenth centuries and again in the late eighteenth and early nineteenth centuries. In each region the impetus to integration derived from a fluid combination of endogenous factors (local population growth, agricultural experimentation, domestic commercial intensification, administrative refinement) and of external factors (the stuff of connective history), among which climatic-cum-demographic rhythms, firearms, and maritime trade seem to have exercised a hegemonic coordinating influence.

I do not pretend that these integrative trends were the only significant constituents of global early modernity; I virtually ignore intellectual, aesthetic, and social comparisons. I am also at pains to emphasize variations in the substance and form of integration both across Eurasia and within its main subsectors. All of Southeast Asia, for example, experienced similar commercial and technological pressures, but whereas in the mainland (present-day Burma, Thailand, Laos, Cambodia, and Vietnam) these pressures encouraged sustained political and cultural integration, in the island world (present-day Malaysia and Indonesia) different geography and novel European inputs after c. 1670 produced quite different results. Thus the notion of a seventeenth-century watershed has qualified validity for the island world but not for the mainland. Even among the six examples of sustained integration, we find gaping differences in the levels of administrative centralization, commercial intensification, post-1300 discontinuity, and so forth. However, I do claim that: *(a)* measured in terms of both elite options and popular self-images, the integrative processes on which I focus were among the most influential constituents of global early modernity; *(b)* they provide a comparative entree into ancillary phenomena not discussed directly; *(c)* according to these integrative criteria, the six countries in question can be organized into continua that cut across any simple European-Asian divide. For example, in terms of post-1300 disruptions, access to external models, and cultural standardization within each kingdom, Vietnam and France had substantially more in common than did Vietnam and her immediate neighbor Siam. An emphasis on multiple axes of comparisons weakens the presentist preoccupation with long-term industrial potential in favor of patterns that were more critical to earlier generations themselves. This schema is obviously compatible with, and in some sense dependent upon, the European metanarrative of the rise of the nation state. But it differs from Eurocentric models (including Wallersteinian schemas) because it regards Western Europe, represented in this case by France, as one of many equivalent, yet peculiar points along very broad continua.

The second essay, by Mary Elizabeth Berry, is both an elegant critique of certain assumptions of the introductory essay—for which reason it seems best to place it immediately after that essay—and an exploration of cultural growth in Tokugawa Japan. Professor Berry cautions against assuming that congruence in outward cultural forms indicated subjective solidarity. On the one hand, she warns that even full conformity in, say, language or religious ritual did not necessarily indicate a sense of shared culture, and she urges us to balance attention to external behavior with a search for evidence of mental habits and orientations. On the other hand, she points out that in Tokugawa Japan (and no doubt elsewhere) standardization of certain practices was accompanied by a countervailing, equally remorseless movement toward more specialized economic, social, and cultural roles that could encourage specialization in self-definition and outlook. In other words, integration and fragmentation were two sides of the same coin, and to privilege one side is arbitrary. By way of illustration, she shows how numerous, highly disparate elements in Tokugawa Japan were accommodated in increasingly comprehensive, but not necessarily more psychologically inclusive systems of knowledge, as represented in maps, travel guides, urban directories, and other "public information" materials. Without rejecting the value of "early modern" periodization, Professor Berry cautions that the complexity of post-1400 culture prevents any simple contrast between medieval fracture and early modern cohesion. Conversely, lest we minimize the distance from the Tokugawa era to modernity, she reminds us of profound Meiji ruptures.

The next four essays also analyze the relation between pre- and post-1400 formations, and I hasten to note that their findings defy a simple East-West categorization. Using the criteria of integration proposed for other Eurasian rimlands, R. I. Moore examines northwest Europe, most particularly during the medieval era c. 1000 and 1400, in an effort to rethink that critical region's geographic and chronological affinities. Geographically he suggests that the transition from the Mediterranean-based civilization of late antiquity to that of medieval Latin Christendom paralleled the emergence of new civilizations farther east, also often in hitherto peripheral areas. And chronologically, within northwest Europe he sees very substantial continuity in sociopolitical dynamics as well as in basic structures from the eleventh to the eighteenth centuries. Thus, for example, early medieval church reform and allied departures in aristocratic family organization created systems of social differentiation and surplus extraction that endured in their essentials through the late 1700s. A principal difference between pre-1400 and post-1400 acculturation was the growing attention to national ethnicity and language, but this, too, Professor Moore views as an intensification of late medieval patterns, and he reminds us that alongside such departures persisted an extraordinarily vital trans-European high culture with roots deep in the eleventh century. Likewise he calls attention to medieval precedents for post-1500 military and technocratic innovation. At least in the political realm, he suggests that such continuities (which appear no less pronounced than in Japan) owed something to Western Europe's immunity from nomad invasion. Thus Professor Moore implicitly joins the critique of the "Asian stasis/European dynamism" dichotomy by modifying less the first than the second half of the formula.

In his analysis of French state building, James B. Collins supports Professor Moore's emphasis on the medieval origins of French institutions and the evolutionary nature of subsequent change. Yet at the same time Professor Collins argues that the period c. 1500–1650 witnessed a number of intellectual and organizational departures that in combination inaugurated a more or less distinct early modern phase. Territories that had been regarded as the collective possession of the royal family were transformed into the king's personal holding at the same time, paradoxically, as the state as an institution become more clearly distinguished from the individual ruler. An earlier emphasis on the king's judicial role shifted to his legislative prerogative, which now became a principal attribute of sovereignty. Fiscal, legal, and military institutions became more centralized, while the state's growing activism increased elite determination to influence lawmaking, especially as it affected property. In the 1600s and 1700s the central apparatus became yet more interventionist and routinized. Hand in hand with the growth of the state apparatus went an intensification of national sentiment, nourished by a sense of conflict and alterity, a sentiment that Professor Collins shows was entrenched by the fifteenth century and that drew strength from the subsequent dissemination of Parisian culture. In short, early modern France boasted highly distinctive features—extraordinarily stable institutions, a concept of legitimacy that depended in part on the consent of the governed, a recurrent concern with the definition of property, an incipient concept of nationality—but the post-1500 acceleration of political integration fits broader Eurasian themes.

The conservatism of French evolution c. 1000–1800 becomes clearer when set against Russian patterns. Valerie Kivelson argues that the shift in the political center of gravity of the Russian lands from Kiev, a principality that reached its peak in the eleventh and twelfth centuries, to Moscow, which began to expand in the fourteenth and fifteenth centuries, involved fundamental changes not only in geography but also in economic life, popular religion, and concepts of authority and administration. Between 1350 and 1700 the profoundly innovative Muscovite state grew in response to a variety of stimuli: early Mongol patronage, constant military challenges along an extensive frontier, the attraction of Mongol and then European military/administrative models, and a demand from both government and nongovernment elites for greater control over a constantly expanding territory and population. Professor Kivelson dissects the self-images and emotional underpinnings of the Muscovite state, exploring those tensions between autocratic ideology and practical limitation. In contrast to West European counterparts, Muscovy emphasized not aristocratic rights but universal service to a merciful royal guardian, partible rather than unigeniturial inheritance, an ideal of minute social regulation and of collective social responsibility. Yet in a wider sense, Professor Kivelson argues that Muscovite centralization resembled its early modern West European counterparts not only in chronology but also in substance: in both regions we find increasingly routinized administrative procedures, more efficient military forces, and more abstract notions of state authority alongside persistently patrimonial modes of political accommodation.

As discussed by John K. Whitmore, Vietnam's post-1400 situation exhibited features intermediate between those of France (and perhaps Japan), on the one hand, and of Russia, on the other. There was no physical or political rupture comparable to that of post-Kievan Russia. However, the Neo-Confucian revolution of the fifteenth century did inaugurate a profound cultural and institutional reorientation that would continue, amid fluctuating fortunes, for some four centuries. Dr. Whitmore analyzes a series of political crises between the mid-1400s and early 1800s, each of which the ruling dynasty resolved by invoking the expertise of Neo-Confucian literati in preference to more strictly patrimonial solutions or Mahayanist or Christian cultural orientations. The literati's long-term durability Dr. Whitmore attributes to three factors: the unique prestige of Chinese models; their enormous practical utility; and economic/commercial growth, which eroded self-sufficient aristocratic estates in favor of a smallholder regime sympathetic to central taxation and regulation. Far from being a literati monopoly, Neo-Confucian social norms and associated dichotomies of "civilized" vs. "barbarian" influenced the wider population and, in combination with military conflicts, contributed to a sense of Vietnamese ethnic distinctiveness. This in turn helped to maintain an overarching, if fragile, political unity in an extraordinarily unfavorable geographic environment.

With David K. Wyatt's essay "Southeast Asia 'Inside Out,' 1300–1800: A Perspective from the Interior," our focus turns from victors to losers and from impersonal measures of early modern change to more psychological indices. His analysis, which complements Professor Berry's in its attention to *mentalités* but which reaches somewhat different conclusions about the relation between fracture and synthesis, uses "interior" in a double sense: the subject matter is more internal, and the physical site is not lowland or coastal Southeast Asia, where the great exemplars of early modern mainland consolidation were rooted, but Chiang Mai in the uplands, an area cannibalized by Burma and Siam. Using a newly edited version of the *Chronicle of Chiang Mai,* Professor Wyatt compares attitudes in the fourteenth century with those in the eighteenth/nineteenth centuries in an effort to uncover "the reality of the Past *as it really was* to those who lived *in* that past." In general he finds a shift from a highly particularistic worldview, in which allegiance and ethnicity were intensely local, social structure relatively simple, and Buddhism still remarkably peripheral, to a view that accorded Buddhism unchallenged primacy, that embraced novel overarching ethnicities (Tai vs. Burmese and Vietnamese), and that naturalized Chiang Mai's subordination to the great king of Siam even as it valued Chiang Mai's growing authority within the northern hills. Accepting the utility of 1300/1400–1800 periodization, he suggests that these new attitudes were associated with wider commercial and political linkages and with large-scale warfare that increased the attraction of royal patrons; and he concludes that forces comparable to those which transformed Japan, Burma, and Siam also operated in the upland interstices of mainland Southeast Asia.

Whether viewing events from the center or periphery, in macrosocial or attitudinal terms, all previous essays considered examples of sustained integration. With Peter Carey's analysis of Java, we turn to a situation where these trends aborted. This is of considerable interest not only because Dr. Carey suggests that Java was representative of much of the Southeast Asian island world after c. 1670—and in some measure, I would add, a larger class of Eurasian societies—but also because as a counter-factual example, his study confirms the lesson from other essays that a stable political center was needed to ratify and to disseminate cultural norms. *Pace* Dutch historiography that emphasized localism and stasis, Dr. Carey shows with exquisite documentation that the south-central, eastern, and north coastal regions of Java engaged in a complex cultural exchange, a form of homogenization, that antedated Mataram's rise in the late sixteenth century and that continued so long as that great empire flourished, and even beyond. He argues too that pressures familiar elsewhere in Eurasia encouraged the rise at Mataram of "a Spartan polity dominated by the exigencies of war and military expansion." But between 1675 and 1830 unfavorable internal geography joined with growing Dutch and, more briefly British, military and political encroachments both to fragment Mataram and to circumscribe its successor states. Interestingly enough, the island after 1755 enjoyed a multifaceted agricultural and commercial florescence reminiscent of other Eurasian regions, but Dutch political restraints as well as Javanese fiscal and administrative weaknesses prevented indigenous rulers from tapping the surplus. It was only as a result of this political failure that south-central Java in the nineteenth century became culturally isolated, if not embalmed.

Finally Sanjay Subrahmanyam uses his wide-ranging knowledge of South Asia to enlarge our understanding of global early modernity—a category he, too, endorses—in two ways. First, he draws our attention to certain often ignored Eurasian transitions not restricted to Europe, including a new sense of the limits of the inhabited world, a heightening of long-term structural conflicts between settled societies and wanderers (in which category he proposes to include European explorers), new vocabularies of humanism and universalism, and complex changes in the ideology (the "political theology") of empire. More basically, elaborating the last point, he offers a novel contextual explanation for the dramatic expansion of Eurasian empires in the sixteenth century (and perhaps other eras). Although I emphasize the impact of Chinese models on Vietnam and of West European models on Russia, my take on the problem of synchronization assumes that cultural/religious boundaries were most permeable to material goods, and therefore I focus on those bullion flows, firearms, and so forth on which connective history usually rests. Dr. Subrahmanyan, however, marshalls a wide array of evidence from the Christian Mediterranean, the Ottoman, Safavid, and Mughal empires, and Southeast Asia to suggest that the 1500s saw a genuinely pan-cultural exchange of millenarian symbols, myths, and expectations of imminent transformation that helped to inspire imperial projects in superficially distinct areas. Here, then, is a view of connective history that invites a closer synthesis of material and ideological (even short-term ideological) factors, and a new definition of global circulation.

Where, then, does this collection leave us? Of the two overarching problematics—What happened in various areas of Eurasia c. 1400–1800? Why do we find a degree of synchronization between changes in these areas?—obviously the first question tends to dominate, because it is most congenial to established national/area studies disciplines. This approach in turn means that, forays by Dr. Subrahmanyam, Professor Moore, Professor Kivelson, me, and others notwithstanding, our picture of Eurasia is as much one of assembled pieces as of organic interaction. But the virtues of this approach are the reverse of its defects: only specialists can confidentally determine whether c. 1400 to 1800 constitutes a useful historical category in any given area, how variables interacted, why integration was sustained, anemic, or abortive. And only through the juxtaposition of comparable phenomena in different places can a reliable global periodization begin to emerge.

The category "early modern" can be problematic for three reasons. *(a)* The checklist of telltale traits usually varies from one account to another. *(b)* "Modern" often carries triumphalist, teleological messages, and "early modern" suffers from guilt by association. *(c)* Although "early modernity" implies "modernity in embryo," in fact the core feature of the twentieth century—massive use of fossil rather than organic fuels,[18] on which a host of economic, social, and intellectual developments necessarily relied—appeared but once in history. This was the result, many argue, of utterly unpredictable contingencies in late eighteenth- and early nineteenth-century Britain. In so far as that transformation was unique and fortuitous rather than the logical outcome of universal processes, Jack Goldstone claims that "global early modernity" is an oxymoron.[19] Despite such problems, most of these essays retain "early modern" as a shorthand description for a moderately distinct period in several regional histories, and by extension, Eurasian history. This period commonly began in the fifteenth century (Professor Moore, of course, offers an earlier starting date), terminated in the late eighteenth to mid-nineteenth centuries, and was defined by the following complex of linked traits: territorial consolidation, firearms-aided intensification of warfare; more expansive, routinized administrative systems; growing commercialization, which (especially from the eighteenth century) contributed to greater social mobility; wider popular literacy, along with a novel proliferation of vernacular texts; more vigorous dissemination of standard dialects and cultural symbols, and an unprecedented intersection between specifically local culture and state power. The fact that many of these features both appeared before 1800 in Western Europe, where early modern is an accepted convention, and anticipated, however feebly, twentieth-century global developments provides some justification for the term *early modern.*[20] Everywhere between c. 1450 and 1830 political and cultural integration reflected an intensifying circulation of goods and ideas—a circulation that was simultaneously local, regional, and global. At the same time, it is obvious that individual elements varied in form, scale, and duration; while in some places one or more traits were entirely absent (political integration in Java, for example). Nor is there any suggestion that any non-European area was on the verge of an autochthonous industrialization.

Naturally these broad claims introduce a host of queries: Why did the degree of continuity between pre-1300 and post-1400 civilizations differ sharply from one part of Eurasia to another? What factors most favored continuity: insulation from invasion, easy access to external models, heavy

18. "Organic" here refers to biomass from crops that could be converted into muscle power for humans and draft animals, and wood fuels.

19. Goldstone, "Problem of the 'Early Modern' World," esp. 261. Cf. Anthony Giddens, *The Consequences of Modernity* (Stanford, 1990); Maurizio Passerin d'Entreves and Seyla Benhabib, eds., *Habermas and the Unfinished Project of Modernity* (Cambridge, 1996).

20. Cf. the logic of Totman, *Early Modern Japan,* xxv–xxvi; McClain, Merriman, and Kaoru, *Edo and Paris,* xvi ff.; Shmuel N. Eisenstadt and Wolfgang Schluchter, "Introduction: Paths to Early Modernities—A Comparative View," *Daedalus* 127, no. 3 (1998): 1–18; Bjorn Wittrock, "Early Modernities: Varieties and Transitions," idem, 19–40.

demographic densities? After c.1400, why did the pace of change vary between regions, and in the same region, in different spheres of activity? What measures are most appropriate in making these judgments? If political integration ceased, did cultural and economic integration normally follow suit? What was the relation between oral and written vehicles of cultural diffusion? How shall we explain the exceptional nature of West European military innovation, and how in turn was that linked to economic dynamism and precocious bureaucratization?

But perhaps the most elusive problem concerns the impact of cultural integration on self-images and subjective identities. In one form or another, this issue recurs in most of the essays. I endorse Professor Berry's warning that to graph the cultural terrain accurately, to avoid an artificial flatness, we must focus stereoscopically on both standardization and specialization, on coherence and fracture. But bear in mind that such alterities did not cancel one another out—this was hardly a case of *plus ça change, plus c'est la même chose*—and that they made sense only in terms of an overarching developmental dynamic. That is to say, whereas in 1400 in each Eurasian region, numerous geographic and social systems enjoyed a relatively high degree of cultural self-sufficiency, by 1830 they had been subsumed within more complex, supralocal reference systems. At the same time, the growing complexity of intellectual, religious, and occupational activity engendered new cultural niches, especially in the cities, that also made sense only in terms of mutual reference and inescapable interdependence. Intentionally or no, new styles of dress, entertainment, religious ritual, and literary composition defined themselves vis-à-vis older modes and new contemporary modes, and thus became subspecialties. In this respect the realm of cultural production was analogous to administration and economics. As administrative systems grew larger and more penetrating, they engendered more elaborate hierarchies and more expert functions. As market linkages grew more extensive, they called forth more specialized niches for agricultural and handicraft producers, transporters, wholesalers, and retailers. Subjectively, specialized actors might regard one another with hostility, collegiality, ignorance, or utter indifference—but precisely to the degree that they were specialized, they depended on the same structures for their livelihood.

The question, then, is under what circumstances cultural or economic interdependence translated into a degree of self-conscious articulated solidarity. And here, I think, this collection suggests at least two prerequisites. First was a stable political center—in turn dependent on favorable geography and external security—that could coordinate patronage, validate religious and linguistic norms, and provide a focus of identity. Here the contrast between Java, on the one hand, and France, Muscovy, Burma, Siam, even Vietnam (with its purely nominal unity) is suggestive. Second, it required a sustained sense of alterity that was rooted in competition for scarce resources and that was able to reproduce itself through structured discourse and acknowledged symbols of group difference. To be sure, such identities constantly struggled with both more cosmopolitan and more local allegiances. Normally identification with the center was stronger among elites with direct access to capital culture and patronage than among peasants. Often, too, it was most pronounced on the military or agricultural frontier. But in the aftermath of repeated invasions or conflicts, a sense of alterity could implicate wide strata and, in combination with denser communications/commercial circuits, could assume an autonomous, self-replicating character. In many of these respects Japan, whose civil wars had no ethnic component and whose geography precluded sustained external warfare, diverged from less protected Eurasian regions. Note that in contrast to post-1789 European nationalism, the typical early modern fusion of state power and local culture not only coexisted with, but depended upon notions of rigid hierarchy, dynasticism, and "realm-specific" religious universalism.[21]

As for the second grand problematic, that of global synchronization, our essays suggest several lines of inquiry. Two grand temporal movements, one cyclic, the other linear, dominated the history of most of the regions covered in this volume. During the thirteenth to fourteenth centuries, the sixteenth century, and again in the mid- to late eighteenth century, political systems collapsed. Yet over the long term, I have emphasized that fluctuations went hand in hand with a sustained strengthening of commercial, cultural, and (outside Java) political linkages.

Dr. Subrahmanyam's theory of ideological circulation offers one promising approach to synchronism, but another focuses on the shifting intersection in each region between global economic stimuli, domestic economic stimuli, and local political responses. It is increasingly clear that demographic cycles across Eurasia were influenced by hemispheric climatic fluctuations, which in turn probably reflected a combination of changing solar radiation, modifications in the tilt of the earth's axis, and oscillations in the heat economy and circulation of ocean currents. One might imagine that a warmer global regime would have harmed agriculture in tropical or semitropical areas, but in fact, theoretical and empirical evidence (some as-

21. Cf. claims that collectivity was incompatible with hierarchy, religion with realm-specific loyalty, and popular mobilization with pre-industrial social conditions: Anderson, *Imagined Communities*, esp. chs. 2, 3; Ernest Gellner, *Nations and Nationalism* (Ithaca, 1983), esp. chs. 1, 2, 6; E. J. Hobsbawm, *Nations and Nationalism Since* 1780 (Cambridge, 1990), chs. 1, 2. Nor, *pace* Anderson, was print-capitalism a necessary condition for strong collective political identities.

sembled after the completion of the other essays in this collection) argues that the same periods of global warming that extended the growing season and aided population growth in much of Europe and Russia correlated with enhanced monsoon flows, hence cereal production, in southern China, South Asia, and Southeast Asia.[22] Across key sectors of Eurasia (the position of Japan and the Mideast is less clear) temperature and climate thus conspired to boost population and agricultural output c. 900–1300, c. 1450–1600, and c. 1720–1800, and to reduce, sometimes sharply, the rate of growth in intervening periods. In each sector population changes in turn affected reclamation, domestic exchange, and cultural production. Associated modifications in long-distance trade—an activity that has dominated scholarly explanations of global interaction, but that prior to c. 1500 was often more symptom than cause of demographic growth—impacted even those regions whose domestic economies were relatively sluggish. Either because immunological patterns had their own rhythms or because climate modified the behavior of pathogens and disease vectors, some epidemics also had a recurrent character.

The net result: political structures across much of Eurasia faced coordinated cyclic pressures. In periods of famine and population decline, conditions were obviously hostile to centralization. Ironically, however, political systems also had difficulty adjusting to very rapid growth, either because inflationary pressures and more intense intra-elite competition overstrained fiscal and organizational capacities à la Goldstone,[23] or because military overextension and intensifying warfare had the same effect. Thus, across much of Europe, South Asia, and mainland Southeast Asia political collapse in the late thirteenth/fourteenth centuries, the sixteenth century, and the second half of the eighteenth century climaxed periods of economic expansion. Frequently, collapse then inspired a compensatory explosion of political and military energy under a new, more competitively selected leadership.

Such cyclic tendencies aside, it is also clear that in key Eurasian areas a variety of pressures favored an increasingly durable integration whose foundations were at once material, institutional, and psychological. Substantial net population growth between c. 1400 and 1830 contributed to frontier

22. For these correlations and possible explanations of the underlying dynamics, see besides Lieberman, "Transcending," n. 95, Raymond S. Bradley and Philip D. Jones, eds., *Climate Since* A.D. 1500 (rev. ed., London, 1995); Henry F. Diaz and Vera Markgraf, eds., *El Nino* (Cambridge, 1992), esp. section B; Elizabeth Nesme-Ribes, ed., *The Solar Engine and Its Influence on Terrestrial Climate* (Berlin, 1993); J. T. Houghton et al., eds., *Climate Change 1995* (Cambridge, 1996); T. M. L. Wigley, M. J. Ingram, and G. Farmer, eds., *Climate and History* (Cambridge, 1981), esp. 465–78; and David S. Godley, "Flood Regimes in Northern Thailand: An Inter-Disciplinary Approach" (M.A. diss., Monash University, 1997), chs. 5–7.

23. Goldstone, *Revolution and Rebellion*.

colonization, regional specialization, technical innovation, and denser market networks, all of which gave leaders who controlled privileged economic zones a cumulative advantage over local rivals. Carefully preserved local advances in military and administrative organization had much the same effect. After c. 1500 expanding international trade also disseminated "best practices"—administrative, military, mining, and shipbuilding techniques—along with New World crops and rising imports of New World bullion. Buoyed by rapid population growth, especially on Eurasian frontiers and in the New World, by larger bullion supplies, new commercial institutions, and by an accelerating Smithian specialization that was both regional and global, between 1720 and 1820 alone the volume of trade at the chief ports of mainland Southeast Asia, Russia, and France alike rose five- to tenfold.[24] Although still dwarfed by domestic trade and still influenced by climatic fluctuations, maritime exchange accelerated local growth, buttressed established centers in most regions,[25] and thus powerfully reinforced Eurasian coordination. As internal consolidation and external warfare grew, self-interest led local elites to support their capital counterparts in broadening (and in many cases institutionalizing) central powers of patronage, military recruitment, revenue collection, rural control, and status regulation. For instrumental and expressive, social and psychological reasons, cultural standardization was normally part of this integrative project. Meanwhile denser communication circuits, wider literacy, and the rise of vernacular literatures also favored capital elite cultures over provincial alternatives. More dependent on invisible, capillary processes than on royal intervention, cultural exchange tended to be less fragile than administrative centralization, but often had much the same emotional impact. Gradually—and in the aftermath of periodic crises, spasmodically—integration thus came to be seen as the normal state of affairs. In Western Europe, Russia, and mainland Southeast Asia alike, the most obvious result of this intersection between cyclic and secular forces was that successive breakdowns tended to become less prolonged and less threatening to central institutions.

The ensuing essays will explore these connections and attempt to flesh out the abstractions.

24. Anthony Reid, "Introduction," in Reid, ed., *The Last Stand of Asian Autonomies* (New York, 1997), 12; Arcadius Kahan, *The Plow, the Hammer and the Knout* (Chicago, 1985), 164–65, 265, giving ruble values unadjusted for inflation for the second half of the eighteenth century; and James B. Collins, *The State in Early Modern France* (Cambridge, 1995), 179–83, 219-20, giving eighteenth-century trade volumes.

25. This was true in Russia, Siam, Burma, and most of Western Europe, but in Mughal India and archipelagic Southeast Asia, and with more ambiguity in Vietnam, frontier development and commercial growth had devolutionary implications.

Transcending East–West Dichotomies: State and Culture Formation in Six Ostensibly Disparate Areas

VICTOR LIEBERMAN

Binary Histories

Although the question has assumed at least two principal forms, most scholars who would compare the history of Europe and Asia have long been absorbed with a single query: Why was Asia different?

On the one hand, a tradition of macrohistorical sociology starting with Montesquieu, John Stuart Mill, Karl Marx, and Max Weber sought to establish 'despotism' as a general form of Oriental civilization whose historic immobility contrasted with the restless innovation of Europe. In more recent years Immanuel Wallerstein, Jean Baechler, John A. Hall, Michael Mann, E.L. Jones, Daniel Chirot, and Geoffrey Parker, among others whose expertise is in Western history, have pursued implicitly or explicitly the same theme of European, or more precisely West European, exceptionalism. If we may extract an explanation common to many of these later observers, it is that of cultural entelechy, the peculiar centuries-old legal-cum-political heritage of the West: its multiplicity of competing power networks, its unusually strong legal guarantees for personal property, the consequent strength of market mechanisms and commercial institutions.[1]

On the other hand, influenced by these broad concerns but usually focusing on more circumscribed problems of institutional or social

[1] See Weber, *Economy and Society* (Berkeley, 1978), II, chs 10–15; Perry Anderson, *Lineages of the Absolutist State* (London, 1974), 397–402, 462–549; Wallerstein, *The Modern World-System*, I (Orlando, FL, 1974); Baechler, Hall, and Mann (eds), *Europe and the Rise of Capitalism* (Oxford, 1988); John A. Hall, *Powers and Liberties* (Oxford, 1985); Jones, *The European Miracle* (Cambridge, 1987); Chirot, 'The Rise of the West,' *American Sociological Review* 50 (1985): 181–95; Parker, *The Military Revolution* (Cambridge, 1988); Karl Wittfogel, *Oriental Despotism* (New York, 1981), 374–89.

history, scholars of early modern Asia have explored the degree to which specific European features had analogues in the East. The most popular candidates, not surprisingly, have been 'feudalism' and 'capitalism,' followed more recently by European concepts of the 'public sphere.' Among historians of Japan, even those who opt for narrow definitions usually concede that the late Muromachi period, in particular, exhibited many characteristics of European-style feudalism, while the Tokugawa era produced capitalist features.[2] Scholars of pre-1800 China, South, and Southeast Asia have also marshalled evidence of commercial intensification and greater specialization in production and exchange, features which in some respects recall early modern Europe.[3] Yet on the whole, it is safe to say that the search for recognizably European analogies has yielded rather modest results. With the doubtful exception of Japan, all concede that Asia in 1800 was not moving towards an industrial revolution on the Western model; much effort therefore has gone into finding the culprits responsible for this 'failure.'[4] Nor did European notions

[2] Rushton Coulborn (ed.), *Feudalism in History* (Princeton, 1956); Edmund Leach *et al.* (eds), *Feudalism: Comparative Studies* (Sydney, 1985); John W. Hall and Marius B. Jansen (eds), *Studies in the Institutional History of Early Modern Japan* (Princeton, 1968), 3–51; Gary P. Leupp, *Servants, Shophands and Laborers in the Cities of Tokugawa Japan* (Princeton, 1992); Yasukazu Takenaka, 'Endogenous Formation and Development of Capitalism in Japan,' *The Journal of Economic History [JEH]* 29, 1 (1969): 141–62 [this entire journal issue is devoted to examining the early extent of extra-European capitalism]; Karen Wigen, 'The Geographic Imagination in Early Modern Japanese History,' *The Journal of Asian Studies [JAS]* 51, 1 (1992): 3–29; David L. Howell, 'Proto-Industrial Origins of Japanese Capitalism,' *JAS* 51, 2 (1992): 269–86.

[3] Evelyn Rawski, 'Research Themes in Ming–Qing Socioeconomic Hitory—The State of the Field,' *JAS* 50, 1 (1991): 84–111; Susan Naquin and Evelyn Rawski, *Chinese Society in the Eighteenth Century* (New Haven, 1987); Lloyd E. Eastman, *Family, Fields, and Ancestors* (New York, 1988); Philip C.C. Huang, *The Peasant Family and Rural Development in the Yangzi Delta, 1350–1988* (Stanford, 1990); Albert Feuerwerker, 'Presidential Address: Questions about China's Early Modern Economic History that I Wish I Could Answer,' *JAS* 51, 4 (1992): 757–69; Frank Perlin, 'Proto-Industrialization and Pre-Colonial South Asia,' *Past and Present [PP]* 98 (1983): 30–95; D.A. Washbrook, 'Progress and Problems: South Asian Economic and Social History *c.* 1720–1860,' *Modern Asian Studies [MAS]* 22, 1 (1988): 57–96; Sanjay Subrahmanyam, 'Rural Industry and Commercial Agriculture in Late Seventeenth-Century South-Eastern India,' *PP* 126 (1990): 76–114; *idem* (ed.), *Merchants, Markets and the State in Early Modern India* (Delhi, 1990); Anthony Reid, *Southeast Asia in the Age of Commerce, 1450–1680*, 2 vols (New Haven, 1988, 1993); Victor Lieberman, 'Secular Trends in Burmese Economic Hitory, *c.* 1350–1830,' *MAS* 25, 1 (1991): 1–31; Peter Carey, 'Waiting for the "Just King",' *MAS* 20, 1 (1986): 59–137.

[4] The chief suspects are cultural impediments, political sins of commission (market interference), political sins of omission (failure to provide capital-friendly institutions), and demographically-based equilibrium traps. See previous notes, plus

of individual and corporate autonomy have any close resonance. Although late Ming/Qing China (where the issue has been most closely examined) saw growing extrabureaucratic activity by organizations concerned with public welfare on the local level, the notion of an autonomous 'public sphere,' characterized by critical debate on issues of national policy by individuals enjoying defined rights vis-à-vis the state, had no parallel, certainly not before the twentieth century.[5] In the image of E.L. Jones' widely-received book, Europe was indeed a 'miracle.'[6]

But given the choice of criteria, was any other conclusion possible? Could one really expect to link European and Asian historical experiences by means of phenomena whose definitions were, at bottom, culture specific? How profitable would a discussion of English social organization prove if the template were Indian *varnas*? By and large, the search for European elements outside Europe has been structured to yield the same result as the dynamism–immobility contrast. In both cases we are necessarily left with an image of incomparability, and by implication, Asian deficiency.

Although Russian institutions, particularly after Peter, could hardly be described as static, Russia too has often been assimilated to a binary discourse. Exposed to sustained Mongol–Tatar influence, lacking a powerful bourgeoisie, subject to an extraordinary level of state direction, her educated classes obsessed by a sense of inferiority vis-à-vis the West, Russia has appeared to many indigenous and foreign observers alike as a variant of Asian despotism, an exception, if

Ramon H. Myers, 'How Did the Modern Chinese Economy Develop?' *JAS* 50, 3 (1991): 604–28; Albert Feuerwerker, 'The State and the Economy in Late Imperial China,' *Theory and Society* 13, 3 (1984): 297–326; William T. Rowe in Olivier Zunz (ed.), *Reliving the Past* (Chapel Hill, NC, 1985), 236–96; Mark Elvin, *The Pattern of the Chinese Past* (Stanford, 1973); Tapan Raychaudhuri in Raychaudhuri and Irfan Habib (eds), *The Cambridge Economic History of India*, I (Cambridge, 1982), 261–307, esp. 295; Jeyamalar Kathirithamby-Wells in Anthony Reid (ed.), *Southeast Asia in the Early Modern Era* (Ithaca, NY, 1993), 123–48; Thomas C. Smith, *Native Sources of Japanese Industrialization, 1750–1920* (Berkeley, 1988).

[5] On the public sphere debate, William T. Rowe, 'The Public Sphere in Modern China,' *Modern China* 16, 3 (1990): 309–29; 'Symposium: "Public Sphere" "Civil Society" in China?' *Modern China* 19, 2 (1993); Bin Wong, 'Great Expectations: The "Public Sphere" and the Search for Modern Times in Chinese History,' *Chugoku shigakkai* 3 (1993): 7–50; C.A. Bayly, 'Rethinking the Origins of the Indian Public Sphere,' Univ. of Michigan lecture, Sept. 15, 1995. A similar test of European categories in Asia involves the search for a '17th-century crisis,' *MAS* 24, 4 (1990), special issue.

[6] Jones, *Miracle*. Cf. his later argument for sustained growth in Song China and Tokugawa Japan, *Growth Recurring* (Oxford, 1988).

not the antithesis, to normative Western patterns. Peter Chaadaev's characterization of his homeland as a kind of historic swamp ('Talking about Russia one always imagines that one is talking about a country like the others; in reality, this is not so at all.') inaugurated an approach which in successive Slavophile, Weberian, and Cold War incarnations, has remained remarkably vital into the late twentieth century.[7]

One hardly need rehearse the political benefits—directed as much against self-doubt as against colonial and semi-colonial subjects—that accrued from describing the non-Western world as awaiting the Western kiss of life. Not infrequently 'Asia' as an emblem for unwise policy was also defined by domestic European political debates. But more basically, Eurocentrism said less about political sensibilities per se than about the overwhelming intellectual—nay, emotional—need to explain ever widening power inequalities between Euro-America and the rest of the world during the eighteenth to mid-twentieth centuries. To assimilate comparative historiography to an Orientalist mode; to portray European patterns as some sort of norm whose absence (invariable, yet somehow still puzzling) in other areas had to be explained; to hypostatize and essentialize asymmetries was all too irresistible. Hence the compression of societies that were enormously varied but comparably vulnerable into a single category, 'Asia.'[8] Hence too the contrast between European dynamism and Asian/Russian stasis even among historians with impeccable anti-imperialist credentials. We see this later tendency, for example, in the intellectually bankrupt, but long-lived Marxist notion of the Asiatic Mode of Production as a non-linear, regionally-specific formation.[9] We see it among post-war Japanese academics who held Tokugawa repression and xenophobia responsible for Japan's 'retardation.' We see it in the call by J.C. van Leur and John Smail for an Indies-centered history of Southeast Asia, a call which although strongly anti-colonial, ironically mirrored colonial historiography in its insistence

[7] Quote from Richard Pipes, *Russia under the Old Regime* (New York, 1992), 266. Pipes' book itself offers an essentialist Cold war view. Cf. Liah Greenfeld, *Nationalism* (Cambridge, MA, 1992), ch. 3; Marshall Poe, 'Russian Despotism' (PhD, UC Berkeley, 1993); Valerie Kivelson, *Autocracy in the Provinces* (Stanford, 1996), Intro.

[8] See Edward Said, *Orientalism* (New York, 1978); Anderson, *Lineages*, Note B; Michael Adas, *Machines as the Measure of Men* (Ithaca, 1989); K.N. Chaudhuri, *Asia Before Europe* (Cambridge, 1990), 19–24.

[9] Anderson, *Lineages*, Note B, 462–549.

on the autonomy and extreme conservatism of Southeast Asian civilization.[10]

New Criteria, New Affinities

In the post-imperial, post-Cold War late twentieth century, less dichotomous approaches to Eurasian history seem feasible, if not obligatory. In part the pressure of accumulated empirical studies encourages revision. But most basically the retreat of American power in Asia, East Asia's spectacular economic success, the globalization of information and consumer culture, and the (possibly temporary) erosion of regionally-based political ideologies have combined to weaken the self-confidence, the sensibilities, the psychological assumptions of Eurocentric historiography. Not unlike those sixteenth-century genealogists who furnished upwardly mobile English commoners with aristocratic ancestries, now we may be tempted to reward the latest success stories by emphasizing the early evidence of their achievement. As John W. Hall some thirty years ago observed of Japanese historiography, novel interpretations normally arise less from new evidence than from the preoccupations of a new generation.[11] Such revisionism is in fact already far advanced in Japanese studies. Once despised as an era of backwardness and isolation, the Tokugawa period is now widely praised for having engendered those very patterns of social solidarity, capital accumulation, and agricultural innovation on which Japan's modern industrial success has rested.[12] John P. Powelson, writing over a decade after E.L. Jones, has now accorded early modern Western Europe and Japan the apotheosis which Jones once allowed only Western Europe as exceptions to universal agrarian stasis.[13]

This essay seeks, in preliminary and schematic fashion, to widen the geographic scope of such revisionist approaches, and at the same time to shift their thematic focus. Useful correctives though they

[10] On van Leur and Smail, see my 'Introduction,' this volume, n. 2.

[11] Hall, 'The New Look of Tokugawa History,' in Hall and Jansen, *Institutional History*, 55, corroborating C. Vann Woodward.

[12] On Japanese revisionism, now in fact a new orthodoxy, see *supra* nn. 2, 4, plus Thomas C. Smith, *The Agrarian Origins of Modern Japan* (Stanford, 1959); Chie Nakane and Shinzaburo Oishi (eds), *Tokugawa Japan* (Tokyo, 1991).

[13] Powelson, *Centuries of Economic Endeavor* (Ann Arbor, MI, 1994).

may be, the new views of Tokugawa history provide a basis for Eurasian comparisons no more adequate than classical Eurocentrism, and for the same reason: they employ a criterion, namely the ability to support a precocious industrialization, that by definition was restricted to one or two societies. Preserving intact the chasm between Europe and the rest of the world, such an approach merely shifts Japan from one side to the other.

I propose to substitute what I believe are more neutral, capacious, and ultimately more revealing standards of comparison. In particular, I am interested in the little noted Eurasian pattern between *c.* 1450 and 1830 whereby localized societies in widely separated regions coalesced into larger units—politically, culturally, commercially. I seek both to describe these parallel evolutions, and to relate such departures to changes in demography, markets, urbanization, literacy, military technology, and interstate competition. Now obviously, as intellectual constructs all such categories and processes derive from the Western historical imagination no less clearly than 'feudalism' and the 'public sphere.' But as demonstrable patterns within this now universal mode of viewing the past, sustained integrative patterns were not restricted to Europe, and in some cases found fullest and most dramatic expression outside Western Europe. Such an approach is not incompatible with—nor have I any desire to minimize—European exceptionalism, arguably the central feature of early modern world history. Yet such an approach also permits us to begin viewing European and other regional experiences as peculiar variants of more general Eurasian patterns. Instead of 'failure' or 'success,' we find numerous idiosyncratic sites along very broad continua.

The six geographic areas on which I concentrate are discordant, and for that very reason, instructive. I include the chief realms of mainland Southeast Asia (Burma, Siam, Vietnam), omitted from most world histories, both because I am eager to contextualize my region of expertise and because this region offers truly novel perspectives on global simultaneity. In turn I juxtapose Southeast Asia with Western Europe as typified here by France (but which could have been represented as easily by Britain, Sweden, Portugal, Spain, Prussia, etc.), with the Russian empire, and with Japan. That these regions spanned the northern and eastern rimlands of Eurasia, generally had minimal contact with one another, differed profoundly in demography, popular culture, high religion, administrative and economic structures—but nonetheless experienced remarkably synchronized political rhythms illustrates in stark fashion the thesis of Eurasian interdependence.

These six areas were in fact part of a Eurasian subcategory sharing the following features: (a) Lying on the periphery of older civilizations (in India, the Mediterranean, China), all imported world religions, developed urban centers, and underwent what Barbara Price calls 'secondary state' formation during the latter part of the first or the early second millennium C.E.[14] Principalities founded in this period provided a novel charter for subsequent local states in so far as their religious, cultural, and in some cases, dynastic and territorial traditions were regarded as normative and legitimizing. (b) Following the decay/disruption of these charter principalities, a renewed process of political and cultural integration began at some point between 1450 and 1590 and, in key dimensions, continued to gain in scope and vigor well into the nineteenth century. (c) In partial explanation of this accelerating solidity, each polity enjoyed relatively good internal communications and/or an economic/demographic imbalance between districts that was markedly favorable to the capital area. (d) Throughout the period *c.* 1400–1830 each also enjoyed substantial protection from external invasion, whether overland from Central Asia or by sea from Europe. In their common possession of such features, these six societies constituted an intermediate category between, on the one hand, China, which experienced a uniquely precocious and durable integration, and on the other, Mughal India and island Southeast Asia, where political integration proved less intense and continuous. Among these six case studies the juxtaposition of similarities and divergences allows us to identify variables governing particular outcomes, while the concluding section explores some of the larger contrasts with other sectors of Eurasia. Conceivably societies ignored in the present essay could be assimilated to the same continuum, with the Ottomans perhaps intermediate between the Russian and the Mughal empires, and so forth.

Why use for Eurasian comparison this criterion of political and cultural coalescence rather than, say, broad changes in economic, urban, or intellectual structure? In part, I hasten to acknowledge, because these concerns are most congenial to existing Southeast

[14] Price, 'Secondary State Formation: An Explanatory Model,' in Ronald Cohen and Elman R. Service (eds), *Origins of the State* (Philadelphia, 1978), 161–86. Conceivably parts of West Africa could be included in this schema.

Asian historiography, whose focus remains political and cultural; and in part, I have suggested, because synchronized integration provides a sensitive index of global connections. Is it not puzzling that the multistate systems of Europe and of mainland Southeast Asia, at opposite ends of Eurasia, should have experienced more or less simultaneous oscillations and consolidation? And does not a recognition of such similarities invite reconsideration of processes usually interpreted in a purely regional context? At the same time, a concern with integration can suggest novel connections between ostensibly disparate phenomena—demographic, military, literary, religious—all of which reflected a wider, more rapid circulation of goods and ideas. Note that higher exchange velocities, so to speak, transformed not only the most successful polities within each region, but also less durable contenders—Burgundy, Lithuania, Chiang Mai, Cambodia, and so forth—so that the patterns with which we are concerned are of yet wider application. Beyond this and perhaps most fundamental, trends towards political, cultural, and commercial integration merit attention because for centuries prior to *c.* 1830 they helped to define the political aspirations, self-images, ethnicities, and conceptions of sanctity available to local elites, and also to growing sectors of the general population. Nor is early modern state and culture formation without contemporary implications, although here one must be wary of essentialism.

I am the first to acknowledge, however, that these concerns hardly exhaust the possibilities for what I shall term early modern classification. In its West European context, 'early modern' refers to a complex of traits usually said to include not only standardization within emergent national units—but also an increased emphasis on rationality and secularism, growing literacy, and in the wake of urbanism and denser market relations, a halting movement from familiarity to impersonality, from inherited status to individual merit, from social solidarity and public honor to self-interest and privacy.[15] These six case studies focus on the first element in the above list, that of consolidation. I also emphasize that across much of Eurasia literacy rapidly expanded, popular religions became subject to an unprecedented degree of textually-sanctioned reform, political authority became far more routinized, and particularly after 1750, economic

[15] Marvin Becker, *Civility and Society in Western Europe, 1300–1600* (Bloomington, IN, 1988); *idem*, *The Emergence of Civil Society in the Eighteenth Century* (Bloomington, IN, 1994); Robin Briggs, *Early Modern France 1560–1715* (Oxford, 1977); Isser Woloch, *Eighteenth-Century Europe* (New York, 1982).

growth encouraged social mobility, an erosion of ascriptive categories, and greater commercial influence in elite society. All served to give this era in Eurasian history a distinctive character. But other intellectual and social components of European early modernity—rationalist critiques of religious tradition, elaborated theories of social organization, autonomous associations in the space between family and state, the legal abstraction of authority from the specifics of lordship—receive less attention, chiefly because these features had little or no purchase in Southeast Asia or pre-Petrine Russia.

Yet if one were to examine the most economically developed sectors of Asia, including coastal China and India as well as Japan, other possibilities might open. I have cautioned against efforts at mechanical duplication of European patterns, but one might well find a range of preeminently urban intellectual and cultural developments worthy of broad comparison.[16] Likewise, if one were to use as organizing principles proto-industrialization, commercial networks, marriage and family systems, or tensions between high religion and popular beliefs, groupings of Eurasian regions rather different from those presented in this essay might well emerge. (Clearly, however, many of these also would eschew a simple East–West dichotomy.) In short, this essay approaches the problem of Eurasian coherence from a particular and, I believe, revealing set of perspectives without in any sense pretending to an exclusive prerogative.

In seeking to treat Eurasia as an interactive, loosely synchronized ecumene, I employ William H. McNeill's seminal study of Eurasian epidemiology,[17] climate reconstructions hinting at hemispheric regimens of agricultural productivity,[18] Alfred Crosby, Jr. and James

[16] See previous references to the 'public sphere' debate, which takes on added significance when one compares urban publishing industries in Japan and Europe: Henry D. Smith II, 'The History of the Book in Edo and Paris,' in James L. McClain *et al.* (eds), *Edo and Paris* (Ithaca, NY, 1994), 332–52, and Mary Elizabeth Berry, this volume. According to Karen Wigen, 'Mapping Early Modernity: Geographic Meditations on a Comparative Concept' (MS), the conjuncture of urbanization, wider literacy, voluntary associations, evidential philosophy, and an emphasis on the autonomous self in the arts suggests cultural analogies between late Ming/Qing China and the early modern West. Cf. David Johnson, 'Communication, Class, and Consciousness in Late Imperial China,' in Johnson *et al.* (eds), *Popular Culture in Late Imperial China* (Berkeley, 1985), 34–72.

[17] McNeill, *Plagues and Peoples* (Garden City, NY, 1976).

[18] H.H. Lamb, *Climate Present, Past, and Future*, II (London, 1977), ch. 17; *idem*, *The Changing Climate* (London, 1966); T.M.L. Wigley *et al.* (eds), *Climate and History* (Cambridge, 1981); Takehiko Mikami, 'The Climate Reconstruction of East Asia in the Period *c.* 1500–1850' (MS); T. Mikami (ed.), *Proceedings of the International Symposium on the Little Ice Age Climate* (Tokyo, 1992).

Lee's studies of Columbian exchanges,[19] and a growing literature on international trade, including post-Wallersteinian world systems theories promoted by André Gunder Frank, Barry K. Gills, and Janet L. Abu-Lughod.[20] I also build on Jack Goldstone's pregnant theory of demographically-driven revolts in Western Europe, the Ottoman empire, and China.[21] However, in contrast to most epidemiological, climatic, and world systems theorists, I am as concerned with internal social and institutional evolution as with external linkages, and I adopt an open-ended multifactoral approach. By extension, the Wallersteinian theory of unequal exchange within a global or regional hegemonic system seems to me less useful than the notion of overlapping trade circuits with multiple, fluid centers. I differ as well from Goldstone, both because demography is but one of several key variables and because I am not primarily concerned with periodic collapse. Rather, my six studies focus on secular construction, to which periodic breakdown often provided an acceleratory stimulus.

As for the chronological limits of early modernity: Although I shall refer to early charter polities, the great Eurasian-wide economic upsurge of the mid and late 1400s—and attendant innovations in warfare, politics, and culture—recommend this period as a rough point of departure. A terminal date is more difficult to coordinate across Eurasia and more arbitrary in so far as we have after *c.* 1720 a continuously accelerating series of changes, but the second quarter of the nineteenth century has some claim to attention as the era which saw the irruption of European colonialism in mainland Southeast Asia, more adumbrative external pressures on Japan, and the onset of profound railroad-borne transformations in France. Within this broad era, in some locales one could claim that the mid-sixteenth and mid-eighteenth centuries inaugurated major subperiods.

[19] Crosby, *The Columbian Exchange* (Westport, CT, 1972); Lee, 'Migration and Expansion in Chinese History,' in William H. McNeill and Ruth S. Adams (eds), *Human Migration: Patterns and Policies* (Bloomington, IN, 1978), 20–47; *idem*, 'Food Supply and Population Growth in Southwest China, 1250–1850,' *JAS* 41, 4 (1982): 711–46.

[20] Frank and Gills (eds), *The World System* (London, 1993); Abu-Lughod, *Before European Hegemony* (New York, 1989); Philip D. Curtin, *Cross-cultural Trade in World History* (Cambridge, 1984); Jerry H. Bentley, *Old World Encounters* (New York, 1993); Wolfram Fischer *et al.* (eds), *The Emergence of a World Economy 1500–1914*, I (Wiesbaden, 1986); John F. Richards (ed.), *Precious Metals in the Later Medieval and Early Modern Worlds* (Durham, NC, 1983); William Atwell, 'Some Observations on the "Seventeenth-Century Crisis" in China and Japan,' *JAS* 45, 2 (1986): 223–44.

[21] Goldstone, *Revolution and Rebellion in the Early Modern World* (Berkeley, 1991). Cf. Roland Mousnier, *Peasant Uprisings in Seventeenth Century France, Russia, and China* (New York, 1970).

Territorial Consolidation

What then were the chief parallels among the areas under consideration?

Most visible was the sustained movement between *c.* 1450 and 1830 towards the political and administrative integration of what had been fragmented, localized units. Thus in Europe west of the Dniester and Vistula five to six hundred more or less independent polities in 1450 were reduced to some 25 by the late nineteenth century. In northeastern Europe, Siberia, and the Caucasus, over thirty city-states, princedoms, and khanates yielded to a single Russian imperial suzerainty. In mainland Southeast Asia, some 22 genuinely independent states in 1350 were reduced to three—Burma, Siam, and Vietnam—by 1825, when Europeans began to freeze an ongoing process. In Japan a very large, if fluid, number of proto-daimyo domains and autonomous religious and merchant communities in 1500 had come under unified rule by century's end.

Several aspects of this cannibalization require emphasis. First, although in each region between *c.* 1400 and 1830 the paramount state (and indeed its chief rivals) significantly, in some cases dramatically, expanded its territory, consolidation generally had an episodic rather than continuous character, with repeated collapse yielding to renewed expansion. We shall return to the substantial, though obviously imperfect, correlation between political collapse in different parts of Eurasia during the periods *c.* 1250–1550 and *c.* 1750–1800; and between accelerated annexation in different areas in the sixteenth and late eighteenth/early nineteenth centuries.[22]

Second, all post-1500 movements were in some sense movements of recentralization. That is to say, each post-1500 realm claimed the

[22] Japan knew but one period of sustained breakdown, *c.* 1467–1590. For political/administrative overviews, see Victor Lieberman, *Burmese Administrative Cycles* (Princeton, 1984); William J. Koenig, *The Burmese Polity, 1752–1819* (Ann Arbor, MI, 1990); David K. Wyatt, *Thailand: A Short History* (New Haven, 1982); Le Thanh Khoi, *Histoire du Vietnam* (Paris, 1987); Alexander Woodside, *Vietnam and the Chinese Model* (Cambridge, MA, 1971); John Fennell, *The Crisis of Medieval Russia 1200–1304* (London, 1983); Robert O. Crummey, *The Formation of Muscovy 1304–1613* (London, 1987); Paul Dukes, *The Making of Russian Absolutism 1613–1801* (London, 1990); J. Ph. Genet and M. Le Mêne (eds), *Genèse de l'état moderne* (Paris, 1987); Georges Duby, *France in the Middle Ages, 987–1460* (Oxford, 1991); David Potter, *A History of France, 1460–1560* (New York, 1995); Emmanuel Le Roy Ladurie, *The Royal French State 1460–1610* (Oxford, 1994); François Bluché, *L'Ancien Régime* (Paris, 1993); James B. Collins, *The State in Early Modern France* (Cambridge, 1995); *The Cambridge History of Japan [CHJ]*, III, Kozo Yamamura (ed.), and IV, John Whitney Hall (ed.) (Cambridge, 1990, 1991); Conrad Totman, *Early Modern Japan* (Berkeley, 1993).

dynastic, religious, or institutional heritage of a charter polity (Pagan, Angkor, Dai Viet, Kiev, Capetian France; classical, Kamakura, or Muromachi Japan), and sought to reorganize all or part of the territory controlled by that predecessor. In each case, therefore, collapse at some point between *c.* 1250 and 1550 was in some sense merely the first in a series of progressively shorter interregna extending to the late eighteenth century. At the same time, I shall emphasize that the degree of genuine, as opposed to fabricated, retrospective, continuity between charter and post-1500 polities differed widely. In this respect as in others, distinctions cut across East–West boundaries.

Finally, in the open, sparsely populated frontier societies of mainland Southeast Asia and Russia the possibilities for continuous, accelerating conquests were considerably greater than in Japan, which found colonization of Honshu uninviting and which abandoned a 1592–98 invasion of Korea; or in Western Europe, where hostile coalitions checked rapid French expansion on the east and northeast. In other words, all six societies saw a dramatic consolidation in the late fifteenth or sixteenth centuries, but in Japan and France physical expansion quickly reached a plateau similar to that under the late charter principalities. Thus, whereas in Vietnam, Burma, Siam, and Russia districts under central authority in 1830 were two to four times more extensive than in 1600, in Japan and France post-1600 accretions, by most definitions, were in the order of only 10 to 15%. On the other hand, if we consider New World acquisitions—a not unreasonable proposition in that such acquisitions both enhanced and reflected metropolitan strength—the French parallel to Russia and Southeast Asia is closer.

Administrative Centralization and Social Regulation

At the same time as privileged cores extended their territorial writ, they commonly sought to strengthen their extractive, judicial, and military functions and systems of provincial control. As just indicated, external expansion and internal reform were mutually reinforcing in so far as larger domains required more efficient control, while the concentration of resources that flowed from better coordination facilitated colonization and conquest.

If all these polities, Russia apart, were of comparable size in 1800, their populations and internal geographies differed substantially, along with the potential for centralization. Each Southeast Asian realm contained a population in 1800 of between 4 and 7.5 million, which, despite a respectable proportion of city-dwellers, could not support urban and commercial networks comparable to those of the larger states. Vietnam was also disadvantaged in that its elongated domain lacked a central river artery. On the other hand, although the highlands of western and central mainland Southeast Asia were relatively inaccessible, the Irrawaddy and Chaophraya basins tended to concentrate the population in easily-monitored clusters. France, Russia, and Japan in 1800 each had between 30 and 37 million people, including urban communities considerably larger than in Southeast Asia. With no major mountain barriers, extensive roads, and at least four major rivers, in France problems of control and communication were relatively modest. The extraordinary vastness of the Russian plain posed more obvious problems, but these were offset to some extent by the western concentration of population and by Russia's excellent river systems. The Japanese islands had no central river, but the seas provided regular coastal links, while demographic-transport concentrations in the Kinai region and the Kanto created natural political foci.

At times reinforcing, at times contradicting these geographic and demographic patterns, diverse local imaginations, external models, and interstate pressures produced wide discrepancies in administrative form and penetration. Let it suffice for now to say that whereas France by 1810 had a uniform territorial administration with three levels of appointed officials in all departments between Paris and the frontiers, Siam and Burma remained 'solar polities,'[23] usually with but one layer of appointed officials in the lowlands, with hereditary vassal rulers in inaccessible uplands, and with no clear notion of frontiers at all. The Paris administration, imbued with bureaucratic norms, penetrated French villages to the point where it could conjure standardized communal budgets, rural police forces, and road repairs.[24] By contrast, even in lowland Burma and Siam tax

[23] Characterized by a central 'sun,' 'planets' held by a gravitational pull whose strength varied with distance, and multiple 'moons' for each 'planet.' Cf. 'galactic polity' in S.J. Tambiah, *World Conqueror and World Renouncer* (Cambridge, 1976), chs 6–8.

[24] Isser Woloch, *The New Regime* (New York, 1994); Clive H. Church, *Revolution and Red Tape* (Oxford, 1981), chs 1, 2. I choose post-Revolutionary France to emphasize Eurasian variety, but if 1750 had been the base year, the decentralized, personalized Southeast Asian system would have found closer French parallels.

collections and service rotas normally depended on the uncertain mediation of long patron–client chains.[25] Largely under Western inspiration, Russia struggled to impose a more uniform and centralized system, while permitting indirect rule in privileged borderlands.[26] But the Japanese polity remained no less and possibly more decentralized than the Burmese. The bakufu recognized the daimyo as semi-autonomous rulers in control of some three-quarters of the country's agricultural output. National institutions present in Southeast Asia and yet more developed in France and Russia—treasuries, judiciaries, military forces—remained problematic or absent in Japan.[27] Finally, Vietnam represented the extreme of decentralization: notwithstanding an overarching dynastic loyalty and considerable cultural unity, elongated geography allowed the southern seigneurie to remain effectively independent from 1558 to 1802. Uniform administration in Vietnam's three principal regions was not even attempted until the 1830s. Nor, despite growing routinization, is it clear that 'bureaucracy' accurately describes the central apparatus in either Vietnam or Japan by 1830.[28]

To complicate further Eurasian comparisons, lest one assume that we can effortlessly rank all six societies according to one or two indices of 'state power,' consider that spheres of government vigor could be quite distinct. By the late 1700s, for example, the Russian state was effective in organizing up-to-date military forces, but not particularly interested in local religious observance. In Burma, the situation was more or less reversed.

Notwithstanding such differences in geography, structure, and focus, between *c.* 1400 and 1830 the administrative systems of France, Russia, Burma, Siam, Vietnam, and Japan experienced certain general parallels.

It is convenient to visualize most of these early modern states as closely administered cores, which were privileged demographically or

[25] Lieberman, *Cycles*, ch. 2.

[26] John P. LeDonne, *Absolutism and Ruling Class* (New York, 1991), 112–18, 305–9; Edward C. Thaden, *Russia's Western Borderlands, 1710–1870* (Princeton, 1984), pts 1–2.

[27] Mark Ravina, 'State-building and Political Economy in Early-modern Japan,' *JAS* 54, 4 (1995): 997–1022, analyzing the 'compound state'; Mary Elizabeth Berry, 'Public Peace and Private Attachment,' *The Journal of Japanese Studies [JJS]* 12, 2 (1986), 240, 255, 257.

[28] For different characterizations, see Woodside, *Vietnam* 38, 74–82, 106–7, and *passim*; Nola Cooke, 'The Composition of the Nineteenth-Century Political Elite of Pre-colonial Nguyen Vietnam,' *MAS* 29, 4 (1995): 741–64; Berry, 'Public Peace,' 255, 263–71; *CHJ*, IV, 15.

economically, surrounded by zones of subordinate cities and provinces whose autonomy tended to increase with distance from the center and/or with access to independent resources. The 'solar polities' of Toungoo Burma and of Ayudhya; the division between the Tonkin delta and Thanh-hoa frontier in fifteenth-century Vietnam; the early Muscovite division between central provinces and *namestniki* and *volosteli* areas; the separation between *pays d'élection* and *pays d'États* in *ancien régime* France; and distinctions in Muromachi Japan between the central provinces and semi-independent zones like Kyushu all illustrate the point.[29] In each polity, as consolidation resumed or began after 1450 or 1500, we find a long-term, if halting tendency for peripheral zones and autonomous enclaves to assimilate to the status of intermediate or core provinces, and for systems of extraction and coordination in the core to improve. Thus, for example, independent kingdoms that fell under Burmese and Siamese rule were converted to governor-ruled provinces, while control of governorships and apanages within the core also strengthened. Supervision in the French *pays d'États* gradually approached that in northcentral France. Southern Hokkaido and Kyushu by 1650 were tied to the center as effectively as outer areas of Honshu had been in 1400. In Vietnam during the era of division the northern and southern seigneuries steadily modified internal operations, while, as noted, from 1830s the new Nguyen dynasty sought to standardize provincial administration.

In this extension of control, moreover, a number of broadly comparable strategies and processes were at work. Before the triumph of the central polity over what eventually would become provincial dependencies, the latter typically had been engaged in independent projects of state building. In Burma, Siam, *ancien régime* France, and Japan (and less commonly in Russia and Vietnam), this triumph typically entailed not the destruction, but the preservation in outlying areas of local institutions: executive agencies, tribunals, armies, tax systems. The capital ensured the loyalty of newly annexed organs, first, by controlling the appointment of senior personnel, and second, by subordinating them to an overarching/parallel network of central

[29] John K. Whitmore, 'The Development of Le Government in Fifteenth-Century Vietnam,' (PhD, Cornell Univ. 1968); Horace W. Dewey, 'The Decline of the Muscovite *Namestnik*,' *Oxford Slavonic Papers* 12 (1965): 21–39; Roland Mousnier, *The Institutions of France under the Absolute Monarchy 1598–1789* (Chicago, 1979, 1984), I, ch. 14; J. Russell Major, *Representative Government in Early Modern France* (New Haven, 1980), xiv, 58–96; *CHJ*, III, 201–11.

courts and agencies. If in the short term this 'mosaic' strategy placed obvious limits on integration, it reduced the financial costs of annexation for the capital and the psychological costs for local elites. Moreover, in the long term overarching agencies could proliferate as circumstances demanded. Outside Tokugawa Japan (where, in the absence of external incentives, bakufu revenues declined both absolutely and relative to the national economy),[30] every central authority expanded its resource base through new mobilization techniques, monopolies, loans, direct and indirect taxes. In turn larger income permitted (and reflected) a growth in the number of judges, tax collectors, provincial supervisors (French *intendants*, Russian *voevodas*, Burmese *myo-wuns*, Vietnamese *tong doc*), and soldiers. In Burma between 1500 and 1800 the administration and army both doubled in size, while in Russia from 1632 to 1756 the army increased tenfold. In France between 1515 and 1715 the military multiplied twenty times and officialdom, eleven-fold.[31]

Animating and complementing institutional elaboration were expanded systems of patronage. Although administrative procedure became more routinized, even in France until the late 1700s clientelism remained basic to the operation of the polity. Authorities everywhere sought not to destroy factions, but to balance and incorporate them through centrally-administered pensions, blocs of offices, tax privileges, guarantees of status, concessions of all sorts. Sharon Kettering's description of French patron–broker–client ties as 'interstitial, supplementary, and parallel' to more formal structures can easily be generalized.[32] In lieu of an earlier historiography that saw the early modern state in France, Russia, and Southeast Asia crushing and displacing local elites, this perspective allows for a substantial degree of accommodation between central and regional leaders whose interests in patronage, social regulation, and military effectiveness were basically congruent.[33]

[30] James W. White, 'State Growth and Popular Protest in Tokugawa Japan,' *JJS* 14, 1 (1988), 11.

[31] R.J. Knecht, *French Renaissance Monarchy* (London, 1984), 15; Jeremy Black, *A Military Revolution?* (Atlantic Highlands, NJ, 1991), 6; Charles Tilly, *Coercion, Capital, and European States, AD 990–1900* (Cambridge, MA, 1990), 79. On a comparably dramatic expansion in Ashikaga-Tokugawa armies, Herman Ooms, *Tokugawa Ideology* (Princeton, 1985), 44. Yet no serious increase in Vietnamese army size is apparent *c.* 1600–1800.

[32] Kettering, *Patrons, Brokers, and Clients in Seventeenth-Century France* (New York, 1986), 5.

[33] For such views, and contrasts with earlier historiography, see Michael Mann, *The Sources of Social Power*, I (Cambridge, 1986), 458–63; Nicholas Henschall, *The Myth of Absolutism* (London, 1992); François-Xavier Emmanuelli, *Un mythe de l'absolut-*

But if the state was less autonomous, more subject to faction, negotiation, and paralysis than earlier historians conceded, it is also true that over the long term local prerogatives were substantially modified. Most basic, princes and other regional leaders in France, Russia, and lowland Southeast Asia gradually lost the right to tax without permission, to build private fortifications, to run some independent judicial systems, and—apropos the Weberian definition of the state—to employ unauthorized violence against one another or their subjects. As royal income grew, as status came to be defined in relation to uniform hierarchies, as central armies achieved a clear superiority, ambitious leaders tended to abandon rebellion and 'mighty neighbor patronage' in return for improved access to royal patronage and stronger support for their rights vis-à-vis local rivals and/or over the local peasantry.[34]

In all six societies between *c.* 1500 and 1830 religious organizations likewise came under more effective regulation. Personnel and, in some cases, doctrine were monitored more closely by appointed officials. In Burma, Russia, Japan, and France (the latter most dramatically, but not exclusively, from 1789), church lands or income were reduced, at times severely. State resources widened accordingly, while religious groups were curtailed or eliminated as institutionalized political actors. Ironically, in some cases efforts to increase religious conformity intensified even as the power of the church waned, because the state assumed wider responsibility for monitoring social behavior.[35]

isme bourbonien (Aix-en-Provence, 1981); David Parker, *The Making of French Absolutism* (New York, 1983); William Beik, *Absolutism and Society in Seventeenth-Centry France* (Cambridge, 1985); Robert Harding, *Anatomy of a Power Elite* (New Haven, 1978); Roger Mettam, *Power and Faction in Louis XIV's France* (Oxford, 1988); Nancy Shields Kollmann, *Kinship and Patronage: The Making of the Muscovite Political System 1345–1547* (Stanford, 1987); Robert Crummey, *Aristocrats and Servitors* (Princeton, 1983); Kivelson, *Autocracy*.

34 Previous note, plus Ronald G. Asch and Adolf M. Birke (eds), *Princes, Patronage, and The Nobility* (Oxford, 1991); Wyatt, *Thailand*, chs 4–6; Busakorn Lailert,'The Ban Phlu Luang Dynasty' (PhD, Univ. of London, 1972); Akin Rabibhadana, *The Organization of Thai Society in the Early Bangkok Period 1782–1873* (Ithaca, NY, 1969); *CHJ*, III, chs 1–6, IV, chs 1–5; Mary Elizabeth Berry, *Hideyoshi* (Cambridge, MA, 1982), chs 4–6.

35 Victor Lieberman, 'The Political Significance of Religious Wealth in Burmese History,' *JAS* 39, 4 (1980): 753–69; Pipes, *Russia*, ch. 9; Donald Ostrowski, 'Church Polemics and Monastic Land Acquisition in Sixteenth-Century Muscovy,' *Slavic and East European Review [SEER]* 64, 3 (1986): 355–75; Paul Bushkovitch, *Religion and Society in Russia* (New York,1992), chs 3–5; Eugenii V. Anisimov, *The Reforms of Peter the Great* (Armonk, NY, 1993), 203–17; Isabel de Madariaga, *Russia in the Age of Catherine the Great* (New Haven, 1981), 111–27, 515; Edwin O. Reischauer and Albert M. Craig, *Japan* (Sydney, 1979), 77, 87; *CHJ*, IV, 359–72; Knecht, *Francis I*,

Indeed, typically from the seventeenth century, authorities in Russia, France, Burma, Japan, and Vietnam attempted to regulate more aspects of daily life, not least as these affected lower social strata. Determined in varying degrees to increase revenue, to assure cheap grains, and/or to coopt powerful merchants, virtually every rimland state fixed prices, standardized weights and measures, and granted monopolies (at least until the late 1700s, when a liberalizing trend appeared in many countries). To cement ties with local powerholders, to promote order, to defend hierarchy, to ensure service and tax payments, and to advertise the power of central authorities, vigorous attempts also were made to strengthen hereditary status divisions, to integrate them into a theoretically universal system, to define deviance, and to extend legal regulation and criminal punishment, at least in those cities and core provinces subject to effective control. In Russia, Burma, Siam, Vietnam, and Japan, these measures included energetic efforts to curtail social and/or geographic mobility among the workforce, although again these efforts often ran into difficulty from the late 1700s. Such programs required expanded censuses and cadastres, and greatly increased flows of information to and from each capital.[36]

In turn the growing scope of government action, the extension of authority to new territories, the sheer increase in the volume of documents joined with wider literacy (see below) to encourage changes in political culture. In all six countries secretariats gradually expanded, the court as it outgrew the ruler's household became more elaborate, and the royal (or shogunal) position became more elevated. In varying degrees, in Burma, Siam, (pre-1600 and post-1800)

51–65; Mousnier, *Institutions*, I, ch. 7; François Furet, *Revolutionary France 1770–1880* (Oxford, 1992), 80–5, 226–8; Collins, this volume. Of course, the French church remained a key political actor to 1789. On Vietnamese controls, Nguyen Ngoc Huy & Ta Van Tai, *The Le Code*, 3 vols (Athens, OH, 1987), Articles 152, 215, 288, 301.

[36] Previous note, plus Robert Muchembled, *Popular Culture and Elite Culture in France 1400–1750* (Baton Rouge, LA, 1985), emphasizing state–church cooperation in popular regimentation *c.* 1600–1750; Collins, *State*, 3–4, 184–95, emphasizing the state's expanded welfare and regulatory powers from Louis XIV; Richard Hellie, *Enserfment and Military Change in Muscovy* (Chicago, 1971), pts I–II; J. Michael Hittle, *The Service City: State and Townsmen in Russia, 1600–1800* (Cambridge, MA, 1979); Paul Bushkovitch, *The Merchants of Moscow 1580–1650* (Cambridge, 1980), ch. 9; Crummey, *Formation*, 234–41; Anisimov, *Peter*, 217–43; Berry, *Hideyoshi*, ch. 5; Totman, *Early Modern Japan*, 101–59; Hitomi Tonomura, 'Punish and Discipline: Criminalizing Sexual Relations' (MS); Lieberman, *Cycles*, ch. 2; Akin, *Thai Society*, chs 2, 4, 5; Whitmore, 'Le Government,' chs 4, 5; Insun Yu, *Law and Society in Seventeenth and Eighteenth Century Vietnam* (Seoul, 1990).

Vietnam, Russia, and France, the prerogatives of the royal family as a whole were curtailed in favor of those of the paramount ruler. At the same time, most visibly but by no means only in Western Europe, government procedures tended to grow more impersonal, routinized, and professional. In Japan the transition from fief to stipend and from personal to quasi-bureaucratic authority was one of the crucial transitions of the Edo period.[37] In Vietnam the halting, contested introduction of Chinese norms at the expense of older, more personalized systems of loyalty provided a leitmotif throughout the period under review.[38] In Russia as early as the 1640s, well before Peter's reforms, the public, the nomothetic, the impersonal began to emerge as the privileged mode in lieu of the private, the merciful, the particular.[39] Even in late Ayudhya and Chakri Siam, where the personalized discourse of monarchy never faced serious challenge, David Wyatt has argued for a growing emphasis on abstract Buddhist morality in the conceptualization of law and governance.[40]

Cultural Integration

This discussion of political culture leads to a third general index of integration within each rimland society: a growing, if highly imperfect and uneven, uniformity of religious, ethnic, and other cultural symbols.

Following Ernesto Laclau, Chantal Mouffe, and Tessa Morris-Suzuki, I regard regional or national culture not as a 'coherently structured whole,' but as an 'unsutured' complex of identities that normally fluctuated according to locale, class, corporate group, even individual.[41] At the same time, within any stable population, by

[37] *CHJ*, IV, 15, 124; Berry, 'Public Peace,' 255; Conrad Totman, *Politics in the Tokugawa Bakufu, 1600–1843* (Berkeley, 1967), 234.

[38] Whitmore, 'Le Government'; Keith Taylor, 'The Literati Revival in Seventeenth-century Vietnam,' *Journal of Southeast Asian Studies [JSEAS]* 18, 1 (1987): 275–97; Woodside, *Vietnam*, esp. chs 1, 3; Nola Cooke, 'Nineteenth-Century Vietnamese Confucianization in Historical Perspective,' *JSEAS* 25, 2 (1994): 270–312.

[39] Valerie Kivelson, 'The Devil Stole His Mind,' *American Historical Review* 98, 3 (1993): 733–56; Borivoj Plavsic in W.M. Pintner, D.K. Rowney (eds), *Russian Officialdom* (Chapel Hill, NC, 1980), 19–45.

[40] Wyatt, 'The "Subtle Revolution" of King Rama I of Siam,' in Wyatt and Alexander Woodside (eds), *Moral Order and the Question of Change* (New Haven, 1982), 9–52.

[41] Laclau and Mouffe, *Hegemony and Socialist Strategy* (London, 1985), chs 3, 4; Morris-Suzuki, 'The Invention and Reinvention of "Japanese Culture",' *JAS* 54, 3 (1995): 759–80. Cf. Clifford Geertz, *The Interpretation of Cultures* (New York, 1973).

definition, rituals, symbols, vocabularies, and practices permitted a measure of intercourse and common identification. The main point is that in the early modern societies under review, such features became more standardized.

In theory standardization could be of two types: (a) lateral, elite standardization, in which a complex of linguistic, ritual, and stylistic practices spread from central to provincial elites; elite practices as whole thus remained more or less distinct from those of subordinate classes; and (b) vertical, demotic standardization, in which some features characteristic of elites spread to lower social strata (or vice versa), so that the entire population of the country/kingdom became more distinct from people in adjacent countries.[42] Lateral integration often involved the partial absorption of one literate complex by another. Nobles and bourgeois in Languedoc assimilated to north French styles, Lao and Khmer tributaries adopted (even as they helped to modify) select elements of central Thai culture. Although vertical, demotic integration also could involve literate displacements, more frequently it exposed illiterate folk traditions to literate norms. Popular dialects, identities, and religious practices were marginalized, or at least challenged. Oftentimes as well, demotic change had a misogynist thrust, rejecting females' claims to supernatural access, subordinating women more completely to male legal power.

Put baldly, we see tendencies towards lateral standardization in all six countries; reasonably sustained movements of vertical, demotic integration in Japan, France, and Vietnam; and weaker vertical tendencies in Burma, Siam, and Russia. It is at once apparent that these complex patterns, like the rhythm of territorial consolidation, showed scant respect for East–West divisions. Moreover, in almost every case ethnic self-definitions underwent rapid change starting in the fifteenth or sixteenth century. Moving from the most to the least homogenized societies, let us sketch these developments. For the time being we shall say little about the underlying dynamics of change, or about the subjective meaning local actors attached to such changes.

Japan's physical insularity may well have minimized alien influences throughout its history. Yet despite the conservatism of institu-

[42] Cf. Anthony D. Smith, *The Ethnic Origins of Nations* (Oxford, 1986), 76–89, opposing lateral and vertical *ethnies* as stable communities, rather than as evolutionary processes.

tions and symbols dating from the late first millennium, not until the fourteenth to sixteenth centuries was there an embryonic sense of what Barbara Ruch terms 'national community,' marked by the vigorous popularization of Buddhism and the tentative vertical diffusion of attitudes and practices from aristocrats and warriors to clerics, merchants, and other commoners.[43] Even so, cultural divisions by occupation and class, and within each social level by province and community, remained profound. Notwithstanding samurai efforts to impede such changes, during the Tokugawa period, particularly from the mid 1700s, the gap between the cultural-recreational activities of the elite and of plebeians, and of cities and hinterland contracted. Spurred by new schools, an elaborate communications system, and an intensive publication industry radiating from the cities, literacy and learning spread among samurai, townsmen, and well-to-do peasants alike. Most books for popular consumption were printed in Japanese *kana* syllabary (or with *kana* alongside Chinese characters), whereas writings for administration and scholarship, originally the preserve of the samurai, were in Chinese characters. Nonetheless, the diffusion of learning, even of higher culture, cut increasingly across class lines, so that in the realm of speculative thought the gap between elite and mass virtually disappeared. So too regional differences in dialect and custom, as between Honshu and Kyushu, eroded, most notably among the samurai. By 1830, according to John W. Hall, this class 'was fused into a single cultural homogeneity,' while the 'cultural styles of the great urban centers became standard for the other major cities of the entire country.'[44]

I find no data by which to measure whether by 1800 dialect and custom differences in France were greater than those in Japan, but both societies moved in a comparable direction. Since the thirteenth century in northern France a growing strand of what Robert Bartlett has called 'politicized linguistic consciousness' became intertwined with an emergent 'royal religion' focusing on the unique sanctity and

[43] Barbara Ruch, *CHJ*, III, ch. 11, esp. 501. Cf. Osumi Kazuo, *ibid.*, 581–2; Bito Masahide, *ibid.*, IV, 378; Conrad Totman, *Japan Before Perry* (Berkeley, 1981), 93–117.

[44] Hall, *CHJ*, IV, 30. See *CHJ*, IV, chs 8, 14; Totman, *Early Modern Japan*, chs 6, 10, 16, 19; Mary Elizabeth Berry, this volume; essays by Katsuhisa Moriya, Tatsuro Akai, and Chie Nakane in Nakane and Oishi, *Tokugawa*; Reischauer and Craig, *Japan*, 86, 99–107.

ancestry of the French king.[45] The last phase of the Hundred Years War, it has been argued, widened sentimental attachment to the crown in parts of central France. In this period and throughout French history to a greater degree than in Japan, political identity was defined by opposition towards an external 'reference society' (England, Spain, the Empire).[46] Such identities remained fluid, in rivalry with flourishing regional (Breton, Provençal, etc.) patriotisms—and most intense among economic and educated elites. As late as 1789, 50% of Frenchmen still did not speak Parisian French at all, relying on either *patois* or such distinct languages as Occitan, Basque, or Breton, and only 12–13% spoke it 'correctly.' The kingdom—which James Collins terms a 'polyglot empire'—remained a collection of *pays* and seigneuries, with their own customs, laws, as well as linguistic patterns.[47] Nonetheless, in the 1600s and 1700s French cultural and political identities—the two were often interdependent—spread deeper and more widely, not least in southern and western towns and their hinterlands, where Parisian French steadily replaced both Latin and local tongues in elite speech and in rapidly proliferating popular publications. Knowledge of Parisian dialect and culture was critical both to upward social mobility and to participation in the national, urban-centered sphere of high culture and political debate, with its emergent notions of citizenship. Revolutionary leaders tried to yoke language and political allegiance yet more closely, charging that 'federalism and counter-revolution' spoke low Breton, German, and Basque.[48]

[45] Bartlett, *The Making of Europe* (Princeton, 1993), 201 and 197–242 *passim*; Colette Beaune, *The Birth of an Ideology* (Berkeley, 1991). Cf. Jacques Krynen, *Idéal du prince et pouvoir royal* (Paris, 1981), 241–77; Bernard Guénée, *States and Rulers in Later Medieval Europe* (Oxford,1985), 50–65, 216–20; Joseph Strayer, *The Reign of Philip the Fair* (Princeton, 1980), 387–92.

[46] Reinhard Bendix, *Kings or People* (Berkeley, 1978). See Bernard Chevalier and Philippe Contamine (eds), *La France de la fin du XVe siècle* (Paris, 1985), 265–81, 301–11; Beaune, *Ideology*; Christopher Allmand, *The Hundred Years War* (Cambridge, 1988), 136–50; *idem* (ed.), *Power, Culture, and Religion in France c. 1350–c. 1550* (Woodbridge, UK, 1989); P.S. Lewis, *Later Medieval France* (London, 1968), 60–77, 374–80.

[47] Collins, *State*, 5. On cultural/linguistic integration *c.* 1500–1830, A. Brun, *Recherches historiques sur l'introduction du Français dans les provinces du Midi* (Paris, 1923), pts 1, 2, 5; Myriam Yardeni, *La conscience nationale en France pendant les guerres de religion* (Paris, 1971), esp. 13–73; M. de Certeau *et al.*, *Une politique de la langue: La révolution Française et les patois* (Paris, 1975); Peter Rickard, *A History of the French Language* (London, 1989); Briggs, *Early Modern*, ch. 4.

[48] Jean-Yves Lartichaux, 'Linguistic Politics during the French Revolution,' *Diogenes* 97 (1977): 65–84; François Furet and Jacques Ozouf, *Reading and Writing: Literacy in France from Calvin to Jules Ferry* (Cambridge, 1982), 98–9.

Vietnamese cultural history is less well researched. But we may say that its paradox resided in the simultaneous existence of a cultural/religious fault between the Confucian elite and the lower orders—a divide at least as wide as that in Japan or France—and what would seem to have been (at least in the north and center) a genuinely popular, often xenophobic ethnicity. Both of these phenomena may be traced in part to the Neo-Confucian revolution of the fifteenth century, with its emphases on intensive elite education and on erecting novel cultural boundaries between Vietnamese, on the one hand, and southern 'barbarians' and Chinese, on the other. The cultural system of the monarchy, as it had existed since the eleventh century, thus was substantially redefined. Thereafter, according to John Whitmore, Insun Yu, and Nola Cooke, the principal cultural thrusts involved: (a) the partial diffusion and simultaneous modification of Confucian and Vietnamese ethnic norms among lower social strata, especially in the northern lowlands, through official indoctrination, wider literacy, the expanding use of texts written in Vietnamese *nom*, rather than elite Chinese, characters; and the proliferation of patriotic myths and sanctioned tutelary cults, (b) the southward extension of *both* elite and popular culture into erstwhile Cham and Khmer areas (but not the western highlands) through conquest, deliberate acculturation, and—of critical import—large-scale migration which swamped minority peoples. In 1470 between the Hai Van Pass and Cau Mau it is doubtful whether even 10% of lowlanders spoke Vietnamese, but by 1830 possibly 60% did so. In the Vietnamese empire as a whole in 1830 perhaps 85% spoke a Vietnamese dialect. Yet elongated geography ensured that regional distinctions—political, but also social and religious—remained pronounced, certainly no less than in Japan or France. Moreover, if we recall that Vietnam's population was only a fraction that of the other two realms, integration seems yet more modest.[49]

[49] On integration and divergences, O.W. Wolters, *Two Essays on Dai Viet in the Fourteenth Century* (New Haven, 1988); Whitmore, 'Le Government'; Yu, *Law and Society*; P.B. Lafont (ed.), *Les frontiers du Vietnam* (Paris, 1989), 11–24, 136–55; Nola Cooke, 'Colonial Political Myth and the Problem of the Other' (PhD, Australian National Univ. [ANU], 1991); Li Tana, ' "The Inner Region": A Social and Economic History of Nguyen Vietnam in the Seventeenth and Eighteenth Centuries' (PhD, ANU, 1992); Huynh Kim Khanh, *Vietnamese Communism 1925–1945* (Ithaca, 1982), 26–34; Truong Buu Lam, *Patterns of Vietnamese Response to Foreign Intervention: 1858–1900* (New Haven, 1967); Woodside, *Vietnam*; David E.F. Henley, 'Ethnogeographic Integration and Exclusion in Anticolonial Nationalism,' *Comparative Studies in Society and History [CSSH]* 37, 2 (1995): 286–324.

In Burma as well, vertical and lateral standardization increased, but fourteenth-century invasions and subsequent changes in the structure of the monkhood meant that by comparison with the three previous examples, the link between post-1500 formations and charter kingdoms was weak. As a result both of this 'late start' and of difficult highland geography, imperial cultural unity remained limited, all the more so if one considers that the population was yet smaller than in Vietnam. For some three hundred years after Pagan's fall (1287), no ethnic or cultural current—neither Burman, nor Mon, nor Tai—dominated the Irrawaddy basin. Not surprisingly, Theravada religious traditions remained localized and syncretic. Starting in the mid-sixteenth century, however, northern-based reunification under Burman leadership was associated with sustained military and demographic assaults against the once thriving Mon culture of Lower Burma, with the development of a more popular and self-consciously Burman national literature, and with the promulgation of Theravada orthodoxy as defined by the Burman capital. Arguably the Mon wars were central to the emergence of a sharply defined Burman identity, and by 1830 Mon culture in Lower Burma had been effectively extinguished through repression, Burman migration, and voluntary assimilation. Likewise in the vast highland perimeter, select Burman motifs—calendars, alphabets, rituals, dress, architecture—were mimicked by vassal Tai elites. Yet unlike Mons, upland leaders rarely changed ethnicity, while upland commoners remained yet more insulated. If 85% of those subject to Hue in 1830 identified themselves in some contexts as Vietnamese, probably only 60% of Ava's subjects regarded themselves as Burmans. Even as Burman culture became more articulate and aggressive, therefore, the realm was still conceptualized as a polyethnic Theravada domain.[50]

Like Burma, Siam had a modest-size core ethnie, peppered with alien deportees and surrounded by minority populations whose elites were liable to incorporate selected imperial motifs. So, too, within the Chaophraya basin, vertical integration was reflected in more orthodox Theravada observance, a lively interaction of elite and popular literary styles in Siamese rather than in Pali or Khmer, and a modest diffusion of Siamese ethnicity. Notwithstanding recent large-scale admixtures of alien deportees, in 1830 a majority of

[50] See Victor Lieberman, 'Was the Seventeenth Century A Watershed in Burmese History?' in Reid, *Early Modern*, 240–9, and sources.

Chaophraya basin residents probably considered themselves Siamese in most contexts, and the state, though poly-ethnic and ideologically universalist, was also preeminently associated with Siamese culture. Yet on the whole the link between ethnicity and polity appears to have been weaker than in Burma, and the effort at ethnic (as opposed to religious) patronage less pronounced. In part perhaps this reflected the novelty of Siamese ethnicity itself: whereas Burman ethnicity and culture had roots in the Pagan era, Siamese identity gradually emerged from a blend of Angkorean, Tai, and Mon elements only after Angkor's collapse in the fifteenth century. Indeed, Professor Wyatt has suggested that Khmer remained the preferred court tongue into the 1400s, and a documentary language into the 1500s.[51] In part ethnic boundaries may have been less well defined because Siam—until 1759, when it entered a fifty-year struggle with Burma—lacked a counterpart to the bitter Burman–Mon wars that flared over some three centuries. In part ethnicity was less prominent, because the court, located near the coast, patronized and identified to an unparalleled degree with Chinese and other alien merchants.[52]

The Russian empire offers perhaps the clearest example of limited lateral and vertical assimilation outside the core. From the fifteenth to seventeenth centuries Russian and smaller numbers of Lithuanian, German, and Tatar warriors forged a court culture at Moscow that intersected with provincial traditions chiefly through its emphasis on 'Holy Russia' as a theocratic community under the protection of the Orthodox tsar. To sanction westward expansion, Moscow ideologues later invoked the legacy of Kiev, but in fact Muscovite/Great Russian ethnicity and institutions—like those of Siam—were relatively novel.[53] The interdependence of an emergent Great Russian ethnicity, Orthodoxy, and loyalty to the Muscovite tsar became apparent in sixteenth-century miracle cults; in anti-Catholic,

[51] Personal communication, June 1995.

[52] Wyatt, *Thailand*, chs 4–6; Sunait Chutintaranond, 'The Image of the Burmese Enemy Through History: Thai Perspective,' *Journal of the Siam Society* 80, 1 (1992): 1–32; Thongchai Winichakul, *Siam Mapped* (Honolulu, 1994), ch. 1; Hong Lysa, *Thailand in the Nineteenth Century* (Singapore, 1984), chs 1–4; B.J. Terwiel, *Through Travellers' Eyes* (Bangkok, 1989), 224–33.

[53] Edward L. Keenan, 'On Certain Mythical Beliefs and Russian Behaviors,' in S. Frederick Starr (ed.), *The Legacy of History in Russia and the New States of Eurasia* (Armonk, NY, 1994), 19–40; Jaroslaw Pelenski, 'The Origins of the Official Muscovite Claims to the "Kievan Inheritance",' *Harvard Ukrainian Studies [HUS]* 1 (1977): 29–52; and Kivelson, this volume.

anti-Polish movements during the Time of Troubles, 1604–1613; and perhaps in subsequent associations between Catholicism and witchcraft. Although in constant tension with more local loyalties, by 1600 Great Russian identity seems to have been rooted among townsmen, gentry, and sectors of the Muscovite peasantry. Subsequently, however, in contrast to Burma or Siam but in common with Vietnam, elite exposure to foreign influences weakened vertical ties. The seventeenth-century Schism and the Petrine revolution opened a chasm (that was only beginning to close in the early 1800s) between a secular Westernizing literate nobility and the enserfed peasantry, still illiterate and suspicious of new impositions. No less disruptive, rapid imperial expansion to the late 1800s surrounded the Great Russian core with massive populations of culturally distinct Ukrainians, Poles, Jews, Baltic, Turkic, and Caucasian peoples. Despite Russian immigration and periodic efforts at proselytism, Russification in most outlying zones had but limited success among provincial townsmen and elites (as in the Ukraine), but virtually no rural demotic impact, so by 1795 non-Russians already constituted 52% of the population. Somewhat perhaps as in Burma, a poly-ethnic imperial vision therefore coexisted uneasily with a developing national culture and national concept, in this case, that of the Great Russian nation as distinct from other Slavs and dominant within the empire.[54]

What was the significance of these varied cultural patterns? The diffusion of rituals, dialects, literatures, and so forth was a sign that commercial, communications, and patronage circuits (to be discussed below) were drawing local groups into more sustained interaction. But to go further and assume that conformity in outer behavior necessarily implied an identity of thought or interest is quite unjustified. Old identities and cultural levels rarely disappeared, but came to occupy more restricted niches. Because different strata fit new motifs to particularized world views, or in some cases self-consciously sought to defend older identities against a threatened

[54] Ethnic figures from Paul Werth, personal communication, Oct. 1995. See J.L. Fennell, *The Emergence of Moscow 1304–1359* (London, 1968); Bushkovitch, *Religion*, 34, 74–89, 111–18; essays by *idem* and James Cracraft, *HUS*, 10, 3/4 (1986), 355–76, 524–41; Michael Cherniavsky, *Tsar and People* (New Haven, 1961); Richard Hellie, *Slavery in Russia 1450–1725* (Chicago, 1982), 390–4; Madariaga, *Catherine*, chs 20, 32; Greenfeld, *Nationalism*, ch. 3; Thaden, *Western Borderlands*, pts 1, 2; Zenon E. Kohut, *Russian Centralism and Ukrainian Autonomy* (Cambridge, MA, 1988); Michael Khodarkovsky, *Where Two Worlds Met* (Ithaca, NY, 1992).

loss of status, the spread of texts and urban-based norms might easily multiply interpretations and conflict.[55] Thus in Renaissance France, far from promoting unity, wider literacy helped to breed heresy and civil war. At best we may say that the appearance of networks encompassing larger numbers created a potential identity.

This potential could be critical, however, in several contexts. Most obviously among intellectual and political elites but to some extent among lower strata as well, growing interaction tended to open up more unified fields for discussion and contestation. By definition, standardization provided a superficially similar set of references, an enhanced sense of interaction. Precisely because the same texts and terms meant different things to different groups, negotiation and struggle to determine normative interpretations became more frequent. If the sixteenth-century Wars of Religion in France showed the disruptive effects of wider literacy, they also showed how certain hitherto mute and marginal strata could become embroiled in national debate.[56] Somewhat the same could be said of the religious Schism in seventeenth-century Russia or the late 1700s robe-wrapping dispute over monastic standards in Burma.[57]

Beyond this, in so far as specific languages, rituals, and ethnicities were associated with political centers, assimilation could transform cultural markers into a shorthand for political allegiance. By definition (one is tempted to say), identities require alterity.[58] To the extent that features were universal, they provided no basis for self-conscious association precisely because, like ears, they were unremarkable; within what an external observer might see as a more or less homogeneous space, self-definitions tended to focus on class,

[55] Cf. Roger Chartier's notion of cultural 'appropriation,' *The Cultural Uses of Print in Early Modern France* (Princeton, 1987), esp. 6–9; Natalie Zemon Davis, *Society and Culture in Early Modern France* (Stanford, 1965), ch. 7; and Vincente L. Rafael's notion of (mis)translation, *Contracting Colonialism* (Ithaca, 1988). A.P. Cohen, *The Symbolic Construction of Community* (London, 1985) argues that symbolism owes its versatility precisely to the fact that it carries no inherent meaning.

[56] Yardeni, *Conscience nationale*, pt II.

[57] See Bushkovitch, *Religion and Society*, 70–167 *passim*; Michael Cherniavsky, 'The Old Believers and the New Religion,' *Slavic Review* 25 (1966): 1–39; Lieberman, *Cycles*, 178–9, 238, 262; Maha-dama-thin-gyan, *Tha-thana-lin-ga-ya sa-dan* (Rangoon, 1897), 185ff.

[58] For different versions of this claim, Bendix, *Kings or People*; Partha Chatterjee, *The Nation and Its Fragments* (Princeton, 1993), 138; Prasenjit Duara, 'Deconstructing the Chinese Nation,' *The Australian Journal of Chinese Affairs* 30 (1993): 5–6; Orest Ranum, 'Counter-Identities of Western European Nations in the Early Modern Period: Definitions and Points of Departure,' in Peter Boerner (ed.), *Concepts of National Identity* (Baden-Baden, 1986), 63–78.

clan, village, and so forth (although these often acquired subcultural representation). But sustained contacts—through proselytism, migrations, trade, or most critically, war—with a system that was judged to be external and threatening could modify the equation. During periods of severe dislocation or conflict, contiguous communities were tempted to seize, at times arbitrarily, on common symbols in order to reinforce, or even to erect broad in-group boundaries, which in turn could strengthen their common claim to resources.[59] This was particularly true when (a) war was directed against a foe that could be distinguished easily from the host population by virtue of such markers; (b) the host population could link its cause to an enduring political entity, be it territorial, dynastic, or more abstractly institutional.

Without a formal theory of nationality or a system of sustained mobilization, supra-local identities were likely to recede, or at least lose visibility, once the alien threat disappeared. As noted, such identities tended to affect upper strata more than peasants, towns more than villages; and to use Prasenjit Duara's phrase, ethnic boundaries were typically 'soft.'[60] Over time, however, a repeated sense of external challenge could combine with denser internal communications and commercial circuits to harden boundaries by yoking the welfare of diverse social groups to that of the political center. Such linkages were proclaimed in oral culture through folk tales, ballads, and puppet shows, as well as in 'national' cults devoted to protective saints and tutelary deities—of which early modern France, Burma, Vietnam, Japan, and Russia all offer distinctive examples. Kingdoms were frequently imagined as unique fields of holy sites, guarded by these deities, to whose protection the ruler ensured access by his piety and morality. On a more formal level, in each country (with the apparent exception of Siam), warfare or enhanced competition engendered writings—histories, epics, fictive genealogies—stressing the superiority of domestic over alien culture.[61] For their part, espe-

[59] Cf. Fredrik Barth (ed.), *Ethnic Groups and Boundaries* (Boston, 1969), esp. 86–100; Evelyn Rawski, 'Research Themes,' 95, citing S.T. Leong; C.A. Bayly, 'The Pre-history of Communalism?' *MAS* 19, 2 (1985): 177–203; Cohen, *Symbolic Construction*, 16, 69, 109, 115.

[60] Duara, 'Chinese Nation,' 20–5; *idem*, 'Historicizing National Identity, or Who Imagines What and When,' in Geoff Eley and Ronald Grigor Suny (eds), *Becoming National* (Oxford, 1996), 151–78.

[61] See previous case studies, plus *CHJ* IV, 412, 616–20, 639–42. On national tutelary deities (of decreasing importance in France and Russia after *c.* 1700), Beaune, *Ideology*, pt I; Bushkovitch, *Religion*, ch. 4; Khanh, *Vietnamese Communism*, 31–

cially in contested border districts, leaders sometimes sought to standardize language or cultic practice, in part to improve administrative efficiency, but more basically to strengthen identification with the throne.[62] Thus a discourse of cultural difference helped to structure political thought and action.

To be sure, these political visions outside Europe and those prior to *c.* 1750 in Europe differed from modern nationalism in numerous critical dimensions. Notwithstanding traditions of consultation and even (as in France) of royal election by the great men of the realm, polities were conceived as dynastic entities in which sovereignty flowed not from the people upwards, but from the ruler, sanctioned by the cosmos, downward. In lieu of nationalism's leveling emphasis on citizenship, equal rights, and horizontal comradeship, early modern political ethics were hierarchic, anti-entropic, obsessed with innumerable particularities of status and privilege and with the unequal distribution of patronage. For these reasons, and because by implication subordinates entered the polity not as a collectivity but through individual ties to the sovereign, there was no requirement that minority ethnicities be assimilated or excluded, or even that rulers be of the same culture as the bulk of their subjects. In both Europe and Southeast Asia foreign princes took the throne without murmur, mercenaries figured prominently, alien territories were routinely annexed. Above all, with politics the more or less exclusive preserve of established elites, with self-replicating microcultures enjoying a long-sanctioned autonomy, and with no means of mass communication, official attempts to modify popular culture remained episodic and relatively feeble. In recently annexed areas such efforts normally sought not to extinguish minority cultures, an impractical undertaking, but to assert the ritual primacy of the complex with which the court was most closely associated. Because religion provided the principal sanction of legitimacy, efforts at standardization in *ancien régime* France, Russia, and Southeast Asia focused on ritual practice more than on ethnicity. And by extension, the

2; H. Maspero, 'Etudes d'histoire d'Annam,' *Bulletin de l'Ecole Française d'Extrême Orient* 16 (1916), 17; Melford E. Spiro, *Burmese Supernaturalism* (Englewood Cliffs, NJ, 1967), pt III; H.L. Shorto, 'The *dewatau sotapan*,' *Bulletin of the School of Oriental and African Studies* 30, 1 (1967): 127–41; *CHJ*, III, 140, 147, 455ff.

[62] E.g., Peter Sahlins, *Boundaries* (Berkeley, 1989), 115–27; Victor Lieberman, 'Ethnic Politics in Eighteenth Century Burma,' *MAS* 12, 3 (1978): 455–82; David Chandler, *A History of Cambodia* (Boulder, CO, 1992), 125–7; Madariaga, *Catherine*, chs 20, 32.

notion of discrete national culture, although by no means unknown, was in constant tension both with more cosmopolitan dynastic and religious loyalties and with more particularist identities. Long after annexation, once independent territories retained a keen sense of separate identity, so that multiple loyalties—to Brittany *and* France, to Chiengmai *and* Bangkok—were not merely tolerated, but normal.

Nonetheless, efforts by such theoreticians of nationalism as Ernest Gellner and Benedict Anderson to erect a yawning, unbridgeable gulf between premodern political loyalties and post-1789 (or 1750) European political movements overstate the case, at least so far as the countries under review are concerned.[63] Not only do these authors universalize, but they do so on the basis of some of the most artificial and novel of all twentieth-century political creations, those of Indonesia and certain Arab states. Early modern political identities varied enormously in space and time. But between *c.* 1500 and 1800 the most aggressive and cohesive of the movements under review—in France, Burma, Vietnam, and perhaps Muscovy—shared at least four elements with post-1750/1789 Western nationalism.

First was the aforementioned tendency for cultural features to serve as a badge of allegiance among politically active elements, usually the military or urban elites, but also in periods of invasion or crisis, more popular strata. Often a complex of traits fluctuated depending on the degree of religious or linguistic distinction between would-be in-groups and changing out-groups in border locales. Traits, moreover, could be religious, linguistic, or more broadly ethnic (to risk anachronistic vocabulary), but all tended to serve as political markers. In the fifteenth century, Burmans tended to distinguish themselves from Tai/Shans by language and religious ritual, but during the subsequent Mon wars, hairstyles and body tattoos became the chief indices of loyalty to the Burman court.[64] In western Russia during the Time of Troubles, to distinguish 'Poles' from 'Russians,' people focused on dress, language, hairstyle, and above all,

[63] Gellner, *Nations and Nationalism* (Ithaca, 1983); Anderson, *Imagined Communities*, rev. edn (London, 1991). Also emphasizing modern novelty are Karl Deutsch, *Nationalism and Social Communication* (Cambridge, MA, 1953); Ronald Grigor Suny, *The Revenge of the Past* (Stanford, 1993); E.J. Hobsbawm, *Nations and Nationalism Since 1870* (Cambridge, 1990); Eley and Suny, *Becoming National*, 1–37. Cf. the emphasis on continuity in Smith, *Ethnic Origins*; and John A. Armstrong, *Nations before Nationalism* (Chapel Hill, NC, 1982).

[64] Lieberman, 'Ethnic Politics.'

religion.[65] Vietnamese conflicts with Chams prior to the Neo-Confucian revolution lacked consistent symbolism, but post-1470 efforts to 'civilize' Chams and Khmers tended to single out the latter's dress, speech, hairstyle, and culinary habits as worthy of eradication.[66] In Colette Beaune's reconstruction of the French 'royal religion,' pro-Valois peasants and townsmen sometimes distinguished themselves by their attachment to particular saints and to the sacred image of the ruler. Among French *robins*, nobles, and upper bourgeois by the late 1500s and early 1600s, culture, language, and history began to demarcate what Emmanuel Le Roy Ladurie does not hesitate to call 'national identity.'[67] Such practices anticipated the modern use of language, birth, and history to proclaim nationality, although in France even in the early 1800s such criteria remained surprisingly fluid and indeterminate.[68] I hasten to note that while print capitalism, on which Benedict Anderson lays great stress, clearly accelerated the standardization of language and identity, long before the introduction of popular printed materials in France, Russia, Burma, or Vietnam, oral traditions (combined in some cases with manuscripts) were adequate to maintain stable linkages between culture and political loyalty.

Second, not merely the symbols, but the broader conceptualization of the state, the intellectual and emotional structures of identity, evolved, so that while we can acknowledge the radically novel implications of popular sovereignty in late 1700s France, we can also see that the eighteenth century continued a much older process of sustained redefinition. According to Liah Greenfeld's typology of French nationalism, it passed through overlapping stages of theocentric religious/dynastic loyalty (to the early 1600s), political/royalist identity with vague religious overtones (to the mid-1700s), followed by ostensibly secular notions of popular sovereignty and

[65] Yet no more than in Burma did such distinctions preclude inter-ethnic alliance. S.F. Platonov, *The Time of Troubles* (Lawrence, KA, 1985); Basil Dmytryshyn (ed.), *Medieval Russia: A Source Book, 850–1700* (Ft Worth, TX, 1991), 359–72; Serge A. Zenkovsky, *Medieval Russia's Epics, Chronicles, and Tales* (New York, 1963), 379–87.

[66] John Whitmore, 'A New View of the World' (MS); Chandler, *Cambodia*, 123–32.

[67] Beaune, *Ideology*, esp. pt I, and 323, focusing on the pre-1450 era, but arguing that the French royal religion maintained its peasant hold through 1789; Ladurie, *French State*, 276–83. Similar arguments appear in Krynen, *Idéal du prince*, 269–77; Yardeni, *Conscience nationale*, 43–56.

[68] See Hobsbawm, *Nations and Nationalism*, 18–21, 87–8.

citizenship. These changes were accompanied by more exclusive notions of administrative/political space.[69] In the Irrawaddy basin political-cum-ideological structures obviously were far more conservative, but they were not static. During the 1400s the Upper Burma kingdom was a dynastic entity wherein authority derived from a combination of puissant ancestors, Buddhist sacrality, and protection of the God Indra. Alongside these notions, in the sixteenth century more explicitly Buddhist themes of universal dominion under a World Ruler (*cakkavatti*) became prominent; while by the eighteenth century universal imagery was tempered by explicit claims of Burman supremacy within a polyethnic domain, and Buddhist obligation itself was recast in more abstract, moral terms.[70] No doubt more dynamic intellectual typologies could be constructed for Japan.[71]

Third, difficult to quantify though it may be, as the foregoing country sketches suggest, the proportion of subjects in any given territory willing to identify politically and symbolically with the center, particularly in periods of crisis, gradually expanded prior to 1800, anticipating far more rapid acculturation after the mid-nineteenth century. In many cases, state-centered ethnicities cohered among elites only in the fifteenth or sixteenth century. Modified identities then diffused vertically and laterally in the 1600s and 1700s. In Vietnam, for example, the Confucian redefinition of Vietnamese identity was substantially complete among Tonkin delta literati in the 1400s, but on the Mekong frontier in the mid-1800s this equation was still being contested at all social levels. In France, to return to the *locus classicus* of modern nationalism, we have seen that the Revolutionary-Napoleonic regime, building on long-standing trends, tried to push French identity further into the countryside, but 1790–1815 was actually less of a watershed than 1840–1860. Eugen Weber has argued for another assimilative leap under the Third Republic. [72]

Finally, whereas it is often assumed that the universalizing religious basis of premodern ideologies vitiated their territorial power, in fact the situation was more complicated: both before and after *c.*

[69] Greenfeld, *Nationalism*, ch. 2. On conceptualization of political space, Paul Alliès, *L'invention du territoire* (Grenoble, 1980).

[70] See Inscriptions 848–1076 in Chas. Duroiselle, *A List of Inscriptions Found in Burma*, I (Rangoon, 1921); Lieberman, *Cycles*, chs 2, 5.

[71] Cf. *CHJ*, IV, 89–95, 596–659; Ooms, *Tokugawa Ideology*.

[72] Ted W. Margadant, 'French Rural Society in the Nineteenth Century,' *Agricultural History* 53 (1979): 644–51; Weber, *Peasants into Frenchmen* (Stanford, 1976); James R. Lehning, *Peasant and French* (Cambridge, 1995).

1750 territorial versions of universal religions provided a critical source of legitimacy. The fusion of spatially-bounded doctrines and ethnicity was most obvious in those areas where adjacent peoples tended to support different faiths, which in turn could provide an organizing principle for broad social differences. Such, for example, was the case on the contested Vietnamese/Khmer frontier; or in 1500s Muscovy, surrounded by Catholics, animists, and Muslims. Russia, in the words of ideologues and presumably to some extent even in the minds of peasants, was the last refuge of Orthodoxy on whose fidelity the fate of mankind depended. But also in regions of apparently undivided allegiance—Theravada Southeast Asia, Confucian East Asia, Catholic Europe—a similar logic operated: doctrines were particularized within each polity, said to embody that doctrine in its purest form. The religion of Gotama Buddha shone only in Burma, whose rulers periodically felt obliged to invade Siam and other Theravada realms to clean up impure practices. 'Decadent China, orthodox Vietnam' was a favorite conceit of the emperor Minh-mang (r. 1820–1841).[73] Japanese Confucians claimed for their country the centrality once reserved for China, while in the late Tokugawa era scholars of 'national learning' (*kokugaku*) went further by rejecting much of Chinese culture in favor of expressly Japanese values.[74] Since at least the fourteenth century Frenchmen styled their realm and ruler 'most Christian' and posited a direct link between France and God, derived from the royal blood, that bypassed the Church of the world.[75] Apotropaic cults involving national deities/saints represented a popular version of this same fusion. Nor, one hastens to add, did religiously-based European identities fade after 1789: a sequential opposition between 'religious modes of thought' and 'the age of nationalism' is too neat.[76] Quite apart from the fact that the French nation came to incarnate the sacred and to translate Christian motifs, in Britain Linda Colley has shown that Protestant superiority continued to provide an absolutely critical national bond into the mid-1800s.[77]

While rejecting primordialist notions of nationalism—to repeat, most of the state-focused identities I have described cohered only in

[73] Woodside, *Vietnam*, 121.

[74] *CHJ*, IV, 412, 616–20, 639–42; Totman, *Early Modern Japan*, 366–77; H.D. Harootunian, *Things Seen and Unseen* (Chicago, 1987).

[75] Beaune, *Ideology*, ch. 6, p. 313; Krynen, *Idéal du prince*, 207–39; Collins, *State*, 101–2, 173–4.

[76] Phrases from Anderson, *Imagined Communities*, 11.

[77] Colley, *Britons* (New Haven, 1992), ch. 1, esp. p. 18.

the fifteenth or sixteenth century and long thereafter border populations faced genuine ethnic choices—I therefore think it best to regard late eighteenth-century changes as the most dramatic in a series of transformations involving the symbols and practical reach of supra-local loyalties. And again, basic patterns transcended the East–West divide.

Dynamics of Integration: General Considerations

In sum, between *c.* 1450 and 1830 across mainland Southeast Asia, in what became the Russian empire, in those territories that cohered as France, and in the Japanese islands we find parallel tendencies towards the consolidation of fragmented political units, more efficient systems of extraction and control, and more uniform cultural expression.

But to date we have said little about underlying dynamics. Why was each of these areas more cohesive in 1830 than in 1400? As the history of Eastern Europe, Mughal India, or Muslim Southeast Asia demonstrates, this was hardly inevitable. Why did not some of our six countries unify, others disintegrate, and yet others oscillate in random fashion? In these same countries between *c.* 1400 and 1830 why should subperiods have been broadly synchronized? Finally, how do we explain enormous discrepancies in administrative penetration and levels of cultural standardization?

Existing historiography is of uncertain value in addressing these questions. On the one hand, national histories obviously provide the raw material as well as theoretical approaches from which a larger canvas can be drawn. Yet they often ignore non-military external factors, regard national features as adequate explanation of internal evolution, and thus offer limited insight as to why European—not to mention Eurasian—states followed different trajectories but converged in more integrated structures. At the other extreme, world system theorists, as noted, tend towards an externalist monocausality, often fail to connect global rhythms to local structures, and favor a core–periphery model prior to *c.* 1750 that has no evidential base outside the Western subsystem.

Of greater interest are comparative European schemas, which I would divide broadly into social analyses and geopolitical analyses. Scholars in the first category, represented by Barrington Moore, Jr., Robert Brenner, Perry Anderson, Douglass C. North and Robert Paul

Thomas attribute different political or economic outcomes to variations in social/institutional structure, particularly as the latter influenced property rights and landholding.[78] Thus Perry Anderson explains different forms of absolutism in Western and Eastern Europe by focusing on variable political/economic links among aristocrats, townsmen, and peasants. By contrast, without ignoring internal factors, Theda Skocpol, Samuel Finer, Charles Tilly, and Brian Downing have emphasized the impact on state formation of international competition, as influenced in particular by new military technology.[79] Few of these studies have an extra-European dimension, none is particularly interested in cultural change, and apart from Tilly and Finer, none addresses the question of why local units cohered over time. Yet not only is their identification of variables critical to any wider discussion, but their habit of organizing diverse state-building patterns along unified continua can easily be generalized outside Europe.

I shall approach Eurasian dynamics in several ways. In the next sections I shall discuss in synchronic fashion broad processes promoting consolidation, including what I term the economic, military, and intellectual/institutional dynamics. By analyzing local and external variables governing each process, I seek a general framework within which to explain the strength, extent, and chronology of integration in particular contexts. Thus although my central themes diverge from those of European comparativists, I am no less interested in gradients of difference. I shall then interweave these dynamics in a brief historical narrative designed to suggest how and why political development, that is, collapse, recovery, and acceleration in scattered areas tended to coincide. Finally, in subsequent writings I shall offer case studies that bring these abstractions closer to the ground, dissect the variables, and discuss overwhelming areas of uncertainty.

Economic Growth and Its Causes

Although in any given society there was constant overlap, it may be useful to identify four ideal types of economic growth: (a) 'modern

[78] Moore, *Social Origins of Dictatorship and Democracy* (Boston, 1966); T.H. Aston and C.H.E. Philpin (eds), *The Brenner Debate* (Cambridge, 1987); Anderson, *Lineages*; North and Thomas, *The Rise of the Western World* (Cambridge, 1973).

[79] Skocpol, *States and Social Revolutions* (Cambridge, 1979); Finer in Charles Tilly (ed.), *The Formation of National States in Western Europe* (Princeton, 1975), 84–163;

economic growth,' as understood since the work of Simon Kuznets, in which sustained investment, technological advances, and a favorable political climate created continuous increases in productivity per workday and in total output within a constantly changing production-possibility frontier; (b) 'Smithian growth,' in which greater specialization, wider exchange, and incremental improvements yielded more modest advances in productivity and output, but without creating a new production-possibility frontier; such a growth pattern could accommodate commercial manufacture ('proto-industrialization),' but not industrialization *per se*; (c) 'extensive growth,' in which output expanded through the sheer addition of units, but within a stable technological context and with static productivity per workday; (d) 'involutionary growth,' in which the production-possibility frontier again failed to change but in which productivity per work day actually fell due to excessive demographic pressure on a stable resource base.[80]

Parts of Western Europe, France included, experienced 'Smithian,' 'extensive,' and 'involutionary' growth at various periods after 1400, but by 1830 if not earlier, advanced sectors of the French urban and agricultural economy had entered a phase of 'modern growth.'[81] Russia, which benefited from West European technical and intellectual inputs, would approach 'modern growth' in its industrial sector by mid-century. However, as noted, despite considerable dynamism, few believe Japan in 1850 was on the verge of a Western-style transformation. Clearly Southeast Asia knew only 'extensive' and 'involutionary' expansion and modest 'Smithian' growth. Although post-1600 Southeast Asian textile production, for example, diversified and was accompanied by new marketing structures, technology seems to have been stable. Nor in Burma as late as 1830, despite modifications, was the landmarket free of communal or corporate claims. Symptom and cause of underdevelopment, in both mainland

Tilly in *ibid.*, 3–83; *idem*, *Coercion*; Downing, *The Military Revolution and Political Change* (Princeton, 1992).

[80] This typology I have developed from Kuznets, *Modern Economic Growth* (New Haven, 1966), esp. 490–509; Feuerwerker, 'Address,' 760–62; Joel Mokyr, *The Lever of Riches* (New York, 1990), 3–16; Philip C.C. Huang, 'A Reply to Ramon Myers,' *JAS* 50, 3 (1991): 629–33; *idem*, *Peasant Family*, esp. 11–18; Subrahmanyam, *Merchants*, 2–7; Frank and Gills, *World System*, 81–114, 149–51. On proto-industrialization, see Wigen, 'Geographic Imagination,' 13–15.

[81] Roger Price, *An Economic History of Modern France 1730–1914* (London, 1975); Pierre Léon *et al.*, *Historie économique et sociale de la France*, III (Paris, 1976); Tom Kemp, *Economic Forces in French History* (London, 1971), chs 5, 6.

Southeast Asia and Russia in the early 1800s, indigenous merchants remained extremely weak *vis-à-vis* foreign rivals.[82]

How then do we explain Western Europe's unique vigor? Their low population densities, modest internal demand, and relative isolation from large external markets disqualified Russia and mainland Southeast Asia as serious independent economic contenders, so in a sense West European exceptionalism is only an intellectual problem when compared to the trajectories of such densely populated, urbanized areas as India, China, or Japan. Any number of individual factors have been cited to explain Western Europe's peculiar path, but one suspects that an extraordinarily complex, poorly understood synergy was at work. Abu-Lughod and others have seized on New World discoveries as the key variable. But if Atlantic trade had a major acceleratory role, this thesis cannot explain why Europe and not some other region undertook colonial expansion initially; nor does it address the argument that by 1500 the average West European already enjoyed a major advantage over his Chinese counterpart in access to animate and inanimate sources of power.[83] Francesca Bray suggests that European cereals favored capital-intensive, innovative enterprise more readily than did rice agriculture, but this begs critical differences between France and Russia, or Japan and Siam.[84] E.L. Jones emphasizes the diversity of Europe's ecological 'portfolio,' but it is doubtful whether this *per se* distinguished the region from East Asia.[85] Jones, following J. Hajnal and R.S. Schofield, also calls attention to Western Europe's late marriage age and relatively low birth rates, which may have facilitated capital accumulation and technological investment.[86] But again, if it inhibited immiseration, in post-1700 Japan low population growth by itself was inadequate to permit European-style industrialization.

The most common, and perhaps plausible explanations, to which the opening section of this essay called attention, dwell on cultural

[82] Reid, *Age of Commerce*, II, ch. 5; Alfred J. Rieber, *Merchants and Entrepreneurs in Imperial Russia* (Chapel Hill, NC, 1982).

[83] Abu-Lughod, *Hegemony*, ch. 11. Arguments for European precocity appear in Pierre Chaunu, *L'expansion européenne du XIIIe au XVe siècle* (Paris, 1969), 335–39 (cf. Adas, *Machines*, 21); Mann, *Sources*, I, 373–413, 504 (esp. 377–9), which sees a superior European economic dynamic by 1000. Cf. Elvin, *Pattern*, pts 2, 3. See too Patrick O'Brien's modest quantification of the impact of overseas trade, 'European Economic Development: The Contribution of the Periphery,' *The Economic History Review* 35, 1 (1982): 1–18.

[84] Bray, *The Rice Economies* (Berkeley, 1986), esp. 1–7, 198–217.

[85] Jones, *Miracle*, 226–7 and *passim*.

[86] *Ibid.*,15–21, 226–7.

and institutional patterns: Europe's fragmentation of power, which had political, religious, and economic aspects, is said to have fostered an unusual degree of economic competition, with a resultant premium on innovation and on the mobility of commodity and factor markets. Robert Brenner and Hilton Root in their analyses of English and French landlordism, and E.L. Jones, Richard Pipes, John A. Hall, Michael Mann, North and Thomas in their common emphasis on protected individual property rights, implicitly or explicitly contrast the keen responsiveness to market demand in Western Europe and most especially in England, with more politically or communally restrictive systems farther east.[87] The dynamism of Tokugawa agriculture, which Kozo Yamamura has attributed in part to the break-up of complex tenurial systems in favor of nuclear family farms more sensitive to market incentives, may support this line of reasoning.[88] On the other hand, if there was a difference in this respect between Western Europe and Asia, it was probably less in kind than degree, for the closer one looks at China, India, even Southeast Asia, not to mention Japan, the less harmful government or communal interference with the market appears, the more responsive to market changes producers actually seem to have been.[89] The Chinese economic historian Albert Feuerwerker has suggested that Europe's chief distinction resided less in governmental protection for property and market transactions than in the state's inclination to create monetary, legal, and financial institutions that could shift commercial capital to industrial and fixed capital.[90] But then we are still left to explain this inclination.

The main point of this section is that however different social and institutional contexts and associated productivity patterns may have been, in every area under consideration between *c.* 1450 and 1830 total output expanded, while agricultural and craft production became more specialized and commodified. In one region after

[87] Brenner in Aston and Philpin, *Brenner Debate*; Root, *Peasants and King in Burgundy* (Berkeley, 1987); Jones, *Miracle*; Pipes, *Old Regime*; Hall, *Powers and Liberties*; Mann, *Sources*; North and Thomas, *Western World*. Not all are explicitly comparative within Europe, much less Eurasia.

[88] Yamamura in John W. Hall *et al.* (eds), *Japan Before Tokugawa* (Princeton, 1981), 327–72. Cf. Bito Masahide in *CHJ*, IV, 373–8.

[89] See references to Asian dynamism, *supra* and *infra*.

[90] Feuerwerker, 'State and the Economy.' Without attempting East–West comparisons, Philip T. Hoffman, *Growth in a Traditional Society: The French Countryside 1450–1815* (Princeton, 1996), also sees expansion resulting more from favorable political and trade openings than from peculiar cultural features or property rights.

TABLE 1

Population Estimates, in Millions, 1300–1830

	1300	1450	1600	1720	1830
France	18–20	10–12	19–20	23.2	32
Russia	?5–?10	?7	?17	21	59
Japan	?10	?	12	31	31
Burma	?2.5	?2	3.1	?	5
Siam	?	?	?2.2	?	4.5
Vietnam	?	?	4.7	?	7.5

For each date population estimates are within the boundaries of 1830. For sources, see n. 94.

another, including mainland Southeast Asia, rural markets proliferated and grew more competitive, money infiltrated rural life, bulk trade goods as opposed to luxuries figured more prominently, commercial institutions matured. Most visibly perhaps but by no means only in Europe, the growing frequency of transactions encouraged the codification of procedures concerned with money and credit and with the ownership and transfer of goods. According to Gilbert Rozman's schema of urban networks, between *c.* 1400 and 1800 Russia and Japan, both starting at stage D ('imperial' marketing system), and France starting at stage E ('standard marketing'), all advanced to the highest level of urban/commercial integration, stage G ('national marketing'). Burma, Siam, and Vietnam (whose urban histories have yet to be plotted in detail) probably moved from stage D to E.[91] Finally, as we shall see, with urban growth also came greater social complexity and new urban–rural cultural linkages.

At the most general level, I would suggest that economic growth across Eurasia derived from the interaction of the following stimuli. Most obvious perhaps was long-term population growth. Between *c.* 1330 and 1830 the population grew in France by a factor of about 1.7, in mainland Southeast Asia by perhaps two, in Japan by about three, and in Russia, especially the steppe, six-fold or more (see Table 1). Now Brenner, to whom I just referred, has attacked the

[91] Rozman, *Urban Networks in Russia, 1750–1800, and Premodern Periodization* (Princeton, 1976), esp. 33–40, 84. Cf. Emmanuel Le Roy Ladurie (ed.), *Histoire de la France urbaine*, III (Paris, 1981), esp. 287–389; Jurgen Schneider in Fischer *et al.*, *World Economy*, 15–36. On commercial vigor and specialization in our six areas, see previous notes, plus Lieberman, 'Secular Trends'; Hong Lysa, *Thailand*; Nguyen Thanh-Nha, *Tableau économique du Vietnam aux XVII et XVIII siècles* (Paris,1970); Pierre Chaunu and Richard Gascon, *Histoire économique et social de la France*, I, 1 (Paris, 1977); Daniel Hickey, 'Innovation and Obstacles to Growth in the Agriculture of Early Modern France,' *French Historical Studies* 15, 2 (1987): 208–40; Jan de Vries, *The Economy of Europe in an Age of Crisis, 1600–1750* (Cambridge, 1976);

notion that population growth could be considered as having an unambiguous effect, independent of socio-political structure. In his view, 'different [economic] outcomes proceeded from similar demographic trends at different times and in different areas of Europe' depending primarily on the production incentives that ensued from different landlord/peasant relations.[92] With this general reasoning I have no quarrel, and as noted, there is some suggestion that Japanese experience confirms his emphasis on tenurial arrangements. Yet, as Brenner's critics and others outside the European debate have shown, demographic increase also created certain broad economic potentials that cut across societies. For example, although the level of commercialization might vary, in a variety of landholding systems population growth could encourage the multiplication of production units and an increase in aggregate output, hence taxable resources. Moreover, in those contexts where expansion encouraged Smithian division of labor and specialization of function, a growth in numbers could enhance per capita productivity and the possibilities for commercial exchange. Such was the case, for example, where overflow populations opened areas with novel agricultural or mineral assets, as in the Russian steppe, the Southeast Asian deltas, or the alluvial plains of Japan's largest rivers. Smithian growth also might proceed where *ceteris paribus* an increase in aggregate domestic consumption, hence market demand, encouraged handicraft specialization, or where the growth of urban markets or rural handicrafts quickened the demand for raw materials and commercial foodstuffs. Differences in socioeconomic structure notwithstanding, such effects occurred at one time or another in all six countries.[93]

Arcadius Kahan, *The Plow, the Hammer, and the Knout* (Chicago, 1985); Jerome Blum, *Lord and Peasant in Russia* (Princeton, 1961); Totman, *Early Modern Japan*, chs 5, 8, 12–13, 20–1; Tessa Morris-Suzuki, *The Technological Transformation of Japan* (Cambridge, 1994).

[92] Brenner in Aston and Philpin, *Brenner Debate*, 21.

[93] For theoretical discussions of the relation between demographic growth and economic change, and for divergent case studies, see Julian L. Simon, *The Economics of Population Growth* (Princeton, 1977), ch. 2; Ester Boserup, *Population and Technological Change* (Chicago, 1981), 3–9, 76–7, 94–7; M.M. Postan, John Hatcher, Emmanuel Le Roy Ladurie, and Guy Bois in Aston and Philpin, *Brenner Debate*; Mokyr, *Lever*, 4–6; G. William Skinner, 'Marketing and Social Structure in Rural China,' *JAS* 24, 1 (1964): 3–43 and 24, 2 (1965): 195–228; Emmanuel Le Roy Ladurie, *The French Peasantry 1450–1660* (Berkeley, 1987), chs 1–4; and Japanese data in previous notes.

[94] Figures from Elizabeth Hallam, *Capetian France, 987–1328* (London, 1980), 286–8; Ladurie, *Peasantry*, 8–10, 23, 101, 402–6; Fernand Braudel, *The Identity of France*, II (New York, 1990), 156–80; Collins, *State*, 181; Hellie, *Enserfment*, 304–5

But in turn how do we explain the broad synchronization in population increase, which in many areas was particularly vigorous between *c.* 1440 and 1600 and again (outside Japan) after *c.* 1720? Climatologists have pointed to favorable agricultural conditions at the latitudes of northern France, central Russia, and Japan during much of the period between *c.* 900 and 1300, less notably between *c.* 1450 and 1620, and then again after *c.* 1720; there is some suggestion that these same periods saw increased rainfall, hence yields, in parts of Southeast Asia.[95] To such potential climatic influences on demography must be added epidemiological rhythms: the dramatic recovery in Western Europe and Russia after *c.* 1430 from bubonic plague, which had depressed population by a quarter to a third; the post-1400 recovery in China from comparable depopulation caused by disease and/or political upheavals, a recovery which stimulated migration to Southeast Asia and trade with Japan and other parts of Eurasia; the possible conversion after *c.* 1450 of smallpox, measles, and plague in coastal Southeast Asia from epidemic to endemic character; the virtual disappearance of European plague and the retreat of smallpox from the early 1700s.[96] Goldstone and Ester Boserup claim that long-term mortality was determined less by nutrition than by world-wide disease patterns. In turn Goldstone argues for a strong correlation in northern latitudes between cooler, more variable weather and virulent epidemics.[97]

Yet even if we accept that more benign disease and climate patterns helped to multiply Eurasia's population after *c.* 1450 and again after *c.* 1720, such patterns alone cannot explain secular demographic and economic trends. Consider: over the long term not only population, but commercial integration and specialization grew in

(I extrapolate from Miliukov); Blum, *Lord*, 17, 120, 278; Totman, *Before Perry*, 128; *idem*, *Early Modern Japan*, 140, 251, 467; Lieberman, 'Secular Trends,' 11–12; Reid, *Age of Commerce*, I, 14; Larry Sternstein, 'The Growth of the Population of the World's Pre-eminent "Primate City",' *JSEAS* 15, 1 (1984): 45; Li Tana, 'Inner Region'; Woodside, *Vietnam*, 158–9; Colin McEvedy and Richard Jones, *Atlas of World Population History* (London, 1978).

[95] See *supra*, n. 18, esp. Lamb, *Changing Climate*, 219–20, on Russia; plus Reid, *Age of Commerce*, II, 291–8.

[96] G. William Skinner, 'Presidential Address: The Structure of Chinese History,' *JAS* 44, 2 (1985): 271–92; Eastman, *Family, Fields*, 4; Robert S. Gottfried, *The Black Death* (New York, 1983); Lawrence Langer, 'The Black Death in Russia,' *Russian History [RH]* 21, 1 (1975): 53–67; Carlo M. Cipolla, *Before the Industrial Revolution* (New York, 1980), ch. 5; and sources in Victor Lieberman, 'Local Integration and Eurasian Analogies,' *MAS* 27, 3 (1993), 498, n. 48.

[97] Goldstone, *Revolution*, 180–3, 356; Boserup, *Population*, 94–5.

cumulative, ratchet-like fashion, whereas climate and epidemics had a cyclic or random tendency. Climate, in fact, was most ideal *c.* 900–1300, but virtually everywhere commodification and market integration were markedly more elaborate in 1800 than 1300. Clearly other factors reinforced the effects of climatic/epidemiological amelioration when it occurred, and inhibited collapse in periods of deterioration. Among these factors, almost by definition, was a sustained accumulation of technical, organizational, and productive expertise.

In part this grew from local experimentation. I refer, for example, to extensive trial-and-error improvements in cultivation methods and in rice strains in Burma, Siam, Vietnam, and Japan; and to complex, locally evolved changes in agriculture, mining, handicraft, engineering, printing, banking, and commercial organization in both Japan and Western Europe after 1450.[98] Again, to recall Brenner, technology was not autonomous in the sense that innovation responded to social pressures, that is, production bottlenecks or higher demand, which in turn might reflect population pressures, changing class alignments, political requirements, new overseas markets, resource depletion, and so forth. But an increased stock of knowledge permanently transformed each society's production potential.

Sustained expansion of international exchange after *c.* 1450 had similar implications. By strengthening the demand for imports and diversifying exports, technical experimentation or population growth in one locale could confer benefits on distant centers, so that trade could become the vehicle of a more generalized prosperity. The significance of foreign trade varied with time even in the same area, but in general it seems to have been more important to Siam, southern Vietnam, and France than to northern Vietnam or Japan, with Burma and Russia somewhat intermediate. In Muromachi Japan trade with China reached considerable proportions, but declined thereafter in the face of disruptions and policy changes: in 1700 Conrad Totman estimates total foreign trade was less than 1.5% the value of Japanese agricultural production.[99] By contrast, in coastal

[98] Previous notes, plus Nguyen, *Tableau*, 47–107; Yoneo Ishii (ed.), *Thailand: A Rice-Growing Society* (Honolulu, 1978), chs 1–3; Yoshikazu Takaya, *Agricultural Development of a Tropical Delta* (Honolulu, 1987), chs 1, 4; Nagahara Keiji and Kozo Yamamura, 'Shaping the Process of Unification,' *JJS* 14, 1 (1988): 77–109; Mokyr, *Lever*, chs 4, 5; Ladurie, *La France urbaine*, III, 346–89; Harry A. Miskimin, *The Economy of Later Renaissance Europe 1460–1600* (Cambridge, 1977), chs 3–6; Annie Moulin, *Peasantry and Society in France since 1789* (Cambridge, 1991), 8–11.

[99] Totman, *Early Modern Japan*, 148; 73–9, 141–8. See too the revisionist view of 17th century trade, Robert L. Innes, 'The Door Ajar' (PhD, Univ. of Michigan, 1988).

mainland Southeast Asia, Chinese and Indian Ocean trade grew vigorously, amidst periodic adjustments, from the fifteenth to the mid-nineteenth centuries. Chinese merchants became the most dynamic agents of change, and from the 1600s Chinese maritime influence was reinforced by burgeoning overland contacts.[100] In late seventeenth- and eighteenth-century France the economy—recalling Abu-Lughod's emphasis on Atlantic resources—was effectively divided between a dynamic, increasingly urbanized coastal/riverine sector dependent on international trade, chiefly with the Atlantic, and a far more conservative, demographically stable interior.[101] Notwithstanding the inertia and self-sufficiency of Russian agriculture, in the 1700s and early 1800s West European demand for timber, iron, and especially grain accelerated settlement in the Russian periphery, with broad implications for urbanization and sectoral specialization.[102] In each region international exchange commonly drew strength from—and encouraged—improved ship design and navigational aids, novel commercial conventions, and expanded trade diasporas. Likewise in one region after another commodification and increased bullion supplies were mutually reinforcing. Between 1525 and 1800 the annual production of precious metals from Central Europe, Japan, and the Americas—a production that probably grew more rapidly than global commercial volume but that nonetheless reflected an expansion in real volume—rose at least ten-fold, the great bulk flowing to Western Europe and East Asia.[103]

Furthermore, to return to the issue of technical advance, external contacts provided a principal conduit for new methods and products. The density and competitiveness of West European markets and the excellence of communications help explain the rapidity with which the latest innovations, not least those of England, spread throughout the region. Compared to Southeast Asia, Russia, even Japan, these were among Western Europe's principal assets. But cross-fertilization was hardly limited to that area. During Japan's sixteenth-century boom, Chinese smelting and refining techniques imported via Korea boosted the output of precious metals, which

[100] Reid, *Age of Commerce*, I, II; Lieberman, 'Local Integration.'

[101] Collins, *State*, 179–83, 219–20.

[102] Kahan, *Plow, Hammer*, ch. 4.

[103] Ward Barrett in James D. Tracy (ed.), *The Rise of Merchant Empires* (Cambridge, 1990), 224–54, esp. Fig. 7.1 and Table 7.3; Frederic Mauro in *ibid.*, 255–86; Dennis O. Flynn and Arturo Giraldez, 'Born with a "Silver Spoon": The Origin of World Trade in 1571,' *Journal of World History* 6, 2 (1995): 201–21. See too Richards, *Precious Metals*, pt 3; Curtin, *Cross-Cultural*, chs 6–10.

then circulated throughout East Asia.[104] The introduction to Burma of cotton plants from eastern India, and the growth of Chinese demand for cotton after *c.* 1500, transformed Upper Burma's commerce. In the early 1600s Japanese merchants spurred sugar cultivation in Vietnam. In Russia the introduction apparently from Lithuania of the three-field system starting in the late 1400s constituted what R.A. French termed Russia's most decisive agricultural transformation until the twentieth century.[105]

In this context one must consider Europe's sustained contribution to East Asian economic growth, a contribution that included: (a) the indirect benefits of firearms-aided pacification; (b) the multiplier effect of enhanced demand for tea, textiles, spices, and bullion; (c) the injection of New World silver; (d) the provision of such New World crops as maize, sweet potatoes, and beans, which aided cultivation of hitherto marginal lands.[106] I know of no attempt to quantify this overall contribution for individual countries, much less East Asia. Lest one exaggerate, however, it is unlikely that South China's demographic boom ever depended chiefly on New World crops.[107] At least until *c.* 1750, New World silver within East Asia apparently represented only a modest fraction of regional supplies;[108] and until the mid-1800s Europe's economic role in mainland Southeast Asia and Japan was strictly circumscribed. It is also well to remember that Asian growth aided European prosperity, though as Jan de Vries has argued, this too is easily exaggerated.[109]

Finally, in explaining the cumulative nature of economic growth across much of Eurasia, the increasing sophistication and demands

[104] Nagahara and Yamamura, 'Process of Unification,' 81–2. Cf. Yamamura and Tetsuo Kamiki in Richards, *Precious Metals*, 329–62.

[105] French in James H. Brater and French (eds), *Studies in Russian Historical Geography*, I (London, 1983), 79, 19; R.E. Smith, *Peasant Farming in Muscovy* (Cambridge, 1977), 27–33, 109–25, 203–26.

[106] Crosby, *Columbian Exchange*, ch. 5; Totman, *Early Modern Japan*, 313; Lee, 'Food Supply,' building on Ping-Ti Ho; Dwight H. Perkins, *Agricultural Development in China 1368–1968* (Chicago, 1969), ch. 3.

[107] 'Food Supply,' esp. 738–43.

[108] Barrett in Tracy, *Merchant Empires*, 246; Eastman, *Family, Fields*, 125–30 suggest that prior to 1700 at most 1/3 of China's *imported* silver derived from Europe or the New World. Japan was the chief external source to 1640, and large-scale inflows from Britain to China began only *c.* 1760. But none of these calculations allow for substantial, though ill quantified, *domestic* silver production or *overland* imports from mines in Burma and Vietnam. Cf. Goldstone, *Revolution*, 372–4. Mainland Southeast Asia's reliance on European/New World silver may have been similar to that of China, but Tokugawa Japan obviously was far less dependent.

[109] De Vries, *Economy*, 128–46 *passim*.

of the state in each region must be considered. As subsequent sections will emphasize, the state benefited from demographic and commercial expansion, but in reciprocal fashion it frequently accelerated such growth by improving pacification, concentrating urban demand, and self-consciously seeking to broaden its tax base.

The Political and Cultural Implications of Economic Change

For the time being, let us concentrate on the first part of this reciprocal relation, that is, the impact of economic change on political, and also cultural, integration. Within each region of Eurasia growth was not uniformly distributed. On the contrary, such expansion tended to multiply in cumulative fashion the demographic and commercial advantages of privileged districts—the Irrawaddy and Chaophraya basins, the Red River and Mekong deltas, the Volga-Oka interfluve, northeastern (and later coastal) France, the Kinai basin and the Kanto plain—at the expense of more marginal areas. Even if core and periphery grew at the same rate, the former's initial superiority in manpower and wealth normally ensured a constantly increasing absolute advantage. But in fact, at least in the early phase of consolidation, growth rates in the core often exceeded those of outer zones. Furthermore, the development of national markets, which implied a concentration of higher-level commercial functions in the capital region, meant that even where the periphery and overseas trade became a principal area of growth (as in eighteenth-century Burma, Russia, and France), the center frequently was able to reap major benefits.[110] Thus favored districts often were able to pyramid their powers of military coercion and political patronage.

But in one area after another the nature of the political economy also changed. The widespread transition from subsistence to market production, for which global bullion increases were a precondition, was both symptom and cause of integration. To be sure, adapting Tilly's schema, we can arrange Eurasian societies along a continuum from those like France, where already by the 1400s market forces effectively had eliminated feudal-style military service and where money taxes were becoming the lifeblood of the state; to those like Siam and Burma, where hereditary labor service and apanages remained important in the nineteenth century. The precocity of

[110] Cf. the typology at Wigen, 'Geographic Imagination,' 12–13.

French integration was in part a function of its commercial vigor. Nonetheless, with the partial exception of Japan,[111] in every country we find along with an expansion of market connections, a gradual movement from in-kind and labor taxes to cash taxes, and growing reliance on salaries and commercial favors in the reward of followers. Everywhere this tendency became pronounced from the sixteenth and especially the eighteenth centuries. Thus in Russia in the 1500s commutations became common and some military units began to receive cash awards.[112] In sixteenth-century Siam maritime revenues grew dramatically, while in the late 1700s and early 1800s tax farms, labor and in-kind tax commutations, and cash allocations expanded.[113] In Vietnam as well, long-term commercialization forced cash more and more into taxation until money rather than goods or services had become the basis of Nguyen finances.[114] Such changes helped central authorities to tap a larger share of production, to gain closer control over subordinates, to replace hereditary service with more efficient wage labor and professional troops, and to regularize the provision of arms and matériel.

In a wider social and psychological sense, this same mobility of land and labor helped to erode autonomous networks, while generating a growing receptivity to supra-local political coordination and cultural norms. The issue of capital–local interaction may be considered from the standpoint of patronage and class models, and of diffusionist cultural models. The first approach, associated with such French historians as William Beik and Sharon Kettering, emphasizes the growing dependence of local elites on the state apparatus to define and to buttress their economic and social position.[115] The argument differs from one context to another, but in general the erosion of self-sufficient systems of agriculture; the growing economic importance of tax revenues, contracts, and market access; the

[111] Kozo Yamamura, 'From Coins to Rice,' *JJS* 14, 2 (1988): 341–67.

[112] On the monetization of Muscovite government, Marc Zlotnik, 'Muscovite Fiscal Policy, 1462–1584,' *Russian History* 6 (1979): 243–58; Blum, *Lord*, 131, 142–3, 228–9; Hellie, *Enserfment*, 24–5, 36–8, 158–9; Plavsic in Pintner and Rowney, *Officialdom*, 23.

[113] Wyatt, *Thailand*, 88ff., 131–2; Ishii, *Thailand*, ch. 2; Akin, *Thai Society*, esp. ch. 7; Hong Lysa, *Nineteenth Century*, chs 1–4; Terwiel, *Travellers' Eyes*, 113, 138, 150, 169, 228, 242–3, 253.

[114] Nguyen, *Tableau*, 28, 32–5, 150–1; R.B. Smith, 'Politics and Society in Viet-Nam during the Early Nguyen Period (1802–62),' *Journal of the Royal Asiatic Society*, 1974: 164–5; Woodside, *Vietnam*, 79–80, 139–40.

[115] Beik, *Absolutism and Society*; Kettering, *Patrons*.

professionalization of military functions; the increasing patronage available to central authorities; the recurrent threat of social disorder and foreign incursion; and the state's growing judicial and regulatory ambition—all these factors made it difficult for local leaders (landed, mercantile, political) to maintain their preeminence or to direct affairs without support from the central apparatus. As in Beik's province of Languedoc, they therefore entered into novel arrangements which enhanced the coordinating powers of the crown, but which simultaneously strengthened local privileges and access to wealth.

Outside Western Europe, local privilege and rights of political consultation gained less formal recognition. But as Richard Hellie, Valerie Kivelson, and J. Michael Hittle have shown in the case of Russia and as I have suggested for Burma and Siam, there too the key to centralization lay frequently in the growing inclination of landed and mercantile elites to support, indeed to help engender, an agency that could expand patronage, provide additional land, curb mobility among the workforce, adjudicate status disputes, and regulate trade. In return, local elites tended to assume greater responsibility for collecting taxes and for popular supervision. In other words, to reinforce an earlier observation, in these countries as in France centralization may be seen as more local in origin, more consensual—and the state, by implication, as more vulnerable to a rupture of elite consensus—than was previously thought.[116] If Tokugawa unification was particularly forceful, Philip C. Brown has recently argued that there too reforms in land rights, taxes, village organization, and so forth should be seen as negotiated compromises among village authorities, the domains, and Edo.[117]

The diffusionist concern for cultural standardization, as in the work of French historian Robert Muchembled, emphasizes the multifaceted breakdown of self-sufficient cultural systems under the combined impact of expanding urban–rural trade, wider literacy, urban-based programs of religious reform and repression, and a process of social differentiation by which successful peasants and townsmen sought to advertise their superior status by adopting prestigious motifs. Through contagious imitation, therefore, local dialects,

[116] Hellie, *Enserfment*, esp. pts 1, 2; Kivelson, *Autocracy*, also emphasizing local orientations; Hittle, *Service City*; Lieberman, *Cycles*, chs 2, 5.

[117] Brown, *Central Authority & Local Autonomy in the Formation of Early Modern Japan* (Stanford, 1993).

customs, and religious practices gradually lost ground.[118] Muchembled's schema has been criticized for positing binary elite/popular categories when in fact gradations were innumerable, and for minimizing the resilience, plasticity, and subversive capacity of local cultures.[119] In lieu of unidirectional flows, it is probably more useful to envision a dialectical process in which central norms modified regional cultures, but in which the latter syntheses also influenced the center.

Nonetheless, the general argument that a thickening web of economic, legal, and cultural links 'involved an enlargement of social space and a quickening of exchanges within that space' has wide application.[120] In rural France between 1670 and 1750 unprecedented levels of migration from countryside to town, and from stagnant to prosperous regions lowered dramatically rates of village endogamy.[121] At a higher social level and in a somewhat earlier period, Robert Harding has analyzed the mechanisms of 'social centralization' by which Paris attracted leading provincial nobles through its role as marriage market, site of literary and artistic production, and source of financial credit.[122] In early modern Japan as well, Katsuhisa Moriya and Mary Elizabeth Berry have linked economic and cultural integration. An ever more ramified land and water communications/transport system joined the main towns of Kyoto, Osaka, and Edo; provincial centers with one another; and towns with their hinterlands. Responding from the mid-1600s to the growth of island-wide commerce, this network transmitted political and cultural as well economic information, disseminating urban arts and letters into the countryside and thus contributing to what Moriya terms 'a developing national consciousness.'[123] Suffice it to say that with less intensity and capillary penetration, the Muscovite core and each of the main Southeast Asian basins also experienced a thickening of communication and transport links, along which moved itinerant traders, seasonal workers, monks, popular entertainers, pilgrims, all bearers in some measure of religious and cultural information. Moreover, after *c.* 1600 accelerating frontier colonization often helped to diffuse

[118] Muchembled, *Popular Culture*.

[119] Robin Briggs, *Communities of Belief* (Oxford, 1989), 53–7, 384–402; Jacques Revel in Steven L. Kaplan (ed.), *Understanding Popular Culture* (Berlin, 1984).

[120] Quote is from Jonathan Dewald, *Pont-St-Pierre 1398–1789* (Berkeley, 1987), 284, discussing the erosion of Norman lordships.

[121] Collins, *State*, 43, 156, 184.

[122] Harding, *Power Elite*, esp. ch. 12, focusing on *c.* 1560–1650.

[123] Moriya in Nakane and Oishi, *Tokugawa*, 97–123, quote 122; Berry, this volume; Totman, *Before Perry*, 188–99.

central norms among outlying peoples. Although, as Carol Belkin Stevens has shown in the case of Russia, the frontier could subvert or reject as well as entrench such norms, over the long term sustained immigration into the Russian steppe and the Irrawaddy, Chaophraya, and Mekong deltas created cultural syntheses sympathetic to the heartland.[124]

Rising literacy promoted standardization in all six societies. Most basically perhaps, literacy expanded because increasing wealth and/or the leveling of income differences supported a larger number of schools and encouraged well-to-do commoners to acquire new cultural amenities and forms of sensibility, while the complexity of administration and trade required more voluminous records and more numerous record-keepers. In addition, in mainland Southeast Asia after *c.* 1450 and in France after *c.* 1520 movements of religious reform encouraged a wider social and geographic dissemination of texts. Everywhere reading deepened familiarity with urban or capital norms, challenging and reconfiguring local styles and notions of sanctity. In Professor Berry's words, books and maps 'worked through generic codes of signs and labels that insist[ed] upon the subordination of the particular to the general.'[125] Symptom and cause of expanded literacy were the rise, beginning in Japan and France earlier than elsewhere but everywhere in bloom by the seventeenth or eighteenth centuries, of popular literatures appealing to a wider circle of readers and listeners, displaying greater variety of form, exploring new secular themes, ethical dilemmas and emotional attitudes; and above all, employing vernacular languages and/or syllabaries. Thus in Burma, after pioneering efforts in the 1400s and 1500s, we find especially from the 1700s a proliferation of vernacular-language poems, biographies, devotional works, dramas, and chronicles supplementing more thematically restricted Pali and Burmese compositions. Late eighteenth-century Siam also saw the flowering of vernacular poetry, drama, and literature, exhibiting greater folk influence and a more realistic and commercially-oriented world view than had characterized previous Siamese,

[124] Cf. Stevens, *Soldiers on the Steppe* (De Kalb, IL, 1995); Kahan, *Plow, Hammer*, chs 1, 2, 5; Blum, *Lord*, 247–68, 330–2; Paul Avrich, *Russian Rebels 1600–1800* (New York, 1972); Nguyen, *Tableau*, 111–82; Li Tana, 'Inner Region,' ch. 1; Lieberman, 'Local Integration,' 504–11; Ishii, *Thailand*, chs 1–3.

[125] Berry, this volume. One is reminded of the emphasis in Anderson, *Imagined Communities*, on print-capitalism as an agent of standardized national languages and identities.

Khmer, and Pali writing. In Vietnam, starting in the 1300s but chiefly from the 1600s, an energetic poetry written in demotic *nom* characters and developing novel themes and verse forms supplemented older, more elitist traditions of prose and poetry in Chinese characters. Building on Muromachi traditions of popular literature and commercial book production, Tokugawa Japan saw an explosion of fiction and non-fictional writing in *kana* syllabaries; somewhat as in Vietnam, Chinese characters retained their monopoly for administration and elite expression, but *kana*-based works became far more widespread and vibrant. In France, as noted, Parisian French gradually became the preferred vehicle not only for an unprecedented outpouring of devotional, literary, and political publications catering to popular audiences, but also for elite scholarship and royal administration.[126]

Yet the actual mechanisms of literacy's spread varied widely, as did its relation to urbanism and printing, and the proportion of the population affected. Lowland Burma, where in 1400 literacy seems to have been rare, by 1850 had achieved 50% male literacy on the basis of quasi-universal rural monastic education. Siamese patterns were similar. In the absence of Theravada monasticism, Vietnamese rates probably were lower, but the rise of commercial authorship points to a growing audience there as well. With some Vietnamese exceptions, Southeast Asian texts were not printed, and rural schools and scribes appear to have been as influential as urban.[127] By con-

[126] So too in Russia, although literacy was less common, by 1700 everyday Russian had begun to assert itself in literature at the expense of archaic Slavonicized forms, while the 18th century saw the first Russian dictionaries and the beginning of modern literary culture. On literary/linguistic developments, see Maung Thu-ta, *Sa-hso-daw-mya at-htok-pat-ti* (Rangoon, 1971); Pe Maung Tin, *Myan-ma sa-pei thama-ing* (Rangoon, 1955); Nidhi Aeusrivongse, 'The Early Bangkok Period: Literary Change and Its Social Causes,' *Asian Studies Review* 18, 1 (1994): 69–76; Klaus Wenk, *Thai Literature: An Introduction* (Bangkok, 1995), 6–67; Maurice M. Durand and Nguyen Tran Huan, *An Introduction to Vietnamese Literature* (New York, 1985), chs 1, 5–9; Huynh Sanh Thong, *The Heritage of Vietnamese Poetry* (New Haven, 1979), xxvii–xxxi; Barbara Ruch in John W. Hall and Toyoda Takeshi (eds), *Japan in the Muromachi Age* (Berkeley, 1977), 279–309; Donald H. Shively in *CHJ*, IV, 706–69; Reischauer and Craig, *Japan*, 35–8, 99–107; Roy Andrew Miller, *The Japanese Language* (Chicago, 1967), ch. 3 (note that *kana* arose in the 9th century); Rickard, *French Language*, chs 5, 6; W.D. Howarth, *Life and Letters in France in the 17th Century* (New York, 1965); Chartier, *Cultural Uses*, chs 5–7; Nicholas Riasanovsky, *A History of Russia* (New York, 1984), 285–99, 349–60; Gary Marker, *Publishing, Printing and the Origins of Intellectual Life in Russia, 1700–1800* (Princeton, 1985), chs 5–7.

[127] On mainland SE Asian literacy, Lieberman, 'Local Integration,' 508–10; *idem* in Reid, *Early Modern*, 245–6; Terwiel, *Travellers' Eyes*, 59, 157–8, 179, 251–2, claim-

trast, literacy in rural as well as urban Japan, France, and Russia was tied not only to proliferating schools but to urban publishing industries, which produced perhaps 1000 titles a year in Japan in the 1840s and 1500 in France in the 1770s.[128] In terms of per capita production of texts, thematic diversity, and the institutional complexity of intellectual life, Southeast Asia offered no parallel to France or Japan. Curiously, however, printing did not boost literacy rates beyond those in Burma and Siam: by 1800 French male literacy was about 50%, Japanese 40%, and Russian perhaps 10%.

Before concluding this section, I would make more explicit two paradoxes embedded in these intertwined processes of economic and cultural change. First, international trade and the global spread of technology encouraged cultural integration, but as we have just seen, the language and idiom of written culture within each country tended to become more self-sufficient. In other words, at the same time as long-distance material links grew stronger, those preeminently universal literatures and languages (Pali, Chinese, Latin) that had inspired elite acculturation during the early second millennium C.E. were either displaced or increasingly supplemented by more expressly national forms. One may object immediately that, unlike Latin in Europe, Chinese scholarship in Japan and Vietnam retained an unqualified prestige among the elite; that French itself became a principal vehicle of Enlightenment thought among educated Russians and Germans in the 1700s; that in terms of intellectual substance and geographic spread, European Renaissance humanism and Enlightenment thought were no less cosmopolitan than medieval scholasticism; and that into the nineteenth century Theravada centers remained in close contact with one another as well as with Sri Lanka. All this is perfectly true, but the fact remains that by 1700 or 1800 higher literacy rates and denser communications had engendered a flow of popular writings with little or no early second millennium precedent; and of necessity these new literatures used vernacular media and created more idiosyncratic forms.

Second, most notably perhaps in France, Japan, Russia, and Burma, as culture became more spatially standardized and more

ing 'a very high proportion' of male literacy in central Siam; Alexander Woodside, 'Political Theory and Economic Growth in Late Traditional Vietnam' (MS).

[128] Smith, 'History of the Book,' 335–6. On French and Japanese publishing, cf. Chartier, *Cultural Uses*; Furet and Ozouf, *Reading and Writing*; Briggs, *Communities*; Nakane and Oishi, *Tokugawa*, 61–2, 118–21; Totman, *Early Modern Japan*, 27, 195–211, 354, 401–36.

willing to accept a common set of references, that same culture accommodated unprecedented social and intellectual specialization. That is, as wider literacy and denser commercial exchanges helped to erode local identities, these very circuits fostered more complex economic relationships, more variegated occupational niches, more numerous channels of intellectual expression, and often, more cacophonous public exchanges.[129]

The Military Dynamic

Alongside economic growth, military competition provided a powerful incentive to political integration. Feedbacks between these dynamics—economic expansion, warfare, and political integration—were numerous and complex.

Across Eurasia the collapse or enfeeblement of charter polities and the rise of successor states in the thirteenth to fifteenth centuries ushered in a period of intense competition. The resultant trial-and-error, particularly when reinforced by economic and demographic expansion after 1450, tended to produce more efficient military and fiscal machines. Between *c.* 1430 and 1540, primarily in response to military pressures, we find the following novel systems: in Japan the replacement of an atomized manorial system by consolidated daimyo domains; at Ayudhya, Trailok's ambitious reform of social ranking and departmental organization;[130] in Vietnam the Neo-Confucian transformation of military and civilian functions; in Burma expanded military service and mercantile systems; in Muscovy new apanage controls and the *pomeste* cavalry-cum-land-grant system;[131] and in France a permanent army and lasting taxation during the later stages of the Hundred Years War.[132]

Then, starting in the early 1500s and continuing (outside Japan) intermittently throughout the period under consideration, the dis-

[129] See previous references to the French Wars of Religions, the Robe-Wrapping dispute of Burma, and the Schism in Russia.

[130] H.G. Quaritch Wales, *Ancient Siamese Government and Administration* (New York, 1965); Wyatt, *Thailand*, 70–86 *passim*.

[131] John L.H. Keep, *Soldiers of the Tsar* (Oxford, 1985), ch. 1; Hellie, *Enserfment*, chs 2, 9; Gustav Alef, 'Muscovite Military Reforms in the Second Half of the Fifteenth Century,' *Forschungen zur osteuropaischen Geschichte [FOG]* 18 (1973): 73–108.

[132] Tax and military reforms were adumbrated in the 1360s, but solidified *c.* 1435–1445. John Bell Henneman, *Royal Taxation in Fourteenth-Century France* (Philadelphia, 1976), esp. 274–311; Lewis, *Later Medieval France*, 47ff, 101–10; Collins, this volume.

semination of European-style handguns and artillery magnified the advantages of the wealthiest and most populous principalities in one Eurasian region after another.[133] Thereby guns not only accentuated that concentration of power inherent in renewed economic growth, but provided an obvious and persistent stimulus to further administrative reorganization designed: (a) to marshal resources for external warfare, and (b) to confront the danger of anti-centralizing rebellions that attended the forcible incorporation of ever more far-flung and alien communities.

These processes were preeminently European both in so far as the best weapons in Southeast Asia and Japan derived from Europe, and in the sense that militarily-induced change remained most intense in Western and Central Europe, which drew Russia into its system from the mid-1600s. The stages in Michael Roberts' European 'military revolution' are well known.[134] Although pike-wielding infantry had been making steady inroads, after *c.* 1500 mobile artillery and muskets decisively favored those states that could afford to cast cannon, build artillery-resistant forts, and supply large numbers of handguns. In the late 1600s and 1700s mercenary forces yielded to standing armies, distinguished by their growing size and standardization. In Tilly's formulation, the advantage of Western states like France over smaller city-states and over more agrarian eastern polities derived precisely from their ability to combine large domestic armies with commercial wealth. As fresh rounds of warfare whittled down the number of competing states, survivors were driven to penetrate local society ever more deeply and to bypass or coopt intermediary agents in the hope of enhancing income and curbing protest by overburdened peasants and regional dissidents. Military expenditures typically consumed 60–90% of French and Russian budgets. In turn the state's growing interest in problems of tax exemption and incidence, most notably in France during the 1600s and 1700s, made property-holders more eager to influence the legislative process. In

133 Vietnam *c.* 1600–1778 is an exception in so far as imported guns helped the southern Nguyen regime to hold off the northern Trinh. On the other hand, the Nguyen advanced the Vietnamese ecumene in its broadest sense, and after 1801 guns and French-style citadels bolstered Nguyen efforts at centralization.

134 Roberts, 'The Military Revolution, 1560–1660,' ch. 7 in *Essays in Swedish History* (London, 1953); plus J.R. Hale, *War and Society in Renaissance Europe, 1450–1620* (New York, 1985); William H. McNeill, *The Pursuit of Power* (Chicago, 1982); Parker, *Military Revolution*; Tilly, *Coercion*; Samuel Finer in Tilly, *National States*; Marshall Poe, 'The Consequences of the Military Revolution in Muscovy in Comparative Perspective' (MS).

these ways standing armies, national political cultures, and direct rule tended to nourish one another.[135] In social terms, moreover, by expanding opportunities for professional soldiers, the military revolution enhanced the dependence of the lower nobility (and until the early1700s, of some townsmen) on government employ. Alongside an older stratification based on birth or tenure appeared in Russia as well as France a rival system, based on military and civil rank. By emphasizing written planning, the military revolution also may have encouraged 'technicality' in administration and noble culture generally.

In mainland Southeast Asia military innovation was less intense for a variety of reasons. With a smaller number of initial contenders than in Europe and with broad, inhospitable marches separating the main antagonists, fewer opportunities for conflict arose (at least till the 1780s, when consolidation brought the chief states into more sustained contact). Whereas printing, mercenaries, and a common cultural subtext rapidly disseminated military innovations from the Channel to the Urals, poor communications and the Indian-Sinic divide inhibited a comparable fluidity within Southeast Asia. And, of course, populations were smaller and local economies more sluggish, which was critical in so far as: (a) Southeast Asia lacked the ready resources, including urban credit mechanisms, needed to sustain war machines over a long period; (b) without Europe's global stakes, it lacked the same incentives; (c) it had no serious indigenous gun manufacture, which in turn reduced the pressure for change in tactics, army training, and royal finance.

But if military change was less dramatic, it remained highly significant. Although by 1830 some mainline Southeast Asian troops still lacked firearms, the high cost and efficacy of cannon and matchlocks, and the expense of new forts tended to favor the largest and wealthiest states, especially those with maritime access. As in Europe, after *c.* 1550 gun and firearms-based strategies contributed to a drop in the number of independent polities after each major round of warfare. In the three most successful states, overhauls of taxation and the reform of provincial government commonly came in preparation for war, or in its immediate aftermath.[136] In some ways the social—as opposed to the technical—impact of military change may have been more pronounced than in Europe. In the absence of salaried

[135] Tilly, *Coercion*, 104, 76ff, 99–104; Anisimov, *Peter*, 160–233 *passim*; Collins, this volume; Harding, *Power Elite*, ch. 13; Bailey Stone, *The Genesis of the French Revolution* (Cambridge, 1995).

[136] Lieberman, 'Local Integration,' 492–5, 511–13. Cf. C. Skinner (tr.), *The Battle for Junk Ceylon* (Dordrecht, Holland, 1985).

professionals, most military tasks in Burma and Siam continued to depend on hereditary services from a substantial part of the general population. The resultant emphasis on stratified control joined with the weakness of family property to encourage royally-defined rankings more complex than anything attempted in Russia or France. Here too a growth in record-keeping to aid service rotas may have strengthened literacy.

As for psychological effects, I have already emphasized that in parts of Southeast Asia as well as of Europe intensifying warfare, particularly from the mid-1700s, strengthened popular identification with the crown. This it did by integrating conscripts from different locales, by rendering border communities more dependent on the throne for security, by generating invidious stereotypes and mythic reminders of communal danger and transcendence. By comparison with the twentieth century, such bonding was episodic, but prior to 1790 it may not have been significantly weaker in Burma and Vietnam than in France. In so far as military intensification within each region benefited from the spread of firearms and the growth of trade across Eurasia, we therefore have another partial explanation of the aforementioned paradox that cultural separation and material interdependence waxed simultaneously.

Through intended and unintended effects, interstate competition also helped to stimulate economic growth. Most basically perhaps, warfare intensified each court's interest in resource accumulation and in the expansion of its tax base. 'Mercantilism' confers an artificial coherence on various ad hoc measures adopted by European governments from the sixteenth through eighteenth centuries—tariffs, the sponsoring of new industries and techniques, production subsidies, monopolies, currency manipulations—which were designed to increase national wealth, most particularly through a positive trade balance, in express rivalry with other states. Although mercantilism was concerned with state-building, economic unification, and national prosperity in the broadest sense, it transferred from warfare to economics the assumption that international relations were a zero-sum competition, and as such provided an economic counterpart for a bellicist foreign policy. This was true, for example, of Colbert's work under Louis XIV, and even more so of Peter's pathbreaking support for Russian manufactures.[137] Over the long term in France

[137] Thomas Schaeper in Paul Sonnino (ed.), *The Reign of Louis XIV* (Atlantic Highlands, NJ, 1990), 27–43; François Bluche, *Louis XIV* (Oxford, 1990), ch. 8; Anisimov, *Peter*, 70–86; James Cracraft (ed.), *Peter the Great Transforms Russia* (Lexington, MA, 1991), pt IV.

as well as in Russia, the growing need of the military for equipment, uniforms, and provisions offered economies of scale to private producers, and more especially to traders and financiers, with benefits—real, if often unrecognized—for the general economy. Constant demands for cash taxes, which again were primarily military in purpose, did as much as any deliberate policy to channel peasant production into the market and thus to magnify openings for trade and specialization. Finally, as the French division between a prosperous, colonial-oriented coast and a less dynamic interior, or as Russia's expansion from the economically restricted forest zone into the black earth region of the south and along the Baltic coast suggest, an aggressive external policy could confer truly major benefits in resources and markets. To be sure, war also could inflict severe damage, armies were hardly ideal targets of investment, while short-term profits and the deficiencies of economic theory wrecked numerous state initiatives. Nonetheless, Jan de Vries concludes that in seventeenth- eighteenth-century Europe, 'one cannot help but be struck by the seemingly symbiotic relationship existing between the state, military power, and the private economy's efficiency.'[138]

During this same period Southeast Asian governments encouraged foreign trade, with numerous spin-off economic benefits, in order to boost general income but also for the express purpose of obtaining military revenues, strategic metals, and firearms. To enhance offensive or defensive capacities, as in Siam and Burma during their recurrent wars, each state organized massive deportation, agricultural, and resettlement schemes, including in some cases the building of irrigation works. Across the mainland the accelerating move to cash taxes, particularly from the early 1700s, helped to drive peasants to the market; here too military demands were often critical. And in all three countries the conquest of new agricultural districts, including the rich Mekong and Irrawaddy deltas, and the subjugation of rival commercial centers made warfare in some contexts an economically rational activity (which is not to deny the admixture of prestige and religious motives).[139] Although quantification is unusually diffi-

[138] De Vries, *Economy*, 242–3, and chs 7, 8. The mutual stimulation of war, economic growth, and state-building receives emphasis also at Tilly, *Coercion*, esp. chs 3, 4; *idem* in Theda Skocpol (ed.), *Bringing the State Back In* (Cambridge, 1985), 169–91; Anderson, *Lineages*, 32–41; Kahan, *Plow, Hammer*, chs 7, 8.

[139] Lieberman, *Cycles*, 96–107, 250–62; *idem*, 'Local Integration,' 489–519; Koenig, *Polity*, 14–30, 107–18; Hong Lysa, *Thailand*, 38ff, 77, 84; John K. Whitmore, *Vietnam, Ho Quy Ly, and the Ming* (New Haven, 1985), 74–6; Wyatt, *Thailand*, 171–2.

cult and although the technological context was less propitious, in Southeast Asia as in Europe one is thus tempted to posit a circular relation: enhanced revenues, administrative cohesion, and new military technologies joined to intensify interstate rivalry, which spurred political integration and, in some degree, economic growth.

And what of Japan? One can make Japanese history testify to either the marginality or centrality of the military dynamic. On the one hand, as noted, the absence after 1638 of internal or external warfare did not prevent the cultural integration of one of the early modern world's more homogenized populations. It did not preclude the increasing complexity and routinization of both shogunal and daimyo administration. Nor did it prevent the rapid commercialization of the economy in the 1700s and 1800s. As Professor Berry notes, the integrative effects associated with war-making could also flow from peace-keeping.[140] On the other hand, peace helps to explain why the Tokugawa state remained more conservative not only than its European and Southeast Asian counterparts, but also than Japanese polities during the extremely creative Warring States period (1467–1568). Conflict in that era spurred unprecedented economic growth and shaped those domains which, as noted, became the basic governing units of the Tokugawa system. Momentum towards centralization ebbed after the early 1600s, not because the Tokugawa state was incapable of innovation—in domestic peacekeeping James White has shown the shogunate took vigorous initiatives—but, in part, because it lacked military incentives to incur the political costs associated with tax increases and with efforts at more direct rule.[141] In economics as well, if we follow Conrad Totman's logic, the slowing of Japanese growth *vis-à-vis* Europe after *c.* 1700 reflected to some degree Japan's failure to acquire the windfall resources that colonization or frontier conquest afforded European countries.[142] Notwithstanding the rise of 'national learning' (*kokugaku*) and Marius Jansen's claim of an incipient Japanese/Chinese cultural opposition, one could argue further that by denying

[140] Berry, this volume. A similar argument appears in Hayami Akira, 'A Great Transformation,' *Bonner Zeitschrift fur Japanologie* 8 (1976): 3–13; and Kozo Yamamura in Hall, *Before Tokugawa*, 327–72.

[141] See the comparison of military and domestic dynamics in Europe and Japan at White, 'State Growth,' 1–25, esp. 14.

[142] Without invoking European comparisons, Totman, *Early Modern Japan*, chs 12, 13, emphasizes the growing strain on Japan's resource base after *c.* 1700 and the aborted expansion into Ezo.

Japan an accessible alterity, Tokugawa isolation inhibited the politicization of national culture and the development of a sharply defined national self-image.[143] Finally, even post-1600 economic vitality can be attributed during its early phase in part to the benefits of unification, itself a preeminently military achievement.

Intellectual and Institutional Spurs to State Intervention: Additional State Influences on Economics and Culture

Thus far I have sought to explain sustained integration by exploring the linked processes of economic expansion and military competition. No doubt other dynamics—for example, changing social structures—could be examined with profit. In Japan Bito Masahide has argued that the establishment of the house or lineage (*ie*) as the basic unit among peasants and merchants *c.* 1550–1700 was itself fundamental to rising living standards in so far as it engendered a more worldly orientation and an obligation to promote the material welfare of the house.[144] Yet for most of the countries under review Western-language literature is inadequate to compare the evolution of social structures.

Instead I shall conclude this survey by suggesting briefly how integration also drew strength from two better-documented dynamics, namely, the changing intellectual contexts of political action and accumulating institutional expertise.

'Intellectual contexts' refers here to those formal doctrines and informal currents that defined normative state activity, that sanctioned new interventions, and that both interacted with material interest and shaped the perception of those interests. In general new perspectives derived less from changes in economic structure *per se*, than from the challenge posed by recurrent government difficulties; and from the spread of education and wealth among the upper

[143] Jansen, *China in the Tokugawa World* (Cambridge, MA, 1992), 76–88. Cf. Berry, this volume; and Harootunian, *Seen and Unseen*, 36–56, 186–96. David L. Howell, 'Ainu Ethnicity and the Boundaries of the Early Modern Japanese State,' *PP*, 142 (1994): 69–93 argues that after 1600 the categories 'Ainu' and 'Japanese' became more clearly delineated, but less through warfare than the political needs of the Matsumae domain within the Tokugawa system; and the impact on Japan at large appears to have been quite limited.

[144] *CHJ*, IV, 373–8.

classes, the wider circulation of books and manuscripts, and the concentration of literate people in towns, all of which swelled the number of thinkers interested in issues of political and social order.[145]

Among these intellectual departures perhaps none was more precocious or durable than the aforementioned Neo-Confucian revolution in Vietnam, which derived from a juncture of government crises, Chinese intervention, and the internal growth of the literati. As Dr Whitmore shows in this volume, from the fifteenth through nineteenth centuries Vietnamese Neo-Confucianism prescribed an aggressive program of moral, social, and economic, no less than administrative, transformation. Lacking an external model comparable to that of Vietnam and embracing a doctrine, namely Theravada Buddhism, whose concerns were more narrowly soteriological than social, Burma and Siam adopted a more circumscribed, ad hoc approach to reform. Yet there too growing Theravada textualism supplied a rationale, indeed an obligation, to standardize ritual, to monitor more closely local personnel, and in the process to extend state authority closer to the ground.[146] In Tokugawa Japan a new class of schoolmen, including samurai, monks, declassé warriors, and teachers, constructed a novel Confucian-based discourse that harmonized the regime and justified samurai privilege. Although concerned less with the extension of central authority than with a stable system of domination, this vision of society as consisting of separate and unequal parts underlay legislation and determined how rulers allocated scarce goods.[147] Far more restless than Tokugawa ideology was that post-1600 European system of administrative practices and political ideas which Marc Raeff subsumes under the concept 'the well-ordered police state' (*état bien policé*). In partial contrast to both Tokugawa and late medieval European thought, this system, molded by seventeenth-century philosophy and science, argued that if human reason were harnessed to will and if social institutions were reformed, resources could expand continuously so as to enhance the wealth of both the state and society. At first in a mercantilist mode, and from the late 1700s

[145] Cf. C.B.A. Behrens, *Society, Government and the Enlightenment* (New York, 1985), 161–2.

[146] Lieberman, *Cycles*; Wyatt, 'Subtle Revolution.'

[147] Totman, *Early Modern Japan*, 168–83; Ooms, *Tokugawa Ideology*, analyzing what he terms Japan's first 'fully closed ideology.'

transformed into a more liberal set of prescriptions, these basic assumptions inspired a succession of expansive reforms in both France and Russia.[148]

At the same time as such intellectual visions lent varying degrees of support to policy initiatives, each administration improved its procedures for gathering and processing information, for collecting and disbursing funds, and for monitoring personnel—all of which were preconditions for successful policy execution. Such expertise derived from at least three sources. First was the inheritance from pre-1400 charter principalities. In so far as post-1400 political ruptures in France, Vietnam, and Japan were relatively modest, these countries had more direct access to sophisticated legacies and began the period under review with comparatively elaborate systems.

Second, external models. As noted, Confucian thought aided reform not only in Vietnam, but in Japan, where it allowed the samurai of 1600 to transform themselves into a literate officialdom. In Russia Tatar fiscal and military traditions enjoyed great prestige through the late 1500s, followed by Ukrainian, Lithuanian, and Polish models in the 1600s, followed by Dutch, German, Swedish, and later French; from Western and Central Europe Russia derived both the concept of the *état bien policé* and numerous specific techniques. Siam and Burma may have imitated one another's provincial governance. Late Bourbon experiments with debt, tax, and parliamentary reform owed much to Dutch and English models.[149]

However, during much of the period under review local trial-and-error, our third category, seems to have been the principal source of administrative change in Burma, Siam, France, as well as Japan (which followed Chinese models less closely than Vietnam). This could involve either ad hoc experiments or structured reform based on a wide-eyed knowledge of precedent. The latter approach, for example, describes widespread efforts to curb princely autonomy. Likewise within the more technical departments—treasuries, secretariats, war ministries—the increased volume of transactions, the wider array of concerns, and the expansion of the apparatus itself encouraged specialization and routinized procedure. Even the Toku-

[148] Of course, West European and Central/East European administrative philosophies also differed, as for example, in the latter's greater cameralist emphasis. Raeff, *The Well-Ordered Police State* (New Haven, 1983), pt. 3; *idem*, *Understanding Imperial Russia* (Columbia, 1984), esp. 24–31; Behrens, *Society*, esp. 116–62.

[149] Collins, *State*, 168–70, 264.

gawa apparatus, byword for conservatism, was 'vastly more complex' in 1830 than in 1615.[150]

In short, administrative expertise—like technology or military power—was a resource that could accumulate, and which therefore helps to account for the ratchet-like nature of integration. In combination with demographic, military, and intellectual pressures, enhanced regulatory capacity allowed each state to foster conditions suitable for the continued elaboration of its own authority.

How precisely did this occur? I have already sketched the interaction of economics and warfare, but the state's economic impact was not limited to interventions designed to promote military strength. For one thing, as indicated, economic initiatives also could be driven by doctrinal imperatives and domestic political concerns. Le and Nguyen support for agricultural extension, Chakri encouragement of coffee and other commercial crops, Catherine II's partial liberalization of manufacturing and her patronage of immigration on the Volga and in the Ukraine, Tokugawa irrigation and water-control projects offer typical examples.

Beyond this, as interventionist ambitions and abilities increased, each state shaped the economy in ways which may have been incidental to the original purpose of state action but which nonetheless were conducive to growth. In most if not all six countries, literature suggests that military/political unification lowered commercial transaction costs by reducing brigandage, invasions, tolls, and other impediments to trade; by offering some standardization of measures, currency, and law; by building waterways or roads with commercial as well as strategic benefits, and by easing exchange between zones with unique resource profiles.[151] In Southeast Asia pacification also encouraged population growth by increasing nuptiality and reducing infant mortality.[152] In Vietnam, Japan, and northern France, post-1500 administrative/legal changes tended to aid individual

[150] Totman, *Tokugawa Bakufu*, 234. Cf. Collins, *State*, 145.

[151] See *supra* n. 139, plus Denis J.B. Shaw in Bater and French, *Historical Geography*, 118–42; Chaunu in Chaunu and Gascon, *Histoire économique*, I, 1: 214–24; De Vries, *Economy*, 200–54; Louis Bergeron, *France under Napoleon* (Princeton, 1981), ch. 7; Kahan, *Plow, Hammer*, chs 4–9; Yamamura in Hall, *Before Tokugawa*, 327–72; Robert V. Hubbard and James A. Hafner, *The History of Inland Waterway Development in Thailand* (Ann Arbor, MI, 1977); Li Tana, 'Inner Region,' ch. 1.

[152] M.C. Ricklefs, 'Some Statistical Evidence on Javanese Social, Economic, and Demographic History in the Later Seventeenth and Eighteenth Centuries,' *MAS* 20, 1 (1986): 1–32; Norman Owen in Owen (ed.), *Death and Disease in Southeast Asia* (Singapore, 1987), 91–114.

producers at the expense of less commercially responsive systems of communal or absentee proprietorship. Such changes in turn strengthened the land market, invigorated rural credit, and promoted peasant marketing.[153] Moreover, into the great capital cities of Ava/Amarapura, Thonburi/Bangkok, Hue, St Petersburg, Paris/Versailles, and Edo—most of them founded or extensively rebuilt in the 1600s or 1700s—governments poured money for patronage and construction, while relocating large numbers of officials, retainers, and support personnel. This fostered a remarkable concentration of both public and private demand that spurred all manner of specialization and long-distance exchange and that was a principal feature of early modern economies. The *sankin-kotai* (alternate attendance) system at Edo shows how such arrangements could promote a broad national market, in this case partly by increasing demand with Edo itself, partly by forcing the sale of domainal products to finance the annual movement to Edo. These effects were all the more remarkable in that, as with pacification, the original purpose of *sankin-kotai* was narrowly political.[154]

The same mixture of motives, and the same distinction between intended and unintended effects, applies to government influence on culture, including religious practice, literature, language, and ethnicity. Tilly, Joseph Strayer, and Stein Rokkan have emphasized the instrumentalist value of cultural homogeneity: it coopted ready-made communications systems, facilitated the transfer of expertise, and sanctioned the crown's regulatory function.[155] But intellectual and religious doctrines had an autonomous dynamic.

Again, if the determination of motive is difficult, the practical impact is often clear. Each court took greater responsibility for defining orthodoxy and for regulating ritual: Theravada rulers circulated purified copies of the *Tipitaka*, Vietnamese civil service exams and village indoctrination promoted Neo-Confucian orthodoxy, the

[153] Lieberman, 'Local Integration,' 506–8; essays by Hall and by Yamamura in Hall, *Before Tokugawa*, 211–19, 327–72; Totman, *Before Perry*, 195–9: Howell A. Lloyd, *The State, France, and the Sixteenth Century* (London, 1983), 30–5, 111–13; Knecht, *Francis I*, 308–10; Dewald, *Pont-St-Pierre*, 127–56, 212. Cf. Root, *Peasants*, arguing that the 18th century French monarchy strengthened, rather than weakened, communal forms of peasant economic organization.

[154] T.G. Tsukahira, *Feudal Control in Tokugawa Japan* (Cambridge, MA, 1966); Reischauer and Craig, *Japan*, 94. Cf. De Vries, *Economy*, 206–7; Koenig, *Burmese Polity*, 31, 59.

[155] Essays by Tilly and by Rokkan in Tilly, *Formation*, 40–9 (citing Strayer), 77–80, 581–97.

Bourbon state strongly supported the Catholic Reformation. The other side of the coin was an attack on heterodoxy: pre-Buddhist practices were targeted in the Burmese hills; Old Believers, Bashkirs, and Muslims were subject to assimilationist pressure in Russia;[156] Huguenots, in France; Christians, in Japan. In Burma and Vietnam, provincial unrest sometimes prompted efforts to modify the linguistic/ethnic identity of newly subjugated populations. At a more scholarly level, courts from Ava to Paris sought with varying degrees of determination to standardize orthography and script, to promote approved languages for official documents, and to encourage specific literary and artistic forms.[157] In Vietnam and Russia official patronage broadened into deliberate, sustained, basically successful efforts to impose on local elites foreign norms of dress, social organization, deportment, and intellectual expression.

The indirect cultural effects of government action were no less significant. By appealing to a combination of snobbery and a desire for practical advancement, capital patronage encouraged self-Burmanization, self-Gallicization and so forth laterally and, to some extent, vertically. Although we lack studies outside Europe comparable to Norbert Elias' work on French/European courts as purveyors of a new language of body control, St Petersburg, Bangkok, Ava, Hue, and Edo all functioned as arbiters of taste and as cultural magnets for high provincial nobles.[158] The swell of written documents and legal decisions between provincial and capital agencies must have had a similar integrative effect. In Burma and Siam the rotation of provincial servicemen at the capital offered yet another powerful mechanism, largely unintended, of cultural exchange.[159] And to this must be added the homogenizing cultural effects of persistent government efforts to unify social hierarchies and of government economic action, already discussed.

If we summarize the entire process of cultural standardization, then, it reflected the circular, open-ended interaction of factors that

156 Michael Cherniavsky, 'The Old Believers and the New Religion,' *Slavic Review* 25, 1 (1966): 1–39; Paul Werth, 'Apostasy, Alienation, and the Reconfiguration of Imperial and Religious Space in Russia's Eastern Provinces' (MS).

157 See, e.g., Than Tun (ed.), *The Royal Orders of Burma*, 10 vols (Tokyo, 1983–1990), IV, 130–1, V, 458, 572; Woodside, *Vietnam*, chs 3, 4; Sonnino (ed.), *Louis XIV*, chs 10–14; Anisimov, *Peter*, 217–25; Collins, *State*, 119–22.

158 Elias, *The Civilizing Process*, 2 vols (New York, 1978, 1982), esp. I, ch. 1 and II, ch. 1; Ellery Schalk in Asch and Birke, *Princes, Patronage*, 245–63; Tsukahira, *Feudal Control*.

159 Sternstein, 'Primate City,' 49; Koenig, *Polity*, 107–18.

were simultaneously independent and dependent variables. Where one chooses to break into the circle can be arbitrary. Commercial and demographic growth encouraged a wider and more rapid exchange of goods and ideas, which strengthened supra-local identities and increased the resources of expanding polities. Responding to military, political, and doctrinal imperatives, central authorities undertook measures whose effects, intended and unintended, promoted economic growth and cultural diffusion. In turn, closer cultural links between province and capital tended to aid political integration (although they could also breed localizing resistances). Finally, as states waged war on a larger scale, conflict itself stimulated identification with the throne and intensified the state's own interest in direct rule. The challenge, of course, is to weigh these factors and to chart their interconnections in specific contexts.

Synchronized Chronologies

In these ways, not only long-term trajectories, but the underlying dynamics of integration defied a simple East–West divide. But another basic parallel deserves attention: In all six countries administrative development tended to follow a similar chronology in so far as: (a) its movement was both cyclic and linear, with successive periods of collapse becoming shorter and less anarchic as market connections, institutions, and popular expectations became more secure; (b) as already indicated, these cycles and associated structural changes were synchronized, at times loosely, but in many cases quite closely.

The earliest relevant correlations occurred between *c.* 900 and 1300, during all or part of which period Pagan, Angkor, Dai Viet, Kiev, Capetian France, and the Kamakura bakufu benefited from demographic and commercial expansion and associated organizational changes. The so-called Medieval Warm Epoch of improved climate *c.* 900–1400, and a transformation of epidemic diseases to a merely endemic character, have been invoked to help explain Europe's florescence, but elsewhere evidence in weak.[160] Pagan, Angkor, and Kiev were the earliest extensive polities within their respective regions, whereas Dai Viet, Capetian France, and Kamakura Japan already may be seen as regional successor states.

[160] McNeill, *Plagues*, ch. 3; Lamb, *Climate Present*, II, 435–49.

At various times between 1100 and 1380 all six polities fragmented as external military threats mounted and, more particularly, as power shifted to socially or geographically insurgent elements. In most cases dislocation seems to have reflected economic decay less than the failure of existing institutions to accommodate long-term growth, not least on the frontiers.[161] However, in Western Europe, Russia, and possibly Southeast Asia, it is also true that once devolution was under way, economic and epidemiological conditions during the 1300s and much of the 1400s were often hostile to recentralization. I refer again to problems associated with Mongol incursions in Russia and Southeast Asia, to the spread throughout Europe (and possibly China) of the Black Death, a disease disseminated in part by the Mongols; to unfavorable climate in Europe and parts of East Asia; and to severe bullion shortages, which were both cause and symptom of commercial contraction.[162]

Across the rimlands such changes prepared the way for a phase of vigorous reintegration. In every region a great counter-movement either began or accelerated between 1440 and 1590, exemplified in the fortunes of Valois France, early Ayudhya, First Toungoo Burma, early Le Vietnam, late Daniilovich Muscovy, and late Muromachi/Shokuho Japan. In the last four cases territorial conquest was extremely dramatic. Japan fit this basic pattern but differed in so far as: (a) fragmentation started later and lasted longer, to the very end of the 1500s; (b) the Tokugawa system proved more stable than initial (re)centralizing experiments in France, Southeast Asia, and Russia.

I have already emphasized how fragmentation itself stimulated experimentation, a stimulus reinforced by the dissemination of firearms and by the economic vigor across Eurasia of the 'long sixteenth century,' *c.* 1460–1630. This economic upsurge in turn drew strength

[161] Aung-Thwin, *Pagan*, ch. 9; Ian Mabbett and David Chandler, *The Khmers* (Oxford, 1995), ch. 15; *CHJ*, III, chs 3, 4; George Vernadsky, *Kievan Russia* (New Haven, 1976), ch. 8. Cf. the emphasis on peripheral growth in Norman Yoffee and George L. Cowgill (eds), *The Collapse of Ancient States and Civilizations* (Tucson, AZ, 1988), chs 1, 10. In short, we see *c.* 400–900 C.E. a political/economic shift from Eurasian cores to outlying areas, several of which faced challenges from their own peripheries *c.* 1100–1400.

[162] On disease and climate, previous notes. On bullion and commercial contraction, clearer in Europe than East Asia, John Day, *The Medieval Market Economy* (Oxford, 1987); Harry A. Miskimin, *The Economy of Early Renaissance Europe, 1300–1460* (Cambridge, 1960), 129–34; Blum, *Lord*, 57–73; Richards, *Previous Metals*, pts 1, 2.

from better political control, improved climate, reduced plague, advances in mining and civil engineering, and eventually from New World stimuli to trade and crop diversification. In Russia and parts of Southeast Asia guns joined with frontier settlement after *c.* 1500 to reverse 'barbarian' inroads that had begun two to three centuries earlier. Everywhere population growth, new taxes, minting, or trade monopolies swelled state resources. Sixteenth-century price inflation, once explained solely by enhanced bullion flows but now usually attributed in its early and middle phases to demographic pressures, generally outstripped revenues after 1500, but until then tended to aid governments by encouraging innovation.[163] This combination from the late 1400s or early 1500s of renewed political vitality, market and urban intensification, greater social mobility, wider literacy, and cultural diffusion helped to inaugurate 'the early modern era.'

Recall that the relation—dynastic, institutional, geographic—between these fifteenth- and sixteenth-century states and early second millennium predecessors varied substantially. If Japan, Vietnam, and France showed relatively strong continuities—Georges Duby has gone so far as to claim that by 1223 'the various elements that constituted the political system in France until the end of the ancien régime were all in place'[164]—in the Irrawaddy basin and more especially in the Chaophraya basin and Russia we are talking about substantially new political, as well as cultural, even ethnic systems with only modest connections to charter antecedents (Pagan, Angkor, Kiev). Whereas since at least 1000 fortunate geography had helped to protect Japan, Western Europe, and northern Vietnam against sustained alien incursions, movements of Tai-speakers in western and central mainland Southeast Asia and of Mongol/Tatars in the Russian steppe contributed to a shift of hundreds of miles in the center of gravity (from Pagan to Pegu, from Angkor to Ayudhya and Phnom Penh, from Kiev to Moscow). In part because of these dislocations, but also because of weak commercial networks and thin populations, the new Burmese, Siamese, and Russian political systems also tended to be relatively unstable.

[163] On inflationary causes and effects, again clearest for Europe, Michel Morineau in *Histoire économique*, I, 2, 929–40; Goldstone, *Revolution*, 89, 122, 186–7, 360–94; Jerome Blum, 'Prices in Russia in the Sixteenth Century,' *JEH* 16 (1956): 182–99; Miskimin, *Economy 1460–1600*, 35–46; Crummey, *Formation*, 7–8; Mann, *Sources*, 433–4, 457–8; Flynn and Giraldez, 'Silver Spoon.'

[164] Duby, *Middle Ages*, 298, echoing R.I. Moore in this volume.

All three of these empires, along with the more mature system of France, disintegrated between 1560 and 1612, inaugurating in each case a fresh round of appalling anarchy, rebellion, and foreign intervention. Each historiography tends to focus on weaknesses in the new systems of administration, and on a hubris which the unprecedented scale of sixteenth-century warfare bred in the most successful states.[165] (Hideyoshi's 1592 invasion of Korea offers another example of such overextension, albeit without long-term costs.) In France, the new print culture also fanned destructive religious controversies. Taking a global perspective, one could speculate that the synchronization of collapse owed something as well to demographic growth *c.* 1450–1600, in the order of 50–300% wherever we can measure it.[166] On the one hand, as Goldstone has shown, expansion in total population produced a disproportionately large increase in marginal elite groups competing for patronage. On the other hand, at least in Europe where the issue has been studied, after 1550 population pressure joined with greater bullion flows to stoke inflation and thus to erode the real income of the crown as well as of insistent private elites. Thus demands on the state apparently intensified at precisely the same time as its resources contracted.[167]

In general the disorders of the late sixteenth century were less severe than those of the 1200s to 1400s, but worse than subsequent breakdowns (including the celebrated crises of the mid-seventeenth century). New dynasties in Burma, Siam, France, Russia, and Japan restored order at some point between 1570 and 1620, and proceeded to organize more durable and ambitious political/cultural systems. In lieu of a master plan we usually find ad hoc expedients. Yet in a broader sense most such changes sought to restore a cosmically sanctioned hierarchy and to reduce the confusion and 'excessive' mobility characteristic of recent decades. Bloodletting may have helped by reducing factionalism. More basically in Europe and possibly Southeast Asia, a demographic slowdown *c.* 1640–1710 may have aided stability by eliminating inflationary pressures and slowing the pace of social change.[168]

[165] See Lieberman, *Cycles*, 32–46, 285–6; Wyatt, *Thailand*, 86–98; Crummey, *Formation*, chs 6, 8; V.O. Kliuchevsky, *A Course in Russian History* (Armonk, NY, 1994), ch. 1; Parker, *Absolutism*, 27–45.

[166] See sources for Table 1. China too saw an increase 1400–1600 of *c.* 110%, Eastman, *Family, Fields*, 4.

[167] Goldstone, *Revolution*, 31–8, 63–169.

[168] *Ibid.*, 192–4, 274; Akin, *Thai Society*, 27–31, 172–3.

I have emphasized that the social contexts of these experiments differed widely: at the same time as new serf-like systems sought to freeze mobility in Burma and Russia, in France market pressures had virtually eliminated serfdom along with vassalage. Yet in one context after another we find an elite consensus that the central apparatus should reward its rural supporters, pacify the countryside, allocate privileges, verify claims, and enforce social distinctions more effectively. In several cases regulation was extended to hitherto marginal groups, social or geographic. Thus between *c.* 1620 and 1670 in Russia we find the formalization of serfdom, the organization of Western-style armies, and a rapid expansion of *prikazy* (ministries). Burma saw unprecedented censuses and cadastres, a major extension of the *ahmu-dan* system of military service, and far-reaching provincial reorganization. Siam experienced comparable provincial and mercantile changes. In France we find departures in taxation, military organization, venal officeholding, and provincial patronage, which together began the transition from what Professor Collins terms a judicial/legislative to an administrative monarchy.[169] Finally, in this same period Tokugawa Japan perfected its *baku-han* governance, executed cadastres comparable to those of Burma, and imposed an exceptionally rigid, (theoretically) quadripartite social system that would endure for two centuries.

A yearning for renewed order contributed as well to seventeenth-century efforts to define more closely female roles and to monitor popular religious practice. As noted, the latter efforts shaded into attacks on dissident sects. Standardization typically drew strength from increasing literacy and from the pull of the capital. Yet ironically elite culture—by definition uniquely open to textual and external influences—was itself unstable, so that by 1720 in Vietnam, Russia, and France the split between a semi-secular, literate elite culture and religious, localized popular systems had actually widened in certain respects.

In Japan and to a lesser extent Southeast Asia, the momentum of administrative innovation ebbed after 1650. But across Europe military competition joined with economic growth and novel social theories to encourage fresh experiments. Thus in Russia and France the era *c.* 1670–1770 saw multifaceted innovations in social control, communications, finance, and local government, and a military pro-

[169] Collins, *State*, 3, 61–124 *passim*.

fessionalism that pointed to a widening gap between Europe and the rest of the globe.

Yet for all its strength, Europe in the second half of the eighteenth century endured a Eurasian-wide pattern of renewed turmoil and institutional crisis. Signs of this were widespread indeed, but most dramatic in France, Burma, Siam, and Vietnam, where in every case between 1752 and 1789 dynastic collapse ushered in chaos and civil war. In turn in both mainland Southeast Asia and Europe, late eighteenth-century breakdowns inaugurated a fresh round of massive warfare and competitive centralization.

One source of instability was the continued growth of the state itself. New impositions helped to dislocate peripheral regions. Though not unprecedented (in France anti-tax revolts were more characteristic of the seventeenth century), new fiscal and administrative demands and/or demands for cultural assimilation sparked vast anti-centralizing revolts between 1740 and 1774 on the Ural–Volga frontier, in Lower Burma, and in southern Vietnam.[170] At the same time the growing scale of eighteenth-century warfare severely strained the tax and service systems, while holding dynastic prestige and popular confidence hostage to battlefield success. In Burma, France, and (more briefly) in Siam, foreign reverses sapped the morale of the dynasty and its supporters.[171]

Of no less fundamental importance, and in various ways defining administrative problems, was the demographic and commercial surge which started in many areas in the 1720s or 1730s and continued (despite local downturns) well beyond the period with which we are concerned. Outside Japan, which experienced commercial intensification but a demographic slowdown, this period could be compared to the 'long sixteenth century.' At the same time the eighteenth century had its own characteristics in so far as in many regions bulk trade in agricultural and primary products figured more prominently, secondary urban centers and rural markets filled the countryside to a novel degree, ancient population ceilings were breached, commerce became more of a multi-class affair, rural manufacture

[170] Lieberman, *Cycles*, 211–24; Li Tana, 'Inner Region,' ch. 7; Marc Raeff in Robert Forster and Jack P. Greene (eds), *Preconditions of Revolution in Early Modern Europe* (Baltimore, 1970), 161–202; Avrich, *Rebels*, ch. 4.

[171] French victory in the American War could not erase debts occasioned by that war and by three earlier 18th century reverses. See *infra* n. 177. On Burma and Siam's military problems, Lieberman, *Cycles*, ch. 4; Wyatt, *Thailand*, 124–38.

expanded, and the scale of enterprises grew notably. In northern France by 1800 'modern economic growth' had begun to characterize pockets of agriculture and industry, while 'Smithian' and 'extensive' growth were common in extensive areas of South and East Asia. What were the causes of this new expansion? Again, it derived *inter alia* from more favorable climate in Europe and perhaps parts of East Asia, the continued spread of novel technologies and New World crops, markedly increased worldwide bullion production,[172] and more effective state interventions. Quickening long-distance trade in the Atlantic, Indian Ocean, and South China Sea served to generalize the prosperity of Eurasia's most commercialized regions, including southern China, on which Southeast Asian exchange depended heavily.[173]

If over the long term this latest round of expansion aided political and cultural integration, it also entailed at least six sources of instability (not all, of course, necessarily found in the same area): (a) as in the sixteenth century, land shortages and resource depletion plagued poorer peasants, in France, Vietnam, central Russia, and demographically stable Japan; (b) among frontier peoples accelerated colonization sometimes intensified anti-centralizing sentiment; (c) as in the late 1500s, demographically-induced price inflation reduced the value of government taxation;[174] (d) so too, more competitors for an inelastic number of positions intensified factionalism; (e) enhanced mobility and growing specialization threatened social and regional hierarchies established during the 1600s. In varying degrees 'upstart' traders, entrepreneurs, and/or commercial farmers became more prominent in France, Siam, Russia, and Japan. But the problem also had a geographic dimension in so far as growth tended to favor outlying areas, while (outside Europe) the latter areas' improved access to guns sometimes combined with technological inertia to erode center-periphery military differentials;[175] (f) most notably but

[172] 262%, 1700–1800. Gabriel Ardant in Tilly, *Formation*, 199.

[173] Leonard Blussé, 'Chinese Overseas Expansion and State Formation Processes in Maritime Southeast Asia, 1550–1800' (MS); Wang Gungwu, *China and the Chinese Overseas* (Singapore, 1992), pt. 1; Eastman, *Family, Fields*, chs 4, 6; C.A. Bayly, *Indian Society and the Making of the British Empire* (Cambridge, 1988), ch. 1.

[174] Best documented in France, Goldstone, *Revolution*, 209–10. Cf. Lieberman, *Cycles*, 159–61.

[175] On challenges to existing hierarchies, Goldstone, *Revolution*, ch. 3 and 346; Guy Chaussinand-Nogaret, *The French Nobility in the Eighteenth Century* (Cambridge, 1985); Dewald, *Pont-St-Pierre*, esp. chs 2,4; Jay Michael Smith, 'The Culture of Merit in Old Regime France' (PhD, Univ. of Michigan, 1990), chs 5, 6; David K. Wyatt, 'The Eighteenth Century in Southeast Asia' (MS); *idem*, *Thailand*, 127–32; Teruko

not only in France, expanding literacy, new circuits of communication, and new organs of public debate spread destabilizing intellectual critiques that strained the tether of government control.[176]

How well societies adjusted to such strains depended on the severity of economic dislocation, the strength of political and cultural institutions, political contingency (now a favorite explanatory device of French revolutionary historians), and (to follow Skocpol) success in interstate competition.[177] In Russia unbroken military success and an open agricultural frontier, in Japan isolation and low population growth, cushioned the strains and helped to postpone severe political crises until the mid-1800s.

The main point is that in all four instances of late eighteenth-century breakdown—France, Burma, Siam, and Vietnam—this collapse facilitated, indeed may be seen as a precondition, for a rapid and extremely vigorous recentralization that redressed the structural and personal weaknesses of the previous regime, marshalled resources more effectively, and in so doing made possible an unprecedented territorial expansion. Moreover, in both Napoleonic Europe and post-1760 Southeast Asia, the dangers and opportunities arising from these upheavals compelled experimentation, if not imitation, and thus served to generalize reform throughout the interstate system. In much the same way as the German states and Russia were driven to overhaul their armies and bureaucracies to compete with Napoleon, numerous Siamese reforms sought to defend against continuous Burmese aggression from 1759 to 1811, which was followed by over thirty years of competition with a newly unified Vietnam. In both Europe and Southeast Asia consolidation in this period also drew strength from accelerated economic growth. Sometime between 1767 and 1846 Burma, Siam, Vietnam, France, and Russia all achieved unprecedented territorial expansion, while in Southeast

Saito, 'Rural Monetization and Land-Mortgage *Thet-kayits* in Kon-Baung Burma' (MS); Lieberman, *Cycles*, 156ff, 221; Hittle, *Service City*, 170–1; Blum, *Lord*, 288–303, 361–2, 470–93; Edgar Melton, 'Proto-Industrialization, Serf Agriculture and Agrarian Social Structure,' *PP*, 115 (1987): 69–106; Totman, *Before Perry*, 192–9, 231–2.

[176] William Doyle, *Origins of the French Revolution* (Oxford, 1980), ch. 4; Roger Chartier, *The Cultural Origins of the French Revolution* (Durham, NC, 1991); François Furet, *Interpreting the French Revolution* (Cambridge, 1981); Arlette Farge, *Subversive Words* (Univ. Park, PA, 1992). Cf. Marc Raeff, *Understanding Imperial Russia* (New York, 1984), 58–61, 129–35; Madariaga, *Catherine*, ch. 34; Marker, *Publishing*, chs 4–7; Totman, *Early Modern Japan*, ch. 19.

[177] Skocpol, *States and Revolutions*. See too Behrens, *Society, Government*, 164–5, and Stone, *Genesis of French Revolution*.

Asia this same period marked the apogee of precolonial administrative coherence.[178]

Meanwhile in all six countries market activity and growing literacy continued to mold more mobile societies, in which ideas as well as goods circulated more rapidly and over greater distances. In the face of such persistent mobility, between *c.* 1750 and 1830 economic, social, and legal controls established in the early 1600s tended to erode, with or without government acknowledgement. In the process market-oriented groups gained wider influence, social relations were increasingly expressed in terms of monetary values, and commerce (with the possible exception of Vietnam) tended to acquire greater elite legitimacy. These developments took a most peculiar form in France, where the gradual erosion of corporate identities and the fusion of wealthy commoners with successful nobles culminated in a post-Revolutionary elite which lacked formal hereditary status and which embraced doctrines of civic equality without the most remote Asian parallel.[179] Nonetheless in one country after another, as middle strata become more involved with the market and more literate, cultural production became more broadly based and central norms diffused more widely. I have already referred to the growth, especially during the eighteenth and early nineteenth centuries, of more popular literatures and to the wider circulation of texts in all six countries. In Europe and parts of Southeast Asia more intense warfare also heightened vertical and lateral cohesion. Yet the fact that Japan *c.* 1830 was culturally more uniform than Burma, Russia, Siam, perhaps even France suggests that warfare was less critical in this regard than geography and internal economic networks.

Precis

In sum, then, I am arguing that widely separated areas experienced loosely coordinated linear and cyclic patterns for some three hundred years prior to the Petrine reforms in Russia, and for over four hundred years before the forcible Euro-American opening of mainland

[178] Koenig, *Polity*, ch. 1; Wyatt, *Thailand*,ch. 6; Le Thanh-Khoi, *Histoire*, ch. 8; Geoffrey Ellis, *The Napoleonic Empire* (London, 1991); Church, *Revolution and Red Tape*.

[179] T.C.W. Blanning, *The French Revolution* (Atlantic Highlands, NJ, 1987), 41–9; Roger Price, *A Concise History of France* (Cambridge, 1993), 139–41; Chaussinand-Nogaret, *French Nobility*; Becker, *Civil Society*, esp. pt I.

TABLE 2

A Calculus of Integration in Six Countries

The six rankings represent countries in this order: Burma, Siam, Vietnam, France, Russia, Japan. L = Low, M = Moderate, H = High.

Geographic inducements to internal control and communication:	M	M	L	H	M	M
Population densities:	L	L	M	H	L	H
Level of post-1350 institutional disruption and foreign occupation:	H	H	M	L	H	L
Access to foreign economic technology:	L	L	M?	H	H	L
Access to foreign military technology, *c.* 1600–1830:	M	M	M	H	H	L
Access to external administrative models:	L	L	H	H	H	L
Level of interstate competition, *c.* 1600–1830:	M	M	M	H	H	L
Importance of foreign trade to overall economy:	M	H	L	H	M	L
Commercialization, urbanization, *c.* 1830:	L	L	L	H	M	H
Literacy, *c.* 1830:	H	H	M?	H	L	H
Administrative centralization, *c.* 1830:	M	M	M	H	H	L
Cultural homogenization, *c.* 1830:	M	L	H	H	L	H

Southeast Asia and Japan. But I have also emphasized that if all six countries were more effectively knit together and if central authorities controlled a larger territory in 1830 than in 1450, integration can be judged by several criteria—administrative, commercial, religious, ethnic—and that in any given country these criteria did not necessarily coincide. By the same token, some criteria crosscut Orientalist boundaries. Thus France, Japan, and perhaps Vietnam had as much in common with one another as any of them did with Burma, Siam, or Russia if we consider (a) post-1350 continuities, or (b) levels of cultural cohesion in 1830.

The preceding table seeks to abstract and correlate some of these factors, most of which were simultaneously cause and symptom of integration: commercial networks and urbanization, for example, aided political cohesion, but these same factors were deeply influenced by state action. I would call attention again to the link between good internal communications and intense interstate competition, on the one hand, and administrative centralization, on the other. And between low levels of post-1350 dislocation, pervasive commercialization, and advanced literacy, on the one hand, and a highly homogenized culture, on the other.

Criticisms

This approach is open to at least two major objections. One might argue that the relentless linearity of this master narrative, the apparent concern with the origins of present-day 'nations' exhibits the same teleological bias as Eurocentric or Japanocentric economic historiography: by taking as its starting point current patterns, this approach reads history backwards as prelude to an inevitable culmination. Preoccupied with society's ultimate fate, it devalues patterns that do not betoken change, while elevating those of evolutionary significance.[180] The danger of reifying and eternalizing 'nations' is underscored by my exclusion of East European, West Asian, and Southeast Asian polities that had no direct twentieth-century offspring. Moreover, because the preoccupation with centralization privileges the views of capital elites and victorious cultures, the narratives of subalterns and of entire populations in 'loser' states are automatically marginalized.

No one would dispute that alternate emphases might produce equally valid narratives. Following John Smail, Eugen Weber, or Peter Sahlins, one could focus on the long-term evolution of autonomous local communities on which the influence of distant capitals is easily exaggerated.[181] The virtue of my concern with sustained political-cum-cultural integration derives from the fact that, first, it lets us deploy existing Southeast Asian historiography to compare hitherto incomparable units; and second, it is concerned with the evolution of genuinely critical structures that helped to determine the life choices and self-images of enormous numbers of people, not merely central actors, during the periods in which they lived. To justify studying the evolution of pre-1830 political/cultural units, one hardly needs to invoke their subsequent fates, however intriguing, critical, or irrelevant those linkages may have been (see below). Ultimately, I think, if supra-local histories are impossible outside local contexts before 1830, the reverse is also true.

By itself, moreover, the tracing of long-term changes in identity prior to 1830 implies no essentialism. I have argued not only that most early modern ethnicities arose late, usually not before the fifteenth or sixteenth century, but that even among core populations

[180] See Thomas Kierstead, *The Geography of Power in Medieval Japan* (Princeton, 1992), 6–7, 122–3; Prasenjit Duara, *Rescuing History from the Nation* (Chicago, 1995).

[181] Smail, 'Autonomous History'; Weber, *Peasants into Frenchmen*; Sahlins, *Boundaries*.

such identities remained socially uneven and territorially fluid. Many ultimately unsuccessful states also embarked on projects of consolidation, and with a bit of luck, could have absorbed one or more of the six entities with which we are concerned: in other words, Siamese and southern Vietnamese could have become provincial Khmers. So too, the social assumptions, religious context, and semiotics of identity in 1450 differed from concepts in 1800, and yet more profoundly from twentieth-century 'nationalism,' so while we may talk about 'Russia' in 1400 and 1800, at bottom national continuity is a matter of heuristic convenience. Professor Berry and Professor Wyatt in this volume argue for diachronic inquiries into local psychologies, and I warmly support their call. It should be clear, finally, that the real focus of this essay is not 'nations' *per se* (whose future, in any case, is uncertain) but Eurasia as an internally graduated, evolving, loosely interactive system.

A second charge, more or less opposite to the concern for nationalist reification, is that these sweeping comparisons, driven by an avowedly revisionist instinct—and by a desire to compensate for Southeast Asia's obscurity?—elide genuine particularities. The chief variations allowed are on set grids, grids which, despite anti-Eurocentric protestations, tend to place France at the acme of achievement. The possibility that ostensibly parallel evolutions concealed fundamentally divergent mentalities arouses limited interest. In essence, it could be said, this is a neo-modernization project, encumbered with all the weaknesses of modernization theory itself and allied universal teleologies, namely an insensitivity to local difference, unilinear bias, a privileging of economic and technological causality, a celebratory view of the present.[182]

But if we accept the original goal of comparing European and non-European evolution, we must employ common criteria. The standards I have selected, flattering to France though they may be in some respects, are by no means peculiar to European experience or derivative solely from European historiography. If my revisionist goals have led me to focus on parallels, I have also pointed out major differences in chronology, social organization, economic trajectory, and religious idiom—variations that can easily be extended. Indeed, the fascination of Eurasian parallels derives precisely from their

[182] On modernization theory and its critics, Downing, *Military Revolution*, 5–6; Lynn Hunt, *Politics, Culture and Class in the French Revolution* (Berkeley, 1984), 205–12.

appearance in widely divergent contexts. There is no implication that Vietnam was but a couple generations 'behind' France en route to industrial capitalism. Nor, in contrast to modernization theory and other Enlightenment models—Whig, German historicist, Marxist—is this approach emancipatory or celebratory in its attitude to the present or the impending future: I seek to relax distinctions not only between East and West, but between 'premodern' and 'modern,' regarding both distinctions in their more categorical form as self-flattering conceits.

Other Sectors of the Eurasian Continuum: Concluding Perspectives

Finally, the validity of these particular comparisons derives from these six countries' loosely comparable position within a far wider Eurasian continuum. Now I have already suggested that throughout the era *c.* 1000–1800, France and Japan enjoyed rather greater political and cultural continuity than Burma, Siam, or Russia. Extending these gradations, we find that China represented a yet earlier and more stable pattern. At the other extreme, South Asia and island Southeast Asia were among those areas where, despite numerous economic parallels, political integration proved more short-lived than in any of our six areas. A few brief comparisons follow.

If one were to assume that the shift in the center of economic gravity from the Mediterranean to northern Europe in the later half of the first millennium C.E. resembled the contemporaneous shift from north to south China, and if one were to assume further that French civilization was in some fundamental sense heir to Roman civilization, one could argue that Capetian France stood in a similar relation to Rome as Song to Han China. Yet, while this analogy is not to be dismissed out of hand and while one must resist the essentialist image of China underlying dynastic cliches, by almost any measure—ethnic self-identification, institutions, imperial boundaries—continuities in Europe between *c.* 100 and 1300 C.E. were far less substantial than in the area we know as China.

And in the other five areas of study, contrasts between Chinese continuity and local novelty were yet more pronounced. The Chinese functional equivalent (the Qin-Han empire) to the charter polities of Pagan, Angkor, Kiev, Nara, and so forth arose almost a thousand years earlier, in the third century B.C.E. The dichotomy between 'Han' and 'barbarian' gained full expression in the Han, along with a centralized quasi-bureaucratic tradition, long-lived imperial boundaries, and a quasi-Confucian ideology. The second period of Chinese imperial unity, including the Song (960–1279)—which was contemporary to these rimland charter principalities and which benefited from a related economic upsurge—anticipated yet more specific features of the early modern era. These included the primacy of civil service exams, official recognition of Zhu Xi Neo-Confucianism, a vigorous printing industry and substantial literacy, the intense settlement of south China by ethnic Chinese, a more self-consciously oppositional relation to the non-Han periphery, and a far-reaching revolution in agriculture, in water transport, and urbanization. As China's regional economies became more integrated during the Song, as elite culture grew more uniform, as administrative expertise accumulated, political unity became the norm in a fashion that would not be duplicated in Russia, Burma, Siam, or Vietnam until the sixteenth century or later.[183]

None of this is to minimize the novelty of Chinese developments *c.* 1550–1850—which both deepened and transformed Song patterns—or their similarity to developments elsewhere. After a catastrophic population decline *c.* 1300–1450, China, like much of Eurasia, entered another era of growth, followed by a mid-seventeenth-century decline, followed by rapid economic and demographic expansion from the late 1600s. Society grew more fluid and commercially oriented, increasingly subject to market influences. Greater spatial and social mobility, new educational institutions, and the yet wider circulation of printed texts joined to bring elite and peasant values into closer alignment and to transform literati culture into a more genuinely national culture with a broad urban base. During this same period, much as in Russia and Southeast Asia, accelerated migration, repression, and trade worked to assimilate frontier peoples. Despite novel devolutionary strains caused by China's size and unique population burden, the Qing also extended its borders, while increasing the scope of metropolitan and provincial bureaucracies and the monetization of its affairs.[184] Yet, to repeat,

[183] Elvin, *Pattern*, pt 2; *idem* in P. Abrams and E.A. Wrigley (eds), *Towns in Societies* (Cambridge, 1978), 79–89; John Winthrop Haeger (ed.), *Crisis and Prosperity in Sung China* (Tucson, 1976).

[184] Rowe in Zunz, *Reliving*, 260–83; Naquin and Rawski, *Chinese Society*; Huang, *Peasant Family*, pt 1; Johnson *et al.*, *Popular Culture*; Eastman, *Family, Fields*; G. William Skinner (ed.), *The City in Late Imperial China* (Stanford, 1977), 26–8; T'ung-tsu

these early modern structures lacked the fundamentally innovative character that we find in most of our fifteenth–sixteenth century case studies, with the possible exception of France (and more debatably, Japan).

The Indian subcontinent generated its own precocious state structures and Hindu–Buddhist civilization, which during the first millennium provided a model for most of Southeast Asia in somewhat the same way as China influenced Vietnam and Japan. Also as in China, alien conquest dynasties steadily expanded their power from the early second millennium. However, whereas in China invaders tended to accept the conventions of the host culture, even to present themselves as paragons of that culture, in India they proved rather more innovative and culturally autonomous. The traditions of Central Asian and Indo-Muslim rule as developed by the Delhi Sultanate before its fourteenth-century decay, and by the Afghan Sher Sha (r. 1538–1545), provided the administrative and intellectual foundation of the Mughal empire (established militarily in 1526, administratively by 1600, but in decay by 1720).Turkish and Iranian immigrants were the backbone of the Mughal elite, while Perso-Islamic conventions provided a cultural pillar.

In short, if northern India resembled China in the antiquity of its civilization and its seminal relation to more distant areas of secondary state formation, one might argue that it resembled the latter areas themselves in its three-stage pattern of late first or early second millennium charter principality (the Delhi Sultanate and its antecedents)—breakdown—fifteenth/sixteenth century reintegration.

Like contemporary empire-builders, the Mughals achieved an unprecedented territorial control and level of public order. In John F. Richards' view it 'was an intrusive, centralizing system which unified the subcontinent,' reduced the level of internal violence, and by its administrative practices left its mark on virtually every locality.[185] The Mughals drew strength, in familiar fashion, not only from accumulated expertise, but from the introduction of effective firearms and from the expansion of international trade, which stimulated output and provided bullion needed to lubricate the revenue system.

Chu, *Local Government in China under the Ch'ing* (Stanford,1962); Beatrice S. Bartlett, *Monarchs and Ministers* (Berkeley, 1991); Hans van de Ven, 'Recent Studies of Modern Chinese History,' *MAS* 30 (1996): 225–41.

185 Richards, *The Mughal Empire* (Cambridge, 1993), 1–2 *et seq*. Cf. Chetan Singh, 'Centre and Periphery in the Mughal State,' *MAS* 22, 2 (1988): 299–318.

A combination of improved pacification, government demand for cash taxes, urban markets, and exports encouraged population growth, agricultural extension, and commodity production. Associated systems of capital accumulation and credit were more elaborate than anything in precolonial Southeast Asia. As elsewhere, such trends meant increased reliance on monetary values to express social relations, and greater political influence for commercially successful groups.[186]

Given its early effectiveness and the propitious economic context, why then did a centralized political structure in the subcontinent—alone among those areas thus far considered—collapse permanently in the early and mid-1700s? For one thing, the scale was vastly different. The Mughal empire was seven or eight times larger, and six to 35 times more populous than Japan, France, or any Southeast Asian kingdom—each roughly the size of a large Mughal province—so problems of communication and control were far more severe.[187] If the early Qing and Mughal empires were of comparable size, the Qing inherited a more coherent gentry self-image as well as an administrative pattern less accommodating to local privilege than the Mughals' *zabt* revenue system.[188] Indeed, by any standard, cultural uniformity in the Mughal realm was modest. To be sure, as Richards and C.A. Bayly have emphasized, since at least the early 1500s an all-India military tradition encouraged substantial religious syncretism and ritual coexistence between Hindus and Muslims, while personalized political ties crosscut ethnic and religious categories.[189] Nonetheless, practical difficulties of penetration and patronage, not least in the newly-conquered, poorly-assimilated south; the multiplicity and massive inertia of regional, clan, and caste loyalties; the self-conscious Muslim identity of some later Mughal leaders, resultant Hindu–Muslim tensions, as well as Sunni–Shii rivalries all joined to preclude even among the provincial nobility the same degree of ritualized cohesion that we find in most countries under

[186] Richards, *Empire*, esp. chs 1–4, 9; *idem*, 'The Seventeenth-Century Crisis in South Asia,' *MAS* 24, 4 (1990): 625–38; Marshall G.S. Hodgson, *The Gunpowder Empires and Modern Times* (Chicago, 1972), ch. 2; Bayly, *Society*, ch. 2; and *supra* n. 3.

[187] If Muscovy's domain was more vast, its population *c.* 1700 was barely 8% that of the Mughal realm, and was more concentrated.

[188] Cf. Chu, *Local Government*, chs 1, 10; Richards, *Empire*, ch. 4.

[189] Bayly, 'Communalism,' 181ff; Richards, *Empire*, 3, 53, 60. See too Barbara Metcalf, 'Presidential Address: Too Little and Too Much: Reflections on Muslims in the History of India,' *JAS* 54, 4 (1995): 951–67.

review.[190] Nor did literacy below 10% offer a promising vehicle of wider acculturation.

Yet it was not these tensions *per se* that overstrained central structures, rather the combination of such tensions with (a) military reverses in the south and later invasions from the northwest; (b) a shortage of new patronage lands; (c) succession disputes; and (d) perhaps most important, new social challenges. If we follow André Wink, Muzaffar Alam, Bayly, and others, Mughal decline reflected, at the most basic structural level, not a collapsed economy, but the rise of new forms of wealth and social authority in the provinces that actually had been encouraged by Mughal prosperity but that eventually outgrew Delhi's control. The Mughal elite was transformed and displaced by inferior social groups—Muslim gentry, Hindu landholders and merchants. These insurgent groups profited from sustained commercial expansion, gradually converted prebendal and conditional entitlements to patrimonial property, and developed provincial coalitions that could manage power independently of Delhi. A series of successor states now arose to challenge one another and, in some cases, European powers.[191]

One is thus tempted to suggest that Mughal decline was a precocious version of that eighteenth-century crisis that economic expansion helped to precipitate in other Eurasian areas. After *c.* 1740 commercialization joined with the spread of European-style military techniques to raise the cost of warfare, which inspired Mughal successor states to pursue a variety of fiscal and military reforms, while insisting on the primacy (not exclusivity) of their religious rituals. The resultant interplay of military innovation, mercantilism, and state-sponsored culturalism recalls competition-driven consolidations in Europe and across the Bay of Bengal. If we accept that India always contained a hierarchy of imperial, regional and local states, each with its own aura of sovereignty, and if we avert our gaze from Mughal fortunes to the evolution of these regional entities, the notion of 'decline'—and the contrast with previous examples—loses

[190] Richards, *Empire*, 151ff, 175ff, 218, 284, 290; C.A. Bayly, *Imperial Meridian* (London, 1989), 22; Cynthia Talbot, 'Inscribing the Other, Inscribing the Self,' *CSSH* 37, 4 (1995): 692–722.

[191] Wink, *Land and Sovereignty in India* (Cambridge, 1986); Alam, *The Crisis of Empire in Mughal North India* (Delhi, 1986); Bayly, *Society*, ch. 1; *idem*, *Rulers, Townsmen and Bazaars* (Cambridge, 1983), ch. 1; Richards, *Empire*, ch. 12; J.R.I. Cole, *Roots of North Indian Shiism in Iran and Iraq* (Berkeley, 1988); Stewart Gordon, *The Marathas 1600–1818* (Cambridge, 1993).

some of its force. Some, but not all—for whereas our six polities had been fully independent for centuries, the major Indian states of the 1700s occupied more ambiguous ground. Some were merely metamorphosed provincial governments, while even those insurgent states promoting Hindu or Sikh primacy continued to base their own legitimacy in part on Mughal authority and to preserve Mughal administrative culture.[192] Furthermore, by virtue of British intervention the process of post-Mughal state formation proved unusually short-lived. Indian capital and expertise were drawn into partnership with the English East India Company, which wed commercial and military power in much the same way as Indian rulers, but with greater ambition and success. By the early 1800s British tribute demands, the sale of military power, and British commercial inroads had joined to weaken the foundations of regional and local states in the Indian interior.[193]

I turn finally to archipelagic Southeast Asia (including Malaya). In so far as its high culture derived from India, this area is appropriately grouped with mainland Southeast Asia. Yet by comparison with the mainland, archipelagic geography was unfavorable to centralization. So too, in contrast to our six polities, the archipelago lay exposed to sustained external intervention, in this case European maritime incursions. In both respects therefore we see a certain resemblance to India, although in the archipelago these features tended to be far more pronounced, and the prospects for sustained integration correspondingly limited.[194]

Island Southeast Asia's geographic restrictions included poor inter-island communications, generally infertile soils, and exceptionally low population densities in the western and eastern sectors, features that favored shifting capitals and non-territorial forms of organization. Fertile Java did have populations as large as those in mainland basins, but lacked unifying river arteries comparable to the Irrawaddy or Chaophraya. Accordingly, the chief pre-1450

[192] Previous note, plus Burton Stein, 'State Formation and Economy Reconsidered,' and Frank Perlin, 'State Formation Reconsidered,' *MAS* 19, 3 (1985): 387–413 and 415–80; Bayly, *Society*, 14–18.

[193] Bayly, *Society*, 5, chs 1, 2; Washbrook, 'Progress.'

[194] Discussion of archipelagic Southeast Asia derives from Reid, *Age of Commerce*, I and II; Lieberman, 'Local Integration,' 540–82; *idem*, 'Wallerstein's System and the International Context of Early Modern Southeast Asian History,' *Journal of Asian History* 24, 1 (1990): 70–90; *idem*, 'Mainland-Archipelagic Parallels and Contrasts, c. 1750–1850,' forthcoming in Anthony Reid (ed.), *The Last Stand of the Autonomous States of Southeast Asia*.

principalities in the archipelago—Srivijaya, Kediri, Singhosari, possibly Majapahit—appear to have been more fissiparous and unstable than their mainland counterparts.

As elsewhere in Eurasia, the mid- and late 1400s inaugurated some two centuries of rapid commercial growth, driven in this case by an expansion in transit trade along Eurasia's southern rim, by mounting Indian Ocean and Chinese demand for Southeast Asian products, and by an associated expansion in intra-regional exchange. Anthony Reid has carefully documented this upsurge, together with associated trends towards urbanism, cultural cosmopolitanism of a predominantly Muslim character, and the rise of new political centers. With the introduction of Portuguese and Muslim firearms and improved naval craft after *c.* 1520, and with a consequent intensification of interstate rivalries, indigenous polities (Aceh, Banten, Johor, Mataram, Makassar) grew more administratively ambitious and more self-consciously Muslim. The so-called 'Southeast Asian religion,' quasi-Indian quasi-animist, became subject to textualist pressures as on the mainland. In short, in several parts of the archipelago we see further instances of political and cultural integration, albeit of modest scale.

During the course of the seventeenth century, however, these trends aborted through the interplay of several factors which Reid again has excavated: destructive tensions between interior and coast, price declines, navigational advances that outstripped local capacities, and most critical, unprecedented assaults by the Dutch East India Company. By 1690 all the principal archipelagic states had collapsed or severely contracted, commercial networks had withered, indigenous urbanization had gone into reverse. Attempted revivals starting in the late eighteenth century in central Java, Aceh, and Sulu were relatively anemic. Ironically, however, before *c.* 1830 the Dutch themselves failed to create a stable or extensive order because of their limited political objectives and internal disorganization, and because of mounting British economic competition. Moreover, notwithstanding a degree of syncretism between Dutch and Indies culture and Dutch patronage of Javanese nobles, the religious/cultural divide between the Dutch and indigenous peoples denied Europeans the same bases of authority as local leaders enjoyed elsewhere in Southeast Asia, in Europe, or even Mughal India. As repeated Javanese disturbances in the 1700s and early 1800s suggested, cultural issues had a way of complicating, reinforcing, and reconfiguring material grievances.[195] Finally, Chinese immigrants, despite their growing economic influence, lacked political ambition or extensive inter-island coordination. Thus although the archipelago as a whole clearly participated in the great worldwide economic upsurge of the early modern era and although maritime contacts favored Islam's spread, before 1830 economic and political power tended to remain sundered.

To conclude with a comment on later implications of early modern integration: Anderson, as noted, sees the artificiality of 'Indonesia,' its absolute incongruity with precolonial formations, as arguing for the critical role of intelligentsia agency in the colonial era. Indonesia, in turn, he sees as sufficiently emblematic of non-Western nations.[196] To be sure, as I myself have argued, mainland Southeast Asian conceptions of sovereignty, territory, even ethnicity were fundamentally recast after *c.* 1900.[197] Yet it seems to me no less true that in today's Burma, Thailand, and Vietnam state authority rests on the loyalty of a paramount ethnic group in a fashion rather different from anything found in Indonesia—and that this divergence has major implications for the marginalization and incorporation of minority peoples. In large part, this discrepancy reflects the fact that lowland peoples on the mainland had a long-standing relation to stable state traditions which the Europeans were obliged to respect in their tripartite division of the mainland—but which had no counterpart in the archipelago, even in Java. Whereas in the archipelago the colonial state became the indigenous state, on the mainland (with the partial and curious exceptions of Laos and Cambodia) the situation was the reverse.[198] Within the mainland, moreover, conflicts between lowland and upland peoples obviously bulk larger in Burmese political life than in Vietnamese, and again precolonial tensions, transmogrified by colonial experience, are not hard to discern. By the same token, modernist critiques of primordial nationalism in the former Soviet Union can easily obscure the fact that the fault lines

[195] M.C. Ricklefs, *Jogjakarta under Sultan Mangkubumi 1749–1792* (London, 1974); Carey, 'Just King,' 59–137.

[196] *Imagined Communities*, esp. 114–15, 127–32, 176–85.

[197] Lieberman, 'Ethnic Politics,' 480–2.

[198] Henley, 'Ethnogeographic Integration,' 286–324 also has sought to contrast the Indonesian and Indochinese experience by analyzing differences in precolonial heritage, colonial conquest, and colonial policy; yet he generally fails to consider the degree to which the latter two sets of factors depended on the first.

of political collapse in 1991 between Russia, Belorus, the Ukraine, and the Baltic areas bear an undeniable relation, negative and positive, to state-centered identities that originated in the sixteenth and seventeenth centuries. Again, the challenge is to chart without teleological bias the changing definitions of identity on different social levels.

Was Early Modern Japan Culturally Integrated?

MARY ELIZABETH BERRY

Orientations: Four Questions

In an earlier draft of his essay, Professor Lieberman quoted, with some bemusement, a remark by Edwin O. Reischauer that has flown from the text but stuck in memory. Japan during the Tokugawa era, observed E.O.R., achieved 'a greater degree of cultural, intellectual, and ideological conformity . . . than any other country in the world . . . before the nineteenth century.'[1] The claim is remarkable—no less for its tone than for its unlikelihood (were we even remotely able to test it). Still, the claim is tantalizing, and versions of it, more hesitant, continue to resonate in the survey literature.

The quotation surely appealed to Professor Lieberman because he, too, argues, if guardedly, that Japan saw an extensive 'standardization of culture' in the early modern period. Indeed, this standardization appears more vigorous in Japan than in the other rimlands under discussion. Lieberman's rhetoric mutates on occasion. He sometimes refers to cultural 'consolidation,' even 'homogenization,' and to a growing 'uniformity . . . of cultural symbols.' Yet throughout his pursuit of culture, Lieberman is concerned with the unprecedented formation in early modernity of common 'customs, attitudes, and practices' within national or proto-national units. And this is the subject, in the Japanese case, that I take on as well. Warily.

Lieberman himself is cautious. Skeptical of the very macrohistorical comparison he pursues, he tempers big claims with small qualifications, switching vertiginously from telescope to microscope. But my own wariness has less to do with focus than with the unspoken assumptions framing the project. Let me begin, then, by examining Lieberman's conceptual armature.

[1] Reischauer, in Edwin O. Reischauer and Albert M. Craig, *Japan: Tradition and Transformation* (Sydney, 1979), p. 86.

I. Is Cultural Convergence Any More Pronounced Than Cultural Divergence in the Early Modern Period?
(Or, Thoughts on the Twin Movements of Consolidation and Fragmentation)

A military personnel register, published in 1681, groups the officials directly in service to the Tokugawa shogunate under 230 titles.[2]

A Japanese agricultural manual, completed in 1697, includes separate chapters on each of 19 varieties of grain, 57 vegetables, 11 grasses, 36 trees, and 22 herbs.[3]

A directory to the city of Edo, published in 1687, lists prominent craftspeople, merchants, and providers of services in 97 categories.[4]

A Kyoto publisher's catalog, issued in 1659, lists 1,600 titles in 22 categories. An Edo publisher's catalog, issued in 1696, includes 7,800 titles.[5]

These statements tell two stories—one of convergence, another of divergence. On the one hand, the integrating structures important to Professor Lieberman are everywhere implicit: a centralized polity has generated a capacious, hierarchical officialdom; regional and even national markets have generated both a specialized, commercial agriculture and a specialized, vertically organized workforce. Additional integral forces—reliable transport, urbanization, schooling—lurk behind the statements as well. Indeed, the very tallies and sources I cite are themselves a sign of integration; for classification and quantification were part of a contemporary sociology that presumed pattern and coherence in worldly affairs.

[2] *Tenna gannen koshō-kei Edo kagami*, in Hashimoto Hiroshi (ed.), *(Kaitei zōhō) Dai bukan*, 3 vols (Tokyo, 1965), vol. 1, pp. 156–82.

[3] Thomas C. Smith makes this tally in *The Agrarian Origins of Modern Japan* (Stanford, 1959), p. 89. The manual is the *Nōgyō zensho*, by Miyazaki Antei, in Hirose Hideo *et al.* (eds), *Kinsei kagaku shisō* (Tokyo, 1971), vol. 62, pp. 67–165.

[4] *Edo sōganoko meisho taizen*, pt 6, in Edo Sōsho Hangyō-kai, *Edo Sōsho* (Tokyo, 1916), vols 3–4.

[5] For the 1659 catalog, Shidō Bunko (ed.), *(Edo jidai) Shorin shuppan shoseki mokuroku shūsei* (Tokyo, 1962–64), 4 vols. For discussion, Donald H. Shively, 'Popular Culture,' in John W. Hall (ed.), *The Cambridge History of Japan* (Cambridge, 1991), vol. 4, p. 731.

On the other hand, the disintegrating power of change is no less apparent in the tallies. The figures all speak to the multiplication of differences. These are not only the base differences of class and status, wealth, religion, gender, race. They are the relentlessly elaborated differences inherent to the centralizing process itself. Accompanying political and economic integration was ever-finer discrimination (and distance) between the daimyo and his surveyor of roads, the rice broker and the porter, the embroiderer and the reeler of thread, the tobacco grower and the breeder of silkworms. And differences in skill and station were marked further, of course—not just by training and income, but by the distinctive tools and sites and costumes and vocabularies of distinctive work.

In short, the integration of systems tends to accelerate the separation of people. Here is the paradox of modernity itself, and perhaps the surest link between the early modern experience and our own. Consolidation requires differentiation. Rationalization heightens complexity. New unions invite new fractures. The convergence traced by Max Weber brings the divergence explored by Emile Durkheim.

From a distance, and with the help of abstract models, analysts of polities and markets can (more or less) clarify the principles that unite multiplying parts to systemic wholes. (These principles may be less lively to the actors who are variously ensnared and estranged by systems.) But even dauntless analysts must pause before the challenge of culture; for it is there that the multiplying differences in polity and economy are both expressed and dispersed. The internal logic that may govern markets is elusive at best when we confront the dizziness of cultural activity in early modern societies.

We find in Japan, for example, increasing diversity in diet, architecture, textiles. Entertainment crossed a widening spectrum of dramas and spectacles, tourist travel and shopping, commercial sex and cosseting. Painting, poetry, potting, music—all took multiple directions within multiple organizations of professionals and amateurs alike. Burgeoning schools taught burgeoning curricula.[6] And so forth.

We can detect structural causes and principles of order in such diversity. Variety in culture responded, surely, to greater urbanization as well as to the expansion and redistribution of wealth within a proto-bourgeoisie. And this variety can be organized into sectors

[6] Shively, 1991; Susan B. Hanley, 'Tokugawa Society: Material Culture, Standard of Living, and Life-styles,' in Hall (ed.), *The Cambridge History of Japan* (Cambridge, 1991), vol, 4, pp. 660–705; and Richard Rubinger, *Private Academies of Tokugawa Japan* (Princeton, 1982).

with their own coherence. Nonetheless, cultural practice is ultimately disorderly; for it is Protean in dimension and influenced by incalculable variables. In early modernity, the new and crucial variable was commercialization: culture could be purchased and thus loosed from any tight relationship with class. Almost everything—food and drink, education and books, paintings and ornamental shrubs, theater and music—was on the market. In effect, culture became increasingly a matter of choice and hence susceptible to myriad combinations that correlated imperfectly with income and station. Across income and station boundaries, moreover, culture was loosed from mundane social rhythms to become a matter of private recreation and conscious cultivation. The publishing information I cited in my opening statements may be evidence of macro-social integration through literacy and print networks. Yet the thousands of titles in expanding categories intimate a kaleidoscope of writers and readers ever rearranged (and shaken apart) by ambition, imagination, value, and taste.

Because cultural practices (and economic and political practices as well) resist synoptic treatment, the search for integration in the early modern world entails problems. These are partly, as Lieberman notes, problems of exclusion and emphasis. Concentrating on large patterns of consolidation that anticipate national formation, he elides both the many actors who were not party to various changes (such as subsistence farmers, the almost totally illiterate population of women) and the many competing movements that did not survive modernization (such as a militantly anti-market agrarianism). Lieberman's followers must be lumpers rather than splitters who risk confusing dominance with universality.

But the greater problem, within the context of Lieberman's argument itself, is a temptation toward flatness and away from depth of field. Once we acknowledge that the very process of consolidation involved a twin process of fragmentation, we need a stereoscopic version of change. If we foreground integrating developments, we must do so in a fashion that keeps in view a background of multiplying differences. How we are to do this is the challenge of Lieberman's project.

Let me note, incidentally, that attention to the remorseless complexity of early modern culture precludes any simple contrast with the medieval past. However attractive, a contrast between medieval fracture and early modern cohesion in cultural practice cannot be convincing. Too many new forms of cultural fracture, no less than many persisting ones, spread across the early modern divide.

II. Can We Actually Detect Cultural Convergence?
(Or, Thoughts on Elusive Evidence and Arbitrary Perspectives)

Although his approach is wide, Professor Lieberman looks for cultural convergence primarily in cultural behavior—such as language and religious practice. This approach and these subjects are as important as they are ridden with difficulty.

The most obvious difficulty is an often intractable one in macrohistorical discussion—proof. We may grant that language is a critical bond and that confluence probably increased in early modernity. But we have no good way of measuring either linguistic divergence before 1400 or convergence by 1800. The problem is complicated by the premodern separation in Japan of written and spoken languages, and our consequent reliance on piecemeal evidence (such as folk songs and novelistic dialogs) to recover the oral vernaculars. The presumption of convergence must be undercut, in any case, by the roiling debates over language that opened in the late nineteenth century—debates over whether and how to unite the many written forms of Japanese with the many spoken dialects, debates over who was to control the textbooks and the media and thus impose a national standard on still highly diverse usages.[7]

But even if we could demonstrate the convergence of language in early modernity, we would be left with the problem of perspective. Professor Lieberman's vantage on culture is high and external. He works, as broadly comparative historians must, at a gross level of generalization and with an outsider's attention to long trends. Turning to the religious sphere, then, Lieberman might see in Japan a penetration of Confucian values and a rationalization of Buddhist belief. Insiders might see only the proliferating schools and sects whose fine and finer distinctions in faith and practice marked wide and wider divisions in identity among adherents. So, too, in the sphere of language. Seemingly minor differences in semantics or accent can hew chasms in social filiation. And the point must repeat itself endlessly as we posit commonalities in any sphere of cultural

[7] Mizuhara Akito, *Edogo, Tōkyōgo, hyōjungo* (Tokyo, 1994).

conduct—from marriage ritual to calligraphic style. Whatever standardization we choose to stress may bear lightly on lived experience; for small variations may form the greatest divides. Can we know what really unites and divides peoples?

As Lieberman notes, we tend to glimpse cultural solidarity—and thus what seemingly unites a group—in moments of crisis, particularly foreign crisis. Yet as he also notes, such glimpses are distorted; for crisis invites an uncommon concealment of differences. Just as important, the face of solidarity is usually the face projected by holders of power. Is chauvinistic rallying a test of common culture?

If there are profound bonds of culture, then, the historian's search for them is troubled. Evidence is variously elusive or deceptive. Apparent convergence may mask the fine divergences that matter more. And, in the end, even full conformity in cultural practice tells us little about cultural consciousness: a sameness in behavior is hardly equivalent to a shared mentality—to a *sense* of common culture.

I raise these concerns not to disable inquiry, but to recommend alternative directions and modest goals. Because behavior is hard to track in the aggregate and harder to evaluate as binding or dividing, I would shift the emphasis to thought, and thus search the sources for common mental habits—and orientations—that might underlie differences in experience. Because written sources are partial in reach and myriad in meaning, I would resign any quest for inclusive representations of society or active demonstrations of consciousness. Although cultural 'standardization' seems to me beyond historical proof, we can usefully explore novel ways of thinking that may have gradually, unconsciously connected people.

III. Does the Early Modern Experience Really Matter?
(Or, Thoughts About Continuity and Rupture in Culture)

Professor Lieberman trains his gaze on early modernity because he finds in that period a movement away from medieval fragmentation and toward an integration that anticipates modern statehood. In effect, he emphasizes a break between the medieval and early modern experiences and a continuity between the early modern and modern experiences. We might easily reverse the emphases. I linger over the point since our attention to early modernity requires some groundwork—some comparison with preceding and succeeding eras.

If we retain a high and external perspective, pre-Lieberman Japan (or Japan before 1400) might look reasonably well integrated. The ocean, which acted more as a barrier than a connective artery, formed outer boundaries that were assailed regularly by piracy but rarely by invasion. (The Mongol incursions of the late thirteenth century drew Japan into foreign war for the first time in at least six centuries.) Immigration was not substantial after the early classical period; diplomatic contact remained intermittent; and a distinctive vernacular language, however various its dialects, separated Japan from neighbors.[8] The commonalities resulting from such isolating factors were amplified by material culture. Housing was overwhelmingly detached and single-story wooden construction (because of the threat of earthquake); the diet was dominated by sea products and grains (because limitations on arable land precluded the pasturage of animal herds); the penetration of wet rice agriculture promoted sedentary and interdependent communal formation, discouraged the growth of slavery, and disseminated a common agrarian technology across the three main islands.[9]

In politics, moreover, the centralizing disciplines of the classical state (*c.* 710–1185), though much altered by episodic civil war and the maturation of shogunal rule, exerted an influence throughout the medieval period (1185–1467). An ancient monarchy continued as the font of legitimate authority; rank and title derived from courtly practice; space was ordered by the classical system of provinces, districts, and highways; taxation remained focused on grain and labor; classical legal traditions and habits of litigation persisted.

Across classes, genealogy defined status and inheritance conveyed property as well as profession. Blood was identity. A stem family system organized kindred more insistently than extended or clan systems.[10]

Buddhism, supported by the state and prevalent among the aristocracy from the eighth century, had spread widely by the late medieval period. Although always a manifold phenomenon (for there are many Buddhisms and many interweavings of Shinto and other

[8] Roy Andrew Miller, *The Japanese Language* (Chicago, 1967); and Nakamoto Masachie, *Nihon rettō gengoshi no kenkyū* (Tokyo, 1990).

[9] The best study in English of the early rice regime is William Wayne Farris, *Population, Disease, and Land in Early Japan, 645–900* (Cambridge, MA, 1985).

[10] Jeffrey P. Mass, *Lordship and Inheritance in Medieval Japan* (Stanford, 1989); Murakami Yasusuke, 'Ie Society as a Pattern of Civilization,' in *The Journal of Japanese Studies* 10, 2: 279–363.

traditions), the Buddhist presence quickly affected the national landscape, where temples became the major monuments, as well as the conduct of death, for cremation became the normal manner of interment. Buddhism also legitimated the life of the road.

Perhaps the most significant social movement in pre-Lieberman Japan was the penetration of the country by medieval itinerants. They came in many forms: they were preachers and healers, entertainers and prostitutes, pilgrims and monks soliciting donations to temples. Yet virtually all who left a trace in the record shared a Buddhist identity conveyed by tonsures or robes or names or professed affiliations. These many men and women, all outside society but accorded licence by the Buddhist markings, were the vehicles of cultural integration at the time. They proselytized a vernacular Buddhism, transmitted a popular literature focused on tales of the Genpei war (1180–85), established a repertoire of miracle stories, helped routinize the rituals of death, and carried news across borders.[11]

The experience in pre-Lieberman Japan of foreign encounter (and hence of an alterity that may have shaped national consciousness) was a paradoxical one. In one sense, China saturated Japan: its written language, polity, religions, material and high culture inflected all aspects of the classical Japanese state and retained an influence in the medieval era. A China-consciousness is intense in all scholarly writing (much of it written in Chinese), and conspicuous in much of the tale literature that circulated orally.

Nonetheless, the Chinese presence was tempered by two considerations. First, Chinese forms tended to be altered in Japan and thus to assume putatively native shape. (Even the Chinese language used in Japan for formal writing took on numerous native variants.) Second, the physical—rather than the intellectual—presence of China and the Chinese was rare. From neither side of the Japan Sea was there any unflagging impetus toward diplomacy, settlement, combat, or commerce (with the exception of the piracy that influenced China and Korea more gravely than Japan). Sixteen diplomatic missions went from Japan to China between 607 and 838, for example, but were then discontinued until 1404.

[11] Janet Goodwin, *Alms and Vagabonds: Buddhist Temples and Popular Patronage in Medieval Japan* (Honolulu, 1994); Barbara Ruch, 'The Other Side of Culture,' in Kozo Yamamura (ed.), *The Cambridge History of Japan* (Cambridge, 1990), vol. 3, pp. 500–43.

The simultaneous presence and absence of China created a clear international order even as it permitted the translation of 'the foreign' into a remote other, into an idea and source of ideas that might be managed at will. Whether the Mongol invasions of 1274 and 1281 broke this relationship more than temporarily I do not know. They may have heightened a generally inchoate sense of alien and native while deepening the inclination toward controlled contact.[12]

This brisk survey of pre-Lieberman Japan, though everywhere vulnerable to challenge, suggests that some integration occurred early—at least if we use such gross and lumpish measures as outer boundaries, stable ethnicities, a common parent language, dominant religious and agrarian systems, an ethos of hereditary power, generally durable polities with a single source of legitimacy, and established patterns in foreign relations. Since Professor Lieberman invites us to gauge the acceleration of integrating developments after 1400, this prehistory offers a baseline of comparison.

Post-Lieberman Japan deserves remark as well. Despite the integration I have just imputed to the period before 1400, and despite the gains I shall eventually claim for early modernity, the evidence for the Meiji era (1868–1912) indicates that the new state regarded the work of integration as barely begun. To an extent never before seen in Japan, political disciplines—largely responsive to perceived foreign threats—became the medium of cultural refashioning. Meiji leaders focused on the creation and projection of a national government that had been, if not exactly weak, at least concealed in the Tokugawa period (1600–1868). And much of this labor was necessarily cultural in emphasis: the display of the monarch on train platforms across the country; the invention of anthems and flags and state rituals; the establishment of telegraphs, newspapers, and radio networks to carry information and propaganda; the design of a public school system to nourish good subjects, pliable conscripts, and willing industrial workers; the formation of a state Shinto cult to instil reverence for emperor and nation. The work of nationalism, and the creation of its essentially new symbols, was the work of Meiji.[13]

[12] Studies in English of early Japanese foreign contacts are few. See Robert Borgen, *Sugawara no Michizane and the Early Heian Court* (Cambridge, MA, 1986); and David Pollack, *The Fracture of Meaning: Japan's Synthesis of China from the 8th through the 18th Centuries* (Princeton, 1986).

[13] See, for example, Carol Gluck, *Japan's Modern Myths: Ideology in the Late Meiji Period* (Princeton, 1985); and Takashi Fujitani, 'Japan's Modern National Ceremonies: A Historical Ethnography,' Ph.D. dissertation, University of California,

I need not run through the litany of modernization moves here. But I would like to suggest two points relevant to our discussion of the earlier world.

First, the distance between early modernity and modernity, at least in Japan, really was vast. Much of the scholarship on the Tokugawa period has been concerned with how the gap was apparently closed rather quickly as the result of foundations laid, and preparations made, before 1850.[14] Similar concerns inform the Lieberman project as well. But while it is foolish to deny the importance of foundations, it is overly sanguine (and a-historical) to exaggerate their magnitude and thus miscalculate the Meiji undertaking. If the male literacy rate in the Tokugawa period was 40% and the female literacy rate 10%,[15] do those figures predict or explain a rapid doubling of the literate population during the Meiji years? Similar questions must surround the quantum increases in urban population and agricultural productivity. Certainly we are not dealing with clear cases of historical causation (as, invariably, the China scholars remind us). Nor does the Tokugawa experience speak at all directly to the profound surprises of the Meiji era: the ability to conscript a popular army and win foreign wars after 250 years of peace and civilian disarmament; the ability to contain foreign diplomatic and commercial incursions after 250 years of relative inexperience with state-to-state relations. Just how significant, we might well ask, *was* the Tokugawa experience to modernization?

Second, given the presumption that *some* premodern experiences must have been *reasonably* significant, the isolation of those experiences remains a tough and probably impressionistic job. I have noted already that a certain commonality in language did not preclude convulsions over a standard dialect. We might wonder whether any earlier developments could have prepared for the sundering of a state Shinto cult from Buddhism, or whether the popular adoption of samurai styles was not reproached by the modern injunctions to cut hair, store swords, and learn to waltz.

These are cautionary observations. In entering the world of Lieberman proper, I am wary of discovering a cultural convergence that we

Berkeley, 1986. For discussion of the transition, see Marius Jansen and Gilbert Rozman, *Japan in Transition: From Tokugawa to Meiji* (Princeton, 1986).

[14] The modernization school in Tokugawa studies is best represented in English by Robert Bellah, *Tokugawa Religion* (Glencoe, 1957); Ronald Dore, *Education in Tokugawa Japan* (Berkeley, 1965); and Thomas C. Smith, 1959.

[15] Dore, 1965.

might impute to pre-Lieberman Japan. I am also wary of portraying culture as a cumulative project when, after all, it is an odd creature that may move incrementally or suddenly change skins.

IV. What Are We Looking For?
(Or, Thoughts on the Lieberman Agenda)

Macro-historical comparison tends to focus on fairly well-defined outcomes, which organize the inquiry into origins. Theda Skocpol, for example, examines the conditions of social revolution; Perry Anderson examines the sources of political absolutism.[16] The Lieberman enterprise is more subtle and elusive, and hence more unnerving to contributors.

At the simplest level, Lieberman appears interested in comparison for comparison's sake—which is no mean thing. Without concentrating on outcomes, or on originary principles, he surveys six different countries with open eyes. The resulting detection of parallel forms of integration in these rimlands is an act of intellectual virtuosity of a high order.

At another level, comparison leads Lieberman to (at least) three statements about the trajectories of his rimlands: parallel forms of national integration occurred during a (very roughly) synchronized period that we might call early modernity; such integration seems to have resulted from some similar causes that, though partly internal, were substantially external as well; and, finally, such historical commonalities militate against any binary formulations of separate eastern and western development. But, however cogent at a magisterial level of generality, each of these claims poses problems that Lieberman is the first to acknowledge. For starters, the time-frame of analysis, which exceeds four centuries, is exceptionally elastic. The causal elements are also numerous and dependent: neither an independent variable nor a stable mix of prime factors accounts persistently for the commonalities Lieberman discovers. Thus, the prolonged peace and relative isolation of early modern Japan seem to have achieved results comparable to the periodic wars and international exposure of early modern France. Another difficulty is the loose standard of comparison among the six sample countries: the

[16] Theda Skocpol, *States and Social Revolutions* (Cambridge, 1979); Perry Anderson, *Lineages of the Absolutist State* (London, 1974).

increasing 'integration' claimed for each of the rimlands had locally disparate manifestations and even more disparate limits. If the Burmese and Russian polities assumed such different shapes, have we gained more than a superficial insight by noting their shared concern with centralization?

To overcome caution in the face of such difficulties, and hence join the macro-historical enterprise, we need a clear purpose. Here Professor Lieberman wavers. Sometimes he asks us to look for 'Eurasian interdependence'—to gaze beyond borders at a Eurasia that formed an 'evolving, loosely integrated system' or an 'interactive, loosely synchronized ecumene.' But this project is compromised by Lieberman's attention to discrete local histories, and to their powerful interior as well as exterior imperatives. Eurasia finally looms less large than six countries that were variously embarked on the transition to modern nationhood. In effect, Lieberman's enterprise does seem a 'neo-modernization project'—a quest for the common origins, in Asia as well as Europe, of durable nation states.

We are closer, then, but not close enough, to a well-defined outcome. Like the term 'integration,' 'nation state' is the loosest of common standards of analysis. Even if we grant this denomination to the gang of six, their modern histories diverge wherever we look—whether at political form or philosophy, legal structure, economic organization, military power, colonial experience. . . . So one possible promise of the Lieberman project—that a roughly common course of development might produce states of a certain kind—seems thwarted. Just how, then, are the rimlands comparable? And what are we seeking in their early modern experiences that might account for that comparability?

I think Professor Lieberman reveals his answers in a discussion of the differences between archipelagic and mainland Southeast Asia.

> [I]t seems to me . . . that in today's Burma, Thailand, and Vietnam state authority rests on the loyalty of a paramount ethnic group in a fashion very different from anything found in Indonesia—and that this has major implications for anti-colonial legacies. . . . In large part, this discrepancy reflects the fact that lowland peoples on the mainland had a long-standing relation to stable state traditions which the Europeans were obliged to respect in their triparite division of the mainland—but which had no counterpart in the archipelago. . . .[17]

Lieberman's concern here is nationalism. Unlike the arbitrarily (or colonially) formed countries of the archipelago, the mainland coun-

[17] Lieberman, this volume.

tries were able to connect modern state authority to some sense of peoplehood (or ethnicity) through the medium of loyalty. This is nationalism: a demonstrable relationship between centralized territorial governance and collective identity. Although governance and identity need be neither congruent nor harmonious, they must correspond sufficiently to permit semi-voluntary mobilizations in response to state needs.

The difference of the mainland is, for Lieberman, a difference of history. There the lowland 'peoples' (with an at least latent awareness of peoplehood) had known a 'long-standing relation' (with an at least rudimentary presumption of attachment) to 'stable state traditions.' In sum, modern nationalism was anticipated by what we might call the proto-national consciousness of early modernity.

However multi-valent, Professor Lieberman's work seems to me ultimately concerned with these ties between nationalisms and their antecedents. The search for 'integration' in disparate early modern countries has little to do, in the end, with the exact chronologies or details of political centralization, market penetration, and cultural standardization. Lieberman readily concedes staggering variety in these matters. The search for 'integration' also slights Eurasian interdependence to emphasize the sense of 'alterity'—and hence the sense of local distinction—produced by foreign encounter. So what remains apparently common to the early modern experience of 'integration' in the rimlands (though not solely there) is an intersection between statist power and collective identity.

Summary and Subject

Professor Lieberman invites me, I conclude, to explore the development in early modern Japan of a proto-nationalism, or, more loosely, of the antecedents of a national identity. Was there some construction of peoplehood (or some experience of cultural integration) that was yoked to a stable polity?

My task is complicated by the scruples apparent in my introductory questions. Because I find cleavage inherent to early modernity, it seems misguided to find integration in either the transcendence of differences (through a common parent language or grain regime, for example) or the erosion of differences (through the dissemination of literacy or the samurai style, for example). Although persuasive in general terms, both approaches are forms of denial: they presume the superiority of centripetal over centrifugal forces in human affairs. They also have limited explanatory power. Transcendence invokes commonalities too lofty for routine application. Erosion tends to blur one boundary only to clarify another.

Hence, I duck the search for a cultural integration that occurs when similarity surpasses difference. I am concerned, rather, with how difference gets managed. My subject is the integrative principles that can connect necessarily different units in society—the ideas or mental habits that permit fragmented units to situate themselves in a whole. The effect of such integration will not be cultural unity or alikeness. It can only be the crafting of workable relationships.

The integrative principles at work in early Japan seem to me best revealed in an extraordinary body of printed material that I call 'public information.' This material was part of a publishing explosion that began, by the 1640s, in the three great cities (Kyoto, Edo, Osaka) and then spread to commercial concerns across the country.[18] The Edo publishers' list for 1696, with its 7,800 titles, intimates the dimensions of the enterprise. Religion, philosophy, history, and fiction commanded large places in the industry, but informative and instructional works assumed an increasingly strong position. They ranged from sheet maps and atlases to encyclopedias, word dictionaries, biographical dictionaries, personnel registers, rural gazetteers, urban directories, travel guides, agrarian manuals, surveys of any manner of specialties (from gardening to sericulture), evaluations of professional services (from prostitution to Confucian teaching), and a vast assortment of texts for the education of the young.

This explosion in information was new. It was linked to printing but not to technological discovery. Virtually all commercial printers continued to use the ancient art of woodblock, which was employed in Japan continuously from the seventh century for small editions of Buddhist works. Although movable type fascinated publishers in the early seventeenth century, the aesthetics and economies of woodblock prevailed.[19] Rather than technology, then, printing responded

[18] Discussions in English of Tokugawa period publishing include Shively, 1991; Henry D. Smith II, 'The History of the Book in Edo and Paris,' in James L. McClain *et al.* eds), *Edo and Paris: Urban Life and the State in the Early Modern Era* (Ithaca, 1994); David Chibbett, *The History of Japanese Printing and Book Illustration* (Tokyo, 1977); Katsuhisa Moriya, 'Urban Networks and Information Networks,' in Chie Nakane and Shinzaburo Oishi (eds), *Tokugawa Japan* (Tokyo, 1990), pp. 97–123; and Peter Kornicki, 'The Publisher's Go-Between: *Kashihon'ya* in the Meiji Period,' *Modern Asian Studies* 14, 2: 331–44.

[19] Shively, 1991, pp. 726–7.

to a variety of social imperatives in the early modern world, including a literate market and the ambitions of new, often professional writers. And, in turn, the market and the writers responded to the burgeoning of print.

A similar push–pull effect operated in the area of literacy. The printing industry presumed the healthy readership provided by multiple large cities, even as books stimulated the growth of ever larger readerships. The larger publishers opened provincial branches and significantly expanded their networks through loans: book stores also operated as lending libraries; itinerant lenders with books strapped to their backs worked the village market.

Within the expansive world of early modern print, my emphasis falls on the texts of public information for several reasons. First, they probably reached the reading majority as well as large circles of listeners and recipients of second- and third-hand intelligence. In so far as written materials moved beyond a literate minority to approach anything like common circulation, the information sources provide our surest link between textual and popular cultures. Indeed, they were produced in astonishing volume. Tens of thousands of domestic maps from the Tokugawa period survive today, for example, suggesting that in both productivity and variety Japan was one of the most active mappers among all early modern countries. (Historians count over 1,200 separate extant editions of maps of Edo city alone.)[20]

Further, I concentrate on the texts of public information because their content engaged and organized mundane experience. I focus in this essay on three particular genres in the information category: cartography, travel guides, and urban directories. In each case, the sources resonate with broad social movements and political disciplines to suggest some consonance between their printed messages and practical modes of knowledge. They may point to a culture that was not monopolized by readers alone.

Before I turn to the texts, their context must concern us. It is there that the conditions of change come clearer. And it is there that we discover the integral structures of polity and economy, crucial to the Lieberman project, that shaped cultural exchange.

[20] Iida Ryūichi and Tawara Motoaki, *Edo-zu no rekishi* (Tokyo, 1988), 2 vols. Among the larger and more accessible holders of Tokugawa period maps are the National Diet Library, the Kobe City Museum, the Tenri Library, and the Tokugawa Institute for the History of Forestry (Tokyo).

Contexts: Japan *c.* 1460–1800

Internal Perspectives

The formative experience of early modern Japan was civil war, which raged from 1467 until 1590 (or 1615, if we include two final battles over succession). Although local combat had not been uncommon after 1000, sustained and country-wide upheaval was rare. The upheaval after 1467 rose from dense troubles—from conflicts between urban usurers and rural borrowers, from predatory forms of absentee proprietorship, from the exhaustion of a manorial landholding system without margins for continued extraction and expansion. The upheaval took the form of political rebellion—of breakaway movements for local autonomy that encompassed the martial elite, then minor magnates, and eventually village and sectarian communities.[21]

As cleavages in the medieval polity spread, two alternative patterns of rule began, haltingly, to emerge: the consolidation of small territorial units (previously a patchwork of manorial jurisdictions) into integral domains that were governed—through force and administrative innovation—by daimyo lords; and the denial of all overlordship by self-governing leagues of farmers and village soldiers, religious sectarians, and urban commoners.

Fired by economic and political competition, war became the engine of economic growth. The replacement of atomized holdings by consolidated domains, *and* the reliance of daimyo upon local resources for success in battle, led to coordinated developments. These included the stimulation of agriculture (through large-scale irrigation works and reclamation programs); the encouragement of commerce (through relaxed market laws, the expansion and integration of market circuits); the exploitation of mines (through continental techniques of tunneling and smelting); the improvement of highways and waterways. Population began a climb that would be sustained into the eighteenth century.[22]

[21] John W. Hall, Nagahara Keiji, and Kozo Yamamura (eds), *Japan Before Tokugawa: Political Consolidation and Economic Growth, 1500–1650* (Princeton, 1981); and Mary Elizabeth Berry, *The Culture of Civil War in Kyoto* (Berkeley, 1994).

[22] Kozo Yamamura, 'Returns on Unification: Economic Growth in Japan 1550–1650,' in Hall, 1981, pp. 327–72; Nagahara Keiji and Kozo Yamamura, 'Shaping the Process of Unification: Technological Progress in Sixteenth- and Seventeenth-Century Japan,' *Journal of Japanese Studies* 14, 1: 77–109; Susan B. Hanley and Kozo Yamamura, *Economic and Demographic Change in Preindustrial Japan* (Princeton, 1977).

This economic change in the domains was accompanied by political initiatives. The most ambitious daimyo registered and systematically taxed agrarian properties. They imposed domainal-wide codes of law; they integrated both monasteries and towns into their jurisdictions. The process was jagged. It was also volatile. Daimyo rose and fell in a constantly changing mudscape. The domainal model of rule, nonetheless, proved tenacious, crushing brutally the defiant leagues.

I call civil war the formative experience of early modernity for (at least) two reasons. First, it shaped the domains that became the basic governing units in a national federation established around 1590 by Toyotomi Hideyoshi and led by the Tokugawa house from 1600 to 1868. Hideyoshi's settlement brought roughly 200 semi-autonomous domains into a federal form of union. (The number would increase to over 250 under Tokugawa rule.) Second, the length and gravity of wartime upheaval inspired a polity fixated on peace-keeping.

The Toyotomi and the early Tokugawa used central authority with singular audacity but precise target to cut the roots of turmoil. They disarmed farmers, monks, and townspeople; they leveled fortifications. They removed most samurai from villages to the castle towns of their daimyo, where they became underemployed peacetime stipendiaries. They forbade changes in class and station, monitored physical movement, disciplined belligerent monastic establishments. By 1640, moreover, they had heavily constrained foreign contact.[23]

Let me emphasize the audacity of these measures. The emphasis would hardly seem necessary except that fifteen generations of Tokugawa rule saw few substantial advances on these central powers and, indeed, several retreats. This situation moves Professor Lieberman to remark upon the limits of political integration in early modern Japan, and many scholars to regard shogunal governance as weak.[24] Without rejecting such observations, it seems well to offer modifications. First, the shogun (and, more important, the deputies to whom power devolved by administrative design) maintained for 250 years the most far-reaching polity Japan had known. They protected a

[23] Mary Elizabeth Berry, *Hideyoshi* (Cambridge, MA, 1982); Asao Naohiro, 'The Sixteenth-century Unification,' in Hall (ed.), *The Cambridge History of Japan* (Cambridge, 1991), vol. 4, pp. 40–95.

[24] Mark Ravina reviews the arguments over this matter and includes a good bibliography in 'State-Building and Political Economy in Early Modern Japan,' *Journal of Asian Studies* 54, 4: 997–1022.

federal contract that vested domainal rule in local daimyo and reserved for the center jurisdiction over pacification, daimyo discipline, and the public province (major cities, mines, currency, and so forth). Maintenance of a system is different from weakness.

Second, the shogun and daimyo alike were apparently willing to exchange public order for a certain restraint in rule—particularly in the matter of taxation, which ebbed as a percentage of the agrarian product over time and was never applied doggedly to commerce.[25] The longevity and stability of the Tokugawa peace (although uprisings mounted from the late eighteenth century) is impossible to explain without administrative temperance. And this temperance is poorly explained as simple weakness or fecklessness.

Finally, the audacious structure of pacification imposed around 1600 continued to frame the lives of all residents of early modern Japan. The dynamic and integrative effects that Professor Lieberman associates with war-making, and which we see clearly enough in the formation of Japan's wartime domains, can equally be associated with peace-keeping. If the Tokugawa shogun became largely invisible, the unfolding consequences of their original polity remained everywhere conspicuous: in the urban networks generated first by the removal of samurai (roughly 7% of the population) from villages and then by the requirement that all daimyo reside periodically in Edo; in the commercial agriculture geared to the supply of vast samurai cities; in the patterns of urban investment and alliance with rural capitalists that were pursued by merchants forbidden to buy village land; in the complex social roles that were invented by samurai left with stipends but without military employment (and who variously turned to scholarship, medicine, professional writing, political commentary, and freelance instruction).[26] In short, it is impos-

[25] The classic statement on agrarian taxation in English remains Thomas C. Smith, 'The Land Tax in the Tokugawa Period,' in John W. Hall and Marius B. Jansen (eds), *Studies in the Institutional History of Early Modern Japan* (Princeton, 1968), pp. 283–99. Commerce is explored in William B. Hauser, *Economic Institutional Change in Tokugawa Japan* (Cambridge, 1974); and John W. Hall, *Tanuma Okitsugu* (Cambridge, 1955). Also, see Tessa Morris-Suzuki, *A History of Japanese Economic Thought* (London, 1989).

[26] I know of no extended modern study of the multiple roles of Tokugawa period samurai and the consequences of maintaining a large elite that was over-educated, under-employed, and poorly paid. For portraits of individual samurai thinkers, see Kate Wildman Nakai, *Shogunal Politics: Arai Hakuseki and the Premises of Tokugawa Rule* (Cambridge, MA, 1988); and Olof Lidin, *Ogyu Sorai's Distinguishing the Way* (Tokyo, 1970).

sible to separate polity and economy, polity and society, in Tokugawa Japan.

I have accorded primacy to internal—often political—forces in the genesis of civil war, and in the formation of the alliances that ended combat and the control system that held the peace. The internal issues seem to me crucial. The extent of the slaughter between 1560 and 1590, the scale of campaigns that brought hundreds of thousands of troops to battle, and the phenomenal destruction of great daimyo houses in those campaigns—all disposed former enemies to seek accord for their very survival. And continuing fear of daimyo neighbors and local insurrection disposed them to enforce the strategies of pacification that defined the early modern experience.

The Meanings of Foreign Contact

But if internal factors were central to war-making and peace-keeping in early modern Japan, international factors were, nonetheless, weighty. The question is, how weighty? Was Japan linked 'interdependently' to a Eurasia that formed an 'interactive episteme' and influenced substantially the conduct of war and peace?

Japan's overseas encounters during the Lieberman era crossed several sub-periods that suggest a highly variable attitude toward foreign connection. From 1404 until 1549, an old model of nominally managed contact with China prevailed, although relations were in mounting disarray from the late fifteenth century. In theory, envoys of the Ming court and the Ashikaga shogunate supervised both a trade and a diplomacy with strong tributary dimensions. Formal relations with Korea also occurred through the Sō family of Tsushima (and goods from Southeast Asia entered Kyushu from the Ryukyus).[27] From 1549 until 1640, overseas contacts exploded. Even as Japanese traders and adventurers moved across East and Southeast Asia with unprecedented enterprise (and a freedom sanctioned by domestic turmoil), so foreign bottoms arrived in Japan not only from Asia but from Europe (first from Portugal and Spain, later and briefly from England, finally from the Netherlands). Largely unregulated before 1590, contact was increasingly controlled by the

[27] Wang Yi-T'ung, *Official Relations Between China and Japan, 1368–1549* (Cambridge, MA, 1953); Kawazoe Shoji, 'Japan and East Asia,' in Yamamura (ed.), *The Cambridge History of Japan* (Cambridge, 1990), vol. 3, pp. 396–446.

Toyotomi and the Tokugawa as political unification proceeded.[28] From 1640 until 1853, a policy of strictly managed exchange was resumed. Japanese maritime activity officially ceased (smuggling continued); foreign entry through Nagasaki was confined to Chinese and Dutch vessels. (Relations through Satsuma with the Ryukyus, and through Tsushima with Korea, continued.) Despite this constrained contact, trade volumes grew well into the seventeenth century before flattening and then ebbing around 1700.[29]

In judging the importance of foreign contact to Japan across these periods, the value of trade itself has served as one too obvious—and misleading—a measure. In wartime as in peacetime, trade centered on the exchange of Chinese silks (thread, floss, raw and finished fabrics) for Japanese metals (first copper ore, then, overwhelmingly, silver). When China relations were broken for a time after 1550, disparate Asian and European merchants carried the continental silks to Japan. But while this trade was certainly heavier than any earlier exchange, efforts to calculate its annual value in the fat years of the seventeenth century have reached modest verdicts: Conrad Totman concludes that imports may have had 'a value equivalent to less than 1.5 percent of domestic agricultural production.'[30] Seemingly limited in value, the trade was also suicidal. It depleted metal resources virtually to the break point, when domestic clamor forced curtailment of silver exports. A silver flow of immense importance to Eurasia as a whole was damaging to Japan.[31]

We might better gauge foreign impact, however, by considering the general circulation of both goods and ideas and their rippling consequences. The above account is heedless, for example, of the multiplying effects in Japan of major imports and exports: Chinese silks organized the luxury textile market, as silver demand organized a huge mining industry, until the late seventeenth century. The account is also heedless of the disproportionate importance of commerce to its main parties: trade income loomed large, for example, to the early shogun who licenced Japanese mariners, created a silk

[28] Ronald P. Toby, *State and Diplomacy in Early Modern Japan: Asia in the Development of the Tokugawa Bakufu* (Stanford, 1984); Charles R. Boxer, *The Christian Century in Japan* (Berkeley, 1951); Jurgis Elisonas, 'The Inseparable Trinity: Japan's Relations with China and Korea,' in Hall (ed.), *The Cambridge History of Japan* (Cambridge, 1991), vol. 4, pp. 235–300.

[29] Toby, 1984; Robert LeRoy Innes, 'The Door Ajar: Japan's Foreign Trade in the Seventeenth Century,' Ph.D. dissertation, University of Michigan, 1980.

[30] Conrad Totman, *Early Modern Japan* (Berkeley, 1993), p. 148.

[31] Innes, 1980; Totman, 1993, pp. 140–8.

thread monopoly, and controlled the mines.[32] More critical, though, is attention to the many items, and the even greater knowledge, that bore lightly on trade accounts but heavily on social change.

In wartime, European arms (copied in Japan by the 1550s but fired with imported saltpeter) profoundly altered combat and mercilessly increased casualties, thus hastening the peace. Chinese mining technologies accelerated recovery of the mineral resources indispensable to war's victors. And Chinese coins fed monetization of the market (even as they deferred intensive domestic minting).[33] In peacetime, a range of introduced products became agrarian staples—the sweet potato above all, as well as South Asian cotton and new world tobacco, for example. The books and objects funneled through Nagasaki were conduits of cartographic and optical science, medical and botanical knowledge, painting and pottery styles, philosophical and historical ferment.[34]

This catalog, though perfunctory, begins to suggest the intricate and incalculable effects of overseas connection. None of these effects was definitive of war or peace, nor were they collectively greater in force than the Chinese impact on classical and medieval Japan. But such comparisons lead in futile directions. Consider the hypothetical Japanese farmer of early modernity who grew cotton, raised her children on Confucian primers, and wore spectacles to refill her pipe. Here 'foreign' elements have become part of a normal domestic order virtually unimaginable without them. This form of encounter had very old traditions in a Japan never sealed from influence. Again, a Eurasian 'interdependency' is hard to claim. A great permeability, and a steady adaptation of culture, is patently clear.

Was this flow of goods and ideas conducive to domestic integration? I am doubtful but not sure. Christian proselytism—the most dramatic foreign arrival—was divisive during the fifty years it was

[32] These are the principal subjects of Innes, 1980.

[33] The seventeenth-century military historian Yamaga Sokō reconstructs the major battles, with notes on muskets and casualties, in *Buke jiki* (Tokyo, 1965), pp. 749–1189. For coinage, Kozo Yamamura and Tetsuo Kamiki, 'Silver Mines and Sung Coins,' in J. F. Richards (ed.), *Precious Metals in the Later Medieval and Early Modern Worlds* (Durham, 1983), pp. 329–62. For mining and smelting, Kobata Atsushi, *Kingin bōeki-shi no kenkyū* (Tokyo, 1976).

[34] Research on such exchange is eloquently called for, and pursued by, Karen Wigen. See 'Mapping Early Modernity: Geographical Meditations on a Comparative Concept,' *Early Modern Japan* 5, 2: 1–13; *The Making of a Japanese Periphery, 1750–1920* (Berkeley, 1995); 'The Geographic Imagination in Early Modern Japanese History,' *Journal of Asian Studies* 51, 1: 3–29.

permitted; Christian persecution may have been fortifying to statist power but ineffective in guaranteeing cultural orthodoxy. The anti-Christian policies enforced a degree of religious conformity and fostered habits of compliance to statist demands, even as they taught believers and sympathizers alike the lessons of secrecy. Indeed, foreign learning taught the lessons of intellectual struggle. Tokugawa scholars would split regularly on questions of eastern and western science, Chinese and native philosophy.[35]

The shogunate's attention to ideology raises a larger subject, and the one most germane to the Lieberman project: the relationship between foreign affairs and state formation. At the simplest level, the control of contact—through licences, laws, monopolies, and force—served a legitimating function important to military leaders since the thirteenth century. Although state-to-state relations were secured only with Korea (after 1636), foreign consent to Japanese policy identified the hegemons as protectors of the realm.[36] This role was not new, but both its Eurasian scope and its superior tone were. As Professor Lieberman notes, a once deferential posture toward China gave way to a chauvinism that would inflect historical writing and philosophy as well.[37] The international order was now wide, and Japan's position in it was unbowed.

For a while, Japan's position was also bellicose. After threatening to invade both Taiwan and the Philippines, Toyotomi Hideyoshi twice sent invading armies to Korea in the 1590s with the ultimate intention of 'entering China, spreading the customs of our country to the four hundred and more provinces of that country, and establishing there the government of our own imperial city unto all the ages.'[38] Ruinous to Korea, the invasions failed—but without closing the possibility of resumed Japanese aggression in Asia. The Tokugawa shogun contemplated war with the Manchus on the Korean peninsula in the 1620s, and war with the Spaniards in Manila during the 1630s.[39] They were already waging the equivalent of war on Christians in Japan. Some 3,000 local converts and foreign mission-

[35] George Elison, *Deus Destroyed* (Cambridge, MA, 1973); Peter Nosco (ed.), *Confucianism and Tokugawa Culture* (Princeton, 1984).

[36] Elisonas, 1991; Toby, 1984.

[37] Bob Tadashi Wakabayashi, *Anti-Foreignism and Western Learning in Early Modern Japan* (Cambridge, MA, 1986).

[38] Berry, 1982, p. 208.

[39] Totman, 1993, pp. 113–14.

aries would be killed by 1660 for defiance of a xenophobic regime.[40] Although complex in circumstance, these episodes shared an exceptional background: Japanese leaders commanded immense and domestically triumphant armies of up to 300,000 men;[41] and they operated within a changed world of Manchu conquest, European expansion, and pan-Asian piracy. Japan might have remained within this international arena as one more dangerous player.

Instead, the early modern Japanese state was defined for two centuries by withdrawal. Why? A long history of managed contact with non-intrusive powers was doubtless important. More critical, I think, was a paramount concern with order. Megalomania and a desire to amplify his daimyo's holdings probably led Hideyoshi into Korea. But temptations toward international violence were ultimately resisted by a shogunate more wary than welcoming of trouble. The internal imperatives shaped by lacerating civil war led the unifiers to uncommon policies of domestic pacification. As foreign disturbance swelled—from militant evangelism at home to confrontation among mariners abroad—a secure peace seemed to require uncommon international controls as well.

Thus, Japan's place in the 'interactive ecumene' fell at the isolationist extreme, which was one position on a spectrum of choices posed by the maritime age. But there can be no doubt that an isolationist polity formed the Tokugawa state as decisively as foreign engagement formed other rimlands. The 'great peace' and the absence of foreign menace underwrote authority. The anti-Christian policies inspired the statist disciplines of annual registration and interrogation of the population. An agrarian ideology, unchallenged by mercantilism or an export-driven emphasis on industry, remained dominant. Such systemic consequences of seclusion could be multiplied many times. And the mundane consequences—for everything from dress styles to vocabulary—could be entertained endlessly.

* * *

Japan's place on the isolationist extreme prompts two final questions, which I raise but can barely address here. First, how could Japan

[40] Boxer, 1951, p. 448; Jurgis Elisonas, 'Christianity and the Daimyo,' in Hall (ed.), *The Cambridge History of Japan* (Cambridge, 1991), vol. 4, p. 370.

[41] Among the clearest figures are those available for Hideyoshi's first Korean campaign. See Berry, 1982, p. 209.

successfully maintain that place? There are salient if not fully convincing answers on the domestic side—including the disadvantageous trade in metals, the continued access through Nagasaki to foreign learning, the power of internal propaganda, and the adaptability of the political economy to constraint. But the answers on the international side seem to me elusive and deserving of attention. Surely they include Japan's geographical remoteness and limited resource base. Are such answers sufficient if we posit a genuinely interdependent Eurasia?

The second question was raised by Professor Lieberman in personal correspondence. 'Given its relative insularity, why didn't Japan follow an internal trajectory entirely different from [the other rimlands]?' Put differently, if continuing international contact was not a primary impetus to integration of the polity, economy, and culture, what *did* drive the integrative process in Japan? And can we generalize the importance of such factors? Schematically, and without making rules, I would draw attention to four internal factors that guided Japan's early modern development.

Crucial was the centripetal force of three monster cities (Edo with a population in the eighteenth century of one million, Kyoto and Osaka with populations approaching 400,000) that required production and marketing organization across the country. Production and distribution were encouraged, moreover, by a taxation system that stopped short of confiscating the agrarian surplus and mercantile wealth. (Indeed, the Tokugawa period is remarkable for a certain income leveling that narrowed the gap between samurai—whose stipends were reduced through inflation and unimproved by tax gains—and the more prosperous commoners.)[42] Further, economic gains were protected by the contraction of population growth from the early eighteenth century.[43] Finally, and fundamentally, those gains were made possible by the agrarian revolution chronicled by Thomas C. Smith. The revolution was sustained not by mechanical change or government planning, but by incremental improvements in method, a transition to very small farms worked by disciplined family units, and the dissemination of knowledge by independent agronomists and cultivators themselves.[44]

[42] Gilbert Rozman, 'Edo's Importance in the Changing Tokugawa Society,' *Journal of Japanese Studies* 1, 1: 91–112; *Urban Networks in Ch'ing China and Tokugawa Japan* (Princeton, 1974). Also, see n. 24.

[43] Thomas C. Smith, *Nakahara* (Stanford, 1977); Hanley and Yamamura, 1977.

[44] Smith, 1959.

These remarks move us from the international to the domestic arena, and from state policy to social change. The Tokugawa experience was structured by remarkable statist initiatives: federation, seclusion, class laws, the transfer of samurai to cities, the requirement that daimyo reside periodically in Edo. But the Tokugawa experience was also redefined daily by both the unforeseen effects of these initiatives and the dynamic responses of many actors.

Cultural Integration

My survey of the early modern context in Japan has emphasized integrity in structure. Yet as I begin the discussion of culture, let me return to my opening theme. Tokugawa governance was predicated on differences—on making them and enforcing them. Distinctions of class were primary—ordained in laws covering everything from residence and land ownership to dress and drink. Differences were also elaborated officially among religious organizations, schools and academies, even theatrical troupes and highway lodgings.[45] And differences were amplified not only by such deep structures as gender and geography but also by economic specialization and cultural choice.

As I suggested earlier, integration in a society of difference could not occur primarily through the erosion or transcendence of boundaries. Rather, integration required workable principles of relationship between disparate social units. Some such principles appear in the texts of public information generated by the publishing explosion. I turn to them now to explore culture as an expression of social connection. Distinctly early modern sources, the texts belong to the sphere of entrepreneurship. If Meiji leaders were obsessed with the mission of nationalist indoctrination, the Tokugawa authorities were a distant party to the work of cultural integration.

Cartography and the Taxonomic Imagination

Before 1600, mapmaking in Japan was an uncommon enterprise, limited in subject and function. The roughly 200 examples of early

[45] See, for example, the laws cited by David John Lu, *Sources of Japanese History* (New York, 1974), vol. 1, pp. 199–232; Tetsuo Najita, *Visions of Virtue in Tokugawa Japan* (Chicago, 1987), pp. 60–98.

cartography that survive today describe a practice focused on discrete manorial holdings and the internal disputes—principally boundary quarrels—within them.[46] By the latter part of the seventeenth century, however, mapping in Japan flourished on all fronts. Cartographic energy flowed, originally, from the state. The shogunate conducted four national surveys in the seventeenth century alone, gradually spreading the cartographic habit to each of its administrative units: urban magistrates, jurists, local daimyo, and village heads became prolific mappers of everything from fire lanes to procession routes, from forest resources to irrigation works. Private patrons acquired the taste as well. They commissioned the scrolls and screens and finely painted sheets that constituted the luxury end of the cartographic trade, with subjects that tended to mansions and gardens, coastal and highway scenes, historical battle sites, and the great lost cities of the past. It was commercial printers, however, who flooded the public market with maps. Maps of the nation, of the major cities and highway routes, predominated. Maps of famous places and scenic sites, of elite residences and brothel quarters, of mountain trails and pilgrimage routes, of burial grounds, spas, individual neighborhoods, and religious complexes were ubiquitous.[47]

The most obvious effect of the cartographic revolution was the creation, and circulation, of synoptic statements about physical and social geography. The basic statement is the most important: space and place are knowable and known, not mysterious, and capturable in a total graphic representation. The statements about particular spaces then unfold. In the many variants of national maps, for example, a 'Great Japan' comprising the principal islands is framed by water, and set against Korea and China (typically indicated by coastlines and labels) as well as more remote countries (typically named in long verbal indices with notations about travel distances).[48]

[46] For a census of premodern maps, Nishioka Toranosuke, *Nihon shōen ezu shūsei*, 2 vols (Tokyo, 1976–77). For further analysis, Kokuritsu Rekishi Minzoku Hakubutsukan (ed.), *Shōen ezu to sono sekai* (Tokyo. 1993).

[47] Basic surveys with extensive illustrations include Namba Matsutarō *et al.* (eds), *Nihon no kochizu* (Tokyo, 1969); Akioka Takejirō (ed.), *Nihon kochizu shūsei* (Tokyo, 1971); Unno Kazutaka *et al.* (eds), *Nihon kochizu taisei* (Tokyo, 1972). Also, see Hugh Cortazzi, *Isles of Gold* (Tokyo, 1983); J. B. Harley and David Woodward (eds), *History of Cartography*, vol. 2, pt 2: *East Asia* (Chicago, 1994).

[48] See, for example, illustration 31 in Unno, 1972. National names (including Honchō, Yamato) tend to appear on the coverings of the maps, rather than on their faces. Ezo, or Hokkaido, rarely appears in national maps before the eighteenth century. The indices list both Asian and European countries, sometimes in Chinese characters, sometimes in a phonetic syllabary.

The domestic space of these maps is defined less by natural topography than by the overlapping systems of integration that are the cartographic subject. The sixty-six provinces first plotted by the classical state and still units of local identity order the background (sometimes in contrasting colors, otherwise with boundary signs and labels). Dispersed on this provincial base are standardized markers of the Tokugawa polity: symbols and labels for castle towns (accompanied by the names and titles of their daimyo as well as numerical totals for annual domainal productivity); exaggerated symbols and labels for the main cities held directly by the Tokugawa. And connecting all parts, however far-flung, are the arteries: highways and roadways punctuated by official post stations (with distance markers and notes on portage fees); rivers and sea lanes served by ports and ferry crossings (with similar markers and notes).[49]

Although we might catalog at length the further messages of national and small area maps alike, the point is clear enough. Maps served up to the Tokugawa public highly patterned visions of itself. Indeed, maps helped create the very possibility of a Tokugawa public by converting the infinitely discrete details of local experience into uniform categories embracing a total population.

Here, of course, is the deeper significance of the cartographic revolution. Apart from their individual statements, maps represent an epistemological conversion—a movement from the immediate to the categorical apprehension of phenomena, and from esoteric to analogical learning. Maps emerge from the twin processes of inventorying and classifying worldly phenomena. And they operate through generic codes of signs and labels that insist upon the subordination of the particular to the general. The codes create essentialized, and therefore reductive, modes of definition to impose structure on the landscape. So experience is not, the code declares, unfathomably myriad but governable by *genera* and fixed variables.[50]

The conversion to a routine cartography began with the unifiers of the early modern state. Cartographic learning itself was certainly not new. The impetus and will to use maps prolifically in the reinvention of power was. A desultory medieval cartography gave way to the intense and prescriptive surveying of hegemons who saw in carto-

[49] These conventions derive from the shogunal surveys. The most important is the identification of daimyo power with an urban headquarters and a productivity figure, rather than with a bounded territory.

[50] I rely on Denis Wood, *The Power of Maps* (New York, 1992); and David Turnbull, *Maps are Territories: Science is an Atlas* (Deakin, Australia, 1989).

graphic codes a means to order knowledge and define a still nascent authority. Maps anticipated, and helped impose, a polity in formation. Their immediate audience was not a 'public' but the contentious body of daimyo and ranking military retainers. Official cartography, nonetheless, formed the basis of the commercial mapping that drove—and was driven by—public desire.[51]

This desire is the most interesting aspect of the map revolution. It came, I suspect, from the same source that provoked the mapping impulse among the unifiers—from the need for orientation in a world torn apart and under reconstruction. The ordeal of war and pacification required mass mobilizations and demobilizations, forced relocations and status changes, and attendant shifts of pervasive character. Such crises eroded customary frameworks of attachment and identity, creating large populations of strangers bound by the very broad associations (such as class, occupation, tax status) that emerged from the early modern settlement. Paradoxically, perhaps, maps confirmed their readers as strangers; for the map is an impersonal tool needed by outsiders who learn from symbols what they do not know from experience. But, at the same time, maps initiated their readers into a holistic mode of knowledge that implied access to—and participation in—worlds larger than themselves. If maps locate their users in physical space, they more emphatically locate them in systems of political and social meaning.

Maps also responded to, and fed, curiosity, the trustiest agent of connection. Tokugawa maps were loaded with information. Maps of Kyoto, for example, identified all the residences of the courtly and military elites (with names and incomes), the locations of theaters and brothels, the sites of religious institutions (with notes on income, history, icons). Indices offered lists of special products and manufactures, guides to the festival calendar, all the measurements of Hideyoshi's Great Buddha (length of ear-lobes, nose . . .).[52] However useful to the stranger in need of orientation, such maps surpassed practical needs to transform secrets into popular currency. The voyeur could possess expansive social knowledge. And social knowledge could become social membership.

[51] Ōshikōchi's Dōin's surveys of Edo for the shogunate were printed commercially in the 1670s, and atlas versions of the shogunal surveys of the nation were printed by the 1660s. Some official urban surveys, particularly of castle fortifications, remained sensitive and did not circulate. Protection of cartographic secrets (such as Inō Tadataka's coastal surveys) was most pronounced in the nineteenth century.

[52] See, for example, illustrations 83 and 84 in Unno, 1972.

Here, certainly, is the reason why officials failed to censor commercial maps, and even cooperated in their creation. Maps are so seldom subversive, and so effective as propaganda, because they naturalize artificial systems of power. Mixing, blurring physical and social geography, they make a castle town or a palace seem as natural and inevitable as a mountain. A jurisdictional boundary appears as real as a river; a label like 'Lord Shimazu' is as just as a label like 'Mount Fuji.'

For the Tokugawa public, then, maps taught the lessons of authority—the lessons of political integration and encompassing social codes. They discriminated relentlessly: between villages and great towns, major daimyo and minor officials, the neighborhoods of commoners and the compounds of princes. But the classification of parts illumined the structure of a whole. And the habit of classification—the essential taxonomic imagination of cartography—could be brought to new structures. Although Meiji maps of power would replace Tokugawa maps of power, they addressed readers well schooled in cartographic relationships.

Travel Guides and the Accessible Landscape

'Famous places' (*meisho*) were almost always marked on large-area maps of Tokugawa Japan and quite copiously laid out in a cartographic genre of their own. They were central to the prodigious literature of local geography (from travel guides to gazetteers) and indispensable to the imagery of poetry, drama, and fiction.[53] The famous place was all but unavoidable.

Originally a trope in classical literature and painting, the *meisho* was a place with a name made somehow remarkable by a poet's notice, an historical poignance, an uncommon beauty. These places increased in number and variety over time, only to proliferate in the early modern era. Growth was driven in part by expectation and competition. Once the category of 'famous place' became conventional in local maps, ethnographies, school primers, and such, pride dictated profusion.[54] Once travel guides became a publishing staple,

[53] Baba Akiko *et al.* (eds), *Meisho: Hare kūkan no kōzō (Shizen to bunka 27)* (Tokyo, 1990).

[54] In the various village reports (*meisai-chō, fūzoku-chō*) that daimyo periodically required from villagers themselves, *meisho* was one of many standard categories of local description. See Shōji Kichinosuke (ed.), *Aizu fūdoki, fūzokuchō*, 3 vols (Tokyo, 1979–80).

authors took pains to invent for a new Edo a roster of sites not incommensurate with those of an ancient Kyoto. Growth was driven, too, by a culture of movement—for pilgrimage, seasonal employment, the transport of goods—and by a culture of commerce. Temples displayed treasures to paying visitors, publishers generated ever fresh series of landscape prints. The *meisho* was commodity, entertainment, education, source of prestige.

Travel guides served as catalogs of famous places and most bore the term *meisho* in their titles. By far the most numerous of their notable sites were temples, but 'fame' was lavished, too, on shrines, battlegrounds, burials, ruins, sensational or scenic spots (or individual trees, rocks, waterfalls). Amply bestowed, fame was also, of course, relative. Some places were very famous. They claimed the longest entries in guides, appeared at the top of the 'self-guided tours' recommended in appendices to guides and maps alike, and dominated the souvenir trade. They included the major pilgrimage sites (for example, Ise shrine, the temples of Mount Kōya), the big religious attractions in important cities (the Great Buddha and Kiyomizu temple in Kyoto), imperial and shogunal monuments (the palace, the Tokugawa memorials at Nikkō), and natural sites (Mount Fuji, Yoshino, the Nachi Falls).[55]

Famous places worked variously as binding agents in Tokugawa society. The most popular sites (Ise above all, where millions of visitors congregated in special pilgrimage years) linked through experience the people of every station and locale who actually traveled to them.[56] Such sites bound people vicariously as well; for villagers sponsored lotteries to send representative delegations, and homebound pilgrims visited nearby simulacra (most notably artificial versions of Fuji and scaled-down counterparts to the circuit of thirty-three Kannon temples of Shikoku).[57] And the elaboration of locally important places joined most communities to the continuum of fame (everybody had *some* claim to eminence), just as local excursions joined modest to heroic travelers in the business of discovery.

Actual discovery may not have been essential to the social role of *meisho*, however. Indeed, many sites could be viewed (if at all) only from a distance and through a barrier of walls. It was the presentation of famous places in guides and maps, as well as the dissemina-

[55] The most helpful survey of the guide literature is Wada Mankichi *(Shintei zōhō) Kohan chishi kaidai* (Tokyo, 1968).

[56] Shinjō Tsunezo, *Shaji sankei no shakai keizai-shi teki kenkyū* (Tokyo, 1964).

[57] Hirano Eiji, *Fuji Asama shinkō* (Tokyo, 1987); Shinjō, 1964.

tion of the *meisho* image, that probably bound society more emphatically than travel itself.

Consider the treatment of the shogunal castle in Asai Ryōi's 1662 *Guide to the Famous Places of Edo.* One of eighty entries that cover seven volumes and a riotous spectrum of high and low life, the castle entry opens with the 1440s, during the time of the Retired Emperor Go Hanazono, when 'the influence of the Kanrei Uesugi Ukyōnosuke Noritada spread over the ten eastern provinces.' Noritada's son built the first ancestor of Edo castle. A dense chronology and genealogy of change—replete with era names, challenging proper nouns and official titles—leads the reader to the defeat by the Tokugawa of Hōjō Ujinao, at the battle of Odawara, on the sixth day of the seventh month of the eighteenth year of Tenshō (1590). There follows a paean to the Tokugawa shogun, the peace they brought to the country and the prosperity they brought to the city, and, finally, an overview of the current castle itself. Although Ryōi lingers a bit over the main gate, the rise of maples between the main and western circles of the castle, and the bustle of upright samurai always entering and leaving the scene, physical detail surrenders to mood.[58]

This entry is emblematic of the guide material in general. It describes a place, whether open or closed to actual public entry (the castle was closed), that opens to the public imagination. The reader is meant to know of the place, to want and deserve mental access to it, to share rightful information rightfully provided. And that information is historical. The reader, either literate or educable in a high historical terminology (sometimes glossed phonetically), watches the procession of imperial and military players *as if* it is perfectly natural to do so. What we might consider an elite history (and most *meisho* were steeped only in elite history), appears in the guides as a common history—not the peculiar possession of the Uesugi or Hōjō or Tokugawa, but something available, even necessary, to the consumer of the public place. So, too, the imperial palace or the great burial ground of Kōya is made of dates, personalities, and dramas that belong to any casual visitor or compulsive savant.

The approach carries over to religious establishments. Although sectarian affiliation is mentioned (and sometimes serves as a principle of organization in the guides), temples are lifted out of exclusive associations with worship or belief. Their icons and miracle stories are historicized, their founders located in a pantheon of public

[58] Asai Ryōi, *Edo meisho-ki* (Edo Sōsho Hangyō-kai, 1916), vol. 1, pp. 3–5.

figures, their major rituals converted into part of a public calendar of events. The readers of guides and maps are even counseled to plan travel to coincide with religious festivals, which might as well be secular spectacles.

We might speculate usefully, though inconclusively, about the transforming power of the famous place. Perhaps a dispersed geo-piety, attached both to local and national monuments, came to unite a people and a landscape. Perhaps a historical consciousness, inclusive of disparate actors over many centuries, came to unite a people and a shared past. The disclosures of the guidebooks focus, however, not on feeling but on access and choice. The many *meisho* and their thick histories are available, and available in the same terms to anyone who wants them for any reason. Ise is available to the pious prince or curious merchant or pleasure-seeking farmer. No transformation in soul or identity is required.

The relations described in Tokugawa cartography were structural, integral, and largely vertical: generic parts of greater and lesser importance were located in a whole. The relations described in Tokugawa guidebooks were elective, diffuse, and largely horizontal: myriad places with multiple associations were opened to all claimants.

Urban Directories and the Complex Society

Urban directories, particularly for the cities of Kyoto and Edo, began to appear in regularly revised editions from the latter part of the seventeenth century. These were exhaustive, multi-volume works that cataloged urban phenomena in manifold ways, primarily for the use of local residents themselves.[59]

For example, the *Dappled Fabric of Edo* (1687) includes a list in 22 categories of 292 physical features (important rocks, streams, bridges, embankments); the annual festival calendars of both the military houses and the commoners; a list of 360 art objects in 22 categories held by private collectors; a list in 11 categories of major Buddhist and Shinto icons (statues of Yakushi, Inari, Fudō); a description of over sixty shrines, with historical notes; a description

[59] The most copious and regularly revised directories were versions of the *Kyoto Brocade (Kyō habutae)* and the *Dappled Cloth of Edo (Edo ganoko)*. See Shinshū Kyōto Shōsho Hangyō-kai (ed.), *Shinshū Kyōto sōsho* (Kyoto, 1968), vol. 2; and Edo Sōsho Hangyō-kai, 1916, vols 3–4.

of over 100 temples, organized by sect, with historical notes; a street-by-street survey of the city, with inventories of residents, employments, and frontages; a list of famous vistas; a list of over 300 prominent artists, teachers, and providers of services in 43 categories (doctors of various specialties, poets of different schools, masseurs, removers of ear wax), all with addresses; a list of over 200 prominent craftspeople and merchants in 32 categories (the gold and silver guildsmen, textile specialists, incense blenders, handlers of Buddhist goods, tea merchants), all with addresses; and a list of 22 trade associations. Other editions of this work include lists of all military and civilian office holders in the city.[60]

The scope and detail of this directory are impressive in themselves. But of central concern to me here is the disaggregation of the urban world into many constituent parts. In addition to physical features, urbanity embraces distinctive streets and neighborhoods as well as distinctive work and workers. It embraces disparate religious communities and several festival lives. It embraces an orderly officialdom and bodies of affluent connoiseurs. It embraces numerous outlets for consumption and entertainment.

These constituent parts are also overlapping. As a reader, I might find myself many times in the directory's lists. Perhaps I am a resident of a particular block where my civic and ritual life centers, a vertical flute master listed first among several colleagues, an adherent of a particular temple, a subject of a well-defined military administration, a client of some art fancier, an occupant of a uniquely configured topography, a buyer of silk and a fancier of the twelve views of Zōjōji and a frequenter of the theater quarter. Like the dappled Edo itself, I am a creature of many colors and intersections.

Thus, one message of the directories concerns the differentiation I have seen as inherent to early modernity. Jurisdictions and domains of action are bounded. Divisions among and within status groups are clarified (as addresses, titles, specialties convey distinctions in wealth, training, culture). The sources of, and forces behind, urban diversity become conspicuous.

Yet another message of the directories concerns patterns of connection. My hypothetical flute master has plural identities and plural attachments—which are variously determined and voluntary, vertical and horizontal, institutional and commercial, long and short in

[60] *Edo sōganoko meisho taizen*, literally 'The Dappled Cloth of Edo: Encyclopedia of Famous Places,' from Jōkyō 4, in Edo Sōsho Hangyō-kai, 1916, vols. 3–4.

duration, close and distant in intensity. Hence, early modernity sees not just multiplying difference but multiplying relationships. These relations, many of them ambivalent, do not constitute some organic social union. The directories break down totalizing conceptions of community to replace them with a pluralist and dynamic sociology. But precisely because of this pluralism and dynamism, individuals can construct the diverse ties that make societies resilient.

Concluding Thoughts

Resilience was one of the primary characteristics of Japan's transition from the Tokugawa to the Meiji periods. The polity broke while society did not. Civil wars over the locus and exercise of power led neither to anarchy nor to a pathological immobility.

The resources for survival are impossible to calculate well. The vitality of a 'proto-national consciousness' may be as apt a summary as any of the psychological resources that were surely indispensable. But I am reluctant to assign any particular content to that consciousness, and even more reluctant to cast it in universal or salutary terms. So I have searched the archive of public information less for belief systems than for durable mental habits that might have encouraged notions of relationship, and thus cohesion, in society.

In cartography, I found a structural imagination that required the classification and integration of parts. The map constructs a bounded and labeled physical world (The Great Japan, for example); transforms discrete experience into generic categories (political roles, class identities, economic sectors, communications arteries); and then assembles all parts into a unified system of natural and social geography. Although they may indoctrinate readers with particular cultural visions, maps also teach habits of orientation—of generic analysis and holistic conception—that are adaptable to changing geographies. In the guide literature to 'famous places,' I found the appropriation of a putatively common history and shared landscape. The guides take countless monuments—humble and heroic, closed and open to view—and make them mentally accessible to a 'public' assumed to want, and deserve, such access. Although they may celebrate particular iconic sites, guides also teach habits of popular cultural proprietorship. And in urban directories, I found a pluralist sociology that reflected both intense social differentiation and multiple social connections. The directories expose the plural identities and attachments—of politics, neighborhood, work, belief, patronage, clientage, and culture—that link otherwise atomized individuals in versatile ways. Although they may describe a particular scene, the directories also teach habits of complex perspective on societies too permeable to have a single, simple configuration.

In a polity predicated upon differences and discriminations, these and similar sources insisted on social relationship. Did they forge a sense of 'peoplehood' yoked to a statist administration? Certainly a stable government loomed forever in the shadows of the texts—in the political structure of the maps, the histories of the famous places (many of them military monuments), the lists of officials (and official clients) in the directories. And perhaps a people is implicit in a public, in a network of flexible ties. But to exaggerate these concepts is to miss an essential distinction between modern nationalism and its presumptive antecedents.

Nationalism is the product of hard and manipulative work by determined governments and their servants. It presumes the active identification between rulers and ruled that involves appeals to a common destiny, and the consequent implication of subjects in the rhetoric and conduct of power. It requires, in short, the projection of the state to a people consciously taught peoplehood and the intertwining of the two. The Meiji success in this work doubtless drew on the early modern experience. But that experience was different in kind. The sources I cite were not driven by a state, nor did they serve a people implicated in rule and imagined as a national community.

The principal story of the sources is one of complex social cohesion, which perhaps comes close enough to Professor Lieberman's cultural integration. We find in the texts a Tokugawa public with an extraordinary amount of well-crafted information about itself. If that public did not share a common culture, it was relentlessly scrutinized—and held up for display—by commercial writers looking for patterns, classifications, and connections. Interaction, interrelationship was as much their subject as Professor Lieberman's, though in a domestic setting at the far edge of the Eurasian ecumene.

The Birth of Europe as a Eurasian Phenomenon[1]

R. I. MOORE

Although they still differ considerably in their willingness to acknowledge it, specialists in the history of north-western Europe in the eleventh and twelfth centuries CE are increasingly treating it as that of the emergence of a new civilization in what had previously been a peripheral region of the Mediterranean-based civilization of the classical west, rather than as a continuation or revival of that civilization itself. In this light Europe, or Latin Christendom as it saw itself, offers a number of striking resemblances to the developments which Lieberman discusses. The most dynamic regions of the new Europe—north-western France, Flanders and lowland England, north-eastern Spain, northern Italy, southern Italy and Sicily—were all peripheral, though in various senses, both to the long-defunct classical civilization and its direct successors, the Byzantine and Abbasid Empires, and to the transitional and much more loosely based ninth- and tenth-century empires of the Franks and Saxons (Ottonians). To this one might add that by the end of the twelfth century the remaining rimlands of the Eurasian continent in a purely geographical sense—Scandinavia, including Iceland, and still more the southern coast of the Baltic and the areas dominated by the rivers which drained into it—were developing very rapidly indeed.[2]

The chief source of this dynamism was precisely the concentration of political and economic power on much smaller territorial bases than previously, and the accompanying coalescence of 'localized soci-

[1] I should like to express my gratitude to Ian Brown and Victor Lieberman for inviting me to take part in an extraordinarily stimulating conference, and to Victor Lieberman and Elizabeth Redgate for their comments on drafts of this paper.

[2] Outstanding general accounts include Jacques le Goff, *Medieval Civilization* (1964, Engl. trans., Oxford, 1988); Malcolm Barber, *The Two Cities: Medieval Europe, 1050–1320* (London, 1992); Robert Fossier, *Enfance de l'Europe, Xe–XIIe siècles: aspects économiques et sociaux* (2 vols, Paris, 1982); J.-P. Poly and E. Bournazel, *La mutation féodale* (Paris, 1980, trans. *The Feudal Transformation*, New York, 1991), all with excellent bibliographical information.

eties in widely separated subregions into larger units—politically, culturally, commercially'.[3] At the heart of these changes was a combination of newly privileged groups of clerics, soldiers and administrators in the service of ambitious regional potentates (as *potentiores*, indeed, they sometimes described themselves) strongly reminiscent of those uncovered by Bayly and others in so many regions of later traditional Eurasia,[4] producing a 'strengthening of judicial and fiscal systems and mechanisms of provincial supervision' very much as Lieberman describes it. The establishment of a universal learned culture, much more widely and closely integrated than its predecessors, the growth of markets at many levels and their deeper penetration of the structures of rural as well as urban life, stimulated both by rapid intensive and extensive changes in agrarian production and by a dramatic increase in the variety and volume of long-distance trade, were integral and essential to these developments, which were accompanied by sustained though probably not spectacular long-term demographic growth; it is generally thought that the population of Europe approximately trebled between 1000 and 1250.

As this implies, developments closely resembling those which Lieberman identifies as characteristic of his 'rimland' subcategory of Eurasian polities are also visible in the Europe of the eleventh and twelfth centuries. The conversion of the region to Christianity, begun when it was imported from the Mediterranean during the Roman period, was completed by the foundation of bishoprics and archbishoprics to serve as centres for the evangelization and organization of eastern and northern Europe, all the way from Estzergom (1001) to Trondheim (1029). Everywhere the thoroughgoing reorganization ('reform') of the Church on a far more centralized and hierarchical basis than previously, under the authority of the Roman see, enormously increased the range and penetration of its social, political and cultural influence. A network of true urban centres was formed for the first time in transalpine Europe. Even in Italy (Milan being the only significant exception) the earliest and most dynamic urban centres—Venice, Genoa, Pisa, Florence, Amalfi, Salerno—had no, or no important Roman past. The same is true of Barcelona, and of Dubrovnik (Ragusa), equally the earliest and most dynamic commercial centres in the western Mediterranean and on the eastern shore of the Adriatic, respectively. It was from the eleventh century, and

3 Lieberman, this volume.

4 As summarized by C. A. Bayly, *Imperial Meridian* (London, 1989), pp. 35–74.

not before, that north-western Europe experienced its urban revolution in the full sense of that term.[5] If the Carolingian and Ottonian Empires were 'charter polities' in having secured legitimation and formative guidance from the perceived successors and representatives of the Roman Empire, the Byzantine (East Roman) Emperors and the Bishops of Rome, their decay provided space for a renewed and greatly intensified process of political and cultural integration in the form both of the nascent nation states of France, England, Scandinavia and the Iberian peninsula and the city republics of northern Italy. Relatively good internal communications were plainly essential—most obviously in riverine and coastal navigation, but it is also noteworthy that the development of the facilities associated with the Alpine passes brought the Great St Bernard into use as a major European route in the middle of the twelfth century, and the Simplon and St Gotthard early in the thirteenth.

If 'a strong core–periphery potential' is implied by the abundance of new land available for clearance and exploitation both internally and at the frontiers, and by burgeoning urban demand for both agricultural and primary products, then that, too, is a universally acknowledged and essential foundation of the vigorous growth of European societies in this period. Effective protection from invasion was secured by the fact that expansion took place precisely into the regions from which invasion had previously come. The former invaders from the north and east were assimilated, while those from the south had troubles of their own to contend with. The Almoravides, Almohades and Saljuq Turks affected Christendom only at the margins and Latin Christendom hardly at all. The chance which spared Europe the serious attentions of the Mongols may have been

[5] That is to say, in the sense of V. Gordon Childe, *What Happened in History?* (Harmondsworth, 1942), meaning the appearance of 'citied' or complex civilization, though not with all the implications of Childe's rather mechanistic Marxism. For most European medievalists the phrase 'urban revolution' evokes, more straightforwardly, the world of Henri Pirenne's *Medieval Cities* (trans. F. D. Halsey, Princeton, 1925, revised 1952). For current vigorous debate on the distinct but related argument whether there was a 'feudal revolution' around the year 1000, as adumbrated particularly in the writings of Georges Duby (e.g. *The Three Orders*, Chicago, 1980) and Pierre Bonnassie (e.g. *From Slavery to Feudalism in Northwestern Europe*, Cambridge, 1991), a view now powerfully challenged by Dominique Barthélmy, 'La mutation féodale, a-t-elle eu lieu? (Note critique)', *Annales ESC* xlvii (1992), 767–77; *La société dans la comté de Vendôme de l'an mil au XIVe siècle* (Paris, 1993), see Thomas Bisson, 'The Feudal Revolution', *Past and Present* 142 (1994), and discussion by D. Barthélmy, S. D. White, T. J. Reuter and C. Wickham to appear in *Past and Present*, nos 152–4 (1996–97).

important enough to constitute the greatest single obstacle to the assertion of a common 'early modern' periodization for Eurasian history, if their conquests are held to have marked a radical discontinuity in that of other parts of the landmass. Conversely, to the extent that the present argument is persuasive in suggesting that Liberman's emphasis on common and unifying threads in the history of the Eurasian continent as a whole may be applicable to the entire period between the transformation of the classical civilizations in the early centuries of the common era and the onset of modernization from the middle of the eighteenth century (a proposition far more powerfully supported, for example, by Chaudhuri's *Asia Before Europe*)[6] the significance of that and other catastrophes will be modified.

The first parallel which Lieberman finds among the areas he compares is 'the sustained, generally accelerating movement . . . towards the political and administrative integration of what had been fragmented, localized units'.[7] The Old English state created by the assimilation of the kingdoms of East Anglia, Northumbria and Mercia by the sons and grandsons of Alfred of Wessex was probably the richest and certainly the most fiscally sophisticated in tenth-century Europe,[8] but by the early eleventh century its capacity to assert power in the localities had been fatally undermined by repeated invasion and conquest. There were clear signs in the middle decades of the century of disintegration into territorial lordships of the kind so much in evidence in the west Frankish kingdom at the same time. The Norman conquest of 1066—itself a by-product of those same developments—reversed that process and created a powerful centralizing monarchy which by the end of the thirteenth century had established England, within more or less exactly its present boundaries, as a unitary state. Its consequences also included substantial development towards the construction of similarly unitary political entities in Wales, Ireland and Scotland, all fragmented between various 'kingdoms' and 'nations' at the beginning of this period, and laid the foundations for long-term hegemony over them.[9]

[6] K. N. Chaudhuri, *Asia Before Europe* (Cambridge, 1990).

[7] This volume.

[8] J. Campbell, *The Anglo-Saxons* (Oxford, 1986); *Essays in Anglo-Saxon History* (London, 1987); H. R. Loyn, *The Governance of Anglo-Saxon England* (London, 1984); P. Stafford, *Unification and Conquest* (London, 1989).

[9] M. Chibnall, *Anglo-Norman England, 1066–1166* (Oxford, 1986); J. le Patourel, *The Norman Empire* (Oxford, 1976); R. R. Davies, *Domination and Conquest: The Experi-*

Even more spectacular in the eyes of contemporaries was the achievement of the Capetian monarchy, which by the end of the thirteenth century had subdued the numerous warring lordships of eleventh-century west Francia into a single ruthlessly governed kingdom, within boundaries approximating to the familiar hexagon—a consummation which, notwithstanding a powerful tradition of national historiography, was by no means written in the stars.[10] One possible variant was pre-empted when the kingdom of Aragon was confined to the Iberian peninsula after military defeat at Muret in 1213. There by 1300 it was one of four kingdoms (with Navarre, Leon-Castile and Portugal) which had absorbed the numerous conquerors of the many and transient Muslim *rei taifas* of the tenth-century Caliphate of Cordoba.[11] Without pursuing the point into the tangled regions of northern and eastern Europe it may reasonably be said that this pattern offers a salient contrast (though in some respects it is a superficial one) to that displayed by the Imperial heartlands of Germany and Italy during the same period.

'At the same time as privileged cores extended their territorial writs', says Lieberman (using the word which is perhaps more evocative than any other of the growth of English government, and in Latin [*breve*] of all government, in this period, 'they frequently sought to strengthen their extractive, judicial and military functions and systems of provincial control'. That 'external expansion and internal reform were mutually reinforcing ... while the concentration of resources that flowed from better coordination facilitated colonization and conquest'[12] is precisely the argument of one of the most acclaimed works in European medieval history of recent years, Robert Bartlett's *The Making of Europe*.[13] By the end of the twelfth century the Anglo-Norman and Norman-Sicilian kingdoms possessed bureaucracies which, though not in any complete sense Weberian, were certainly to a recognizable degree staffed by trained professionals exercising a public function, capable of intervening far more

ence of Ireland, Scotland and Wales (Cambridge, 1990); Robin Frame, *The Political Development of the British Isles, 1100–1400* (Oxford, 1990).

[10] Jean Dunbabbin, *The Making of France, 843–1180* (Oxford, 1985); E. M. Hallam, *Capetian France, 987–1328* (London, 1980); G. Duby, *France in the Middle Ages, 987–1460* (Oxford, 1991).

[11] J. F. O'Callaghan, *A History of Medieval Spain* (Ithaca, 1975); Bernard F. Reilly, *The Medieval Spains* (Cambridge, 1993).

[12] This volume.

[13] Robert Bartlett, *The Making of Europe: Conquest, Colonization and Cultural Change, 950–1350* (Princeton, 1993).

rapidly and forcefully in local matters and of tapping the agrarian and commercial activities of their subjects far more effectively than any European monarch could have dreamed of 150 years earlier. Since they owed that ability in large part to the administrative sophistication respectively of their Old English and Arab predecessors, it directly reflected their 'rimland' status in relation to the French, German and Italian successor polities of the Carolingian heartlands.[14] More generally the remarkable number of very long reigns in the thirteenth century (56 and 35 years in England, 43 and 44 in France, 63 in Aragon, 35 and 32 in Leon Castile, 54 in Sicily) illustrates a transition from charismatic to bureaucratic monarchy which made possible among other things the successful conduct of minorities, almost as a matter of course. All the accompaniments which Lieberman notes—the extension of the authority of appointed officials over that of hereditary nobles, the standardization of legal custom in royal codes, the closer regulation of religious bodies and lands, and of commerce, the increase of central revenue, the tendency to definition of local status by national hierarchies and the resolution of local conflicts by national bodies—are the bread and butter of the European political and administrative history of this period.[15]

The transformation of western Europe in the eleventh century upon which these structures rested lay in the changes in social organization which were necessary for (and/or brought about by—the order of causation is not entirely clear) the extension of cereal cultivation, and of other marketable crops among which the vine was generally the most important. A population (for the most part) free and self-sufficient, typically sustained by domestic, cottage-style cultivation supplemented by foraging, was reduced to servitude and reacculturated as an agrarian labour force.[16] The necessity to which this process gave rise for the definition of territorial boundaries and sustained management of the land apparently suggested to the aris-

[14] V. H. Galbraith, *The Making of Domesday Book* (Oxford, 1961); W. L. Warren, *The Governance of Norman and Angevin England* (London, 1987); Donald Matthew, *The Norman Kingdom of Sicily* (Cambridge, 1992).

[15] For example, Harold Berman, *Law and Revolution* (Cambridge, Mass., 1983); W. C. Jordan, *The French Monarchy and the Jews* (Philadelphia, 1989); Robert Bartlett, *Trial by Fire and Water: The Medieval Judicial Ordeal* (Oxford, 1988); R. I. Moore, *The Formation of a Persecuting Society: Power and Deviance in Western Europe, 950–1250* (Oxford, 1987).

[16] Marc Bloch, *French Rural History* (1931, Engl. trans., London, 1966); G. Duby, *Rural Economy and Country Life in the Medieval West* (London, 1968); Robert Fossier, *Peasant Life in the Medieval West* (Oxford, 1988).

tocracy, on the model of the monastic estates where these developments were pioneered, the desirability of securing the transmission from each generation to the next of undivided estates, by ending *de facto* (but not, crucially, *de jure*), the partible inheritance which had been customary, and excluding younger sons and daughters from claims on the patrimony. This created the patrilineal and dynastic family structure which has characterized the European aristocracy in general, and importantly, though far from completely, European society at large.[17] The help of the church in securing the legal and ideological transformation necessary to secure it, notably through the sacralization of monogamous marriage, the promulgation of an extremely severe definition of incest which enabled the contracting of marriages to be tightly controlled, and the idealization of male as well as female chastity, was rewarded by the 'restoration' into ecclesiastical hands of between 20 and 30% of landed property and a tithe of all agricultural produce. In return, a guarantee of clerical celibacy ensured that this wealth would not fund the development of a rival hereditary aristocracy, and would remain available in future generations to provide compensation to a substantial proportion of the younger sons and daughters whose previously legitimate expectations had been sacrificed, together with the freedom of the peasantry, to provide the essential foundations of the new Europe.[18]

In combination the restructuring of the aristocratic family and the 'reform', as it was called, of the church, neither of which could have been achieved without the other, established a dual system of tenure for both land and office, the one based upon transmission through blood and violence, the other by ordination and merit, and the essential criterion of eligibility in each ineligibility in the other. In human terms these arrangements represented a different accommodation. The establishment of male primogeniture required the exclusion from their claims upon the patrimony of daughters and younger sons, as well as those now classified as bastards. Some of them were liberally compensated through the settlement with the church just described, but it remained the case, then and thenceforward, that

[17] G. Duby, *The Chivalrous Society* (London, 1977); D. Barthélmy, 'Kinship', in G. Duby (ed.), *A History of Private Life, II, Revelations of the Medieval World* (Cambridge, Mass., 1988), pp. 85–155; James Casey, *The History of the Family* (Oxford, 1989).

[18] There is no agreed account of these connections, but see G. Duby, *The Knight, the Lady and the Priest* (London, 1983); R. I. Moore, 'Duby's Eleventh Century', *History* 69 (1984), 36–49; David Herlihy, *Medieval Households* (Cambridge, Mass., 1985); Jack Goody, *The Development of the Family and Marriage in Europe* (Cambridge, 1983).

many younger siblings were forced from their families, more or less brutally according to circumstances, to fend for themselves as best they could, and usually, whether in the secular or the ecclesiastical sphere, under the protection of a patron who was not a close biological relative. This meant not only wandering through Christendom in search of heiresses, as the troubadours told it,[19] but less glamorously taking service at the court of whatever prince or prelate offered, and devoting oneself to his service, and the extension of his power, with all the idealism and ruthlessness that desperation could engender.

This breaking of the link between those who became the architects and bearers of bureaucratic power and their biological families constitutes a fundamental contrast to the vital relationship between careers in the imperial bureaucracy and family prosperity in China, which seems to have become increasingly close at this very period, in the generations after the Jurchen overran the Northern Song in 1126.[20] It was accompanied by the creation of a universal high culture firmly distanced from local society, based on the formalization of teaching and learning in the new institution which became the university, and the comprehensive restatement of Catholic faith and doctrine which it sustained.[21] Its creation marks a sharp divergence from the pattern of relations between religion and society, focused on local centres of piety and charity without systematic hierarchical control over the provision of either learning or religious services (to make a somewhat anachronistic distinction) that had hitherto characterized both western Europe and the central Islamic lands: until the twelfth century they resembled each other a good deal more closely in these respects than the traditional historiography of either has usually acknowledged.[22]

[19] See the famous essay of G. Duby, 'Youth in Aristocratic Society: Northwestern France in the Twelfth Century', *The Chivalrous Society* (above, n. 17), pp. 112–22.

[20] Robert P. Hymes, *Statesmen and Gentlemen: The Elite of Fou-chou, Chiang-hsi, in Northern and Southern Sung* (Cambridge, 1986); J. K. Fairbank, *China: A New History* (Cambridge, Mass., 1992), pp. 94–5. The general contrast with Europe suggested here holds, whether the primary dependence of the elite is supposed to be on the office (Ho Ping-ti, *The Ladder of Perfection in Imperial China* (New York, 1962), pp. 92–125) or on the land (Hilary J. Beattie, *Land and Lineage in China* (Cambridge, 1979); Patricia B. Ebrey, *Family and Property in Sung China: Yuan Tsai's Precepts for Social Life* (Princeton, 1984), pp. 15–17).

[21] For a masterly account which gives full weight to these social dimensions, R. W. Southern, *Scholastic Humanism and the Unification of Europe* (Oxford, 1994).

[22] For a strong case against the alleged analogy between the Islamic madraseh and the European university as both developed in the twelfth and thirteenth centur-

These developments, here summarized in an excessively general and schematic fashion, were under way in most regions between the Rhine, the Ebro and central Italy in the two or three decades before and after the millennium, and were complete in their essentials by the end of the twelfth century. In this way the surplus of agricultural production and the social differentiation necessary to the establishment (or, in the Mediterranean regions, re-establishment) of citied civilization was secured. The manner in which it was done, and the terms upon which the various parties to the new arrangements defined, with widely differing degrees of volition, their future relationships with one another—not through the promulgation of any overt or conscious general plan or policy, but by the accumulation of innumerable and similar solutions to innumerable and similar problems—structured the development of European society in the second millennium.[23] In particular it governed the formation of the social and cultural elite, to which the disinherited offspring of the old nobility provided not only, as we have seen, the 'oratores' and 'pugnatores'—the first two estates of what by the thirteenth century is clearly recognizable as Europe's *ancien régime*—but the 'laboratores' (now become 'negotiatores') as well, for it is now generally accepted that the urban patriciate, also firmly entrenched in legal privilege by the same time, frequently originated in the same eleventh-century reconstruction of the noble family.

This was the basis of the 'renewed process of political and cultural integration' which eleventh- and twelfth-century Europe also shared with Lieberman's early modern rimlands. The increasingly widespread use of common rituals, symbols, vocabularies and practices is so much taken for granted as a familiar and fundamental fact of this period that it has been the subject of little systematic comment, but examples of it abound on every hand.[24] The elevation of the cross at the pre-eminent symbol of Christendom—in frontier regions of militant Christendom, rampant against Muslim and heathen—reflected the growing emphasis on the incarnation and crucifixion of Christ in the new theology, and of the eucharist in forms of religious service themselves given new regularity and universality by the movement for ecclesiastical reform. The programme of that move-

ies, see Michael Chamberlain, *Knowledge and Social Practice in Medieval Damascus, 1190–1350* (Cambridge, 1994), pp. 69–90.

[23] G. Duby, *The Three Orders* (above, n. 5).

[24] For everything connected with the church in this period, Colin Morris, *The Papal Monarchy: The Western Church from 1050–1250* (Oxford, 1989).

ment was codified and given legislative force for the whole of Latin Christendom in the canons of the great general Council of the Church in 1215, the fourth to be convened at the Pope's Lateran headquarters since 1059, attended by some 1,200 bishops and abbots from all over Europe. These canons also specified that clergy should not only behave but dress so as to set themselves apart from the laity—and that Jews and Muslims should wear distinguishing marks on their clothing: as Lieberman comments, identity requires alterity. Already by 1215 hundreds of the churches in which the mass was celebrated, not only cathedrals and great abbeys but simple parish churches (the parish system itself being another legacy from this period) were built in the Gothic style which is the single most familiar and universal legacy of medieval Europe. Whereas the Romanesque style which it superseded had developed gradually since Carolingian times in many centres and many forms, shaped as much by local traditions and materials as by aesthetic and liturgical considerations, credit for the invention of the Gothic is customarily given to a single man, Abbot Suger of St Denis near Paris, who supervised every detail of the construction between 1135 and 1144 of the abbey church which he had designed to give physical expression to the religious symbolism of the ninth-century neoplatonist theologian, John Scotus Eriugena.[25] Suger was the chief minister of the Capetian kings of France, Louis VI and Louis VII, to the glorification of whose dynasty his abbey and abbacy were devoted; the spread of Gothic in the second half of the twelfth century matched that of its prestige. None the less, it is worth noting that the essential technical features of the style were already present in another great church begun by a chief minister of the other great aggressive dynasty of the period, Ranulf Flambard, the chancellor of William II of England, at Durham in the 1090s. Even more worth noting in view of this essay's insistence on the autonomy of the new civilization from its distant Mediterranean forebear is that Gothic reached Italy only belatedly and (Milan with its cathedral again the only really significant exception) on the whole unimpressively.

The churches and their decoration provide the most obvious and familiar reminder that the reconstruction of Catholic Christianity as the social, intellectual and spiritual foundation of the new

[25] E. Panofsky, *Abbot Suger on the Abbey Church of St. Denis and its Art Treasures* (2nd ed., G. Panofsky-Soergel, Princeton, 1979); O. von Simson, *The Gothic Cathedral* (Princeton, 1956); P. Frankl, *Gothic Architecture* (London, 1962); K. J. Conant, *Carolingian and Romanesque Architecture* (London, 1959).

Europe's elite, clerical and lay, was accompanied by vigorous and sustained attempts to impart its consolations, and its disciplines, to the mass of the population.[26] It was now, as we have said, that the parish church became everywhere the centre of the community and, as the regular place of baptism, marriage and burial, the site of the crucial rites of passage in every life. The Lateran Council of 1215 decreed that every adult of both sexes must confess to their priest every year before Easter. Those who defied this progress—and in many places they commanded a ready audience—were condemned as heretics, at first only when they insisted on confrontation, but from the mid-twelfth century being sought out with increasing determination and juridical ingenuity.[27] Condemnation as heresy was also the primary instrument for the 'marginalizing of local sources of sanctity and preliterate religious norms in the face of textual orthodoxy' to which Lieberman referred in the earlier version of his paper, and which he connected with the acceptance of capital identities.[28] The assertion of universality is also visible in the increasing popularity of long-distance pilgrimages such as those to Jerusalem, Rome and Compostela—the latter, strikingly, an invention of this period whose rise closely parallels that of transalpine Europe itself—in the concentration of the cult of saints upon a small number of universal figures, the Virgin pre-eminent among them, and in the assertion of papal, bureaucratic, control over the process of canonization itself, including the recognition of miracles.[29] Just as in the eleventh century the cry of reform had provided the occasion for the assertion of the authority of Rome and St Peter over the bishoprics of Latin Europe, from Ambrose's Milan downwards, so in the twelfth and still more the thirteenth, the cry of heresy assisted the new breed of bishops which the reform engendered to assert their control in turn over the local communities, parishes and parish priests in their dioceses.

[26] Rosalind and Christopher Brooke, *Popular Religion in the Middle Ages*, its title notwithstanding, is a good general account of the religion taught to the laity. James A. Brundage, *Law, Sex and Christian Society in Medieval Europe* (Chicago, 1987) is a minute but enthralling account of its most intimate intrusions.

[27] R. I. Moore, *The Origins of European Dissent* (London, 1977), pp. 243–62.

[28] Lieberman, MS.

[29] Historiography in this area is uneven. R. C. Finucane, *Miracles and Pilgrims: Popular Belief in Medieval England* (London, 1974); Benedicta Ward, *Miracles and the Medieval Mind* (London, 1982); P. A Sigal, *L'Homme et le miracle dans la France médiévale* (Paris, 1985); and J. Sumption, *Pilgrimage: An Image of Medieval Religion* (London, 1975), offer interesting information, analysed with mixed success.

Lateral integration, in Lieberman's terminology, was no less evident in its secular than in its religious aspect. Territorial expansion was notoriously driven on every frontier by armies of knights identically organized, trained and equipped, and symbolized and secured by the identical castles from which they rode. The knights themselves were recruited from the same heartlands, and often from the same families, as were many of the peasants attracted by promises of land and liberty to bring the new territories under the same plough—the same system of market-oriented cereal agriculture—that supported the urban revolution in the valleys of the Rhine and the Mosel, the Seine, the Loire and the Po. The grain was sold in towns built on the same plans, privileged with the same laws and again often colonized by the same people, as their heartland counterparts and models.[30] In short, though much in the areas of dress, manners and social conventions is incapable of investigation, and much more remains uninvestigated, it is enough to murmur phrases such as 'university', 'clerical discipline', 'chivalry',[31] 'christian life' to demonstrate that there can be no serious doubt of the creation in this period of a universal and pervasive high culture in Latin Europe. To add the mention of 'the bourgeoisie', and of bread, wine and cloth is to be reminded of the extensive and intensive cultural implications, well below the salt as it were, of the rapid growth of a network of markets which was rapidly and decisively extending its regular operations to the daily necessities.[32]

The role of interstate competition, notoriously crucial to the spectacular growth of European commerce, ingenuity and institutions in the ages of enlightenment and revolution, was no less central to the emergence of the European world, especially in respect of the stimulus given to fiscal, administrative and political development by the cost of advanced military technology. While, predictably enough, there is room for disagreement about their places in the order of causes, there is no doubt that from around the millennium a series of connected military advances, notably the couched lance, the crossbow and the castle, with their corollaries, contributed substantially both to social differentiation and administrative growth in the heart

[30] For a splendid account of all this, Bartlett, above, n. 13, *passim*.

[31] Maurice Keen, *Chivalry* (New Haven, 1984).

[32] P. Spufforth, *Money and its Uses in Medieval Europe* (Cambridge, 1988), pp. 74–131; M. Montanari, *The Culture of Food* (Oxford, 1994), pp. 38–67; Lester K. Little, *Religious Poverty and the Profit Economy* (London, 1978); Jacques le Goff, *Your Money or Your Life* (New York, 1988).

of north-west Europe, and to the expansion of Latin Christendom in every direction.[33] Whether military competition between Latin Christendom as a whole and any of its rivals was a significant factor is more difficult to say. There is certainly a case for the view that the raising and equipping of crusading expeditions (a more continuous activity in twelfth- and thirteenth-century Europe than the conventional reference to the best publicized occasions by number suggests) represented a demand on fiscal and administrative resources which contributed decisively to their rapid development in the kingdoms of Europe during this period.[34] As so often with this argument, it is difficult to see a basis for deciding whether the ostensible (and, of course, rhetorically overblown) need for the raising of money and the extension of royal institutions was in fact the reason for it, or the rationalization. The rhetoric of crusade, like that of heresy and antisemitism, and against sodomy, prostitution and usury, and indeed when it served their turn the cry for law and order, had a useful place among the battery of considerations with which courtiers might present to their masters, and the masters to their subjects, the continuing necessity for higher taxes, wider powers and a more insistent invasion of local communities and overriding of local custom. The same may be true of the increasingly evident and increasingly intense military competition within Europe, for example between the Plantagenet and Capetian monarchies from the middle of the twelfth century onwards, which had all the implications and consequences for state formation, the fostering of ethnic consciousness and all the rest of it, that have been associated with interstate warfare in every subsequent century. Here is continuity with a vengeance.

The obvious difference between this account of political and cultural integration in twelfth- and thirteenth-century north-western Europe and Lieberman's of his fourteenth- to eighteenth-century protected rimlands lies in my careful avoidance of the word 'ethnic' which to Lieberman is so crucial. The easy way to put it would be that what he describes as early modern phenomena of state formation were paralleled, at a more general level, in an earlier process of civilization formation. Leaving aside all the questions which that formulation would beg, I am not sure that we can shrug the issue

[33] P. Contamine, *War in the Middle Ages* (New York, 1984).

[34] See Simon Lloyd in J. Riley Smith (ed.), *Oxford Illustrated History of the Crusades* (Oxford, 1995), pp. 34–65.

off quite so easily. On the one hand, the sense of 'Latin Christendom' displayed in the twelfth century many of what might be regarded in other contexts as functions of ethnicity, in the use of the idea of holy war, for example, and of the growing hostility it fostered towards Greek Christians as well as Muslims, of the justification of colonization by cultural superiority,[35] or in the development and exploitation of antisemitism. On the other, something very like ethnicity was also present, and at least by the later part of the period, many would argue, making rapid progress, in the future national subdivisions (as defined by language) of Latin Christendom. The same developments which made Latin the repository and the instrument of the dominant culture made it also a clear and self-consciously asserted conceptual frontier both between Latin Christendom and its Celtic, Slav, Greek and Muslim neighbours, and within Latin Christendom, between the elite and the masses: in the twelfth century the words 'rusticus', 'paganus', 'hereticus' and 'illitteratus' were used interchangeably, and, as far as most of us can tell, indifferently.[36] The vernacular poems and sermons of tenth- and early eleventh-century England are greatly admired today, but those who used Old English, or for that matter Old Norse or Icelandic, as a literary language did so because they, or if not they, their audience, knew no better. On the other hand, by the thirteenth century the modern vernacular literatures were in their first fine flowering, and the chivalric romances which so eloquently affirm the universality of knightly values also record in their content as well as their language both the presence and occasional awareness of ethnic difference within it. At the beginning of the thirteenth century the Occitan language and its literature were clearly identified, on both sides, with the heretical civilization of the Languedoc which was brutally suppressed, in the early years of the thirteenth century, by the Albigensian crusade, launched by the papacy but destined, if not designed, for the aggrandizement of the French monarchy; near its end, Italian was chosen by Dante for what he meant to be his greatest work in conscious preference to Latin, because it was a mother tongue.

Nevertheless, Ernest Gellner's model of the 'agro-literate bureaucracy', which Lieberman implicitly rejects as finding insufficient

[35] John Gillingham, 'The Beginnings of English Imperialism', *Journal of Historical Sociology* 5/4 (1992), 392–409.

[36] Brian Stock, *The Implications of Literacy* (Princeton, 1983), e.g. at pp. 244–52; R. I. Moore, 'Literacy and the Making of Heresy, c. 1000–c. 1150', in P. Biller and A. Hudson (eds), *Heresy and Literacy, 1000–1530* (Cambridge, 1994), pp. 19–37.

place for pre-industrial ties of ethnic solidarity, describes the society of Europe in the eleventh and twelfth centuries with great accuracy.[37] In particular, the tension which is explicit or implicit in so many of its expressions and operations is not that between universalist and proto-ethnic or proto-national themes, even if such tensions can occasionally be identified, but between the high culture which was created and promulgated by the new elites and the local or regional values and solidarities which it overrode in the process.[38] If in other times and places national or ethnic sentiment was stimulated or invoked as a means of disguising class divisions, no such inclination was indulged here: the universal culture was firmly identified with, and as firmly served to unify, universal privilege. The case of the Languedoc proves my rule in the proper, medieval sense. Romantic nostalgia notwithstanding, the social cohesiveness which Occitania displayed in face of the Albigensian crusade was one indication among many that this was not an advanced society in its time but an archaic one.[39] One might say—it has indeed been one of the principal rationalizations of the dominant historiography—that Simon de Montfort and his successors dragged it, as Edward I did Wales, kicking and screaming into the thirteenth century.[40]

On that basis the birth of Europe may appear as part not of Lieberman's 'early modern' rimlands phenomenon, but rather of an earlier and distinct phase of Eurasian history. On the other hand, the culture and institutions of north-west Europe were subjected to nothing like the same discontinuities by the Mongol conquests and their immediate aftermath as were those of the central and eastern parts of the landmass. Nor were they transformed by the systems collapse that did not quite happen in the mid-fourteenth century, nor by the upheavals of the sixteenth. Terrifying as the mortality sown by the Black Death was, in Europe as in China and in the central Islamic lands, and devastating as its economic, social and even political consequences were, the population had recovered to its pre-plague levels in most regions by the early sixteenth century. Perhaps more important, none of the structures or institutions whose emergence we have

[37] Ernest Gellner, *Nations and Nationalism* (Oxford, 1993), pp. 8–18.

[38] Alexander Murray, *Reason and Society in the Middle Ages* (Oxford, 1978).

[39] Malcolm Barber, 'Catharism and the Occitan Nobility: the Lordships of Cabaret, Minerve and Termes', *The Ideals and Practice of Medieval Knighthood*, ed. C. Harper-Bill and R. Harvey (Woodbridge, 1986), pp. 1–19.

[40] James Given, *State and Society in Medieval Europe: Gwynnedd and Languedoc under Outside Rule* (Ithaca and London, 1990).

in this discussion identified with the birth of Europe was replaced or overthrown. The tripartite division of privileged society between church, aristocracy and bourgeoisie remained in place; within it the same monarchies, more or less, as before, deployed the same instruments of governance and patronage against the pretensions of the same noble families and ecclesiastical potentates, more or less, as before, and they sought to tap the wealth generated by the same cities from the same sources, more or less, as before. Latin Christendom was divided by the Protestant Reformation of the sixteenth century, to be sure, but the same scholastic culture which had shaped its elites since the twelfth century continued to do so until it gave way to a compound of renaissance humanism and eighteenth-century enlightenment whose essential unity was scarcely compromised, let alone fractured, by the confessional divide. That is not to say that there was no change. Of course there was, and nobody would dispute that over two or three centuries it was of transforming, even world-transforming, importance. But it grew from old roots, and most of it grew pretty straight.

The history of Europe in the period of its formation as an autonomous civilization clearly lends itself to description in terms of Lieberman's 'sustained integrative patterns'. Having imported and adopted a world religion in late antiquity (and having in some senses declined to adopt three others, Judaism, Manicheeism and Islam) north-western Europe developed urban centres and experienced secondary state formation during the eleventh, twelfth and thirteenth centuries, generating at that time a self-sustaining momentum in virtually every aspect of social, cultural and political development which, despite the checks inflicted by the economic and ecological catastrophes of the later Middle Ages, continued to gain in scope and vigour right up to the onset of modernization, to which its relationship is not an issue here. Most of the general considerations invoked by Lieberman are applicable both to the initial impetus and to its continuation. From the point of view of the present discussion, the main significance of this assertion of essential continuity in European history from the eleventh to the eighteenth century (whether these centuries are to be called a prolonged medieval period or a precocious early modern one) is that there was no caesura between, on the one hand, the establishment of a dominant high culture, with its accompaniments of social differentiation and administrative intensification, at the cosmopolitan or 'civilization' level which is so obvious in the eleventh and twelfth centuries, and on the other, the emergence within it of the ethnicity based polities to which Lieberman directs attention, already in some important respects well under way in the thirteenth. That is one manifestation of the roller coaster pace of development to which north-western Europe was committed by the voracious appetite for power with which the children of its first, urban, revolution were endowed.

There can be no doubt that the events and developments briefly sketched in this essay had an essential Eurasian context. The appearance of citied civilization in north-western Europe—for the first time, let it be repeated—was an aspect of the general recovery after the decline of late antiquity, the geographical extension and social and cultural deepening of Eurasian civilization which was precipitated by the simultaneous expansion and meeting of the Tang and Islamic worlds. The East Roman (Byzantine) Empire was a full participant in the new world order which followed. Western Europe was not, but its development in the ninth and tenth centuries was continuously and profoundly influenced, if not shaped, by the fringe benefits, as it were, of finding itself at the margin of this enormous and rapidly developing trading region. The Vikings and the Rus, Venice and Ottonian Germany, were among those who made rich pickings, as both traders and raiders.[41] The establishment of the new agrarian regime in western Francia upon which the urban revolution was founded arose in part from the loss of the opportunity to share in that booty by means of frontier warfare which had sustained the Carolingian monarchy in its eighth- and ninth-century greatness.[42] That loss both weakened the monarchy and sent the nobility in search of new sources of wealth, all the more urgently for the opportunity of participating in the delights of the new and expanding long-distance markets. Hence, the economic takeoff of the eleventh and twelfth centuries, providing the conditions that allowed north-western Europe to have become a fully functioning part of an integrated hemispheric trading system by 1250, as Janet Abu Lughod has documented so thoroughly, though it might be argued that it happened at least a couple of generations earlier.[43]

But 'up to the onset of modernization' leaves a question, especially in the context of an observation which arises from Lieberman's paper, as well as from the perspective of European history presented

[41] Maurice Lombard, *The Golden Age of Islam* (Amsterdam, 1975); *Les métaux dans l'ancien monde du Ve au VIe siècle* (Paris, 1974); Karl Leyser, *Medieval Germany and its Neighbours* (London, 1982), pp. 69–101.

[42] T. J. Reuter, 'Plunder and Tribute in the Carolingian Empire', *Transactions of the Royal Historical Society* 5/35 (1985), 75–94.

[43] Janet Abu Lughod, *Before European Hegemony* (New York, 1989).

and implied in this one. The long-term changes which both have addressed are to be seen as recurring intensifications rather than as the once-for-all step changes associated with the categories in which classical social theory has tended to discuss comparative history. The differences between the processes described here as 'state formation' in eleventh- and twelfth-century Europe and those in the sixteenth and seventeenth centuries which are very commonly so described are differences of degree, not of kind, in the subordination of local to 'national' allegiances and powers, the extraction of greater surplus and the consolidation of a dominant high culture; the 'military revolution' of the earlier period was very similar in its general causes, course and consequence to that of the later[44]—and so on. Indeed, the omission of only a few phrases will suffice to make a definition of social revolution offered as a defining characteristic of 'modern' world history entirely applicable to what we have described in this paper as 'the birth of Europe':

> Social revolutions have been rare and momentous occurrences in [modern] world history. [From France in the 1790s to Vietnam in the 1970s] these revolutions have transformed state organizations, class structures and dominant ideologies. They have given birth to nations whose power and autonomy markedly surpassed their own pre-revolutionary pasts and outstripped other countries in similar circumstances.[45]

It would be tedious to labour a point of which examples abound in every paper in this collection. But if these recurring intensifications in so many fields of social action are more or less continuous features of European history between the eleventh and the nineteenth centuries, and of other histories still later, where is the significance of the fact that they occurred 'simultaneously'—but also recurrently—in other regions of Eurasia? Does not the question become whether, instead of discussing what western Europe experienced in the period of its making merely as a local or regional development, we should regard it as an aspect of the reshaping of complex civilization in Eurasia after the decline of its ancient empires—of the 'other transition' from antiquity to what we no longer care to call feudalism?[46]

[44] Compare Bartlett (above, n. 13) with Geoffrey Parker, *The Military Revolution* (Cambridge, 1988) or W. H. McNeill, *The Pursuit of Power* (Oxford, 1983).

[45] Theda Skocpol, *States and Social Revolutions* (Cambridge, 1979), p. 3.

[46] Chris Wickham, 'The Other Transition: from the Ancient World to Feudalism', *Past and Present* 103 (1984), 3–36; 'The Uniqueness of the East', *Journal of Peasant Studies* 12, 2/3 (1985), 166–96, reprinted in J. Baechler, J. A. Hall and M. Mann (eds), *Europe and the Rise of Capitalism* (Oxford, 1988), pp. 66–100.

If so, we lack a name for it: it would be altogether too Eurocentric to borrow that which was given to a classic account of the process in Europe itself, 'The Making of the Middle Ages',[47] but for all its merit in drawing attention to the diffusion of technical, cultural and commercial advances from south Asia from around the fifth century CE, 'southernization' seems unlikely to stick.[48] Any attempt to propose such a label will inevitably be accompanied by renewed and doubtless inconclusive controversy about both the chronology and the characterization it implies, but since European historiography has suffered increasingly in recent decades from a surplus of data and a shortage of new questions, and that of the rest of Eurasia (as it appears to an outsider) rather from the reverse, the prospect is by no means an unwelcome one.

[47] R. W. Southern, *The Making of the Middle Ages* (London, 1953). The once greater temptation represented by the title of a similarly classic account of the European experience, Marc Bloch's *Feudal Society* (Paris, 1941, Engl. trans., London, 1963) raises even greater difficulties as a general description, whether the word feudal is employed with its Marxist connotations (as by Wickham or Perry Anderson, *Passages from Feudalism to Antiquity* (London, 1974)), or as Bloch preferred, with reference to a shared set of legal principles relating the tenure of land to the holding of public office and the performance of public obligation, which is no longer generally thought applicable even to western Europe itself in the period under discussion: cf. Susan Reynolds, *Fiefs and Vassals* New York, 1994).

[48] Lynda Shaffer, 'Southernization', *Journal of World History* 5, 1 (1994), 1–21.

State Building in Early-Modern Europe: The Case of France

JAMES B. COLLINS

Between the fifteenth and eighteenth centuries, Western European political units shared with political units elsewhere in Eurasia both underlying structural factors—population trends, bullion influx, an increasingly integrated world economy—and challenges, above all the rising costs of military activity. Western Europe reacted in ways similar to other regions to the stresses of the fifteenth through eighteenth centuries: greater territorial integration (most notably in France, England, and Spain), stepped-up efforts to establish cultural hegemony in given territorial units, higher levels of taxation, increased military spending and larger military forces, sharply more standardized institutions and administration.

At the same time, Western European propertied elites shared a fundamental political concern—the maintenance of a central political entity that would best define and preserve their private property—that seems to have set them apart from their Eurasian counterparts. The transformation from multiple identity central political units to more simply defined ones, that is, the evolution to the nation-state, required a solution that would protect this private property; the solutions, in England, France, and Holland, reflected the primacy of the consent of the governed in the construction of political legitimacy, and the critical balance between rights of private property and state authority. In the long run, this solution led to the creation of nation-states in which property holders guaranteed themselves control over the legislative process, which allowed them to create the definition of property and then to protect such property from the state, yet simultaneously to use the state to protect their property from the propertyless. The early modern conflict stands in clearest relief in the evolving relationship between the public good, the *res publica*, and the central state—in France, above all, the king.

The wide range of factors affecting state development ensured considerable local and regional variation within Western Europe. The significantly improved military capacities of Europe vis-à-vis other regions of the world, moreover, went hand-in-hand with a remarkable resurgence of cultural hegemonism, a hegemonism specifically sponsored by states. This cultural hegemonism functioned both within states, in a process Robert Muchembled has called the 'invention of modern man,' and without, in the rise of Europeans' belief that, as Antony Pagden has said, they were 'lords of all the world.'[1]

Some of our fundamental assumptions about Western European exceptionalism, however, must be re-examined carefully before we can make useful comparisons with other regions. For most of the period 1400 to 1800 the fundamental political units of most of Western Europe can more accurately be described as empires or as dynastic states of varying sizes rather than as nation states. These political units combined four distinct elements: family property, empire, nation, and state. The families of European rulers of the fifteenth or sixteenth century followed reproductive and lineal strategies entirely similar to those of the peasant families over whom they ruled. In France, the final stage of the shift from the Valois family to the individual king as the dominant unit took place in 1515, when the last of the five male lines of the royal family inherited the throne. With the accession of Francis I, France became much more of a monarchical state focused on a single ruler.

France the family corporation was also France the empire, at least in a cultural sense. The King of France ruled over a polyglot empire, with several major languages (Flemish, Breton, French, Occitan, later, German), and a host of dialects and *patois*. Spain was much the same; the King of Spain ruled the peninsula as joint king of Castile and of Aragon: the latter kept separate institutions—tax system, Cortes, law—until the early eighteenth century.

The critical shift toward the nation state took place in the sixteenth century, when Western European polities redefined the *res publica* to be the state, and increasingly identified the state with the central government. Four key elements—the commonwealth, the state, the government, and the citizen—underwent profound transformation between 1500 and 1650. That such a development was not predetermined can be seen in the Polish case; there, the com-

[1] R. Muchembled, *L'invention de l'homme moderne* (Paris, 1988); A. Pagden, *Lords of All the World. Ideologies of Empire in Spain, Britain and France, c. 1500–1800* (New Haven, 1995). The many works of Norbert Elias also emphasize the dramatic change in European cultural attitudes in the seventeenth and eighteenth centuries, what he has called the 'civilizing process.'

monwealth remained apart from, and above, the state. The political consequences for the Polish state, however, were disastrous: it ceased to exist in the eighteenth century.

In France, we can see the evolving relationship among these concepts not only in the political theory of Jean Bodin or Michel de l'Hôpital, but also in two key changes in ceremonial life. Francis I changed the order of royal entry processions, which traditionally had ended with the king, followed by a representation of France, and then God; beginning in his reign, the new order became, and remained, France, king, God. The second key shift took place in 1547, in the coronation oath of Francis's son, Henry II: the king changed the *ordo*, adding a clause stipulating that the king married his kingdom, that is, took France as a bride. These two changes suggested to all that the king was God's agent in protecting the kingdom (that is, the commonwealth), and that the king's authority over the commonwealth was that of the *paterfamilias*: benevolent but essentially without limits.

If absolutism is a myth, as it surely is in most respects,[2] we still must respect the profound implications of this important shift in the sixteenth century. The titanic theoretical struggle bore witness to dramatic practical changes as well. In order to understand more fully this fundamental shift in the sixteenth century, we need briefly to summarize the evolution of political life in Capetian and Valois France. When, for example, did France become a nation? Was early-modern France a nation-state? What institutional transformations heralded the emergence of a sovereign state? France is a useful model for west European polities both because of its centrality to European politics during this time and because France, along with England, has long served as one of the two models of European state-building.

Medieval Antecedants

As R.I. Moore has suggested elsewhere in this volume, the early-modern central states in Western Europe owed much to their

[2] The absolute sovereign could act with remarkable arbitrariness, often to accomplish a limited, specific goal; royal prerogative in foreign policy made such arbitrariness a particular danger there. We must certainly reject the notion that 'absolute' monarchs imposed a state system on their subjects. They worked out a compromise with local elites that protected the mutual interests of the central states and the

medieval predecessors. By 1300, the two political units that would become the prototypes of most studies of European state building—England and France—had achieved a remarkably high degree of coherence over relatively large (by existing Western European standards) geographic areas. These units differed fundamentally from the old empire of Charlemagne, built on war and tribute; they rested instead on discernable permanent state institutions. Around 1120, Louis VI, *rex Francorum*—the king of the Franks, the titular ruler of this entity, used for the first time the title, *rex Franciae*—King of France.[3] As Georges Duby suggests, this replacement of the concrete (the Franks) by the abstract (France) marked a dramatic shift in the nature of the monarchy and heralded the development of a national consciousness, because the monarchy sought to get agreement on the very existence of an entity over which it ruled. Louis VI simultaneously described himself, in a charter issued to the Cluniac order, as charged with the 'public defense' of the kingdom; that is, the king defended not his personal interests, but those of the commonwealth. Louis naturally sought reaffirmation of such rulership from the most powerful inhabitants of the commonwealth, the great regional lords. A year after routing Louis VI at Brémule (1119), the duke of Normandy, who had hitherto refused to do homage for his duchy, relented and became the king's man.

Geographically, the 'France' of which Louis VI and his successors claimed to be king expanded far beyond the traditional meaning of the Ile-de-France, preserved still in some village names of the area. The new geographic entity ran from Flanders in the north to the county of Barcelona in the south, and from the Atlantic to the river line of the Schelde, Meuse, Saône, and Rhône in the east.[4] France, as meant in the term King of France, thus included many areas then not French, by ethnicity or language. France, from its birth, there-

elites. Two case studies of French 'absolutism' in practice are: W. Beik, *Absolutism and Society in Seventeenth-Century France* (Cambridge, 1985), and J. Collins, *Classes, Estates, and Order in Early Modern Brittany* (Cambridge, 1994).

[3] C. Beaune, *The Birth of an Ideology*, trans. S. Huston (Berkeley, 1991), 284, notes that this title became official in royal documents in 1254. G. Duby, *France in the Middle Ages*, trans. J. Vale (Cambridge, MA, 1991), 129–31, suggests it became normative in other sources, such as monastic chronicles, by the middle of the twelfth century.

[4] The line of towns along or close to the border would run from Sedan, down to Verdun and Toul, thence to Langres, Dijon, Beaune, Chalon-s-Saône, and Lyon. The King of France lost suzerainty over the county of Barcelona in 1162, to the kingdom of Aragon.

fore, had to be both inclusionist—it could not define itself by culture, language or ethnicity—and exclusionist—it did define itself as Christian. Jews had no place in this 'most Christian' France; kings expulsed them from the kingdom in the thirteenth and fourteenth centuries, and from newly acquired territories (such as Provence, which had a large Jewish community), at the end of the fifteenth century. Religion thus formed the first, at some level the only, element of cultural integration in this early France. French kings sought to create a cultural unity within their territorial unit by encouraging worship of saints associated with their house and by encouraging the use of the French language, a process that accelerated rapidly after the appointment of the first lay chancellor in the 1290s.

The first step in the creation of a 'France' was the acceptance of the principle of royal overlordship by the great territorial princes, such as the duke of Normandy. On this issue—creation of a pyramidal, organized structure—the twelfth century marked a decisive turning point both at the national and regional levels. The King of France, like territorial rulers, increasingly got his immediate subordinates to do homage to him for their holdings. This recognition of overlordship, essentially a new phenomenon in the late eleventh and twelfth centuries and not really a holdover from earlier times, had profound consequences for French state development.[5]

Once the great princes had done homage for their territories, the King of France obtained lordship rights. Two of these rights—mediation of disputes and supervision of inheritance—proved critical in the expansion of the royal demesne and thus in the territorial integration of France. The supervision of inheritance rights—including the right of the overlord to a piece of the inheritance in cases of indirect (female) succession—enabled the King of France to expand the royal demesne, just as John Lackland's failure to appear before the court of barons (1202) allowed Philip to confiscate his fiefs: Aquitaine, Normandy, Anjou, and Maine.

These massive additions to the royal demesne between 1190 and 1210 made institutional expansion, so necessary to the maintenance of territorial integration, much easier. Structural changes, above all the growth of towns in the twelfth century, also contributed mightily

[5] The number of fiefs holders in the bailiwick of Troyes (Champagne) doing homage to the count rose from 47 to 78% between 1172 and 1204/10. T. Evergates, *Feudal Society in the Bailliage of Troyes under the Counts of Champagne, 1152–1284* (Baltimore, 1975), 93.

to institutional expansion. The new wealth and size of towns encouraged the creation of 'communes,' self-governing towns; a shift in power toward (urban) bishoprics and away from (rural) monasteries,[6] and the introduction of town-based royal assizes, made monthly in the demesne lands by Philip Augustus (1180–1223) and universal in the kingdom by Louis IX (1226–70). The growth of this grass-roots administration led first to *ad hoc* central arrangements, like the early 'parlements' of Louis IX and the financial commissions of Philip I, and then to the creation of a permanent, kingdom-encompassing superstructure of 'sovereign' courts that grew out of the royal council: the Parlement of Paris (permanently bearing that name after 1278) and the financial Chamber of Accounts (*c.* 1300), which examined the books of all royal officers who handled money.[7] By the early fourteenth century, France shared with England a wide range of such institutions—representative assemblies, court systems, tax systems, quasi-permanent armies, a unitary head of government (king)—which suggests the consonance of underlying conditions that called them into being. It should be relatively unsurprising that these parallel developing systems spent much of their time in conflict with each other.

Louis VI's dual actions of 1119–1120 remind us of the contrast between the state as the central government and the state as the administrator of the *res publica*, of those interests common to all households living in a given polity, to borrow the definition of Jean Bodin (1576). France, like the other central governments of Western Europe, came, by the early fourteenth century, to possess the structures necessary for systematic action in three key areas: (1) protection of physical welfare and property; (2) adjudication of disputes; and (3) paying for the first two functions. European polities used intermediate or parallel institutions—guilds, town councils, seigneuries, provincial estates, churches—to provide a wide range of other commonwealth services, such as education and poor relief. These institutions also carried out local police, both in the modern sense of maintaining civil order and in the early-modern one of

[6] The government relied heavily on the institutional structure of the Church; it used the geographic boundaries of bishoprics for the first territorial jurisdictions of French taxation, the *élections*. Brittany and Languedoc kept the bishopric as their basic unit of fiscal geography until the Revolution.

[7] See J. Strayer, *The Reign of Philip the Fair* (Princeton, 1980) and J. Baldwin, *The Government of Philip Augustus* (Berkeley, 1986).

supervision of daily activities. Central governments may not usually have regulated economic production until the seventeenth or eighteenth centuries, but entities chartered by them, such as guilds, did so under their aegis long before that.

The medieval French state made major strides toward an identification of the central state with the guardianship of the *res publica*. The King of France acted in three careful steps: first, Louis VII (1137–80) made himself the guarantor of settlements reached by contending vassals *before* his intervention; then, by about 1200, Philip Augustus, through his baronial court, mediated the disputes, that is, *he* proposed the terms of the settlement; finally, by the time of Philip the Fair (1283–1314) at the latest, the government actively prosecuted those who violated royal ordinances or who interfered with royal officials performing their duties. After the successful enforcement of the judgment against King John (1202), the King of France had new latitude in imposing the judgments reached by his court (the great barons, later, the Parlement). The permanence of the Parlement makes this new royal power abundantly clear, just as the need for a Chamber of Accounts implies substantial tax revenues by the 1290s.

By 1300, the French polity had accepted important principles of central state building. Practical limitations to central state action, of course, severely curtailed prerogative rights. The simultaneous political debates about the locus of authority in lay (king versus Estates) and religious (Pope versus Church Council) circles alert us to the growing strength of central institutions in fourteenth-century Europe, and to the obvious movement toward consolidation of power. The key issue of legitimacy lay at the core of all European political developments between the fourteenth and nineteenth centuries: What was the basis of the legitimacy of rule? Who should hold authority? What sort of authority should they hold? Who decided the answer to such questions? That the power would exist was not in question, nor was the source of its legitimacy in doubt: power came from the ruled, and, to be genuinely legitimate, then received divine sanction. In France, these two principles received overwhelming reinforcement in the early fourteenth century, when the great lords and bishops of France *elected* Philip of Valois to be King of France in 1328. This election paralleled the one raising the Capetians to the throne in 987; baronial-episcopal assemblies elected by acclamation all Capetian kings through Philip Augustus. As the barons shouted three times at the election and consecration of Philip I (1059): 'We approve, we wish it. May it be thus!'[8] Philip VI received the divine sanction at the coronation ceremony, in Reims, where the archbishop anointed him with the miraculous oils of the Holy Chrism. That ordinary people believed only this ceremony made a man king seems little in doubt; Jeanne d'Arc, for example, always referred to Charles VII as the 'Dauphin' (king's oldest son) until he was anointed at Reims, just as the chronicler Jean Froissart used that term for Charles V before his coronation.[9]

The 'ruled' had a critical input into who held legitimate authority, but the 'ruled' in this sense encompassed a relatively small group: rural landlords (who, in medieval assemblies, represented their peasants, free and serf, as well as themselves) and town leaders. Western European polities had profound debates about political legitimacy, rulership, the nature of the state, and the stewardship of the commonwealth, debates that led to armed conflict in many places, such as Flanders and England.[10] In France, Philip IV had established the principle of consultation with representative assemblies for levying taxes. He did so out of pragmatism—their approval made it easier to collect the money—but also from principle: the king had no right to tax the serfs of other lords without the permission of those lords. The self-governing communes, too, demanded that they give consent to taxation. John II and Charles V (both as Regent and later as King) used local, regional, and supra-regional estates to vote taxes and to help with their collection; later kings used these votes of the Estates General of Langue d'Oc and Langue d'Oïl to justify permanent taxation.[11] The battle over permanent taxation reached its peak in the

[8] Cited in J. Le Goff, 'Reims, ville du sacre,' in P. Nora (ed.), *Les Lieux de Mémoire. La Nation* (Paris, 1986), vol. 2, pt 1, 115.

[9] Beaune stresses the royal government's efforts to get people to accept the idea that the king became king as soon as his predecessor died, but I would agree with M. Bloch, *The Royal Touch*, trans. J. Anderson (New York, 1961, 1989), 128–9, that everyone from nobles to peasants agreed that the coronation alone made the king, the king. French royal mythology held that the Holy Chrism at Reims miraculously replenished itself with oils in time for each new coronation. The Chrism and oil were a gift from God to Saint Remigius, who used the oil to anoint Clovis as King of the Franks in the early sixth century. The custom of coronation at Reims only began with the third Capetian, Henry I (1027); the Pope officially recognized the sole right of the archbishop of Reims to anoint the king about fifty years later. Only two later French kings—Louis VI (1108) and Henry IV (1589)—did not receive their crowns at Reims.

[10] W. TeBrake, *A Plague of Insurrections* (Philadelphia, 1993); M. Mollat, P. Woolf, *Ongles Bleus, Jacques et Ciompi* (Paris, 1971).

[11] P. Cazelles, *La société politique sous Philippe de Valois* (Paris, 1958), as well as the many books and articles of B. Guenée, E.A.R. Brown, and J.B. Henneman, offer

various Estates meeting between 1355 and 1363; the Jacquerie of 1358, a massive peasant rebellion crushed by the nobility, enabled them to force a key compromise on the royal government. Nobles themselves would receive exemption from direct taxes (in the north) and serfs would pay a lower rate than free peasants; in return, the king got the right to tax directly even the serfs of other lords. Kings often questioned this principle of noble tax exemption—in her *Book of the Body Politic* (*c.* 1405), royalist historian Christine de Pizan wrote: 'the rich . . . are exempt from taxes, and the poor who have nothing from the king have to pay . . . It is a strange custom that is used nowadays in this kingdom in the setting of taxes'[12]—but, royal desires to the contrary notwithstanding, nobles kept this direct tax exemption until 1695.[13]

Everywhere, at every level of society, people fought about representation and legitimacy. In towns, guilds fought merchants; in the church, bishops fought the Pope, on one hand, and cathedral chapters on the other. In larger territorial units, landlords and townsmen fought to preserve their right to approve taxation. They preserved this right in many areas; even in those, such as much of northern France, where they did not, the monarchy at least argued that the original grant of taxation had been voted by a representative body: it claimed the *taille* dated from a vote in 1439, one that mirrored Charles VII's abolition of most seigneurial *tailles*, which set in motion the movement toward royal monopoly on taxation. Later, the king would not interfere with town taxation based on immemorial rights—the so-called patrimonial levies—but he would rigorously enforce his absolute right to approve any other form of taxation.

Toward a Unified Monarchy and a National Identity, c. 1400–1515

The long struggle for territorial integrity known as the Hundred Years' War accelerated institutional growth. When he inherited the

details on these issues. The term Estates General refers really to supra-regional assemblies—the Estates General of Langue d'Oc (south) and of Langue d'Oïl (north)—and not to national bodies.

[12] C. de Pizan, *The Book of the Body Politic*, ed. and trans., K. Langdon Forhan (Cambridge, 1994), 20.

[13] Nobles, except those actually fighting in the king's army, had paid taxation; the disaster at Poitiers led many to question the noble exemption. Froissart tells us that the Jacques claimed the 'nobility of France . . . were disgracing and betraying

throne in 1461, Louis XI had the institutional framework for a unified state: a system of appellate courts, all deriving their authority from him, covering most of his realm; a tax system producing revenues unparalleled in Europe (or in previous French history);[14] and an effective standing army. Rival political entities, such as the territories ruled by the duke of Burgundy, had similar institutions, although they were often not so well rooted as the French ones. Louis had dispensed with any sort of national or super-regional representative bodies in northern France, but he continued to consult provincial estates in many areas (such as Normandy) and the great regional Estates of Languedoc.

Louis XI's centralist policies almost immediately touched off a rebellion among the great nobility, who combined in the *ligue du Bien public*—the League of the Public Good. The name of the league amply demonstrates everyone's understanding of the key issue at hand, the claim of the king to be the sole guardian of the commonwealth. The noble rebels believed the commonwealth stood above the king, and that they shared in its protection. Christine de Pizan had written of the nobles: 'Are they not guardians of the prince and the people of the country, and the champions that shed their blood and life for the honor of the prince and the public good?'[15]

Various factors militated in favor of the king in this contest, above all the disunity of his opponents and the ever-increasing solidity of royal institutions. Louis's success against the principles of the League of the Public Good marked the definitive culmination of the long campaign started by Louis VI in 1119. That success made it possible for his sixteenth-century successors to assert with confidence that the king was the sole guardian of the *res publica*, but they still had to redefine the *res publica* to mean the state.

The theoretical proposition supported by the League of the Public Good had much in common with conditions as they actually existed in the fourteenth and fifteenth centuries. The great men of the kingdom believed they collectively guarded the *res publica*; the main

the realm' and that 'those knights and squires who returned from the battle (Poitiers) were so blamed and detested by the commons that they were reluctant to go into the big towns.' P. Geary (ed.), *Readings in Medieval History* (Peterborough, 1991), 746–7.

[14] E. Le Roy Ladurie, *L'Etat royal, 1460–1610* (Paris, 1987), 53, dates the dramatic increase in taxation from Louis XI, not from the official institution of taxes in the 1360s.

[15] De Pizan, *Body Politic*, 50.

guardians, of course, were the members of the royal family, in all its branches. The French monarchy of the fourteenth and fifteenth centuries resembled nothing so much as a peasant family's enterprise. The head of the family parceled out the elements of the family holdings to his sons (more parsimoniously to daughters). The male members of the family pushed for and obtained (in 1316 and again in 1328) a rigorous patrilineal system of inheritance for the core family property.[16] A generation later, the apologists of Charles V would trumpet the Salic Law as the justification for these actions; in time, Charles VII would make it the law of France. This male-only family corporation consistently divided up its landed property, i.e., the kingdom: royal sons got apanages in Berry, Burgundy, and the Orléanais. Because the *apanagiste* received all revenue from his apanage, and often named its 'royal' officials, this policy reduced the relatively unified France of Philip VI into a set of fractured family fiefs. This practice makes sense only when we consider how weak was the legal claim of the Valois to the throne, and how they needed family support against the claims of rival lines.

Between 1328 and 1515, however, the French commonwealth changed from being the hereditary property of the Valois family into the responsibility of a single person, the king, and of the state constructed around him.[17] Louis XI fought for that proposition in the War of the League of the Public Good, but it received practical confirmation only with the consolidation of the royal family into a single line in 1515. That consolidation and the elimination of the last great principalities—Brittany, obtained by forced marriage of its heiress to the king, and the Bourbon lands, confiscated after the treason of the constable in 1521—transformed France from a corporation into

[16] The men dispossessed first Jeanne of France, daughter of Louis X (d. 1316) and her son, Charles of Navarre, and then Isabella of France, daughter of Philip IV, and her son, Edward III of England. French customary law rarely barred male heirs of women from landed property, but the Estates General of 1328 did just that, selecting Philip of Valois. The so-called Salic Law, supposed law of the Salian Franks that denied inheritance of kingship through a woman, had no bearing on the decisions of 1316 and 1328; Charles V's lawyers dredged it up in the 1350s. The French throne passed out of the direct male line of the king in 1498, 1515, and 1589: the three new kings married, respectively, the widow, daughter, and sister of their predecessors.

[17] French customary law gave the family clear rights to the landed property of all members; the lands given by the royal family to the apanagiste thus reverted to the Crown if his line of direct male issue expired. Although customary law invariably had a similar rule about direct issue, the rights of daughters varied widely by geographic region, and by their status (noble/commoner).

a personal holding at precisely the moment when the central government began to make a distinction between the state itself and the individual ruler. That distinction became clear in the early 1520s, when the king created a new official, the Central Treasurer, to handle the state's money, and thus established a division between state revenue and the king's private income (handled, as before, by a separate official, the *changeur du Trésor*). The royal government also abandoned the traditional terminology about revenues: prior to the 1520s, all revenue from taxation was called 'extraordinary'; 'ordinary' revenue came from the king's demesne. In the 1520s, the revenue from regular taxation—the *taille*, the salt tax, etc.—came to be called ordinary. All of these developments pushed France toward a more modern state; at the same time, a second key element in the transformation of the *res publica*, the nation, became more clearly defined.

Georges Duby would have us accept the existence of a 'France' from the early twelfth century: after all, Louis VI could not be King of France unless some people had an idea of what this 'France' was.[18] Recently, Colette Beaune has posited the existence of a French national consciousness in the fifteenth century, one tied tightly to an ever-evolving spectrum of saints connected to the monarchy. Twelfth-century people may not have entirely understood this broader definition of France, but, by the fifteenth century, there can be little question that even ordinary peasants had a sense of living in France, and held a loyalty to the kingdom of France—a loyalty carefully nurtured by the royal government, as Beaune suggests. In Brittany, as elsewhere, early-modern vocabulary made a useful distinction between different types of outsiders: local people (and royal documents) referred to those from other parts of France as 'forains' (outsiders), whereas they reserved the term 'estrangers' (foreigners) for those who did not come from the kingdom.[19]

Beaune's examples of the medieval veneration of given saints as symbols of that unit provide obvious evidence that townspeople espe-

[18] Beaune, *Origins*, 285, cites the phrase 'douce France' from the *Chanson de Roland* (*c.* 1100) as meaning the larger France (liasses 54 and 55, for example), yet in liasse 65 the meaning of the 'Francs de France' or the 'Franceis de France' seems clearly to be the smaller France. The poet suggests that Charlemagne's capital, at Aachen (Aix) is in France, which implies the larger unit. As in so many other matters, the *Chanson* remains ambiguous.

[19] Two recent books offer important insights into the issue of citizenship in early-modern France: C. Wells, *Law and Citizenship in Early Modern France* (Baltimore, 1994) and D. Bell, *Lawyers and Citizens* (New York, Oxford, 1994).

cially and even peasants identified in some larger sense with 'France.' The persistence of local festivals celebrating local victories of national importance, or festivals clearly associated with national victories, above all that of Bouvines (1214), further documents the idea of attachment to a larger entity, to the kingdom of France. Fifteenth- and early sixteenth-century French royal documents that discuss the English invariably describe them as 'our ancient enemies, the English,' a phrase that Beaune shows had tremendous resonance even at the level of a local parish. The story of the peasant Jeanne d'Arc, with her naive patriotism on behalf of the rightful king and the unity of the kingdom, can serve as an *exemplum* of this attitude. The literature of the fifteenth century, such as de Pizan, makes ample use of the term 'France,' and demonstrates a mature chauvinism toward the superiority of its customs and people. In later times, kings or their governments did not hesitate to appeal to a national sentiment, as in the case of the capture of Francis I (1525) or in that of Louis XIV's appeal to his people in 1709, an appeal read from the pulpit of every church in the kingdom. The documents from Brittany from the sixteenth through eighteenth centuries demonstrate conclusively that Bretons knew that they were part of France and that France was not England or Spain. Bretons and other seafarers held a particularly strong animus against the English, one that persists to this day among Breton fishermen.

The term 'France' gradually acquired a dual meaning in the thirteenth and fourteenth centuries, that is, at the same moment at which the central state institutions of the second France came into being. This medieval kingdom of France held a powerful sway over the imagination of French elites: the 'imagined' France of someone like Louis XIV, for example, always included Flanders, even though France had definitively renounced legal right to Flanders at Câteau-Cambrésis in 1559. We must not associate too closely the area over which the central French state held sway and 'France'; that is, we should be reluctant to attach too quickly the term nation state to the political entity over which the King of France ruled.

The four centuries preceding the accession of Francis I (1515) therefore provided the kingdom of France with some key elements both of a central state and of a nation. The central state had powerful, broad roots by 1515. State-building continued ceaselessly at all levels; often, the central government took over the institutions created by local and regional governments, thus amalgamating the state-building process and making the word 'state' mean the central government. Many medieval developments paved the way for such a shift: Philip Augustus's use of bailiffs and his fiscal reforms; Louis IX's assertion of his right to ban private war (that is, he made war a specifically public matter, over which he, as guardian of the *res publica*, had complete authority); Philip the Fair's massive taxation increases, laicization of administration, and standardization of practices (as with the Chamber of Accounts); Charles V's creation of permanent taxes, with an administration; Charles VII's reestablishment of the standing army and expansion of the authority of the tax administration, as well as his creation of regional Parlements; Louis XI's consolidation of the policies of his predecessors and massive increase in the fiscal resources of the crown; and finally the consolidation of the many lines of the royal family into a single line by 1515.

France, the nation, existed too by 1515. The long, slow process begun by Louis VI, in his shift from King of the Franks to King of France, had borne fruit during the Hundred Years' War. French national identity certainly was forged under the white heat of that conflict; French people felt French in part because they knew they were not English and in part because they believed themselves to belong to a community whose definition, the royal government increasingly got them to accept. Not long after the revival of France, symbolized by The Maid, peasant rebels in Normandy terrorized their English occupiers in the name of the 'true' king; the English responded by the time-honored use of summary executions, with the usual result of enhancing the patriotic feeling they sought to stamp out.[20]

The Commonwealth and Sovereignty in the Sixteenth Century

This real sense of French nationalism, combined with the underlying structural changes (social, economic, political), gave Francis I a remarkable opportunity to transform fundamentally the nature of the French state. Like other rulers of his time, he could rely on printing to enhance efforts at cultural integration. He could rely on his massive financial resources, dwarfing those of even the greatest lords in his kingdom, to pay for an equally impressive military apparatus. He immediately sought to use these financial and military

[20] Beaune, *Birth of an Ideology*, 146.

resources in precisely the same way that Charles VIII and Louis XII had done; he invaded Italy on behalf of the Valois family corporation. He sought to make good his 'rightful' claim to foreign subsidiaries, obtained through marriage when his own branch of the family had not held the French throne.

Public opinion—in Francis's time, that meant essentially noble opinion—believed in the justice of the king's cause, and further identified the public good and the cause of the king as one and the same. Indeed, here French public opinion and learned scholars relied precisely on Aristotle; as Christine de Pizan had said, 'the good prince ought especially to love the public good and its augmentation more than his own good, according to the teachings of Aristotle's *Politics*, which says that tyranny is when the prince prefers his own good over the public good.'[21] In a sixteenth-century biography of Louis de la Trémoille, a knight 'without reproach,' we learn de la Trémoille wanted to die in a 'bed of honor, that is, in the service of his king in a just war.' Later, when his son dies, the funeral oration summarizes the qualities of the good death: the young de la Trémoille died 'as a man of virtue, in the company of worthy men . . . not among brigands and pirates, but in a just war . . . not in the service of tyrants, but in that of his king; not in reproach, but honestly, covered with honor, enveloped by his good name and by the love and grace of God.' Later, the father wrote to his wife that their son died in an act of virtue, fighting for the 'public good in a just quarrel.'[22]

The young de la Trémoille, and those like him, died fighting for their king *and* the public good. In the first half of the sixteenth century, the two remained coterminous, but the Wars of Religion raised the most troubling of all possible questions: what would happen if the king's quarrel were not just? In the 1570s, the Huguenot nobles returned to the distinction between the public good and the king, arguing that the public good—the true religion—stood above the king. In the 1590s, the Catholic League took precisely the same position, this time in opposition the Protestant Henry IV.[23]

[21] De Pizan, *Body Politic*, 15–16.

[22] J. Bouchet, *Le Panegyric du Chevallier sans reproche ou Mémoires de la Trémoille* (Paris, 1820), volume XIV of the *Collection complète des mémoires relatifs à l'histoire de France*, ed. Petitot, funeral oration by Claude de Tonnerre, bishop of Poitiers, cousin of the deceased, 509–10, letter of Louis de la Trémoille to his wife, Gabrielle de Bourbon, 511–13.

[23] On the importance of this shift, see, among others, D. Crouzet, *Les guerriers de Dieu* (Paris, 1991), 2 vols; J. Pocock, *The Ancient Constitution and the Feudal Law*

Francis I also acted in ways that affirmed a new conception of kingship. His government shifted the focus of kingship away from the king's judicial role, mediator of disputes and preserver of the peace, toward his legislative role. The king now made law for the commonwealth. Francis's activism went hand-in-hand with fundamental changes in political philosophy, although the normative texts appeared after his death. Let us turn briefly to this critical redefinition of terms, because these new definitions came to dominate western European political discourse for centuries to come.

Jean Bodin began his seminal *Les Six Livres de la République (Six Books of the Commonwealth*, 1576), with a definition: 'Commonwealth is the right government of several households, and of that which is common to them, with sovereign power.'[24] In searching for the origins of the modern state, we do well to heed Bodin's advice to begin with definitions in our examination of early-modern times, by trying to understand terms like 'absolute power' (*puissance absolue*) used by sixteenth- or seventeenth-century writers or royal officials by thinking what *they* meant by such a term. For Bodin, as for his contemporaries, the power of the sovereign prince was both absolute and limited.[25] Bodin argued that the 'first mark of the sovereign prince is the power to give law to all in general and to each in particular,' yet he also stated clearly that the sovereign prince is bound to his contracts because 'the absolute power of sovereign princes and seigneuries does not in any way extend to the laws of God and of nature.' In short, divine and natural law bound the sovereign prince quite as much as they bound the subject.[26] The king, through the mechanism of the central state, had the obligation to make sure his subjects obeyed divine and natural laws (as well as his laws); alas for them, while the king was bound by these laws, no human agency could hold him to them.

Bodin offered a coherent definition of sovereignty: 'the absolute and perpetual power of a Commonwealth,' one that was, and had to

(Cambridge, 1957), J. Franklin, *Jean Bodin and the Rise of Absolutist Theory* (Cambridge, 1973).

[24] J. Bodin, *Les Six Livres de la République* (Paris, 1576; Geneva, 1961 reprint), 1. My translation.

[25] As Nannerl Keohane has argued most eloquently about Bodin's work, 'his discussion of certain limitations on the sovereign appears at first glance to be inconsistent . . . In fact, these limitations are essential parts of the theory itself.' N. Keohane, *Philosophy and the State in France from the Renaissance to the Enlightenment* (Princeton, 1980), 71.

[26] Bodin, *République*: definition of sovereignty—122; lawmaking—221; contracts—152–3; primacy of divine and natural law—133.

be, indivisible, inalienable, and perpetual. This definition became normative in Western European political discourse, among authors as varied as John Locke and Robert Filmer. The term 'sovereign state,' that is a political entity constructed around a central government possessed of unlimited lawmaking authority, evolved from Bodin's principles. The enormous shift in emphasis toward the central political unit implied an assumed commonality of identity between that unit's responsibilities and the stewardship of the *res publica*. Royal propagandists then sought to make the *res publica* coterminous with the state, that is, the central government, that is, the king. Bodin's own position was more subtle, and other writers of his time—first the Huguenots of the 1570s and then the radical Catholics of the 1580s and 1590s—took up on it: the preservation of the *res publica* was the purpose of kingship. That argument, of course, leads to the assumption that the *res publica* is separate from and above the kingship, an argument Bodin himself does not really make, but one that contemporary philosophers like Etienne Pasquier or François Hotman would use.

Bodin's arguments rested on assumptions radically different from those of traditional French politics. He argued that positive (man-made) law must come from one source, the state, which, in France, meant the king. In this sixteenth-century definition of kingship, the king did not discover the law, as he had in medieval political theory, he made it. Bodin believed that it was the purpose of the law to regulate the *res publica*, the things held in common by the 'several households' (*plusieurs mesnages*) that made up the commonwealth, that is, those things shared by the several households that constituted it. Society consisted of a mixture of these public things—regulated by law, provided by the state—and private things, regulated in a different way, by divine, natural, and fundamental laws. Customary law provided the knowable outlines of these regulations of the private sphere.

Bodin's identification of lawmaking with sovereignty paralleled remarks made by chancellor Michel de l'Hôpital to the Parlement of Paris in the 1560s; his theoretical emphasis on legislative kingship also paralleled real developments in the sixteenth-century monarchy. Francis I vastly increased the scope and volume of royal legislation. In both practical and theoretical terms, the French monarchy shifted sharply from its traditional medieval emphasis on the judicial role (as de l'Hôpital pointed out in another speech, unlike the seals of other medieval kings, that of the King of France showed him sitting in judgment, not sitting on a war horse) to this new theoretical and practical emphasis on legislative action: making law. The 1539 edict of Villars-Coterets, in which Francis I mandated the use of French in all courts, should alert us to the vast new scope of royal legislation, and to the king's efforts to create cultural unity within his kingdom.[27]

De l'Hôpital shared Bodin's perspective on the centrality of lawmaking to kingship. Speaking to the Estates General of 1560, he argued:

> the subjects . . . [owe the king] true obedience, which is to guard his true and perpetual commandments, that is, his laws, edicts, and ordinances, and not wishing to make themselves equal to him, by dispensing themselves from the said laws and ordinances, to which all must obey, and to which they are subject, except the king alone.

Yet de l'Hôpital admitted the king's obligation to obey Divine law and recognized that the laws of men (i.e., those made by the king) could not 'change or silence the laws of nature.'[28]

This exception for divine and natural laws, as well as Bodin's similar beliefs about so-called fundamental laws (such as the inalienability of Crown lands, made a fundamental law by the Edict of Moulins in 1566), had profound practical consequences for state development. In a political society in which the position of elites received fundamental protection from their rights and privileges, duly guaranteed by a contract with their prince, the idea that the king had to keep his contracts (because he had to keep the Ninth Commandment) meant that his so-called absolute lawmaking ability rarely threatened the position of anyone of real importance in society. Until the eighteenth century, the sacrality of kingship, evident in every aspect of French ceremonial life, gave elites strong confidence in protections sanctified by divine law. The desacralization of the monarchy in the eighteenth century thus had profoundly destabilizing effects, because it undermined the very foundation of walls of privilege that protected elites. They could no longer accept their position as citizens without sovereignty, to borrow Daniel Gordon's apt description.[29] A desacralized king (and kingship) could not be relied upon to respect divine law, particularly because contraventions of divine law carried no temporal sanctions on the king himself.

[27] Prior to 1539, many southern courts used Occitan; the Parlement of Toulouse used Latin.

[28] R. Descimon (ed.), *Discours pour la majorité de Charles IX* (Paris, 1993).

[29] D. Gordon, *Citizens without Sovereignty* (Cambridge, MA, 1993).

Eighteenth-century elites wanted surer protection; they wanted protection of their property by means of positive law that would bind *everyone*, including the king. In short, they wanted control of the legislative process, thus stewardship of the *res publica*, as their *cahiers de doléances* for the Estates General of 1789 make abundantly clear.

Property, Taxes, and State Building through Louis XIV

The King of France theoretically had a greater range of prerogative than his English counterpart, especially in his ability to levy taxation.[30] Yet Bodin and other political theorists always believed taxation rested on some form of consent, because taxation without consent represented a violation of God's law (i.e., it was theft). The royal government explicitly accepted this view in the *pays d'Etats* and implicitly accepted it for the *pays d'élection*, because it always referred to the mythical vote of the *taille* by the Estates General of 1439 as the justification for that tax. The government even explicitly accepted this position in the great reforming ordinance of Orléans issued by the king in response to the Estates General of Orléans (1560), and it sought votes by the Estates General of 1560 and 1576 for new taxes.[31]

In the *pays d'Etats* (areas with Estates), provinces such as Brittany or Languedoc, the king always sought a specific vote by the Estates before levying a tax. He never introduced into these provinces the pre-existing taxes levied elsewhere in the kingdom; in Brittany, for example, which legally became part of France between 1491 and 1532, the king never sought to introduce the *taille*, the salt tax or the indirect taxes then levied elsewhere in the realm. Breton privileges, guaranteed by contract (and, in their case, by a specific treaty signed by Francis I and by the Estates of Brittany in 1532), would not allow the king to do so. Even in the so-called absolute realm of taxation, therefore, the King of France had significant restrictions on his freedom of action. He had little choice but to consult with elite opinion about tax policy.

[30] P. Campbell, *The Ancien Regime* (London, 1990), offers interesting comparative insights into this question; in England, political discourse called these royal lawmaking powers the prerogative.

[31] The *tailles* fell primarily on land, but the local tax assessors—selected by the villagers themselves—also considered other forms of wealth.

The administrative diversity of France represented an intelligent compromise with the divergent local and regional political (and socio-economic) realities. France did develop a much higher level of institutional integration between the sixteenth and eighteenth centuries, but full-scale integration would have been political suicide. France achieved institutional integrity only in the sense that it had a few integrationist principles on which all agreed—for example, that the king was the sole source of man-made law—and in that the regional manifestations of diversity, such as regional Parlements, obtained their legitimacy from the king. French kings did not try to impose a single set of laws on their kingdom—the great redactions of French law in the late 1660s, for example, made no effort whatsoever to overturn the customary laws of Normandy, Brittany or any other province. The king stuck to his accepted realm of prerogatives: diplomacy, military affairs, civil order, royal demesnes, and, to a lesser degree, such elements of the *res publica* as woodlands. Above all, royal ordinances confined themselves to administrative procedure within the royal bureaucracy. Even the revolutionary 1695 imposition of the capitation, levied on all lay Frenchmen, betrayed this bias: the list of 22 classes of taxpayers consisted overwhelmingly of individual enumerations of the obligations of royal officials holding given offices or commissions.

The fundamental attribute of 'absolute power' as Bodin or any other early-modern Frenchman would define it, was the king's unlimited power to make positive (man-made) law. Everyone accepted the king's unique ability to make law, yet courts everywhere in France effectively made law all the time. They did so in precisely the same manner as English courts: by issuing rulings related to local customary law. Interpretation of custom easily segued into lawmaking, a constant complaint of users of French courts.[32] Virtually every European polity relied on custom for its most important civil jurisprudence: customary law regulated property exchange in almost every case. Kings, whether theoretically absolute in their lawmaking ability

[32] Historians are about to revise completely the long-accepted model of royal legislative sovereignty. D. Parker, 'Sovereignty, Absolutism, and the Function of the Law in Seventeenth-Century France,' *Past and Present*, 122 (1989): 36–74, and Z. Schneider, 'Social Order and the State: Local Courts in the France of Louis XIV' (Ph.D. diss., 1997, Georgetown Univ.). Parker's new book, *Class and State in Ancien Régime France. The Road to Modernity?* (London and New York, 1996), reached me only after I had finished this essay. All readers interested in these matters will want to consult it.

or not, could *not* change these customs.[33] The ambiguity of customary laws, of course, allowed courts the discretionary power to intervene; as royal courts coopted seigneurial ones, that element of state power represented by the royal government did increase its ability to regulate property transfer, albeit within limits prescribed by the community itself. Royal officials used this power to mediate successions and, through their power to interpret customary laws, to take control of local land markets. At least in Normandy, local judges consistently manipulated tutelary and testamentary arrangements to enable them and their allies to buy up the land of those unfortunate enough to end up in courts.[34] Moreover, the cooptation of seigneurial courts took place above all at the level of personnel; that is, seigneurial judges came overwhelmingly from among lawyers practicing in royal courts and from among petty royal judges. Whatever the source of authority of a given court—a royal viscounty or the seigneurial court of the duke of Longueville, to cite a Norman case—a tight-knit circle of specific individuals administered its 'justice.'

Any discussion of early-modern European polities must emphasize that the fundamental regulation of property within the community lay in the hands of the community itself, through norms it established by means of its customary law. At no time did a central political entity seek to impose such norms, a sharp contrast to the situation in Russia (see the Kivelson essay). The strongest central political units, such as the French monarchy, did supervise the redaction of the customs, as in sixteenth-century France, but the extensive documentation about those legislative commissions—made up overwhelmingly of local judges (usually royal ones) and of local lawyers—does not contain many complaints about royal interference with or abrogation of local custom. Comparisons of the sixteenth-century redactions with earlier ones from the same provinces suggest overwhelming levels of continuity.

These political entities divided the public sphere—the *res publica*—which theory and practice increasingly consigned into the hands of the central state, and the private sphere, whose rules emanated from the community itself (although, after 1650, at least in France, the agents of the central state enforced these rules). The drive of elites to assure their control over the lawmaking process was a

[33] Louis XIV gave closer scrutiny to the marriages of titled nobles than most kings, thus getting some control over that fundamental form of property transfer.

[34] Schneider, 'Local Courts,' chaps 3 and 8. In effect, local judges made the law by interpreting custom, and then took advantage of their own rulings.

fundamental reality of early-modern Western European state development. The increased interference of the agents of the central state in the *private* sphere—that is, in the transfer and regulation of property—made control over the lawmaking functions of that central state absolutely essential for elites. The twin abiding fears of propertied elites were the threat of civil disorder to property, which dominated their views, for obvious reasons, in the sixteenth and early seventeenth centuries, and the threat of increased taxation. Once the internal disorders had calmed down, in France, by the time of Louis XIV, the real threat came from taxation, as the central state vastly increased its financial demands on society to pay for war. The obsession with order so typical of the sixteenth and seventeenth centuries shifted toward concerns about the central government itself in the eighteenth century, although arguably later in France than in England and the United Provinces.

All of these developments flowed naturally from the definitional parameters established by Bodin and his successors, and from the course of events themselves. The connection among war, taxation, and property rights literally forced the hand of elites on the lawmaking front. The issue became all the more critical because of Western European society's dramatic definitional transformation with respect to the meanings of property itself. Everywhere traditional forms of property came under attack as west European elites struggled toward a unified definition of property. Different societies attained this unified definition, one that had to abolish feudal property and redefine that of the church, at different times; in England and the United Provinces, this shift had taken place by the middle of the seventeenth century, although by no means did local society entirely abandon its traditional mores.[35]

The first great shift in property rights came in the sixteenth century, when central states everywhere began to confiscate church property in the name of the *res publica*. Rulers such as Henry VIII and the German Protestants confiscated in the name of the commonwealth and redistributed the land to elites, but Catholic rulers, such as the Kings of France and Spain, also confiscated or mortgaged church property to help preserve the *res publica*. In France, the king used as his justification the need to combat Protestantism. Peasant rebels, such as the Germans of 1525, viewed church property, includ-

[35] For one example among many of the persistence of the common people's attitudes toward law in England, see R. Manning, *Hunters and Poachers* (Oxford, 1993).

ing the tithe, as community property, to be spent on behalf of the community. In such a situation, the wonder was not that the church lost so much property (in 1520, it owned 22% of the land in England and an even higher percentage in German lands), but that it kept so much. In the seventeenth century, it was the turn of feudal property in England; in 1789, the French state abolished feudal property and confiscated the remaining church property to pay off state debts, relying on the premise that church property belonged to the *res publica*.

Property lay at the heart of the struggle over state finances. The vastly more expensive military establishments of the sixteenth through eighteenth centuries demanded much higher levels of taxation.[36] The government of Francis I recognized the necessity for more professional financial management by the 1520s; he completely reordered the financial system between 1523 and 1545. Francis, like other rulers of his time in Western Europe, sought out new sources of revenue and more efficient mechanisms for *state* finance. Just as there was a 'financial revolution' in the Habsburg (really Burgundian) Netherlands in the early sixteenth century, so, too, there was a revolutionary shift in France.[37] Francis I made four major changes: (1) he began the systematic royal sale of offices (standardizing a pre-existing practice); (2) he created an entirely new financial administration, clearly separating state and royal finances and establishing much more effective lines of authority and oversight; (3) he initiated new methods of borrowing, getting away from the over-reliance on the personal credit of the chief royal financial officials; and (4) he vastly increased the monarchy's reliance on foreign capital.

Henry II (1547–59) pushed all of his father's policies to new limits. With respect to the annuities guaranteed by the revenues of the city of Paris (created in 1522), for example, he issued a capital value of over 6 million *livres* in 12 years, as against the 0.72 million issued by his father in 25 years. Henry created new courts, such as

[36] See, for example, C. Tilly, *Coercion, Capital, and European State, 990–1990* (Cambridge, MA, 1990), Table 3.2 and the surrounding text, and Le Roy Ladurie, *L'Etat royal*, pp. 48–53. Le Roy Ladurie estimates the silver tonnage amassed by French taxation to have risen from about 100 to 135 tons in the time of Louis XI to 190 tons under Henry II, then to 1,000 tons under Mazarin and to 1,600 tons under Louis XIV. These figures may not be entirely accurate, but they do give a reasonable sense of order of magnitude.

[37] J. Tracy, *A Financial Revolution in the Habsburg Netherlands* (Berkeley, 1985).

the Parlement of Brittany and the country-wide presidials (intermediate courts), selling the offices for millions more; he established a centralized system of borrowing money from foreigners at the fairs of Lyon, the so-called *Grand Parti de Lyon*. Henry's policies did not succeed in the short run—the pressure of war finance led to the bankruptcy of the *Grand Parti* in 1557—but these policies did take root for the long run. Reorganized financial syndicates took the place of the 1557 failed one, this time securing their loans to the king directly from tax revenues by themselves becoming the tax farmers. In the early seventeenth century, the syndicate shifted from Italian to French hands; in time, the syndication of individual tax farms—like the salt tax—led to the creation of a single tax farm syndicate, the General Tax Farm, that had control, save for some brief interludes, of almost all French indirect taxation and royal monopolies from the time of Colbert onward.

Francis I and Henry II both added substantial surtaxes to the regular direct levies, again establishing a precedent their successors would follow. Henry III (1574–89) and Louis XIII (1610–43) levied particularly heavy direct taxes; in both cases, that policy led to financial ruin. Here again, the French case paralleled that of other Western European states. When Colbert set out to reduce French dependence on unreliable, difficult-to-collect direct taxes on the peasantry, he looked to Holland (and to the French *pays d'Etats*, such as Brittany) for an example. In those areas, he found a much greater reliance on indirect taxes, mainly on consumption. Starting with Colbert, and permanently into the eighteenth century, French state finance shifted sharply in this direction, with a preponderance of revenue coming from indirect, rather than direct taxation. In England, land tax peaked as percentage of revenue in 1696 (52%) and dropped steadily thereafter, to a mere 20% by the 1770s.[38]

Methods of taxation tell us much about the nature of states in the early-modern period. Among the European powers, only the United Provinces seems to have relied primarily on indirect taxes, mainly on consumption, in the sixteenth century. The other powers did increase indirect taxation between 1550 and 1630, but it remained second in importance to direct taxation. Many of these powers also relied on

[38] J. Brewer, *The Sinews of Power. War, Money, and the English State* (New York, 1989), figure 4.2. The French case is discussed in J. Collins, *The State in Early Modern France* (Cambridge, 1995).

state monopolies, especially the sale of salt (which produced substantial income in both Austria and France) and, later, tobacco. At the end of the seventeenth century, however, France and England went over to the Dutch model, relying more heavily on indirect taxation (and state monopolies) than on direct taxation. Austria lagged well behind the others, as the share of direct taxation in total revenue remained 59.4% as late as 1749, but it, too, changed policies in the late eighteenth century. By 1784, direct taxes produced only 41.9% of Austrian crown revenues.[39] The higher reliance on indirect taxation in the most advanced economies surely was not coincidental.

England and Holland also evolved excellent systems of state credit, in each case guaranteed by revenues in the control of representative assemblies. That system was already in place in the Low Countries in the middle of the sixteenth century, and came into full force in England in 1694. France resembled its two rivals in its extensive use of indirect taxation, but it had to rely on a much less satisfactory system of state credit, one of its main disadvantages in the wars of the eighteenth century.[40] In Western Europe, taxation remained primarily a matter for accommodation between ruler and ruled, even in France, which had the least consultative system. Unlike the situation in China, in Europe, the Church, not the state, exacted a tribute (the tithe) in kind; efforts to use such a system in state finance, often proposed in eighteenth-century France, invariably met with profound hostility from elites.

In France, the heavy reliance on indirect taxation and the monopolies (leased together to the tax farmers), gave those who dominated the General Tax Farm all the more leverage because such revenues were not collected by the government itself. The General Tax Farm, a semi-private corporation, collected the largest share of

[39] P.G.M. Dickson, *Finance and Government under Maria Theresa 1740–1780* (Oxford, 1987), table 3.6. In the seventeenth century, the Spanish monarchy similarly relied most heavily on direct taxes in the kingdom of Naples: A Calabria, *The Cost of Empire* (Cambridge, 1991), figure 3.3. Calabria shows an important shift around 1600; direct taxation in Naples dropped by stages from 80% of resources in 1550 to 55% between 1616 and 1638.

[40] R. Huang, *Taxation in Sixteenth-Century Ming China* (Cambridge, 1974), indicates that the Chinese state had 'no regular means of obtaining credit' in the fifteenth and sixteenth centuries. China resembled sixteenth-century European states in its heavy reliance on direct taxes (grain tribute) and on a salt monopoly. On French credit problems, see J. Riley, *The Seven Years' War and the Old Regime in France* (Princeton, 1986).

government revenue and, not incidentally, also provided the largest single source of employment in the country.[41] Many innovations associated with the modern state began with this semi-private entity; for example, in the late eighteenth century, the General Tax Farm created a system of retirement annuities for its employees.

The number of French financial officials grew exponentially in the sixteenth and seventeenth centuries; tens of thousands of people worked part-time for the system and thousands more held permanent posts. More people meant more siphoning off of money into payments to royal officials, greater possibilities for tax exemption for officers (and their families), more corruption in local tax assessments. More people also meant greater local integration into the central state: as Roger Doucet long ago noted, the expansion of the royal administration gave the monarchy a broad and solid base of support within the country.[42] The military provided a similar source of employment for thousands of nobles.

The expansion of that army, of course, stands as the most obvious symbol of the rise of the central state's power. Francis I rarely fielded 30,000 men at a time, whereas Louis XIV could raise ten to twelve times that many. The key shift in European armies took place in the seventeenth century, whether or not one accepts that shift as a 'military revolution.'[43] In France, the transformation took place in two key stages: the end of the *compagnies d'ordonnance* in the 1620s, and their replacement by the regimental system; and the reforms of Louvois, creating a far more standardized and centralized military apparatus. The second set of reforms is much better known, thanks to the work of generations of French military historians, but we know almost nothing about the first change. The royal army created by Charles VII in 1445, the *compagnies d'ordonnance* (the companies created by the ordinance), consisted of cavalry companies that contained, in theory, 100 lances of four men per lance. In practice, these companies were little more than private units at the beck and call of their commander; in most cases, the officers and most of the lancers were relatives or noble clients of the commander. When he died, if he did not have a male relative of appropriate age and rank to succeed him, the company often disbanded. These companies had an alarming

[41] Brewer, *Sinews of Power*, table 3.4, shows the Excise house increased its share of government revenue employees from 47 to 63% between 1716 and 1780.

[42] R. Doucet, *Les institutions de la France au XVI siècle* (Paris, 1948), 2 vols.

[43] G. Parker, *The Military Revolution. Military Innovation and the Rise of the West, 1500–1800* (Cambridge, 1988).

tendency to be loyal to the commander, rather than to the king. In the 1620s, the companies ceased to exist; regiments took their place. The regimental structure still relied heavily on the noble clientage network—and would continue to do so until the end of the Old Regime—but the royal government had much greater control over the finances and administration of the new units. The conflicts between the intendants of the armies and the army administration and the noble commanders—the most famous example is the quarrel between Louvois, Louis XIV's War Minister and the viscount of Turenne, commander of the royal army—alert us to the fact that the army had begun to be more loyal to the king than to unit commanders. After the Fronde (a series of revolts between 1648 and 1653), no royal unit commander ever again successfully used his force against the royal government.

By the time Louis XIV took personal power in France (1661), the French state had broad-based support in all three key areas of royal government: military, judicial, and financial. French elites, whether noble or commoner, owned offices in the government, provided it with firm support, and shared important interests with it. These elites, for example, owned a substantial portion of the public debt, so they had just as much interest in timely payment of taxes as did the king. The capital value of royal offices ran into the hundreds of millions of *livres*, so the stability of the government, and hence of the value of its offices, was of the greatest possible importance to all office holders and their families. The last great general disturbance in the kingdom, the Fronde, broke out precisely because of a royal threat to the capital value of judicial offices.

The many sides of the Fronde point the way to an understanding of the French state in the middle of the seventeenth century and after. The first Fronde broke out because the government issued an edict compromising the capital value of royal offices; the government rescinded the edict and never again threatened the value of offices in this way. The second Fronde, the Fronde of the Princes, broke out as a quarrel within the royal family, much as royal minorities had led to such quarrels in 1561–62 and 1610–17. In all three cases, the same family—Condé branch of the Bourbon house—started the problem. In all three cases, they sought a military solution to their goal of capturing control of the state. Here we must emphasize that the Fronde certainly did *not* represent an effort by a disgruntled aristocracy to return to some Golden Age of the nobility; the Prince of Condé wanted control of the central state, not its weakening. In

1715, by way of contrast, the princes of the blood did not rebel militarily during the royal minority; instead, they sought to take control of the royal ministries by means of a conciliar system designed to maintain the government but to wrest control of its decision-making from the hands of the ministers, placing it instead in the hands of the high nobility.

The year 1649—military revolt, 1715—administrative coup: there we have a clear-cut demonstration of the changed nature of the French state by the early eighteenth century. The traditional nobility still served in the military under Louis XIV (if anything, their numbers increased because of the king's emphasis on noble military service), but they could no longer use their military experience and connections to start a provincial revolt, even under a royal minority. The nobility had moved to Paris and Versailles and had given itself wholeheartedly over to Court society. In the provinces, where early seventeenth-century kings had played off the military nobility against the robe nobility (judicial officers), eighteenth-century kings had to deal directly and uniquely with the latter, many of whom had obtained titles from the Crown in the mid to late seventeenth century. Judicial officers did not plot military rebellions; they subtly subverted royal authority by means of the legal system. In time, the stalemate between the judicial officers and the royal ministries created a governmental crisis, one resolved only by the French Revolution.[44] The ministers wanted a more *dirigiste* solution to the problems of French government and society, whereas the judges feared the repercussions of an overmighty central government. Their weak attachment to principles reminds one of the debates of the 1580s and 1590s; René de Maupeou, First President of the Parlement of Paris in 1766, ardent defender of its privileges, became a royal minister shortly thereafter and convinced Louis XV to abolish the Parlements.

King and Nation in the Seventeenth and Eighteenth Centuries

The seventeenth- and eighteenth-century French monarchy made unparalleled use of its authority to create cultural hegemony in the

[44] The complex intertwining of ministers and judges, and the constant shifts in alliances as ministers came and went, are documented in two excellent new books: J. Rogister, *Politics and the Parlement of Paris under Louis XV, 1754–1774* (Cambridge, 1994) and J. Swann, *Louis XV and the Parlement of Paris* (Cambridge, 1995).

territory it ruled. Those efforts focused on the nobility in the seventeenth century. Court society, above all, sought to tame the nobility in a socio-cultural sense. The effort worked not because of any miraculously Machiavellian machinations on Louis XIV's part, but because a wide range of social, cultural, and economic factors pointed in the direction of the new sensibilities. Montaigne did not need the Court to tell him that it was more pleasant to eat off porcelain than off a trencher of bread; he had only to experience porcelain ware in Italy to want some for his table. Taste in food changed dramatically in the seventeenth and eighteenth centuries; cuisine relied now on butter, on new foods and beverages (coffee, chocolate, sugar), on a wider range of vegetables, and, in time, on the essence-based sauces so familiar to us today. With the new table ware, new utensils (like forks), and new food, came a new etiquette of the table. As money spread more evenly through society, refinement came to take on a greater and greater place in the establishment of the social hierarchy.

A wide range of institutions sought to regulate behavior. The churches in all Western European countries stepped up efforts to establish doctrinal unity and to make popular behavior conform to religious norms. These efforts had a mixed success at best. They did succeed in getting people to marry in churches before living together (reversing an immemorial pattern, at least in France) but they could not make city workers go to Mass instead of to the tavern. Churches, like governments, sought to get people to internalize certain values, which reduced the level of required behavioral coercion. The extensive historiography on the issue of control and the extremely varied response of society to that control, suggests that everywhere society accepted those elements of control that it judged useful and rejected others. No more than the Catholic church, the government simply could not impose its will in this area, but it did give direction and unity to a movement much to its advantage. In France, perhaps the best example of an effective use of such control at the elite level was the Académie Française, founded by Richelieu in the 1630s to oversee French culture. It issued its official dictionary in the 1690s. Through the Académie, the state obtained some control over the French language at a critical time in its development, at a moment when, all over Europe, language came to be identified with nation.[45]

[45] A.-M. Mercier Faivre, 'La nation par la langue: philologie, nationalisme et nation dans l'Europe du dix-huitième siècle,' in *Nations and Nationalisms: France, Britain, Ireland and the Eighteenth-century Context*, ed. M. O'Dea and K. Whelan (Oxford, 1995), 161–80.

In the eighteenth century, the king and the people thus both approached the concept of nation in new ways. The people came to associate nation with a group having a shared history and language, as opposed merely to individuals living in a geographic region ruled by a given prince (in their case, the King of France). The king gradually came to identify his interests with those of the nation, not those of the nation with his own; the latter underwent its last, desperate excesses during the War of the Spanish Succession. Louis XIV certainly had good reasons to want to expand his eastern boundaries to protect Paris and the heart of the kingdom, but his personal obsession with the restoration of the 'true' France, i.e., one that included Flanders, and his strong sense of family obligation played central roles in his foreign policy. That personal element in foreign policy tended to die out in the eighteenth century, with its most pathetic, almost comical final gasp the ill-fated War of the Polish Succession, in which Louis XV defended the rights of his father-in-law, Stanislas Lesczynski, to the Polish throne. Even there, a French candidate for the Polish throne was an old refrain, a long-standing element of a foreign policy not at all rooted in dynastic issues.

This foreign policy initiative points us in the direction of France's consonance with political developments in the Eurasian world between 1400 and 1800 and with its dissonance as well. Like many other territorial entities of that period, France in 1400 or 1500 was an amalgam of nation, state, empire, and family property. These elements did not disappear overnight. In France, the imperial element took two paths; internally, it meant a hegemonic imposition of French, specifically Parisian culture on the entire geographic area ruled by the King of France. The state allied with the Catholic church and with elites to establish this cultural hegemony over the mass of the population. In a political sense, French administrative integration led to territorial integration, allowing the imperial aspect of French government to become less pronounced. In time, this imperial impulse shifted overseas, where it ever retained a cultural element.

The political demise of the family corporation, and the concomitant transmogrification of the imperial element of French politics, left two key elements of the original, fifteenth-century kingdom of France: the nation and the state. The state evolved clearly to mean the central state, both in practical and theoretical terms. After Bodin, there could be no more question on the theoretical level that 'state' meant the central government. In a practical sense, the royal central government kept up a constant attack on local and regional institutions, seeking less to destroy them than to coopt them. In the 1560s, for example, the king shifted jurisdiction in most urban cases away from municipalities and gave them to royal officers (provosts, bailiffs, seneschals). In the seventeenth century, in many French towns, like Nantes, leading royal officials *became* the mayors, duly elected by the citizens. Similarly, in the seigneurial countryside, the king did not abolish the courts, but his officials slowly, almost insidiously took over the court system. They did so not by following some royal directive, but by following the logic of political, economic, and social forces then on the ground.

By the turn of the eighteenth century, the various elements of the royal administration came increasingly to resemble bureaucracies, in the modern sense. Patronage still played an overwhelmingly powerful role, to be sure, but the increased routinization and professionalization of the ministries is evident by the 1720s, if not earlier. The most modern of all elements of this bureaucracy was probably its semi-private segment, the General Tax Farm. John Brewer has suggested that precisely the same thing went on in England, and one could point to similar developments in the Austrian lands, so the trend in this matter extended beyond France.

In the eighteenth century, the final element of the fifteenth-century French quadrille, the nation, stepped forward to share center stage. Throughout the century, theorists and jurists alike spoke of the 'nation'; the *cahiers de doléances* of 1789, those of all three orders, invariably referred to the 'nation.' Many of them make it the source of all sovereignty, taking up the argument proffered by the Parlement of Paris in the 1760s. Again and again, the *cahiers* ask for God's blessing on the nation and the king, invariably in that order. The message was clear, even before the Revolution broke out: the nation was *above* the king. The property owners, that is, those with the real power in French society, had never doubted that the king was merely the prime defender of order, but the shift in focus in the eighteenth century shows us that elites, in France as elsewhere in Western Europe, had come to view the government itself as the prime threat to their property. Early-modern European state building evolved in response to that changed dynamic, one made possible by the substantial modification of the early multiple identities of their political units. The power of the state element of the nation-state simply had to be curbed by the nation; that, as much as any specific crisis, is what led to the French Revolution and to modern European political life.

Merciful Father, Impersonal State: Russian Autocracy in Comparative Perspective

VALERIE KIVELSON

Comparative analyses traditionally have done Russian history no favors. Invidious comparisons have situated Russia firmly in a context of backwardness relative to the West. The term 'medieval' customarily applies to Russia until the era of Peter the Great, that is, until the early eighteenth century, and even the least condemnatory scholars point out similarities between Muscovite Russia of the fourteenth through seventeenth centuries and early medieval tribal formations of northern Europe. Along with 'backwardness,' comparative history has customarily found in Russia an example of extraordinarily oppressive autocratic despotism, while at the same time, and somewhat contradictorily, decrying the incompetence and rampant corruption of the central state apparatus. These and other unflattering comparative generalizations arose in the observations of Western travellers who recorded their impressions of Russia in the early modern period and have continued in the writings of scholars and journalists to this day.[1]

This unrelieved condemnation has not gone unchallenged, of course. Many historians have felt uncomfortable with purely negative comparisons, and various attempts to rectify the picture have emerged. Such correctives range from the Slavophiles' and Eurasianists' efforts to celebrate Russian particularism, to more anthropologically inclined scholars' attempts to understand Muscovite customs in their own context. Victor Lieberman's analytical structure, however, allows for a very welcome and much broader way to understand Muscovite Russia in a Eurasian framework. First, it is a curious experience for a Russianist to find Russia exemplifying a 'Western' rather than an 'Eastern' variant, in this broadened comparative spectrum. Second, by acknowledging the areas of Western European

[1] Marshall T. Poe discusses these Western myths about Russia in his ' "Russian Despotism": the Origins and Dissemination of an Early Modern Commonplace,' (Ph.D. dissertation, University of California, Berkeley, 1993).

exceptionalism, Lieberman allows for spheres of profound difference, while at the same time seeking alternate areas of focus that instead highlight similarity. This generous revisionism allows the significant similarities to rise to the fore, leading to the third and most welcome contribution of this very new comparative setting. Lieberman's formulation illuminates the aspects of Muscovite Russia that constituted a typically early modern, rather than 'primitive,' 'barbaric' or 'backward' state formation. Like its contemporaries east and west, Muscovy launched integrative, universalizing cultural programs, bureaucratizing, centralizing, administrative growth, and central state negotiation and alliance with local elites.[2] As in other early modern states, all of these developments contributed to state-centralization, concentrating increasing power in the hands of the monarch.

Focusing on two particular dimensions of early modern Russian state-building, I would like to follow Lieberman's expansive approach, albeit on a much narrower scale, and examine the Russian state's construction of an effective administrative machine and its bids for legitimacy over the course of a broad swath of time, from Kievan Rus' to the beginning of the Imperial period, that is, from about the tenth to the early eighteenth century. In conjunction with this investigation of the rise of the Russian state, I will also consider the tools and methods contributing to the state's efficacy, on the one hand, and the various factors limiting its ability to penetrate and control society on the other.

Kiev Rus', the first site of a Russian state and Lieberman's 'classical' first center, comparable to Pagan or Angkor, figures in later Russian historical conceptions as the 'Golden Age' model from which later eras descended, both in the sense of heritage and of diminution. Kiev flourished due to a fortunate combination of its location on

[2] I think it is appropriate to apply the term 'bureaucratic' to Russian administrative practices from the mid- or late-sixteenth century on. Although clearly not yet reaching the heights of Weberian bureaucratic development that the nineteenth century would produce, Muscovite and Imperial Russian administrations fit many of Weber's definitions for bureaucratic structures. They were characterized by regularized procedure, specialized and highly trained staffs, explicitly specified hierarchies and posts, distinct jurisdictions and functions (albeit with significant grey zones and areas of overlap), and constant reference to written norms, records, and orders. For a thought-provoking discussion of this issue, see Borivoj Plavsic, 'Seventeenth-Century Chanceries and their Staffs,' in Walter McKenzie Pintner and Don Karl Rowney (eds), *Russian Officialdom: The Bureaucratization of Russian Society from the Seventeenth to the Twentieth Century* (Chapel Hill, 1980), 21–45.

and participation in lucrative international trade routes, its internal position as the spiritual and manufacturing center of all the Rus' principalities, and its willingness to participate in the cultural richness brought to it through its international contacts.[3] The great Kievan state, particularly during the reigns of Grand Prince Vladimir, who brought Christianity to Rus' in 988, and his son Iaroslav the Wise, who propagated it, governed a vast 'empire,' to use George Vernadsky's term, spanning from the Volga to the Dniester and from Novgorod in the Northwest to the Black Sea in the south. The grand princes of Kiev are credited with enacting the first law codes, undertaking enormous building and education projects in conjunction with the burgeoning Orthodox Church, supervising lucrative international trade and conducting complex international relations, mainly through the mediation of their many marriageable daughters and sisters, with their brother-princes and kings throughout the Eurasian world. The Kievan era has been highly romanticized in historical hindsight as an age of political pluralism, commercial vibrancy, exuberant, life-affirming Christianity, cosmopolitanism, and cultural receptivity.[4]

More recent revisionist approaches have seriously undermined many aspects of this image of the Kievan Golden Age. Not only was the putative period of greatness ludicrously short—lasting at most the span of two princely reigns before lapsing again into the chronic interprincely warfare that characterized the Kievan and later appanage eras—but the unity, the administrative control, and even the imperial ambitions of the so-called state apparatus tend to evaporate under closer scrutiny. The grand princes of Kiev appear to have had little or no conception of a state as a bounded territorial

[3] On Kiev's economic role, see David B. Miller, 'The Kievan Principality in the Century Before the Mongol Invasion: An Inquiry into recent Research and Interpretation,' *Harvard Ukrainian Studies* 10 (1986): 215–40; Thomas S. Noonan, 'The Flourishing of Kiev's International and Domestic Trade, ca. 1100–ca. 1240,' in I.S. Koropeckyj (ed.), *Ukrainian Economic History: Interpretive Essays* (Cambridge: Harvard Ukrainian Institute, 1991), 102–46. On its spiritual role see Omeljan Pritsak, 'Kiev and All Rus': The Fate of a Sacral Idea,' *Harvard Ukrainian Studies* 10 (1986): 279–300. I cannot comment on the relative importance of these various factors, nor will I hazard any guesses about demographic growth or decline. Population figures for Russia are too unreliable to put to meaningful use until the seventeenth century. The best work on Muscovite demography is Ia. E. Vodarskii, *Naselenie Rossii v kontse XVII–nachale XVIII veka (Chislennost', soslovno-klassovyi sostav, razmeshchenie* (Moscow, 1977). For vastly inflated figures for the early period, see George Vernadsky, *Kievan Russia* (New Haven and London: Yale University Press, 1948).

[4] Vernadsky, *Kievan Russia*.

unit governed by a single sovereign entity, aspiring to administer, tax and control its people. Rather, the territory of the Kievan polity remained amorphous and fluid. The concept and title of 'grand prince' of a unitary Kievan realm entered Kievan vocabulary and political consciousness slowly, as an import from Byzantium.[5] The polity itself (if there was one) was constituted imprecisely around a loosely defined people ('the Rus') and was ruled piecemeal by interconnected competing and conflicting branches of the princely line. Grand princely deathbed testaments demonstrate that the goal of princely politics remained personal, familial, rather than encompassing any broader aspirations toward unified sovereignty or territorial rule. After struggling against brothers and cousins throughout his rule, each successive grand prince lovingly divided his realm among his sons upon his death, commending them to the protection of their mother and eldest brother, optimistically entreating them to love one another and maintain peace.[6] Christianity contributed an important layer to the rhetoric and legitimation of princely rule, adding to the charismatic quality that both Scandinavian and Khazar traditions had lent the ruling dynasty.[7]

Fitting awkwardly, if at all, into any standard models available from Western history, Kiev shares much with the 'solar polities' of Southeast Asia, and this useful model illuminates much that is otherwise difficult to conceptualize about Kiev's political complexities.[8] In Kiev, however, sovereignty was divided not only among multiple princes but also among other empowered bodies, particularly the *vech'* or public assembly and the *druzhina* or princely retinue. Power was shared in complex ways, sometimes hierarchically, sometimes in nested nexuses, and most frequently in loosely defined and flexible ways which varied according to particular circumstances. The earli-

[5] On the late development of a concept of Kiev as a grand princely political entity, see Andrzej Poppe, 'Words that Serve the Authority: On the Title of "Grand Prince" in Kievan Rus',' *Acta Poloniae Historica* 60 (1989): 159–84; Pritsak, 'Kiev and All Rus': The Fate of a Sacral Idea,' 279–90.

[6] For the testaments, see Samuel Hazzard Cross and Olgerd P. Sherbowitz-Wetzor (trans. and ed.), *The Russian Primary Chronicle: Laurentian Text* (Cambridge, Massachusetts: The Medieval Academy of America, 1968; rprt of 1953 ed.), e.g. 142.

[7] Peter B. Golden, 'Aspects of the Nomadic Factor in the Economic Development of Kievan Rus',' in I.S. Koropeckyj (ed.), *Ukrainian Economic History: Interpretive Essays* (Cambridge: Harvard Ukrainian Research Institute, 1991); Hanak, W., 'Some Conflicting Aspects of Byzantine and Varangian Political and Religious Thought in Early Kievan Russia,' *Byzantinoslavica* 37 (1976): 46–55.

[8] Victor Lieberman, 'Transcending East–West Dichotomies,' this vol.

est Russian laws applied primarily to the grand princes' immediate dependants and retinue, only gradually extending, even in principle, to a broader population.

Where Rus' began or ended or whom it included were open questions. In its early years, the term Rus' evidently referred to a largely Scandinavian but inclusive and multiethnic trading/raiding corps, and only gradually came to refer to the largely Slavic inhabitants of the Russian lands.[9] As any nominal unity disintegrated in the appanage period, various parts of the territory split off, appropriating for themselves the name Rus' (as in Galicia), or discarding it altogether in favor of local titles (as in Volhynia).[10] Furthermore, with the adoption of Christianity, Rus' identified itself in both a universal Christian idiom and as a distinct and special entity, and its complicated relationship with Byzantium blurred its political and spiritual boundaries still more.[11] Kiev Rus', then, was far from a codified, territorial state entity, and rather formed around strategies of family enrichment and inheritance, bolstered by economic preeminence, Orthodoxy and cultural supremacy.

Concomitant with this absence of a state vision was an absence of regularized administration. The startling work of both Simon Franklin and I. Ia. Froianov demonstrates that the administration of Kiev Rus' elaborated minimal paperwork, if any. Official interactions only very rarely assumed written form, and when they did, the writing demonstrated ceremonial rather than communicative function. Franklin describes the use of written inter-princely treaties in ritual settings, where princes expressed a sense of betrayal by hurling parchments recording their 'cross-kissed oaths' at the betraying party. In this case the written artifact itself, rather than the information contained on it, was made to communicate a point. Documentary record keeping, on the other hand, essentially did not exist in the Kievan period.[12]

[9] Omeljan Pritsak, 'The Origin of Rus',' *Russian Review* 36 (1977): 249–73.

[10] Pritsak, 'Kiev and All Rus': The Fate of a Sacral Idea.'

[11] Ellen Hurwitz, 'Metropolitan Hilarion's Sermon on Law and Grace: Historical Consciousness in Kievan Rus',' *Russian History* 7 (1980): 322–33. The presence of universalist Christian elements in Rus' culture appears to serve more the integrative function that Lieberman describes than the function of consolidating elite privilege that R.I. Moore sees in Western Europe.

[12] Simon Franklin, 'Literacy and Documentation in Early Medieval Russia,' *Speculum* 60 (1985): 1–38; I.Ia. Froianov, *Kievskaia Rus': Ocherki sotsial'no-politicheskoi istorii* (Leningrad, 1980).

Muscovy, by contrast, emerged as the quintessential documentary state. From at least the late fifteenth century, censuses attempted to record the wealth and location of the entire population. From the mid-sixteenth century, lists governed the lives of Muscovites of all ranks, and standing on various lists determined the options open to any given individual.[13] Lists categorized military service status, genealogical seniority, honor, tax obligations, social estate, and geographic affiliation. Prodigious growth in the number, training, specialization and professionalization of a literate administrative staff characterized both the sixteenth and seventeenth centuries. From an informal, ad hoc system of minimal governance, consisting of armed and mounted princes and boyars backed by a tiny core of slave-clerks, the Muscovite administration burgeoned into a highly articulated, if not clearly differentiated, system of chancelleries (*prikazy*), staffed by full-time, generally hereditary clerks, schooled through practical, on-the-job training from childhood. The first few chancelleries formed in the first half of the sixteenth century: the *Posol'skii prikaz*, the Chancellery of Foreign Affairs, and the *Razriadnyi prikaz*, supervising the service obligations and remuneration due to members of the military service class. By the end of the seventeenth century, these modest departments had ballooned into a massive administrative establishment, with dozens of chancelleries, some of them ad hoc and temporary, many with overlapping or ill-defined jurisdictions, but all with highly hierarchical organization, large staffs, and extensively documented procedural guide-lines. The handful of clerks of the early sixteenth century had grown to hundreds by the end of the century and thousands by late in the next. According to Borivoj Plavsic's provocative thesis, the late Muscovite chancellery system worked far more efficiently and professionally than its Petrine successors, which diluted the humble but highly specialized clerical corps with rising parvenus from the service nobility, who achieved administrative posts through Peter's Table of Ranks.[14]

[13] Marshall T. Poe, 'Elite Service Registry in Muscovy, 1500–1700,' *Russian History* 21 (1994): 251–88.

[14] Plavsic, 'Seventeenth-Century Chanceries and their Staffs'; N.F. Demidova, 'Gosudarstvennyi apparat Rossii v XVII veke,' *Istoricheskie zapiski* 108 (1982): 109–55; N.V. Ustiugov, 'Evoliutsiia prikaznogo stroia russkogo gosudarstva v XVII v.,' in N.M. Druzhinin (ed.), *Absoliutizm v Rossii (XVII–XVIII vv.). Sbornik statei k semidesiatiletiiu so dnia rozhdeniia i sorokopiatiletiu nauchnoi i pedagogicheskoi deiatel'nosti B.B. Kafengauza* (Moscow, 1964), 134–67; A.A. Zimin, 'O slozhenii prikaznoi sistemy na Rusi,' in *Doklady i soobshcheniia Instituta Istorii (Akademii Nauk)* 3 (1955): 164–76.

The bureaucratization of Muscovy occurred in synchrony with that of the other Eurasian rim states that Lieberman discusses and was a typically early modern phenomenon, but Lieberman challenges us to go beyond that observation and to try to identify the origins and influences that provoked such parallel developments in such disparate areas. Did the growth of Russian state administration take place because of some interlinked causal impetus that encouraged bureaucratic development throughout Eurasia? Were the various proto-bureaucratic developments across the globe causally connected or simply chronologically coincidental? These big questions, I fear, cannot be answered, at least in the Russian case, where information on demography, disease, climate and so forth is sparse. More specific questions allow for clearer answers. Was Russian administrative growth inspired by ideas and models imported from Western, Eastern or Southern neighbors? Was it a reactive or defensive growth, designed to make first Muscovy and then Imperial Russia competitive with neighboring states? Was it, perhaps, an indigenous phenomenon, developing of necessity, dictated by the increasingly complex demands of administering an ever-expanding territorial mass with an ever-growing and increasingly diverse population? The answer to each of these questions is yes; Muscovite central administration grew in response to foreign military challenges, in imitation of Western models, and in consequence of its own international expansion, but no one of these explanations alone suffices to explain the rise of the Muscovite centralized state administration. Mutually reinforcing elements of each contributed to Muscovy's development, and none can be isolated from the others without simplifying and misrepresenting the historical process.

These issues have received some attention in the scholarly literature but have not, to my satisfaction, been resolved in any definitive way, mainly because the answers themselves are necessarily diverse. The Mongol conquest has served as the favorite explanation for the chasm between the glories of Kiev Rus' and the oppressive rigors of the Muscovite period. Every nasty Muscovite innovation, from the death penalty, to techniques of collective responsibility and mutual surveillance within communities, to the sequestering of elite women, to Russia's failure to share in the benefits of the Renaissance, is cheerfully attributed to the Mongol Yoke. Few of these claims hold up under serious scrutiny.[15]

[15] Charles J. Halperin, *Russia and the Golden Horde: The Mongol Impact on Medieval Russian History* (Bloomington: University of Indiana Press, 1985).

Regarding Mongol influence on state centralization and administrative practice, however, scholars have formulated a rather strong case. In general outline, the Mongols played an undeniable role in promoting the minor, backwater principality of Moscow over its rival principalities during the chaotic period of interprincely rivalry known as the Appanage Period. During the epoch of Mongol domination, the prince who was designated Grand Prince obtained his patent of rule from the Khan, first the Great Khan in Karakorum, later the local khan of the Golden Horde at Sarai. Although the grand princely title did not suffice to unify the warring princedoms in any significant way for several hundred years, the office of Grand Prince did confer on its holder, and consequently on his principality, some very concrete advantages. Primarily, the Grand Prince bore responsibility for collecting the taxes and tribute demanded by the Khan from all of the Rus' lands. This role as tax-collector afforded the Grand Prince and his minions opportunities to skim off the surface and to enrich themselves in the service of the Khan. Moreover, with an interest in maintaining the status of their revenue-collectors, the Mongols backed their designated Rus' representatives with military might, intervening directly when their chosen Grand Prince met internal opposition. For the first century or so of their rule, the Mongols managed to play the field skillfully, backing first one principality and then another, playing the Russian princes against each other and never allowing one to achieve overweening power. However, in the early fourteenth century, the tiny, undistinguished principality of Moscow managed to turn the tables on its Mongol patrons, manipulating the forces of the Golden Horde against rival Russian principalities, particularly the far older and more eminent principality of Tver'. After 1327, when Mongol forces demolished Tver' upon the instigation of Prince Ivan Kalita of Moscow, Moscow held the grand princely patent almost without interruption. Thus, the Mongols provided Moscow with the military might and financial resources necessary to assert control over all of the other Rus' principalities and, eventually, by the fifteenth century, to consolidate the Russian lands into a force mighty enough to displace the now decaying, fragmented successor states of the Golden Horde.[16]

One might even say that Moscow not only displaced, but even replaced the Golden Horde as the sovereign power within the Rus'

[16] The case for Muscovite manipulation of the Horde in pursuing internal rivalries is most strongly articulated in John Fennell, 'The Tver Uprising of 1327: A Study of the Sources,' *Jahrbücher für Geschichte Osteuropas* 15 (1967): 161–79.

lands, for the mantle of Chingisid imperial legitimacy continued to hold considerable sway in the Rus' political imagination well into the Muscovite era. Muscovite grand princes and tsars played with images and rituals demonstrating their direct connection to their imperial Mongol forbears. Ivan III sported a Tatar crown and occasionally designated himself 'White Tsar' (a reference to the Mongol use of White to signal 'western' and 'tsar' meaning 'Emperor,' a term reserved exclusively for Greek, Roman, Byzantine, and Mongol emperors, prior to its adoption for Muscovy in the late fifteenth and sixteenth centuries). Ivan IV, the Terrible, added substance to his grandfather's imperial claims when he conquered and incorporated Kazan' and Astrakhan', major heirs to the Golden Horde. Around the same time, he or his advisers commissioned a cycle of frescoes in the Archangel Michael Cathedral, the princely necropolis in the Moscow Kremlin, which glorified not only his saintly and princely relatives of the Kievan past but also his Mongol heritage, a heritage of office and legitimacy, rather than of blood.[17]

In more concrete terms, the Mongols may have introduced Russia to the notion of a population census and other administrative practices. One historian, Donald Ostrowski, argues that Muscovy adopted its administrative organization *in toto* from Mongol models.[18] Whether or not Ostrowski's wholesale adoption of a Mongol model of administration took place, linguistic evidence of selective incorporation of Mongol loan words concentrated in the areas of trade, military organization and equipment, tax and customs collection, and administration argue for significant borrowings.

Not only Mongol overlords but also competition and interaction with other neighbors contributed to the subsequent growth of the Muscovite and Imperial Russian state apparatus. The international scene in which Muscovy found itself after the late fifteenth century was a radically changed one, with the key focus lying to the West rather than to the East. First Muscovite grand princes and then Russian emperors found themselves entering a diplomatic and military arena in which Western firearms, and Western infantries, as well as Western commercial corporations, called the shots. Responding to

[17] Michael Cherniavsky, 'Ivan the Terrible and the Iconography of the Kremlin Cathedral of Archangel Michael,' *Russian History* 2 (1975): 3–28; Edward L. Keenan, 'On Certain Mythical Beliefs and Russian Behaviors,' in S. Frederick Starr (ed.), *The Legacy of History in Russia and the New States of Eurasia* (New York, 1994), 19–40.

[18] Donald Ostrowski, 'The Mongol Origins of Muscovite Political Institutions,' *Slavic Review* 49 (1990): 525–42.

this new context, Ivan III consciously modeled his court ritual and imagery on the court of the Holy Roman Emperor, even copying the Emperor's double-headed eagle as his own crest.[19] From the early seventeenth century Muscovites invited Western mercenaries to train and command Russian troops, foreign arms were imported, and foreign munitions manufacturers were recruited. Where Mongol practice may have served as a model for Muscovite administrative development in earlier centuries, Polish–Lithuanian and somewhat archaic Byzantine models rose to the fore in the sixteenth and seventeenth centuries. The 1649 *Ulozhenie* law code, the most massive codification of laws in Russian history until the early nineteenth century, drew upon Lithuanian statutes, Byzantine and canon law as well as upon earlier Russian secular and ecclesiastical legislative precedents in establishing the ultimate law of the land.[20] Foreign models thus undoubtedly contributed to shaping Russian administrative practice, even providing the names for officials, institutions and forms from the Mongol *iarlyki* (patents) and *tamozhnye* (customs officials) to the Petrine *burgomeistry* (town officials) and *gubernatory* (governors).

Charles Tilly's model of military competition explains a great deal about what impelled Russia to adopt these forms and practices.[21] From the late sixteenth century on, as the key theaters of military competition shifted from the nomads and tribal peoples of the eastern border to the more technologically advanced Western arena, Russia was forced to improve the efficiency and efficacy of its military and of the state apparatus that supported its war efforts. In order to compete successfully and protect the borders of the tsardom against Poland–Lithuania and Sweden, Muscovy would have to increase its revenues and retool and retrain its army, both of which would necessitate internal administrative reform. Military needs propelled even

[19] Gustave Alef, 'The Adoption of the Muscovite Two-Headed Eagle: A Discordant View,' *Speculum* 41 (1966): 1–21.

[20] *The Muscovite Law Code (Ulozhenie) of 1649. Part 1: Text and Translation* (trans. and ed. by Richard Hellie (Irvine, CA); and Hellie's series of articles providing commentary on the 1649 law code: 'Early Modern Russian Law: The Ulozhenie of 1649,' *Russian History* 15 (1988): 155–80; 'Ulozhenie Commentary—Preamble,' *Russian History* 15 (1988): 181–224, esp. 183–4; 'Commentary on Chapters 3–6 of the *Ulozhenie*,' *Russian History* 17 (1990): 65–78; 'Commentary on Chapter 11: The Judicial Process for Peasants of the *Ulozhenie* of 1649,' *Russian History* 17 (1990): 305–39.

[21] Charles Tilly (ed.), *The Formation of National States in Western Europe* (Princeton, 1975).

more stringent reorganization of administration and revenue-collection in the eighteenth century, when Peter the Great faced one of the greatest powers in Europe, Sweden, in an on-going military showdown.

In spite of the importance of the contests with better-armed foes, military competition offers only a partial explanation for the innovations adopted in the early modern period. The impulse to reform was not unidirectional. As Lieberman states, the process is a self-reinforcing loop: 'territorial expansion and internal reform were mutually reinforcing, and the concentration of resources that flowed from coordination permitted the subjugation of more distant principalities.'[22] In the Muscovite case, the interactive quality of the two (or more) sides of the equation seem clear. Muscovite state build-up began before clashes with neighboring powers actually necessitated the introduction of more modern arms and warfare. Ivan the Terrible's mid-century experiments with improving the efficiency of tax collection and local policing antedated his major clashes with Livonia, and coincided more closely with his triumph over a traditional eastern foe, the Khanate of Kazan'. Moreover, the bulk of Muscovite expansion took place haphazardly, often accidentally, in the eastward direction, across Siberia, where improved record-keeping and administration rather than military competition against technologically or strategically advanced enemy forces proved to be the key to successful control. In other words, the need to create a powerful and efficient state infrastructure in the newly expanding realm derived as much from internal administrative needs as from the exigencies of war and interstate competition. The sheer size and sprawling diversity of the tsardom spurred the state to reform. Even within the military sphere itself, the logistical challenges of a vast, unsettled frontier engendered reforms as directly as did any competitive advantage of the foe.[23]

Prior to the need to defend and extend the borders of the state, a concept of a territorial state entity had to develop. Had Muscovites continued in the patterns set by their Kievan antecedents, the entire notion of administrative personnel and procedure would have remained irrelevant. As long as princely rule consisted of controlling and exploiting ill-defined territories through a combination of

[22] Lieberman, 'Transcending East–West Dichotomies,' this vol.

[23] On military reforms engendered by logistical problems, see Carol Belkin Stevens, *Soldiers on the Steppe: Army Reform and Social Change in Early Modern Russia* (DeKalb, IL, 1995).

raiding, trading and collecting tribute and taxes, and as long as the long-term goal of reigning princes continued to be the division of resources among their sons, notions of registering, supervising, regulating and policing society remained altogether alien. Eleventh-century Kiev had prospered without need of any kind of elaborate administrative structure, while Moscow based its rise to preeminence among the rival principalities of north-east Rus' on precisely such administrative structures, derived in part from Mongol models. The alteration in the basis of power and dominance reflected fundamental changes in economy and social structure parallel to (although not identical with) the ones described by R.I. Moore in the early medieval West.[24]

Prior to the twelfth century Kievan social and political elites, in this case, princes, boyars and merchants, derived their wealth and power from non-agricultural pursuits, largely a mixture of trade and plunder, and from collection of tribute, taxes and other fees from a largely free and self-sufficient agricultural population. Kievan nobles and princes were almost exclusively urban creatures, without landed estates or manor houses in the surrounding countryside. As far as can be discerned, the Rus' of all social standings practiced partible inheritance in this period. Under the circumstances of partible inheritance and the irrelevance of landed property, long-term preservation of familial manorial estates was a non-concept. Property, territorial jurisdictions, and management of agricultural land and population were largely irrelevant, in turn rendering a sophisticated administrative structure irrelevant.

As the center of Rus' moved north from Kiev to the Suzdalian and Novgorodian lands, agriculture and the exploitation of property assumed more salient roles in elite economies, and the agrarian laboring population gradually lost autonomy, as in the West. Borders, boundaries, properties and territorial jurisdictions all became not only relevant but crucial ingredients of Rus' society and economy, and law codes outlined increasingly fine rules regarding agricultural practice and property holding.[25] In contrast with large parts of Western Europe, however, primogeniture remained unknown and traditional practices of partible inheritance, sometimes even including daughters, continued among the elite. Only the ruling house of

[24] R.I. Moore, 'The Birth of Europe as a Eurasian Phenomenon,' this vol.

[25] Daniel H. Kaiser, *The Growth of the Law in Medieval Russia* (Princeton, 1980), 180–1.

Moscow, the Danilovich princes, switched over to primogeniture, and that appears to have occurred largely by accident, with some timely help by the Black Death in eliminating lateral branches. A civil war in the mid-fifteenth century cemented the practice, and as Edward Keenan puts it, later Muscovite grand princes and tsars devoted significant effort to 'pruning the family tree,' imprisoning and killing inconvenient uncles, brothers and cousins in order to preserve unquestioned the pattern of direct descent.[26] The Danilovich practice of primogeniture in a land of partible inheritance served the dynastic interests of the Moscow house, setting it apart from rival princely lines and sparing it the internal divisions that weakened other principalities. In the absence of a custom of aristocratic primogeniture, the grand princely house together with monastic and other ecclesiastical establishments worked to safeguard the uninterrupted transmission of property by marking it, surveying it, registering it, and administering it.

The rise in state administrative apparatus thus followed fundamental shifts in the social and economic outlines of the Russian state, and with a major alteration of the notion of state, territory and property. Yet it is difficult to make the argument that the shift to an agricultural, landed princely and aristocratic economy in any direct sense caused the rise of a centralized state apparatus, because the timing does not fit this scheme. Where monastic and princely landholding became widely established already in the late twelfth century, the truly explosive growth of Russian administrative ambitions and accompanying inflation of staff and structure did not occur until the sixteenth century, long after the collapse of Kiev, the end of the Mongol Yoke and the rise of Moscow.

By the dawn of the Muscovite era, not only the socioeconomic profile of Russia discussed above, but also the ideological bases of grand princely legitimacy had significantly altered. The rift between Kievan and Muscovite Rus' was so sharp that Edward L. Keenan dismisses the myth of their common heritage as a phantasm. He perceives no meaningful common features or continuity between the two and asserts that Muscovites themselves saw no link to a Kievan past until the seventeenth century.[27] Muscovite grand princes and tsars came to cast themselves, in literary texts, fresco cycles,

[26] Edward L. Keenan, talk presented at the Annual Convention of the American Association for the Advancement of Slavic Studies, Philadelphia, November 1994.

[27] Keenan, 'On Certain Mythical Beliefs and Russian Behaviors.'

legislative dicta, public decrees, and carefully staged ceremonies, as divinely appointed spiritual shepherds to their flocks and earthly protectors of their children.

This mode of justifying grand princely rule necessitated a broader vision of princely intervention and control in the internal life of the realm. The Grand Prince assumed responsibility for maintaining a godly, pious, ordered society. At the same time, this broader and grander vision of the role of the Grand Prince in society required tremendous outlays in wealth to provide a seemly backdrop for a divinely appointed imperial ruler, the appropriate cast of characters to maintain his dignity and strength, and the requisite staff to ensure law and order, compliance and service from all subjects of the tsardom. The tremendous building programs, impressive architectural ensembles, massive literary and legal compilations of the Muscovite era testify to the impulse to build a physical setting in Moscow suited to the new, grandiose claims about rulership.

This greatly expanded vision, of course, required both capital and manpower, and these two requirements become the driving forces behind Muscovite and Imperial Russian state expansion. In order to fill its army with armed, fully provisioned cavalry officers without draining the meager resources of the treasury, Ivan III created the *pomeshchiki* or gentry, a class of conditional landholders who supported their mandatory cavalry service by farming the parcels of land granted to them provisionally by the state. In order to keep track of all of the lands, service assignments, and servicemen, the state established first the Chancellery of Military Affairs and later the Chancellery of Conditional Landholding. Landholding, however, did gentry cavalrymen little good if they were off in service and could not farm the land themselves. Thus, short of providing the impossible amount of money that salaries would have required, the state found itself faced with the necessity of securing a peasant labor force for the support of its cavalry. The requirements of the cavalry corresponded to the state's growing need for more efficient tax collection in order to support its constant wars, as well as to an increasing bureaucratic interest in simply knowing how many tax-paying subjects inhabited the land, where they resided, and how much they could conceivably afford in taxes. The path toward enserfing the peasantry, and thereby satisfying both the cavalry's needs and the administration's interests, met with some formidable opposition, however. Members of the noble and ecclesiastical elite maintained an interest in retaining the legal mobility of the peasants, so that they could prey on the labor forces of more vulnerable lesser landholders. More significantly, the state itself held conflicting views on the value of a mobile population; the expanding frontiers of the growing realm required flexibility in deploying troops and manpower to the newly acquired borderlands. Consequently, the state issued a sequence of contradictory decrees from the last decades of the sixteenth century through the late seventeenth century, alternately enforcing peasants' obligations to remain on the land and allowing movement of populations to towns, forts and frontiers.

The conjunction of the interests of several groups in favor of binding the population to the land reached a high-point in the years between 1645 and 1649. In 1645 the state launched a nation-wide census, promising to assign peasants and other tax-payers permanently wherever they were listed in the census. With this pledge still unfulfilled in 1648, an outbreak of urban uprisings throughout the realm voiced both townspeople's and provincial gentrymen's concern with the erosion of their taxpaying and labor forces. Spurred by the rebellions, the 1649 law code bound both urban and rural populations wherever registered in the census, prescribed penalties for harboring runaways, and abolished the statute of limitations on the recovery of runaways, thereby ending the time-limited nature of peasant bondage. For the rest of the century, gentry landlords and urban communes agitated for increasingly active state intervention in enforcing these norms, recovering runaways, penalizing those who harbored fugitives, and closing loopholes for escape into border regiments and frontier towns. Thus the state administration in Muscovy appears to have grown largely in response to internal demand from both government personnel and society at large for greater state control and surveillance over a constantly expanding population and land mass. These requirements in turn reflected both increasing military needs and an aggrandizing political ideology.

Tsarist claims for legitimacy did not merely remain on paper, but also offered Muscovites compelling new ways to conceptualize their subordination to a powerful ruler. New conceptions of rule engendered new conceptions of the meaning of membership in the tsar's Orthodox realm. The motley assortment of princes and retinues, warrior-traders, urban citizens, and free peasants of the Kievan era gave way to a society based firmly on the paired principles of service and Orthodox piety. If the tsar cast himself as stern yet caring father of his people, guardian to his 'orphans,' and patron to his defenseless 'slaves,' then the orphans and slaves in turn were cast in new roles.

Muscovy emerged as what Max Weber labelled a liturgical or service state, a state in which all members fit into a cohesive hierarchy of service to God and tsar. The highest nobles of the land, the old Moscow boyars, boasted that their ancestors had served the princes of Moscow since the formative fourteenth century. As Moscow engulfed the other Rus' principalities in the fourteenth and fifteenth centuries, former regional princely and grand princely lines moved to Moscow and shifted their service to the Moscow princes. There they adopted the title of 'service princes' and attempted to equate their more recent relationship of service to that of the older Moscow boyar clans. Members of this boyar and princely elite proudly designated themselves 'slaves' of the Grand Prince, and aggressively abased themselves before their ruler in rituals of submission, emphasizing the service element in the relationship. Foreign observers reported on this practice with horror and fascination, deducing from it that the Muscovite nobility was a degraded and powerless one, a poor excuse of an aristocracy. From the Muscovite point of view, however, serving as a slave to a great and Orthodox master redounded to the credit of the servitor. The higher the social standing of the 'slaves,' the more obvious the status and power of the master.[28]

The positive valence of servitude in Muscovite culture may have derived in part from the mimetic ideal of following the role of Christ, gaining glory through humility, serving the supreme master. More pragmatically, the ethos of constant service allowed the Muscovite nobility to continue its practice of partible inheritance, compensating for the perpetual subdivision of estates by allowing each generation to augment its inherited lands with newly granted service lands. Where Western European elites generally adopted some form of unigeniture to keep their estates intact from generation to generation, Muscovite rulers and nobles developed a model of noble service to preserve the economic viability of their descendants. Persistent commitment to partible inheritance produced a very different family

[28] This idea is advanced by Edward L. Keenan, 'Muscovite Political Folkways,' *Russian Review* 45 (1986): 142–3. Muscovites of all ranks further abased themselves, in the eyes of Western observers, when they petitioned the grand prince or tsar by submitting *chelobit'ia*, literally, by 'beating their brow' to the ground, kowtowing. This term dates to the mid-fourteenth century. I.I. Sreznevskii, *Slovar' drevnerusskogo iazyka*, reprint edition (Moscow, 1989), vol. 3, pt 2, cols 1488–89. For a peculiar recent reading of Russian self-abasement, see Daniel Rancour-Laferriere, *The Slave Soul of Russia: Moral Masochism and the Cult of Suffering* (New York, 1995).

structure and a very different relation between elites and rulers than those developing in the West.[29] Reflecting the same model of a service society, each social stratum filled a service role, whether in the military, in the administrative ranks, in the clergy, the merchantry, or the peasantry.

Powerful and all-encompassing as it was, however, the new imagery did not promote a conception of the tsar as unlimited autocrat, nor did it envision untrammeled despotism. The tsar's divinely-appointed rule entailed the weighty responsibilities of fatherhood or guardianship. God's commandments obligated the tsar to rule sternly yet mercifully, to protect the meek from the strong, and to remain receptive to the wishes of his people. To bolster the legitimacy of major administrative reforms, tsarist decrees explained that the people had requested the changes and boasted of the tsar's merciful granting of the people's wishes. For instance, in the mid-sixteenth century when the regime altered the basis of provincial administration by replacing a system of appointed vicegerents with communal self-administration and self-policing, the publicized edicts represented the reform as a generous response to popular requests for just such a shift. A century later, the preface to the *Ulozhenie* law code in 1649 prominently recorded the role of 'all the land' in formulating the code's provisions.[30] Throughout this same period, calls to 'Assemblies of the Land,' at which the ruling circle floated plans for war, peace, or new taxation policies, similarly publicized the tsar's interest in and responsiveness to popular sentiment. (Similar assemblies were called to advise the state or to give public assent to important decisions throughout the eighteenth century.)[31] Far from representing political decision-making as the single-minded whim of an all-powerful autocrat, Muscovite official propagandists stressed that tsarist policy stemmed from fruitful interactions of tsar and

[29] See Jack Goody, Joan Thirsk and E.P. Thompson (eds), *Family and Inheritance: Rural Society in Western Europe, 1200–1800* (Cambridge, 1976), and my 'The Effects of Partible Inheritance: Gentry Families and the State in Muscovy,' *Russian Review* 53 (1994): 197–212.

[30] For examples in English, see 'Anti-Brigandage Charters and Decrees,' in Horace W. Dewey (comp., trans., and ed.), *Muscovite Judicial Texts, 1488–1566* (Ann Arbor, 1966), 23–44; *Muscovite Law Code (Ulozhenie)*, preamble.

[31] On Assemblies of the Land: I.I. Ditiatin, *Rol' chelobitii i zemskikh soborov v upravlenii Moskovskogo gosudarstva* (Rostov-on-the-Don, 1905); A.I. Zaozerskii, 'K voprosu o sostave i znachenii zemskikh soborov,' *Zhurnal Ministerstva Narodnogo Prosveshcheniia* 21 (1909): 299–352. On the on-going tradition of the eighteenth-century: O.A. Omel'chenko, *'Zakonnaia monarkhija' Ekateriny II: Prosveshchennyi absoliutizm v Rossii* (Moscow, 1993).

people, and played up the ability of the simple people to communicate their needs to a receptive and responsive paternal ruler.

The new rhetoric of Orthodox tsardom reached its target audience, displaying demonstrable effect in shaping popular as well as elite conceptions of the relationship between subject and tsar. As evident in the language and conduct of the ruled, the concept of reciprocity of guardianship and service entered the popular imagination in powerful ways, as did the tsarist divinely mandated obligation to rule piously and mercifully. When people felt that the tsar or his officials failed to act mercifully, they did not hesitate to say so, and, by phrasing their complaints in the officially sanctioned language of Orthodox paternalism, they frequently achieved satisfaction. The court could not repudiate its own publicly broadcast moral standards. In the central Russia town of Shuia, for instance, in 1657, the townspeople petitioned to the tsar against their current and previous governors about fire prevention regulation: 'By your order governors come to us, your orphans, and order us not to heat our homes and bathhouses, and metal smiths [are ordered not to build fires] in their smithies.'

> And at this time, Sovereign, from cold and from hunger, without bread, our women in childbirth and sick people are dying unnecessary deaths, and our artisans, smiths and bakers and sword-makers are abandoning their crafts. And the governors are inflicting great extortions and losses upon us. And the governor puts in jail those, Sovereign, poor townspeople who have to heat their homes and bathhouses for sick people and for mothers in childbirth, and beats [them] with cudgels and exacts from them in addition a fine of 2 rubles per person.[32]

In their petition, the residents of Shuia appealed to the tsar's obligation to protect his 'orphans' from exploitation by his own powerful officials, and their appeal was successful.

When bonds of reciprocity appeared violated, when standards of tsarist piety and mercy seemed to be abrogated, so too could the obligations of the subjects to serve and obey be set aside. The urban riots and Cossack rebellions that peppered the seventeenth century were uniformly mobilized by use of language and norms established and legitimized by elite conceptions of tsarist rule. Orthodox standards of service, protection and mercy could be turned against the state and the tsar himself, used as a double-edged sword to affirm

[32] *Russkii Gosudarstvennyi Arkhiv Drevnikh Aktov (RGADA)* [Russian State Archive of Ancient Acts], Moscow, *fond* 210, *Prikaznyi stol*, no. 51, fol. 198.

popular rights and notions of legitimacy. Thus, the very ideology that provided a powerful basis for tsarist legitimacy simultaneously set moral limits on that rule, limits understood by elites and commoners alike.

With theoretical limits set on autocratic rule by official ideology, at one extreme, and practical ones set by popular expectations at the other, we turn to the question of how effective the tsarist administration was in actually controlling and regimenting the population. As mentioned above, Russia has been disparaged from two vantage points. On one hand, from the fifteenth century until the fall of the Soviet Union, western commentators inveighed against Russia as the ultimate manifestation of over-centralized, over-bureaucratized, crippling, dehumanizing despotism. On the other hand, the same commentators frequently derided the incompetence of the Russian administration and the inability of the state to rein in its own corrupt operatives or to control the population at large.[33] As is often the case with stereotypes and generalizations, each of these apparently contradictory judgments contains some truth. By the mid-seventeenth century, the Muscovite state administration aspired to control the lives and movements, decisions and actions of its subjects to an extraordinary degree. Social legislation related to the advent of serfdom increasingly bound people not only to a single geographic location but to a discrete, definable social category: serf, state or 'black' peasant, townsperson, merchant. Economic measures constrained the abilities of merchants or entrepreneurs to expand or innovate, crushing successful traders and manufacturers under enormous burdens of debt and service responsibilities.[34] Civil regulation specified precise penalties for allowing dogs off leashes, singing off-color songs about the tsar, or smearing garlic on someone else's bird blind. A complex system of internal and external passports regulated movement. Samples of travel passes, issued by local officials and by landlords for their peasants, survive, as do numerous court cases involving unlicensed vagrants and wanderers. These cases are particularly revealing of the extent and capability of state penetration into the lives of its subjects. Wanderers and vagrants generally reached the attention of the authorities not because of any kind of

[33] A good example is B.N. Chicherin, *Oblastnye uchrezhdeniia v Rossii v XVIIom veke* (Moscow, 1856).

[34] Samuel H. Baron, 'Who Were the Gosti?' *California Slavic Studies* 7 (1973): 1–40; Paul Bushkovitch, *The Merchants of Moscow, 1580–1650* (Cambridge, 1980).

official sweep of the countryside designed to find them, but rather because villagers and townspeople had a tendency to report them.

One might legitimately wonder what impelled peasants and urban residents to turn in drifters, even those who served some function useful to the community. Itinerant healers and minstrels, two categories targeted by official legislation in the seventeenth century, were particularly at risk for betrayal by their host communities. Here lies the genius of the Muscovite state, perhaps what deservedly earned its reputation as a ubiquitous and insidious police state. Understanding that despite the rapid growth of the state administrative staff, the country remained understaffed and undergoverned, Muscovite leaders built on indigenous traditions of collectivism and mutual responsibility to develop complex systems through which to coopt the population into the process of its own subjugation. Techniques of collective responsibility guaranteed that communities would supervise themselves and discipline recalcitrant members. The tax reforms of the mid-sixteenth century, for instance, granted control over internal allotment and collection of taxes to local communities, which allowed communities to avoid at least one area of exploitation by corrupt governors. The reverse side of the coin, however, was that the state assessed taxes from the community as a collective unit. Although leaving the particulars of collection to the locality, the state demanded full payment of the total sum. Thus, if individuals should flee from the community, their share of the tax burden would fall to those who stayed. If someone chose to risk a chancy investment or potentially fruitful innovation, the risk would fall upon the entire community. Thus, communities shouldered the burden of supervising their members, preventing any untoward behavior, and, particularly in the case of the urban communes, actively agitating to curtail the movement of their own members, effectively calling for their own enserfment. Similarly, collective responsibility for policing communities pushed peasants and townspeople to inform on vagrants and wanderers, whose illegal presence might endanger the standing of the entire community in the eyes of the law.[35] Other uses of collective responsibility held clerks and minor officials accountable for the honesty and loyalty of their superiors and made communities answerable for treasonable acts or words of

[35] Horace Dewey and Ann Kleimola, 'Suretyship and Collective Responsibility in Pre-Petrine Russia,' *Jahrbücher für Geschichte Osteuropas* 18 (1970): 337–54; Richard Hellie, 'The Stratification of Muscovite Society: The Townsmen,' *Russian History* 5 (1978): 119–75.

their members. Such mutual accountability produced a highly developed network of spies and informants for an over-extended and understaffed state. State demands for information met with willing response. Individuals and communities throughout the country initiated suits against vagrants, runaways, rebels, and the whole gamut of offenders who transgressed against the state's definition of social order. Cases of *slovo i delo*, Sovereign's word and deed, which were essentially cases of sedition or lèse majesté, filled the tsar's courts. Denunciations poured in from all parts of the land, primarily from lower-class informants.[36] Muscovite autocrat rule thus clearly secured an impressive degree of hegemony and mobilized an important element of popular support.

Mutual responsibility was not unique to Russia. Many obligations and financial burdens were borne collectively by peasants and villagers in France, for instance, but the Muscovites appear to have instituted a higher and more pervasive, perhaps more coercive, degree of collectivity than elsewhere in Europe.[37] Examining peasant family economies in the eighteenth and early nineteenth centuries, Steven Hoch suggests that the Russian version of harshly patriarchal family collectivism resulted from the need to put survival ahead of any other measurements of family success. The premium placed on survival may serve to explain Muscovite collectivism as well.[38]

The picture of a Muscovite autocracy that functioned within powerful ideological limits and won the willing support of its subjects has emerged in a spate of recent revisionist works on the nature of tsarist rule, and is well on its way to becoming entrenched as a new sort of orthodoxy, the accepted wisdom in the field. In response to the new orthodoxy in the field of Muscovite studies (to which I have contributed) that represents tsarist rule as limited, responsive, and

[36] Mark Charles Lapman, 'Political Denunciations in Muscovy, 1600 to 1649: The Sovereign's Word and Deed' (Ph.D. diss., Harvard University, 1981).

[37] On mutual responsibility in France, lasting into the eighteenth century, see Hilton Lewis Root, *Peasants and King in Burgundy: Agrarian Foundations of French Absolutism* (Berkeley, 1983). I cannot comment on the phenomenon elsewhere in Eurasia.

[38] Steven L. Hoch, 'The Serf Economy and the Social Order in Russia,' in M. L. Bush, ed., *Slavery and Serfdom: Studies in Legal Bondage* (Cambridge, 1996). On mutual responsibility in Kiev and Muscovy, in addition to Dewey and Kleimola, 'Suretyship and Collective Responsibility in Pre-Petrine Russia,' see H.W. Dewey and A.M. Kleimola, 'Russian Collective Consciousness: The Kievan Roots,' *Slavonic and East European Review* 62 (1984): 180–91, and Horace W. Dewey, 'Russia's Debt to the Mongols in Suretyship and Collective Responsibility,' *Comparative Studies in Society and History* 30 (1988): 249–70.

merciful, it is imperative to remember that the crucial ingredient undergirding the tsarist state was coercive might.[39] While it is now clear that Orthodox culture imposed moral limits on the tsar and that the populace shared expectations of pious and merciful rule, it is also important to bear in mind the degree to which ideological limitations could be and actually were ignored. The threat and implementation of physical punishment, inflicted 'forcefully' and 'without mercy,' provided the solid foundation of this system of mass cooptation and allowed the state successfully to extend its reach into society by utilizing society against itself. Most dramatically and hideously displayed during Ivan the Terrible's savage *Oprichnina*, an 'exceptional' period when the monarch set aside established customs of rule and waged war on his own country, coercion always formed the grim background of Muscovite state control. Ivan's excesses, reportedly involving boiling men alive and frying them in special man-sized frying pans, raised violence to an elaborate and gruesome art, but the bread-and-butter cruelty of officially prescribed punishment is also stunning.[40] The courts sentenced offenders to be beaten and thrown in jail for the most prosaic infractions. Punishment by righter (daily beating on the shins) formed another staple of routine discipline. Exile was commonplace. Torture by hot pincers, the rack, water and fire enter court records with dulling frequency. Execution, generally by beheading for men (with drawing and quartering for the most notorious offenders) and live burial up to the neck for women, awaited criminals convicted of a wide range of offenses, particularly recidivists. Demonstrative punishment, public dismembering of the body of the criminal was not, of course, unique to Mus-

[39] Some of the most powerful statements of this new view of the limits of tsarist autocratic power are found in Daniel Rowland's articles, 'The Problem of Advice in Muscovite Tales about the Time of Troubles,' *Russian History* 6 (1979): 271–2, and 'Did Muscovite Literary Ideology Place Any Limits on the Power of the Tsar?' *Russian Review* 49 (1990): 125–56. A concise and convincing precis of the state of the literature is found in Nancy Shields Kollmann, 'Honor and Society in Early Modern Russia,' ch. 5, unpublished manuscript, 1995. I would like to thank her for permission to cite her unpublished work. For my contributions to this view, see 'The Devil Stole His Mind: The Tsar and the 1648 Moscow Uprising,' *American Historical Review* 98 (1993): 733–56.

[40] For lurid contemporary descriptions of the *Oprichnina*, see Albert Schlichting, ' "A Brief Account of the Character and Brutal Reign of Vasil'evich, Tyrant of Muscovy" (Albert Schlichting on Ivan Groznyi),' *Canadian–American Slavic Studies* 9 (1975): 204–72; Heinrich von Staden, *The Land and Government of Muscovy* (Stanford, 1967). For more scholarly analyses, see S.F. Platonov, *Ivan the Terrible*, ed. and trans. by Joseph L. Wieczynski (Gulf Breeze, FL, 1974); Hugh F. Graham, 'What Do We Really Know about Ivan the Terrible?' *Russian History* 14 (1987).

covy in the early modern era. Michel Foucault reminds us that coercive might provided underpinnings for other early modern states as well.[41] Although generally applied selectively, against targeted and visible deviants, state violence maintained the logic of compliance. Fear evidently contributed in a very immediate way to enforcing acquiescence from all levels of society. It also, however, resulted in crippling inaction. Exemplifying the problem of over-centralization one provincial governor wrote: 'We have no ink, no candles, no paper, and my last literate scribe has just been conscripted to chase bandits, but without your decree, Sovereign, I dare do nothing.'[42] Local authorities feared even to take action against outright rebellion without central orders, often enduring extended periods of chaos while awaiting communication from Moscow.

With the formidable array of coercive and ideological powers in its arsenal, the Muscovite state might appear to have been unassailable. Yet, despite its claims to religious legitimacy, and its successful deployment of penetrative mechanisms of social control, legislative micro-management, and coercive threat, outright rebellion was not uncommon. Social unrest shook the state at the beginning of the seventeenth century during the period of tsarlessness and foreign invasion known as the Time of Troubles, and urban revolts broke out around the country at mid-century. The great Cossack Rebellion led by Stenka Razin overwhelmed large reaches of the south and east again in 1670–71. Resistance to tsarist rule assumed many different forms, from minor local incidents in which individuals and groups defied central orders or attacked governmental officials to huge, threatening social rebellions, to religious schism.[43]

[41] Michel Foucault, *Discipline and Punish: The Birth of the Prison*, trans. by Alan Sheridan (New York, 1977).

[42] For examples: *RGADA*, f. 210, *Vladimirskii stol, stlb.* 146, ll. 124, 79–89 (1663/4); *RGADA*, f. 210, *Prikaznyi stol*, no. 384, ll. 420–1 (1666).

[43] On local resistance, see my *Autocracy in the Provinces: Russian Political Culture and the Gentry in the Seventeenth Century* (Stanford, 1997), chs 5–6. On rebellions see Paul Avrich, *Russian Rebels, 1600–1800* (New York, 1972); S.V. Bakhrushin, 'Klassovaia bor'ba v russkikh gorodakh XVI–nachala XVII vv.' in his *Nauchnye trudy*, vol. 1 of 4, pp. 204–36 (Moscow, 1952); V.I. Buganov, *Moskovskie vosstaniia kontsa XVII veka* (Moscow, 1969); E.V. Chistiakova, *Gorodskie vosstaniia v Rossii v pervoi polovine XVII veka (30–40e gody)* (Voronezh, 1975); P.P. Smirnov, *Posadskie liudi i ikh klassovaia bor'ba do serediny XVII veka*, 2 vols (Moscow and Leningrad, 1947–8). On the Schism see Michael Cherniavsky, 'The Old Believers and the New Religion,' *Slavic Review* 25 (1966): 1–39; Georg Bernhard Michels, 'Myths and Realities of the Russian Schism: The Church and its Dissenters in Seventeenth Century Muscovy' (Ph.D. diss., Harvard University, 1991).

The frequency of overt defiance of the state control apparatus returns us to the problem of gauging the efficacy of Muscovite rule. To illuminate the complex interrelationship of compliance and rebellion, control and chaos, let us examine in detail not one of the great rebellions, but rather a small but particularly revealing episode that occurred in the towns of Suzdal' and Shuia in central Russia in 1666. In that year, a townsman by the name of Seresha Pigasov, Shuia's former tax-collection officer, mobilized an armed insurgency, aided by his brother Vaska and 'his relatives and friends and clients and debtors who are indebted to him.' In an audacious act of insubordination, Pigasov resisted house arrest, and loosed vicious dogs in the marketplace to interrupt all business. He also forced or convinced his fellow townspeople to file petitions against the town governor and his staff, who, according to the petitions, had been demanding constant bribes in money and kind: candles, firewood, honey, meat, fish, salt, and all kinds of foodstuffs.[44] The governor described the events in his report to Moscow:

> They gathered the townspeople against their will at the local tax collection office and wrote a slanderous, criminally conceived petition against me, purporting to be from all of the townspeople of Shuia. Vaska Pigasov, of his own arbitrary volition, beat one townsperson on the square and instead of putting him in jail, locked him in someone else's market stall and beat the owner out and kept the prisoner there day and night.[45]

The governor then articulated with poignant clarity the isolation and desperate weakness of the tsar's officials in the distant countryside:

> And from such rebels, Sovereign, in Suzdal' great offenses are being perpetrated against many people, and he, Vaska, is defiant to me, your slave. In no other town, Sovereign, are there such insubordinate people as in Suzdal'. The rebels don't want to live under any rules, Sovereign, but want to live by their own will.[46]

The governor's report was inaccurate in at least one important respect: there were indeed such insubordinate people in other towns. In fact, they were everywhere. The effrontery of the Pigasov brothers in the face of representatives of state authority demonstrates the weakness and ineffectiveness of the administrative system when

[44] *RGADA*, f. 210, *Prikaznyi stol*, no. 993, ll. 35–42. (Pigasov case covers ll. 1–107.)
[45] *Ibid.*, ll. 24–6.
[46] *Ibid.*

tested, but more significantly, it shows some of the ways in which Muscovites managed to play the system, pushing the government's tolerance to the limit and yet staying within and benefiting from the economic and hierarchical structures of the society.

Most striking in the wild Pigasov story is the picture it provides of the construction and uses of the Pigasovs' powerful network of followers. As quoted above, the crowd that supported them in their mutiny in the marketplace was composed of their 'relatives and friends and clients and debtors who are indebted to [them].' Debtors formed an important category of their supporters. The wife of one of his supporters testified that 'her husband, Kuzemka, is indebted to Sereshka, and previous to this he frequently came to their home to drink wine.'[47] Although the Pigasov brothers were ordinary townspeople, quite low on the Muscovite social hierarchy, they not only commanded a network of clients, but also controlled significant resources on the local scene. While he was in prison at the local territorial chancellery, before his case was transferred to Moscow, Sereshka initiated a suit against another Suzdalian resident who had failed to repay a loan of 1700 copper rubles, a significant sum.[48] When the Pigasovs were finally brought to trial in Moscow at the Chancellery of Military Affairs, Sereshka petitioned that they be released to take care of their affairs. He complained that they had spent a long time in the Chancellery prison, and their homes and businesses were being destroyed by their absence. 'And my brother and I pay taxes to you, Great Sovereign, on more than forty households.'[49] They evidently held a significant bloc of real estate in Suzdal' and let houses out for rent, hence increasing their importance in the account books of the state and simultaneously building their network of people in their debt in one way or another. In response to their appeal, the brothers were granted parole. The central government proved itself willing to overlook infractions, however major, on the local scene, as long as the more pressing priority of tax collection could proceed uninterrupted. The Pigasovs' value to the state as prosperous tax payers exceeded their liability as criminal insurgents. The Pigasovs' ultimate understanding with the state clearly grew out of a mutual concern for preserving the small-scale economic empire that they had created. In this complicated picture,

[47] *Ibid.*, ll. 18–19.
[48] *Ibid.*, ll. 98.
[49] *Ibid.*, ll. 105–6.

the Pigasov brothers appear in the dual roles of disorderly rowdies and as pillars of the community, local landlords and solid citizens. Wearing the latter hat, they were able to negotiate for their release from prison, while in the former they were able to scoff at the rules and officials that ostensibly controlled their society.

Investigations of Western monarchies have dispelled the old myth that centralized autocratic states succeeded only by dismantling medieval political formations based on personalism and patronage, replacing these irrational, pre-modern forms with rational, routinized, impersonal norms. Typical of the new historiography on the rise of centralized states in Europe is Sharon Kettering's description of early modern France. Kettering argues that reliance on 'interstitial, supplementary, and parallel structures,' such as patron–broker–client ties, was characteristic of incompletely centralized states in which official institutions alone did not suffice to govern the provinces because of the weak hold of royal authority.[50] 'Clientelism . . . served as a transitional bridge from a late medieval political structure in which there were diffuse power centers and strong regionalism to the absolute monarchy of Louis XIV with its strong central government and emerging royal bureaucracy.'[51] Here again, Muscovy fits neatly into the pattern described in Western Europe. Personal connections, whether to a leading boyar, a petty clerk in a governmental chancellery, or to the tsar himself, lubricated the system, allowing insignificant subjects of the tsar to imagine themselves in a highly personalized and responsive relationship, governed by a subjective standard of mercy. The overlap and lack of clear dividing lines of jurisdictions among various chancelleries and branches of administration maximized the flexibility of justice, allowing litigants to maneuver among the authorities, appealing to those who would judge most 'mercifully.' Litigants searched for administrative venues where clerks or judges might be friends or 'brothers,' cousins of neighbors' wives, or at the very least, susceptible to the compelling logic of large 'gifts.'[52] The law had long condemned favoritism, bribery and other inequities in the tsar's courts, yet personalism and

[50] Sharon Kettering, *Patrons, Brokers, and Clients in Seventeenth-Century France* (New York, 1986), 5. On the interstitial development of new phenomena within old structures, see also Michael Mann, *The Sources of Social Power*, vol. 1, *A History of Power from the Beginning to A.D. 1760* (Cambridge, 1986), esp. 32, 436.

[51] Kettering, *Patrons, Brokers, and Clients*, 224.

[52] For example: *Pamiatniki delovoi pis'mennosti XVII veka. Vladimirskii krai* (Moscow, 1984), no. 257: 250; no. 261: 252–3; no. 264, p. 254.

patronage remained the core of the system. High offices were distributed according to calculations of birth and seniority, and positions in both administrative and military service were officially open only to the sons of men already in service. Parallel to the religious model, in which the benevolent intercession of the Mother of God or an appropriate saint secured the favorable attention of Higher Authorities, supplication and intercession were the fundamental modes of Muscovite administrative interaction. Despite the evolution of increasingly regularized procedures and paper formulae, only by identifying and appealing to a concerned patron could one achieve anything in the early modern Russian state system. This rule applied as much to highly placed boyars and nobles as to peasants, Cossacks and townspeople. Given the ambiguities of official practices themselves, and the ambivalence of rules and legislation toward patronage and clientage networks, it is not surprising that what outsiders readily labelled rampant 'corruption' remained an inherent part of political practice for centuries.

Until Peter the Great, the endurance of the legitimately personal element in Muscovite administration mitigated the cold shock of encounter with impersonal bureaucratic norms. John Armstrong's fascinating comparison of the efficacy of eighteenth-century Russian *voevody* (provincial governors) and seventeenth-century French intendants indicates that premature rationalization of bureaucratic routine in fact undermines the efficiency of administration, resulting in a dysfunctional disjuncture between personalized expectations and norms of procedure and the impersonal demands of standardized officialdom.[53] Time and again from mid-seventeenth century on, public mutinies expressed dismay at the creeping routinization and depersonalization of life. Patronage and mercy had allowed a powerful state to grow and develop; attempts to limit and regulate those personal modes of interaction threatened to reveal the new state structure for the paper-bound monster that it truly was. Legal and administrative rationalization certainly had its supporters, as the painstaking production of the massive 1649 codification of laws demonstrates, and Muscovite chancellery personnel drew on deep currents of support for such an enterprise when they pushed for systemic reform. For instance, even within a system in which different laws applied to different social groups, an ancient concern with equal

[53] John A. Armstrong, 'Old-Regime Governors: Bureaucratic and Patrimonial Attributes.' *Comparative Studies in Society and History* 14 (1972): 2–29.

application of those differential laws for all individuals, great and small, powerful and defenseless, sanctioned the promulgation of new law codes. Furthermore, the recognition that networks of personal connections and bribery functioned better for 'powerful people' (a legal category including leading boyars, church hierarchs and monastic establishments) than for ordinary folk brought about a gradual acceptance of the notion of legal and procedural routinization. By and large, however, both state and society continued to discuss the politics of power and social control in the personal idiom of paternalism and piety.[54]

Peter the Great came as a shock to the system. He deliberately stripped the façade of personalism and of mercy, implementing rigid regulation, strict, military discipline, and regularized hierarchies of authority, jurisdiction, and surveillance. Peter and his successors turned explicitly to Dutch and Swedish models in structuring administrative and military reforms. Peter responded to his own perception of Russia's 'backwardness' compared to the West, as well as to military requirements. Military exigencies underlay his efforts at comprehensive overhaul of the Muscovite system, and financing his ceaseless wars became the driving force of his reign. He attributed the impulse behind his reforms primarily to the need to compete with and master western powers at their own game. He acknowledged his arch-rival, Charles XII of Sweden, as his most valued teacher in the arts of war and governance.[55]

Peter aroused deep opposition among his subjects, who portrayed him as the Antichrist supervising demons building a new Jerusalem, or feasting with the Great Whore of Babylon, with the face of his second wife, Catherine.[56] This is not to imply that Peter put an end to reliance on personal connections at court or in dealings with the bureaucracy. On the contrary, they continued apace, with Peter himself as a prime offender, advancing his favorites, punishing those who displeased him, and generally playing on the force of his personality. However, the tenor of the official discourse shifted to favor procedure, routine and system over patronage and connections.

Lieberman's wide, comparative perspective allows us to set aside the various stigmas of 'backwardness' that have relegated Muscovy to

[54] See my *Autocracy in the Provinces*, chs 7–8.

[55] Evgenii V. Anisimov, *The Reforms of Peter the Great: Progress through Coercion in Russia*, trans. John T. Alexander (Armonk, NY: M.E. Sharpe, 1993).

[56] Cherniavsky, 'The Old Believers and the New Religion,' figures 7 and 8.

'medieval' standing, and to analyze Muscovy in the far more germane context of the early modern Eurasian world. Adopting a revised model of the rise of Western European monarchies in the early modern period, we are able to situate even many of Muscovy's 'archaic' characteristics in a comparative context that better illuminates where they parallel and where they diverge from European norms. Muscovy presented a public façade very different from that of other European monarchies in the early modern period. No discourse in Muscovy approximated the language of rights and institutions, of parlements, diets, or constitutions of contemporary states from England to Poland. Local community and the family remained the key sites for contestation. Patronage networks remained crucial venues for popular aspirations and highly localized public life, interacting with and reinforcing, but posing no competition or opposition to centralized rule. Yet alongside this personalized, localized, apolitical mode of operation, a thoroughly early modern centralized monarchy arose and functioned. The Muscovite tsardom and the Imperial regime that followed both rested on a familiar early modern tripod of religious ideology, paper work, and the knout to coerce and cajole, win popular compliance, build legitimacy, conquer new lands, and crush opposition.

Literati Culture and Integration in Dai Viet, c. 1430–c. 1840[1]

JOHN K. WHITMORE

The land of Dai Viet, whose political and cultural heartland lay in what is now northern Vietnam, followed patterns somewhat analogous to those posited in other Eurasian 'rimland' states. The fifteenth to nineteenth centuries saw administrative centralization, territorial expansion, population growth, economic elaboration, a greater emphasis on textuality and moral orthodoxy, and growing cultural standardization. In contrast to France and West European states, however, the Vietnamese achieved this integration less by refining patterns established during the prior 'charter age' (*c.* 900–1400 C.E.) than by adopting a radically new model, that of the contemporary Ming government in China.

Tightly intertwined with these secular trends in Vietnam was the emergence of a new 'class,' the literati, whose existence, by definition, depended on the rise of Neo-Confucian textualism and whose goals took the form of activist, state-oriented service. They were inspired variously by an undeniable sense of moral commitment; by an international perspective, acquired both from texts and from regular embassies to the Chinese capital (where they communicated with their Korean as well as Chinese counterparts); and by their increasingly sophisticated institutional memory, tempered by a certain rough and ready pragmatism. The literati intended that state intervention in the countryside should lead to the physical well-being of the populace, a goal both broader and more narrow than that of a purely Confucian moral order. And in fact much of their accumulating expertise they directed toward the intensification and regulation of the rural economy.

On repeated occasions between 1430 and 1840 the literati were challenged by political actors favoring more personalized, non-

[1] This essay is dedicated to the late Arthur F. Wright, who first asked me, a quarter of a century ago, what the socio-economic basis was for the political-intellectual changes I was describing.

bureaucratic modes of government, but the prestige of the Chinese models, their practical administrative skills, and long-term changes in the economy combined to favor a reassertion of literati pre-eminence, if not dominance. Notwithstanding a relatively sharp elite/mass cultural divide, Neo-Confucian norms also exercised a growing influence on peasant behavior and notions of ethnicity, particularly in the north and center of the country. In effect, therefore, literati ascendancy helped to define the early modern period in Vietnamese political and cultural history. This paper begins by describing trends toward administrative integration and economic elaboration *c.* 1400–1700, followed by a discussion of literati thought and political fortunes in this same period. I then examine the literati's largely unsuccessful efforts to master the economic crisis of the eighteenth century. Finally, I describe how, in the aftermath of this generalized collapse and in the face of competing ideologies, the literati as a status group and Neo-Confucian culture as an ideology resumed an official hegemony in the 1800s.

I. Political and Economic Trends to *c.* 1700

Although the Vietnamese dynasties of the Ly (1010–1225) and the Tran (1225–1400) had incorporated Confucian elements into their ritual complex and personnel selection procedures, their cultural orientation was fluid and eclectic with a predominantly Mahayana Buddhist focus, while their relatively decentralized political systems were dominated by princes and aristocratic estate owners. It was only as a result of the Ming occupation (1407–27) that the Vietnamese countryside came into direct contact with an aggressive bureaucratic system and with Neo-Confucian moral orthodoxy. The new Le dynasty, which overthrew the Ming, combined pre-Ming Vietnamese traditions with prominent elements of the Ming colonial system, most notably the Neo-Confucian schools and legal code. The result, starting in the 1430s, was an unprecedently vigorous move toward Dai Viet's centralization. After more than a half century of turmoil, Le Loi, founder of the Le dynasty, and his entourage acted to lay a new fiscal base for the state. With land ownership greatly disrupted by late fourteenth-century disorders and by the Ming occupation, Le Loi was able to formalize a new pattern of land tenure, in which public lands (*cong-dien*) provided the great bulk of state taxes, while private lands (*tu-dien*) allowed a pattern of independent peasant production to develop.[2]

Fifteenth-century Vietnam experienced neither a shift in its political center of gravity (Thang-long remained the capital), nor a prolonged foreign occupation (the Ming were present barely twenty years). Nonetheless, this new system moved the Vietnamese away from the social order of the pre-1400 era, with its aristocratic tenor and the apparently extensive use of serf cultivators. Allowing a more substantial role for smallholding peasants and for commercial tenants, the new social order would strengthen the central government by providing larger rural revenues and permitting more effective penetration of the countryside. At the same time the demise of aristocratic estates assisted Neo-Confucian literati within the government both by enhancing the capital's ability to reward them economically and by eliminating rival elites. It must be said that we have no clear sense of the long-term factors favoring this material and social transition. For the moment, I must hypothesize that gradual commercial expansion and the formation of groups of independent peasants and tenants prior to *c.* 1370 combined with subsequent political turmoil and aristocratic decimation to open new possibilities in the mid-fifteenth century. In other words, rather than see the Le court 'creating' this new order, it is far more plausible to view it as taking advantage of the new circumstances to ratify and to accelerate longstanding trends.

In his explanation of political and economic change in early modern, i.e. post-1400, Southeast Asia, Anthony Reid has chosen to see external commerce as the 'major independent variable.'[3] Victor Lieberman, too, at one time began with maritime contacts and firearms, but in subsequent writings and in the introductory essay to this volume, he has taken agricultural economy and demography as his starting points.[4] I am convinced that in analyzing early modern Vietnam's development, the starting point also must be the agricul-

[2] J. K. Whitmore, 'Adopting Antiquity, Han Yu and Ho Quy Ly in Fourteenth Century Vietnam' (MS); *idem*, *Vietnam, Ho Quy Ly and the Ming, 1371–1421* (New Haven, 1985); Nguyen Ngoc Huy and Ta Van Tai, *The Le Code, Law in Traditional Vietnam* (Athens, OH, 1987), I, 191–203.

[3] Reid, *Southeast Asia in the Age of Commerce, 1450–1680* (New Haven, 1993), II, 217.

[4] Lieberman, 'Local Integration and Eurasian Analogies: Structuring Southeastern Asian History, *c.* 1350–*c.* 1830,' *Modern Asian Studies* [*MAS*], 27, 3 (1993), 488–521; *idem*, 'Secular Trends in Burmese Economic History, *c.* 1350–*c.* 1830, and their Implications for State Formation,' *MAS*, 25, 1 (1991), 3–12.

tural foundation and the transition from an aristocratic system of serf-run estates to a peasant-based economy. Thus, I resume the argument I made over a decade ago: '. . . it would appear that these monetary flows [and external trade] were generally secondary to the internal socio-economic developments of the country in their influence on Vietnamese life . . . The movement of silver and the growth in international trade . . . seem to have speeded developments already beginning to take place.'[5]

The principal objective of the Le fiscal system as it took form in the 1430s and 1440s and as it continued for almost three centuries, was to keep 'private' hands off the 'public lands' (*cong-dien*).[6] In fact, the government now achieved considerable success in keeping the villages and their resources locally independent and directly linked to the capital. The critical hinge between the central apparatus (which was increasingly subject to what may fairly be termed bureaucratic procedures) and the countryside was an expansion during the 1460s in provincial and sub-provincial personnel appointed by the capital down to the district level. Here, in jurisdictions of 30–70 villages (approximately one-tenth the size of their Chinese counterparts), district officials gathered census data and promoted textually-based Neo-Confucian social norms. The officials' principal new tasks included the encouragement of agriculture, the standardization of weights and measures, and the promulgation of exhortatory moral rescripts. On the sub-district level the 1480s saw a major effort to restructure the role of the village headman, in order both to consolidate district efforts and to bring Neo-Confucian ideology deeper into society. With the aid of headmen, officials attempted to implant among the peasantry respect for patrilineal and primogeniturial norms by linking these concepts to rituals for the dead and to rules governing inheritance of land supporting this sacrificial cult (*huong-hoa*).[7]

The new system of administration and landholding joined with the restoration of peace after generations of severe disturbance to

[5] Whitmore, 'Vietnam and the Monetary Flow of Eastern Asia, Thirteenth to Eighteenth Centuries,' in J. F. Richards (ed.), *Precious Metals in the Late Medieval and Early Modern Worlds* (Durham, NC, 1983), 389.

[6] *Le Code*, I, 191–8.

[7] J. K. Whitmore, 'Transforming Dai Viet, Politics and Confucianism in the Fifteenth Century' (MS), chs 4–5; *Hong-Duc Ban-Do* (Maps of the Hong-duc [Reign Period, 1470–1497]) (Saigon, 1962), 12–49; *Thien Nam Du Ha Tap* (A.334), 'Legal Section' (1480s–1490s); Whitmore, 'Monetary Flow,' 305–6; *Le Code*, I, 203.

encourage that agricultural, commercial, and demographic growth which seems to have been characteristic of the post-1400 era in much of Eurasia. Peasant agriculture fed local markets across the countryside and supported an expanding urban economy in and around the capital of Thang-long (Hanoi). International trade reinforced these trends, but in itself probably was not a major spur. Li Tana has documented over a three-fold increase in the population of the north between 1417 and 1539. Markets and urban areas seem to have grown proportionately, commercial goods became more specialized, and we see the beginning of a chronic shortage of copper cash, which itself was an index of expanding exchange.[8]

Strengthened by population and tax increases and inspired by its new view of the world, Dai Viet in the late 1400s moved to destroy the major threat of its southern neighbor, Champa, and for the first time to expand Vietnamese territory significantly down the coast into what is now south-central Vietnam. Heretofore, the Vietnamese had engaged in a competition with the Chams over the territory lying between their capitals (now north-central Vietnam), at times losing (especially in the late fourteenth century), at times winning. Cultural differences (the Chams were Malayo-Polynesian speakers and more heavily influenced by Indian civilization) had meant little, but now the Vietnamese adoption of the Neo-Confucian sense of 'civilized' vs. 'barbarian' put the Chams firmly in the latter category. With this new moral ideology, Vietnamese leaders moved to annex most of the conquered territory directly, rather than leave a Cham vassal in place, as after previous victories.[9] The results of this new aggressiveness were both more land—a new province, the thirteenth, was carved out—and an enhanced sense of ethnicity. The wars against the Chams combined with the permeation of Confucian ideology to differentiate Vietnamese more clearly from peoples in the southern lowlands and in the western hills. Together with memories of successive resistance against Chinese incursions from the north, these elements helped the 'Vietnamese' to recognize themselves,

[8] Li Tana, ' "The Inner Region": A Social and Economic History of Nguyen Vietnam in the Seventeenth and Eighteenth Centuries,' Ph.D. diss. (Australian National University, 1992), ch. 1; J. K. Whitmore, 'Social Organization and Confucian Thought in Vietnam,' *Journal of Southeast Asian Studies* [*JSEAS*], 15, 2 (1984), 301; Yu Insun, *Law and Society in Seventeenth and Eighteenth Century Vietnam* (Seoul, 1990), 111–12; Whitmore, 'Monetary Flow,' 367–8; Duncan Macintosh, *Chinese Blue and White Porcelain*, 3rd ed. (Woodbridge, UK, 1994), 158–63; *Chinese and South-East Asian White Ware Found in the Philippines* (Singapore, 1993), 38–42.

[9] Whitmore, 'Transforming Dai Viet,' ch. 5, pt G.

although admittedly it is difficult to know how far down the social scale this identity permeated and in precisely what situations it became manifest.

The Hong-duc model (named after the second of Thanh-tong's two reign periods, 'Pervading Virtue,' 1470–97) of the early Le period would serve as the framework for Vietnamese government during much of the next three centuries, but the Le dynasty itself lost effective power in the sixteenth. From 1528 to 1592 a ministerial family known as the Mac took the throne at Thang-long, but evidence from the *Hong-Duc Thien Chinh Thu* ('The Hong-Duc Book of Good Government') and other sources suggests that the Mac maintained the Le commitment to Neo-Confucian primacy and bureaucratic organization.[10] So, too, the combination of natural population increase and state activism would seem to have continued the developments of the fifteenth century through the middle of the sixteenth. Both the attraction of Chinese models and the prosperity of this period are captured in the report of the Portuguese priest Gaspar da Cruz from the 1550s:

> The people of this kingdom in their apparel, policy, and government, do use themselves like the people of China. The country is much inhabited and of much people; it is also a very plentiful country, as can be seen from the fact that although they do not deal with other peoples outside of their own kingdom . . . they feed and dress themselves very well, as they likewise furnish their houses, having many good buildings, all of which argues the fertility, abundance, and prosperity of this country.[11]

Yet, as would be the case through the eighteenth century, this system was able to control only the heartland, that is, the Red River delta and its immediately adjacent area. Border regions distant beyond the delta offered a haven where those defeated in the capital could build a base of opposition, taking advantage of the often rugged terrain and (notwithstanding the growing sense of ethnic exclusiveness) allying themselves on occasion with Muong, Tai, and other minority peoples. In the fifteenth century the Le themselves had used the mountainous territory of Thanh-hoa to the south as a political refuge. Following the Mac overthrow of the Le, the new

[10] J. K. Whitmore, '*Chung-Hsing* and *Cheng-T'ung* in Texts of and on Sixteenth Century Vietnam,' in K. W. Taylor and J. K. Whitmore (eds), *Essays into Vietnamese Pasts* (Ithaca, NY, 1995), 117–30; *idem*, 'Social Organization,' 305–6.

[11] C. R. Boxer (ed.), *South China in the Sixteenth Century* (London, 1953), 73. See also Donald F. Lach, *Southeast Asia in the Eyes of Europe, the Sixteenth Century* (Chicago, 1968), 565.

Neo-Confucian ideology with its emphasis on filial piety and undying loyalty to the ruler and his line encouraged attempts to restore the Le, most notably the anti-Mac, pro-Le insurgency led by the Trinh and Nguyen clans, who were also based in Thanh-hoa. By 1592 these forces had triumphed, forcing the Mac and their loyalists into a temporary haven of their own in the northern mountains protected by the Ming dynasty in China. However, shortly before their victory, the Trinh/Nguyen alliance also began to split, with the Trinh retaining control of the north and the Nguyen finding refuge on the distant southern border.[12] In short, by 1600, when the Trinh established their power over the heartland of Dai Viet with the Le as their nominal kings, the capital of Thang-long faced political rivals on both its northern and southern peripheries.

While politically and geographically separate, the rivals did not reject the central system itself. In the south, the Nguyen felt themselves to be operating within the system established during the fifteenth century, more precisely in the southernmost thirteenth province set up by Le Thanh-tong. They dreamed of reclaiming power in Thang-long; and although coming to exist in the Southeast Asian maritime world, they and their local followers retained a strong sense of themselves as ethnic Vietnamese.

Given the frequent Trinh attempts at conquest from the 1620s to the 1670s, the Nguyen retained their military orientation, gaining forts and arms from the international trade at their thriving port of Hoi-an (just south of Da-nang). More dependent than its northern counterpart on Japanese, Chinese, and European trade in the South China Sea, the southern economy may have pulled Vietnamese down the coast to produce the sugar and pepper demanded by that trade.[13] More basically, however, the famed movement of settlement and colonization known as the *nam-tien* ('southern push') reflected a desire for new, predominantly subsistence rice lands. As Vietnamese moved through the Cham territory of central Vietnam and onto Khmer lands of the Mekong Delta during the seventeenth and eighteenth

[12] Nola Cooke, 'Nineteenth Century Vietnamese Confucianization in Historical Perspective: Evidence from the Palace Examinations (1463–1883),' *JSEAS*, 25, 2 (1994), 284–6; Whitmore, '*Chung-Hsing*,' 122–3; Nguyen Trieu Dan, *A Vietnamese Family Chronicle* (Jefferson, NC, 1991), 166–73, 220–31; K. W. Taylor, 'Nguyen Hoang and the Beginning of Vietnam's Southward Expansion,' in A. Reid (ed.), *Southeast Asia in the Early Modern Era* (Ithaca, NY, 1993), 42–65.

[13] Whitmore, 'Monetary Flow,' 377–85; Nguyen Thanh Nha, *Tableau économique du Vietnam aux XVII et XVIII siècles* (Paris, 1970) 53–4.

centuries, the Nguyen administration encouraged the flow and expanded its simple provincial structure to include all the new territory, eventually half of present-day Vietnam. Li Tana has shown how this area engendered a new way of being Vietnamese, culturally and socially fluid, commercially open, lacking the stable nucleated villages of the Red River delta.[14]

Meanwhile, under the nominal authority of the Le emperors, the Trinh family ruled the north from 1592 to 1789. With the realm split between this heartland and the southern border (and for eighty years the Mac haven near the northern border), the Trinh felt that the main order of business was forcibly reunifying Vietnamese territory. Through the first half of the seventeenth century, the Trinh, whose origins lay in the military frontier, therefore retained a predominantly military orientation and devalued the Le/Mac bureaucratic model. Failure to achieve reunification by the 1660s, however, induced the Trinh and their literati supporters to re-establish the fifteenth-century bureaucratic style of administration, with its emphasis on state encouragement of agriculture. In fact, the end to the north–south wars, the subsequent elimination of the Mac, and the reintroduction of bureaucratic administration appear to have contributed to renewed prosperity. In the course of the late seventeenth and early eighteenth centuries crops became more specialized, markets proliferated, trade and monetization continued to expand. In order to tap this new wealth in reliable fashion, the Trinh central administration moved to reduce further the political prerogatives of headmen, most especially their control over taxation. In the process, however, these reforms made the system more rigid and less flexible. Specifically, in 1664 the government froze the household registers, which until then had been recalculated every three to six years, establishing a set population figure for each village.[15] Although this change helped to make collections more predictable, it coincided with another demographic surge which, we shall see, would contribute in the next century to a serious disjuncture between government operations and social dynamics.

While social and economic life became more complex, cultural and ethnic integration accelerated in the more densely populated delta and lowland areas. Even before Le ascendancy, in the late fourteenth

[14] Li, 'Inner Region,' chs 2–6.

[15] K. W. Taylor, 'The Literati Revival in Seventeenth Century Vietnam,' *JSEAS*, 18, 1 (1987), 1–22; Li, 'Inner Region,' 27; Yu, *Law*, 108–21; Nha, *Tableau*, pt 1, ch. 1, pt 2, ch. 1; Whitmore, 'Monetary Flow,' 368–70.

century a sense of political and moral crisis had induced some literati to attempt to redefine Vietnamese culture so as to distinguish it more clearly from that of their Southeast Asian neighbors as well as from Chinese traditions. We have seen that the Neo-Confucian transformation of the following century brought the Vietnamese strongly within the Sinic dichotomy of 'civilized' vs. 'barbarian.' Simultaneously, cultural reform worked to 'civilize' the Vietnamese population itself, especially in the northern and central lowlands. This appears to have continued under the Mac and was again emphasized by the bureaucratic revival of the seventeenth century. By this time, increased wealth, wider literacy, and a probable proliferation of rural schools would have helped to disseminate literary culture. The schools, of course, sought primarily to prepare students for the state Confucian exams, which offered a critical avenue of social mobility and which served to link rural and urban elite culture more closely. But by no means was all such ferment linked to the exams, nor was it strictly elitist. Although encouraged by print, much cultural activity was also oral, as the tightly rhymed six–eight (*luc-bat*) verse of vernacular literature (*nom*) allowed oral presentations to those who could not read.[16] Recitations of this sort, popular versions of elite texts, and official efforts at Neo-Confucian indoctrination through the formal recitation of maxims in the villages all served to increase popular awareness of Confucian norms, and to deepen the association between Vietnamese ethnicity and Neo-Confucianism, especially in the north and north-center of the country.

At the same time, the growth in wealth, communications, and social complexity led some elements toward other belief systems. The late seventeenth century saw a resurgence in the north of Mahayana Buddhism, based specifically on the contemporary Chinese pattern, and the rise of Catholicism, drawn from the European contacts. The bureaucracy attempted both to rein in what it considered immoral aspects of this novel popular culture and to standardize older traditions so as to reduce subversive potentials. An example of the latter is the effort to bring the local spirit cults under control, in effect splitting them between above ground, exemplary

[16] Huynh Sanh Thong, *The Heritage of Vietnamese Poetry* (New Haven, 1979), xxvii–xxxi; *idem*, 'Literature and the Vietnamese,' *Vietnam Forum* [*VNF*], 9 (1987), 42–4; 'Folk History in Vietnam,' *VNF*, 5 (1985), 66–80; Tran Quoc Vuong, 'Popular Culture and High Culture in Vietnamese History,' *Crossroads*, 7, 2 (1992), 24.

authorized cults and those deemed unworthy, which survived underground.[17]

II. The Establishment and Re-establishment of Literati Culture to *c.* 1700

In sum, then, literati culture may be studied in terms of its influence on administrative, economic, and cultural integration. But literati culture had its own history which also requires comment. At the heart of the literati world stood the triennial civil service examinations, which served both as the chief mechanism of personnel recruitment and as a critical source of government legitimacy. The relatively abundant records of these examinations, in combination with the chronicles, allow us to trace with some confidence the internal evolution and physical dissemination of literati culture in Dai Viet.

The roots of literati culture lay in coastal zones where commercial contacts with China were most extensive, namely the eastern and southern areas of the Red River delta, the provinces of Hai-duong and Son-nam, respectively. Indeed, the Tran dynasty had roots in China, hailed from this same area, founded the first major Sinic-style school, and made the first tentative efforts at a bureaucratic form of government in Vietnam during the middle of the thirteenth century.[18] During the fourteenth century literati culture then spread from the south and east toward the north and west into the aristocratic heartland of Dai Viet. By 1400 it was entrenched throughout the delta, all around Thang-long. The scholars of this pre-Le period—whom we shall designate 'classicists' because they championed classical Chinese texts rather than Neo-Confucian works—continued to wield influence into the mid-fifteenth century. Represented by such thinkers as Nguyen Trai and Phan Phu Tien, they blended the social traditions of the early Le oligarchy with T'ang/early Song intellectual perspectives. In their poetry, Zhuang-zi

[17] Vuong, 'Popular Culture,' 24, 26–33; Minh Chi *et al.*, *Buddhism in Vietnam* (Hanoi, 1993), 148–60; J. K. Whitmore, 'Bureaucratic Control of the Spirits in Vietnam,' Association of Asian Studies, Washington, DC, 1980. Vuong's discussion of *Dao Noi*, the 'Inside (Indigenous) Way,' indicates how Vietnamese popular culture both adapted to the active bureaucratic reality and resisted it. This set of beliefs helped define Vietnamese ethnicity, while allowing local variation in its expression.

[18] Whitmore, '*Chung-Hsing*,' 118–23, 130; *idem*, ' "Elephants Can Actually Swim!": Contemporary Chinese Views of Late Ly Dai Viet,' in D. G. Marr and A. C. Milner (eds), *Southeast Asia in the 9th to 14th Centuries* (Singapore, 1986), 131–3.

appeared more often than Confucius. Yet these classicists also brought the lessons learned by their predecessors during the troubled fourteenth century to bear on the early years of the Le dynasty (1428–1527), particularly regarding the problems of land concentration and population control.[19]

The classicists were succeeded by Neo-Confucian scholars who rose to leading positions at court through the mid-1400s. As noted, the two decades of Ming occupation (1407–27) brought bureaucratic agencies, Chinese legal norms, a strong sense of Neo-Confucian orthodoxy, and Confucian schools more deeply into Vietnamese society. While the Vietnamese violently rejected Ming political control, these literati equated Ming models with modernity. It was they who led the administrative and intellectual transformation of the Vietnamese state, the so-called Neo-Confucian revolution of the fifteenth century.[20] The 1460s saw this new literati culture flower under the patronage of the young Neo-Confucian educated ruler Le Thanh-tong (1460–97). Successful exam candidates, particularly from the four provinces surrounding Thang-long, took office in the capital and the provinces. As Nola Cooke has pointed out, Thanh-tong intended that the examinations would not merely staff the new bureaucratic structure, but would popularize literati norms:

> [Officials], cultural brokers at home in both village and capital, would act as role models and moral exemplars for local society at the same time that they would watch over cultural orthodoxy in Dai Viet's more than seven thousand villages.

By the early sixteenth century, over 70,000 village scholars were in theory eligible for the basic examinations.[21]

What were the significant elements of this literati culture? Textual expertise and an ability to cite classical Chinese precedents remained from earlier generations of Vietnamese scholars. What was new—and what we must assume derived substantially from a closer knowledge of Ming practice and texts—was the intense activism and

[19] Whitmore, *Vietnam, Ho Quy Ly*, 65–7; *idem*, 'Adopting Antiquity'; *idem*, 'Transforming Dai Viet,' ch. 2; Phan Huy Chu, *Lich Trieu Hien Chuong Loai Chi*, tr. Vien Su Hoc (Hanoi, 1992), II, 220, 228, 240–2, 246.

[20] Whitmore, 'Transforming Dai Viet,' chs 2–5; *idem*, 'The Tao-Dan Group: Poetry, Cosmology, and the State in the Hong-Duc Period (1470–1497),' *Crossroads*, 7, 2 (1992), 55–61; *idem*, 'From Classical Scholarship to Confucian Belief in Vietnam,' *VNF*, 9 (1987), 49–58.

[21] Cooke, 'Nineteenth Century Vietnamese Confucianization,' 278–81, quote 280.

the desire to see the government become strongly involved in the affairs, moral and material, of the countryside. A major expression of this outlook was moralistic, didactic commentary on the past. Ngo Si Lien added his comments to the existing chronicle in 1479, forming the *Dai Viet Su Ky Toan Thu* ('Complete Book of the Historical Record of Dai Viet'), and therein expressed the literati's modernist emphasis. In their eyes, the Buddhist-dominated era of the eleventh to fourteenth centuries, with its tolerance for different creeds, its inadequate sense of ritual/social propriety, and its weak central government, provided object lessons of how *not* to proceed. The disasters of the late fourteenth century, marked by Cham invasions and dynastic collapse, confirmed the need for a fundamental reorientation. The literati championed proper ritual and moral action, which would influence the correlative forces binding Heaven, Earth, and Man.[22] They idealized the conscientious and active official, moving throughout the realm and providing direct expertise. They worried, to quote Alexander Woodside, about 'how to bring the comforts of peace to soldiers and peasants, how to make what is advantageous prevail over what is disadvantageous, how to disseminate moral dogma and reform customs, and how to satisfy their superiors and bestow "favors" upon the people.'[23] In the process, the officials were to comb through libraries for answers and to tour their territories for data. The result was a production of detailed reports and an accumulation of paperwork which created a 'documentary state,' perhaps analogous in substance but chronologically earlier than that which Valerie Kivelson elsewhere in this volume has described for seventeenth-century Muscovy.

During Thanh-tong's reign, the court wanted to make 'full use of agricultural potential' and expected the literati officials to get directly involved in economic affairs. Officials had to map their jurisdictions, maintain the public granaries, dikes, water courses, roads, and bridges, keep the land and population registers up to date, and take particular care that locally powerful families did not absorb the public lands. They were expected to offer agricultural instruction and to promote land reclamation. As the economy grew, they also had to regulate and report on new villages and markets, new goods,

[22] Whitmore, 'Transforming Dai Viet,' chs 2–3; *idem*, 'Tao-Dan Group,' 61–7; *idem*, 'Classical Scholarship,' 58–61; *idem*, *Vietnam, Ho Quy Ly*, notes *passim*.

[23] Woodside, 'Central Viet Nam's Trading World in the Eighteenth Century as Seen in Le Quy Don's "Frontier Chronicles,"' in Taylor and Whitmore, *Essays*, 159.

the circulation of people, and, of critical importance, the money supply.[24]

By 1500 the bureaucratic structure staffed by these literati officials was well in place, and their ideology had begun to penetrate the villages, at least in the Red River delta. As noted, although the documentary record for the sixteenth century is weak, the literati seem to have retained their social pre-eminence, and the system they staffed appears to have retained its vigor throughout the period of Mac rule to 1592. Yet, as in the early fifteenth century, tension persisted between these traditions and more personalized, semi-literate, non-bureaucratic forms of rule that found favor among militarized oligarchies on the southern frontier. Among these leaders military skills, concepts of personal loyalty, and the blood oath of allegiance took precedence. The military triumph in 1592 of the Trinh clan, which initially had weak literati ties and which relied on military groups from the southern frontier; the eclipse of literati supporters of the Mac in 1592, and renewed warfare between the Trinh and the southern Nguyen regime to 1672—all worked to end literati dominance at Thang-long in the early 1600s.

As we have seen, however, during the third quarter of the seventeenth century Trinh setbacks in the war against the Nguyen combined with a growing Trinh acclimatization to the social and cultural milieu of the northern heartland to reverse the political situation. In the ensuing realignment, the Trinh lord and *de facto* ruler Tac allied himself with the literati against the military faction and self-consciously reinstated the Hong-duc model of the late fifteenth century. The attractions of the literati, 'poor but erudite,' were several: they depended on the throne for advancement more than did the military leaders, whose lineages and frontier estates gave them considerable autonomy; their learning accorded them enormous prestige within the north; and they alone had the practical expertise needed to implement the Hong-duc model, whose demonstrated historic success promised practical advantages during post-war administrative reorganization. Much as Thalun (r. 1629–48) in Burma and Naresuan (r. 1590–1605) in Siam acted to recentralize administration after periods of disorder, Tac worked through the literati, especially Pham Cong Tru, to achieve this goal. Once again the highest

[24] *Dai Viet Su Ky Toan Thu*, tr. (Hanoi, 1972), III, 173–319 *passim*, quote 276; J. K. Whitmore, 'Cartography in Vietnam,' in J. B. Harley and D. Woodward (eds), *The History of Cartography* (Chicago, 1994), II, bk 2, 481–2; Chu, *Lich Trieu*, II, 221–47.

ranks of government were staffed with the examination graduates, primarily from the Red River delta.[25]

Again, too, literati officials were charged to enhance agriculture and ensure social order. The population had to be registered in the villages, the hydraulic system had to be reconstructed, transportation systems required renovation and expansion. To aid these tasks, administrative maps began to proliferate. The nineteenth-century scholar and encyclopedist Phan Huy Chu indicated the standard economic targets of the late seventeenth-century Trinh government (reminiscent of those of the Hong Duc period): first, the population registers, then tax collection and the money supply, culminating in readjustments in the public land system. Chu's writings point as well to a lively, somewhat novel interest in commerce in this period, although a conscious decision seems to have been made to maintain very light taxes on this sector.[26]

The late 1600s also saw the literati compose their view of Dai Viet's past, eventually bringing the official histories up to 1693. In K. W. Taylor's words, '. . . the Canh-tri history was written to legitimize the dominant position of the bureaucracy in the state, and in particular the power of the literati families from the Hong [Red] River plain who controlled this bureaucracy.' In the process, the scholars, under the direction of Pham Cong Tru, incorporated the work of their fifteenth- and sixteenth-century predecessors (those who served Le Thanh-tong and the Mac) and placed it within the ideological framework of the Trinh. As two centuries earlier, the literati stressed the moral/administrative failings of the Tran era and the normative value of Neo-Confucian learning.[27]

III. Losing Control: The Eighteenth-Century Crisis

During the eighteenth century the revived system of bureaucratic governance faced a novel set of problems deriving this time not from the challenge of military oligarchies, but from a pace of economic growth that outstripped the state's ability to monitor the population and to draw adequate tax revenues from the countryside. A series of

[25] Taylor, 'Literati Revival,' 12–17.

[26] *Ibid.*, 12, 15–16 ; Whitmore, 'Cartography,' 483–96; Yu, *Law*, 126–30; Chu, *Lich Trieu*, II, 222–47, 267–8, 278.

[27] Taylor, 'Literati Revival,' 14; Whitmore, '*Chung-Hsing*,' 130–4.

imaginative, far-reaching reforms in the early 1700s sought to tax private lands and internal commerce; but in the long term these innovations did not work. This failure helped to collapse both the northern and southern regimes, which in turn inaugurated a period of anarchy and rebellion unmatched since the late fourteenth century, and another temporary retreat of literati fortunes.

In part, the commercial expansion of the 1700s had its roots in the success of the 1660s/1670s reform program. The long era of peace after 1672 and the northern government's concerted efforts to advance agricultural production encouraged further population growth and commercial specialization. To some extent, prosperity, not least in the southern Nguyen state, also must have been aided by expanding international demand, and in particular by the relaxation of Ming bans on maritime trade and the prosperity of the south China coast.[28]

By the first decade of the eighteenth century, this growth and the socio-economic changes it entailed began to move beyond the ability of Trinh officials to cope. Actually the government faced four interconnected problems. First, tax registers began to lose touch with demographic realities. The fiscal rigidity of the 1664 procedure eliminated all serious burdens for some villages, but overloaded others. In combination with heavy demographic pressure on limited land and new commercial opportunities, this tended to 'shake people loose' from the stable communities on which the government depended. Vagabonds now headed in a variety of directions: to the protection of increasingly large landholders (i.e. into the growing private realm), to bandit gangs which further disrupted local society and governmental control, to towns and cities where flourishing commerce required artisans, shopkeepers, and laborers; and perhaps to the commercially and agriculturally expanding south. Second, as landholders accumulated tenants and political influence, they began to encroach upon the public lands by converting them to private status. Recall that in 1700 private lands, in contrast to public, still remained untaxed. Third, a variety of commercial activities also remained untaxed or inadequately taxed, although these had long been of increasing importance to the overall economy. Finally, population growth, increased market demand, and growing imports of silver all appear to have contributed to ongoing price inflation and

28 Whitmore, 'Monetary Flow,' 383–7.

to consequent instabilities in the monetary system, which in turn plagued tax collections and commercial exchange.[29]

A series of reform experiments began in 1711. These are important, less perhaps for their practical success—as we shall see, this was modest and short-lived—than for the indication they provide of pervasive economic and social change, and of the problems government officials faced and attempted to solve. The literati's initial goal was to bring the old-style agricultural taxation system under more effective control, most particularly by halting the illegal sale and seizure of the public lands.[30] Yet, within a decade, the officials acknowledged defeat and abandoned the effort to reconstitute the system as it had been established almost three hundred years earlier, in the early Le period. Now they moved to adopt a new plan suited to the increasing commercialization of the economy and the society.

The first step was to reorganize the system of tax collections. This the Trinh regime began in 1718, setting up six 'palaces' (*cung*), which controlled over a hundred different commercial sites or specialties compared to only 46 comparable units (called *hieu*, or 'offices') under the old regime. The following decade saw additional changes in the tax regime. Recognizing that the fixed registers of 1664 had failed to make adequate allowance for changes in population, officials organized new land and population inquests in 1719. This time, however, both public and private lands were to be surveyed, in preparation for the taxation of both categories.[31] To provide a suitable model for this radical innovation, in the early 1720s they selected from the records of the T'ang dynasty in China the scheme of *to-dung-dieu* (Ch. *zu-yong-diao*). In this tripartite system, the *to* (Ch. *zu*) was the land tax, which was levied henceforth on both public and private fields; the *dung* (Ch. *yong*) was the head tax, on individuals, not households; and the *dieu* (Ch. *diao*) was a single cash payment that replaced sundry obligations and payments. With its expanded tax base and its ability to match more closely expenditures to revenues, this system offered a revolution in fiscal thought and a potential turning point in Vietnamese government operations. Phan Huy Chu, almost a century later, saw the new system as 'clearer and more appropriate' than that established in the 1660s, precisely because

[29] Nha, *Tableau*, 41–4, 65–8, 92–107, 130–47; Whitmore, 'Monetary Flow,' 368–9.

[30] Chu, *Lich Trieu*, II, 247–51.

[31] *Ibid.*, II, 232, 273–8.

all lands, public and private (as well as formerly exempt riverbank tracts), became theoretically subject to taxation.[32]

Although based on T'ang precedent, the Vietnamese *to-dung-dieu*, unlike the early Chinese tax, sought to regularize government income in a period not of economic stability, but of rapid change. Striving for a uniform tax, the administration adapted the system to its circumstances—it sought cash as well as in-kind payments, rated public and private lands at different levels of quality, and allowed the royal areas (the capital and the provinces of Thanh-hoa and Nghe-an) favored rates. The stated goal was to insure that land was being used completely and that the population was not straying from the registers.[33]

In the 1720s the Trinh government also began to tax more extensively the burgeoning commercial economy, notwithstanding the government's agrarian bias. It readjusted the system of toll stations for road and river stations, ferries, and river docks. Moreover, between 1720 and 1724 officials imposed taxes for the first time on a variety of commercial staples, including salt—obviously a critical item—various metals, woods, sea and river products, and cinnamon. The edict on salt explicitly stated that it was time to move beyond a fiscal policy based solely on land taxes and to benefit from commerce as well. Or as Phan Huy Chu explained, 'For the first time the profits of the merchants began to enter the state coffers.'[34] In the 1730s and 1740s, in order to provide specie needed for expanding trade as well as for tax collections, the government authorized the use of privately-minted, hitherto illegal, zinc coins. More important, alongside the traditional copper cash, silver—obtained from mines on the China border and from intra-Asian trade—began to gain acceptance as official currency.[35]

These fiscal reforms culminated in the emergence of the concept of what we would call a budget. When the new ruler Trinh Giang took power in 1730, he sought to determine whether revenues and expenses were balanced. Officials were ordered to study how the revenue moved from the six tax 'palaces' into the administration, and to provide detailed reports. Their subsequent memorandum stated:

[32] *Ibid.*, II, 232–7, 254–6, 265; Nha, *Tableau*, 28–35.
[33] D. C. Twitchett, *Financial Administration Under the T'ang Dynasty* (Cambridge, 1963), 24–40; Chu, *Lich Trieu*, II, 232–6; Nha, *Tableau*, 28–32.
[34] Chu, *Lich Trieu*, II, 257–61, 265, 268–70.
[35] Whitmore, 'Monetary Flow,' 368–9.

Finances are the urgent work of the state . . . Recently, it has not mattered if the amounts collected and paid out came out even, and at the end of the year [they] were not even checked. Now [we] respectfully request [that you] choose from among us to work in confidence with officials of the Ministry of Finance to calculate the revenues from last year compared to the expenses of the entire year—to see whether the revenues are sufficient or fall short . . .

The Trinh lord agreed, and 49 instructions were sent to the Ministry of Finance governing disbursements.[36]

However, by this time, the late 1730s, events—social, economic, and political—were beginning to spin out of control. As a practical matter, even the updated registers could not easily keep abreast of population changes, so that discrepancies and inequities began to multiply. In addition to such physical limits on administrative knowledge, powerful local interests resisted the registration of private lands or the return of vagabonds to their original villages. Not surprisingly, exemptions were bought and sold by corrupt or compliant local officials. The growth of factionalism at Thang-long, as between the Le princes and the Trinh lords, only aggravated these problems. Moreover, once taxes were applied to commerce, the government was tempted to make up for chronic deficits by imposing fresh burdens on the most politically vulnerable sectors. As tax demands mounted, they began to stifle market activity. Meanwhile, although demographic trends and their relation to price movements in the eighteenth century have not been studied, there is undeniable evidence of severe monetary instabilities, as well as a growing shortage of arable land in the north and a consequent increase in vagabondage, banditry, and rural unrest.[37] A series of rural uprisings in northern Vietnam, led variously by disaffected scholars, Le princes, Buddhist monks, local peasants, and minority peoples, and pledged to alleviate popular distress and in some cases to restore real power from the Trinh to the Le dynasty, began in the 1730s, peaked in the 1740s, and persisted through the 1760s.[38] As the Trinh diverted energy and funds to suppress these challenges, the reform efforts of the 1720s and 1730s faltered, the maintenance of dikes and registers deteriorated, and power devolved to local families.

[36] Chu, *Lich Trieu*, II, 281–5, quote 281.

[37] *Ibid.*, II, 224–6, 236, 256–9, 266, 270; Yu, *Law*, 130–2; Li, 'Inner Region,' chs 5, 7; Nha, *Tableau*, 157–62.

[38] Nha, *Tableau*, 16; Thomas Hodgkin, *Vietnam, The Revolutionary Path* (New York, 1981), 82–4; Nguyen Khac Vien, *Vietnam, A Long History* (Hanoi, 1987), 96–101.

Meanwhile, although land on the southern frontier was plentiful compared to the north, the southern seignury of the Nguyen in the mid-eighteenth century also experienced recurrent strains as a result of poorly controlled political expansion and economic dislocation. Li Tana has argued that severe price inflation contributed to a sudden, if temporary, decline in Nguyen revenues from foreign trade starting in the 1750s. This in turn led to compensatory overtaxation on the Quy Nhon area, where people already resented the burdens they were expected to shoulder to support Nguyen military expansion into the rich ricelands of the Mekong delta. Quy Nhon was a recently integrated area, not particularly well administered, with a lively local identity. The result in the 1770s was a massive uprising, the so-called Tayson revolt, which quickly overthrew the Nguyen, and then swept into the north where it exploited the manifest weaknesses of the Trinh to destroy that regime as well. Two centuries of Trinh–Nguyen rivalry were at an end. Revealingly, despite their regional base and despite irredentist fantasies involving claims to south China, the Taysons regarded themselves as leaders of a distinctly Vietnamese polity reaching from the Chinese border to the Mekong delta.[39]

The profound sense of social and intellectual disjuncture, even before the outbreak of the Tayson rebellion, is captured in the writings of perhaps the two chief literati thinkers of the eighteenth century, Ngo Thi Si (1726–80) and Le Quy Don (1726–84). Ngo Thi Si's response to the problems of his age was strongly conventional and deeply conservative. He wanted the administrative model of the Hong Duc period restored in all its vigor, including accurate population registers, which he took to be an emblem of social discipline and proper hierarchy; at the same time he tended to romanticize what he considered to have been the natural interaction of village and throne in an earlier age before discipline became necessary.[40] Le Quy Don, while accepting much of Si's critique, was intellectually more adventurous. Buoyed by what Woodside has termed 'an extraordinary cultural pride' and recognizing the inevitability of change in human affairs, Don sought not merely to impose the literary culture from above, but to absorb local traditions. Opening himself to the active potentialities of Vietnamese popular culture, Don

[39] Li, 'Inner Region,' 167–72.

[40] Chu, *Lich Trieu*, II, 10, 29–30, 219–20, 228, 288–9; III, 7, 41.

advocated adjusting literati culture to popular sources of knowledge and thus strengthening it from below.[41]

These speculations were the latest in a series of literati efforts to achieve a proper moral ordering of society. During some three hundred years, from the mid-fifteenth to the late eighteenth century, literati perspectives provided the principal intellectual impetus for administrative innovation, particularly in the northern heartland. To be sure, even in the north, literati culture never went unchallenged. Not only did it have to contend with recalcitrant popular custom, with Christian and Mahayanist religious traditions, and with military networks in varying degrees unsympathetic to scholarly thought; in addition, the literati remained subject to the often arbitrary political control by the four great families, the Le, Nguyen, Trinh, and Mac.[42] Yet throughout these centuries, the key elements—an intensely archival, written administrative culture; civil service examinations; and an interlocking set of moral and social prescriptions—retained their influence, as Chinese cultural models remained synonymous with 'civilization.' After the eighteenth-century breakdown, these features would again prove indispensable to a centralizing state, even one refashioned from the southern patrimony.

IV. Choosing the Literati Option Once More

Each in its own way, the Tayson movement (which by 1789 had overthrown the Nguyen, Trinh, and Le) and the revived Nguyen dynasty (which in 1802 in turn overthrew the Tayson) entertained non-Confucian, non-literati possibilities. The Taysons, for example, hailed from a frontier area poor in literati culture. The Tayson ruler Quang Trung sought to substitute the demotic script *nom* for Chinese characters as the official national language in which all government communications, including the critical mandarin examinations, would be conducted. In keeping with his military background, moreover, key posts went to the generals and for the first time military officials were superior to civil officials at all levels. The first Nguyen ruler of reunified Vietnam was Gia Long, who also hailed from the south, who had taken refuge in Bangkok, whose forces included

[41] Alexander Woodside, 'Conceptions of Change and of Human Responsibility for Change in Late Traditional Vietnam,' in D. K. Wyatt and A. B. Woodside (eds), *Moral Order and the Question of Change* (New Haven, 1982), 119–31, 139–45.

[42] Cooke, 'Nineteenth Century Vietnamese Confucianization,' 277–312.

Chinese, Khmers, Malays, and French, and one of whose sons was allowed to convert to Christianity. As a military figure, Gia Long, like Quang Trung, allocated key posts to his generals and appointed autonomous military viceroys in the north and south of the country. Out of necessity if not desire, he, too, maintained *nom* as the national script; and, as Nola Cooke has shown, the early Nguyen supporters, concentrated in the south and center of the country, hardly came from orthodox, literarily-accomplished Confucian backgrounds.[43]

Nonetheless, to varying degrees both the short-lived Tayson regime and the early Nguyen dynasty (which would remain in power during the French colonial era) chose to adopt Sinic administrative models based firmly on control of the land and population registers. The reason, as Woodside has made clear in his study of the early Nguyen,[44] was Neo-Confucianism's fateful combination of unequalled cultural prestige and unequalled practical utility in controlling a far-flung, inherently fissiparous realm. As early as 1789, notwithstanding his advocacy of *nom*, Quang Trung undertook to reactivate the traditional land registers, to return the population to their villages, and to redistribute communal lands in keeping with Le/Trinh precedents. So, too, Gia Long, despite his personalized rule, his military orientation, and his basic disinterest in mandarinal exams, took control of the traditional administrative tools, including the land and population registers, and in 1812 adopted the unprecedentedly Sinic Gia Long law code. Under Gia Long's son and successor, Minh Mang (r. 1820–41), Woodside has described how Chinese institutions were extended with a grim determination over the whole range of political, cultural, and administrative life. For this, the first sustained attempt to rule directly the entire area from the China frontier to the Gulf of Siam, no alternate administrative model was available. In the 1830s thirty-one standardized provincial administrations were created atop the old structure of prefects and districts, but now with the Chinese practice of rating districts into four grades according to their administrative difficulty. The capital administration, with its six ministries, four great ministers, and suc-

[43] Cooke, 'The Composition of the Nineteenth-Century Political Elite of Pre-Colonial Nguyen Vietnam,' *MAS* 29, 4 (1995), 741–64; Hodgkin, *Vietnam*, 90–103; Alexander B. Woodside, 'The Historical Background,' in Nguyen Du, *The Tale of Kieu*, tr. Huynh Sanh Thong (New Haven, 1983), xi–xviii; R. B. Smith, 'Politics and Society in Viet-Nam during the Early Nguyen Period (1802–62),' *Journal of the Royal Asiatic Society*, 1974, 2, 155–6.

[44] Woodside, *Vietnam and the Chinese Model* (Cambridge, MA, 1971).

cession of secretariats followed Song as well as Qing precedents. The land registers, begun in 1805 throughout the north, were gradually extended to cover the entire country until, with the bureaucratic integration of the south in the 1830s, they were complete. Along with the population registers, these records continued to provide the basis for taxation and military conscription.[45]

In dealing with the recurrent problems of monetary instability and commercial growth, the Nguyen demonstrated much the same curious combination of experimental pragmatism and ideological agrarianism as their Trinh predecesors. The Nguyen made far greater use of silver in their monetary system than had earlier rulers. In 1839 we find the adoption of a straightforward salary program for the bureaucracy, with fixed amounts for each grade. On the other hand, the regime under Minh Mang continued to rely overwhelmingly on land taxes, it sought to alleviate poverty in Binh Dinh by expanding the public lands at the expense of private holdings, it refused to allow foreign merchants to settle in the country, and it remained broadly unsympathetic to commerce.[46]

Cooke has recently argued that Minh Mang's efforts to integrate the northern elite into the imperial bureaucracy failed. Both before and after his reign, pro-Nguyen elites based in the south and the center of the country successfully manipulated Sinic institutions for their own benefit, and the meritocratic ethos of the Hong Duc period was subverted.[47] This is fair enough. Yet in a broader sense, here, too, we find a basic continuity. Whatever its shortcomings, the revived examination system occupied a far more prominent role under nineteenth-century Nguyen administration that under its eighteenth-century southern antecedent. As such, the exams testified both to the continued primacy of Neo-Confucian learning within the literati value system and to the historic southward march of literate, Neo-Confucian culture.[48]

In sum, I view Dai Viet/Vietnam both as one player in the tripartite early modern division of mainland Southeast Asia and as an example of sustained Eurasian integration. Notwithstanding continuities with pre-fifteenth century institutions and cultural systems,

[45] *Ibid.*, 48, 60–168; Hodgkin, *Vietnam*, 91, 101–13; Whitmore, 'Cartography,' 507.

[46] Woodside, *Chinese Model*, 79–81, 267–80; Smith, 'Politics and Society,' 164–6; Whitmore, 'Monetary Flow,' 388.

[47] Cooke, 'Composition of the Elite.'

[48] Victor Lieberman, personal communication.

the Neo-Confucian revolution of that century sanctioned a complex of features—formal academic training and civil service examinations to select the leading officials, Confucian notions of social and familial propriety, a sense of cultural/ethnic exclusivity, detailed land and population registers, agricultural activism—that was relatively novel. And despite later vicissitudes, this complex retained and, in the aftermath of recurrent breakdowns, even increased its prestige well into the nineteenth century. As such, literati culture helps to define the early modern period in Vietnamese history.

Southeast Asia 'Inside Out,' 1300–1800: A Perspective from the Interior

DAVID K. WYATT

Despite the serious studies of the past century, the history of Mainland Southeast Asia is still poorly understood. This is not to say that we do not have numerous studies of particular countries and events in individual countries; but, despite the efforts of Victor Lieberman, Anthony Reid, and others, we still lack a comprehensive sense of the dynamics of the premodern history of long periods on a region-wide basis.

What we are attempting to understand is exceedingly complex, for it involves numerous political units that coalesce into a much smaller grouping of states by the nineteenth century. How can we understand the process by which this occurs? Lieberman has adopted an externalist approach, looking especially at politics and economics, and attempting to discern general patterns of change. This approach is both necessary and useful; but we need also to look at the 'internal' aspect of change, and to raise some fundamental philosophical issues. What I am ultimately arguing for is an approach to the period through cultural and intellectual history—examining (or at least thinking about) what was happening inside people's heads.

This approach comes out of the indigenous sources for this period dealing with the interior of Mainland Southeast Asia, especially in the northern parts of what is now Thailand, and the adjacent portions of Burma, southwest China, and northern Laos. For the most part, these take the form of what has been called 'chronicles,' including both the 'dynastic' chronicles (*phongsawadan*) of places like Siam and the 'historical legends' (*tamnan*) of places like Nan, Chiang Mai, Nakhòn Si Thammarat, and Luang Prabang.[1] The distinction is prob-

[1] Cf. David K. Wyatt, 'Chronicle Traditions in Thai Historiography,' in *Southeast Asian History and Historiography*, ed. C.D. Cowan and O.W. Wolters (Ithaca: Cornell University Press, 1976), pp. 107–22; reprinted in the same author's *Studies in Thai History: Collected Articles* (Chiang Mai: Silkworm Books, 1994), pp. 1–21. For a general survey of the history of Chiang Mai and Lan Na, the reader will find useful Hans Penth, *A Brief History of Lan Na* (Chiang Mai: Silkworm Books, 1994).

ably meaningless, for, as I have argued in introducing the Chiang Mai 'Chronicle,' such sources surely are worthy in many cases of the appellation 'history.'

We must begin by admitting that the local sources surely lend themselves much more readily to the 'externalist' than the 'internalist' approach. The 'local' and 'national' chronicles rarely concern themselves directly with religion, culture, or the subjective aspects of history: at times they even explicitly eschew such concerns.

Take, for example, *The Chiang Mai Chronicle (CMC)*. Best-known from Camille Notton's 1932 French translation,[2] or from the 1971 Thai edition published by the Thai Prime Minister's Office,[3] this lengthy and substantial work attempts to encompass all of Chiang Mai's history from the time of the Buddhist equivalent of Adam and Eve down to the time when the manuscript was composed in 1827.[4] Based both upon an impressive range of manuscripts dating back perhaps to the sixteenth century (or before), upon the memories of those still alive when the anonymous historian wrote in 1827, and perhaps upon some contemporaneous sources, the author used his sources intelligently and critically. Where the author had to rely upon single sources, he seems to have attempted but minimal editing, and therefore the earlier portions of the *CMC* reflect early sources—that is, sources that were written long before 1827. His accounts of the fifteenth-century Lan Na (Chiang Mai) wars with the Chinese of Yunnan, for example,[5] are much like similar accounts in the earlier versions of the Nan chronicles,[6] and the language of earlier portions of the *CMC* is archaic when compared with the language of the portions of the *CMC* dealing with the eighteenth and early nineteenth centuries. More to the point, the *CMC* is sufficiently detailed for us to be able to say that the values—even the culture

[2] Camille Notton, *Chronique de Xieng Mai (Annales du Siam, III*; Paris: Geuthner, 1932).

[3] *Tamnan phün müang Chiang Mai* [The Chiang Mai Chronicle] ed. Sanguan Chotisukkharat (Bangkok: Prime Minister's Office, 1971).

[4] David K. Wyatt and Aroonrut Wichienkeeo, *The Chiang Mai Chronicle [CMC]* (Chiang Mai, 1995), is a new edition and translation of this chronicle, based on a palm-leaf manuscript in the collection of Hans Penth. References are to folios of the original manuscript, which are marked in the new English tradition.

[5] *CMC* ff°. 4.01–4.04.

[6] *'Prawat tang müang Nan [History of the Foundation of Nan; PTMN]'* unpubl. Ms. (no. SRI 82.107.05.045), Social Research Institute, Chiang Mai. This text is described and discussed in David K. Wyatt, *The Nan Chronicle* (Ithaca: Cornell Southeast Asia Program, 1994), pp. 14–23.

and the thought—attributed to the early centuries (a good example is the warfare of the fifteenth century) are very different from the values, culture, and thought with which he describes and analyzes the warfare of later periods (like the warfare of the late eighteenth century through which he lived).

The point is neither irrelevant nor inconsequential, and has a great deal to do with the phenomena with which Lieberman is concerned—the growth and elaboration of political communities, and the interrelations between them, over the half-millennium between about 1300 and 1800. Just how the *CMC* and similar sources shed light upon such developments cannot easily be traced by looking at the single, isolated episodes of which the chronicles are composed. Instead, we have to examine broader contrasts and comparisons; particularly the contrasts and comparisons between the fourteenth-century world depicted in the sources and the eighteenth- or early-nineteenth-century world in which they are set. For these purposes, let us examine three sets of contrasts, involving the following themes: the world, neighboring non-Tai polities, and nearby Tai principalities, all generally falling under the rubric of 'inter-polity relations'; then a group of themes all involving the definitions of the various socio-political groups of local society; and finally religious contrasts between the earlier and the later chronicles. (There are numerous other themes which might be examined here, but for the sake of economy we must confine ourselves to these.)

The two periods defined. The two periods with which we are concerned were both periods of almost-constant warfare. The first of these extends roughly from the death of the great King Mangrai (r. 1259–1317)[7] to the advent of the great warrior-king Tilokarat (r. 1442–1487). This was a troubled period of nine monarchs during which only gradually the kingdom of Lan Na took shape, centered on Chiang Mai. The second, later period extends from the Burmese invasion of Siam and Lan Na in the 1760s through the Lan Na revolt (1775) to the reconstitution of the Lan Na kingdom by the end of the century, the re-foundation, strengthening, and expansion of Chiang Mai, and the end of the wars with Burma (1804). Because the author could have written much of what he has to say on this later period out of his remembered experience, his treatment of this

[7] Hans Penth gives King Mangrai the dates 1261–1311. [*Jinakalamali Index: An Annotated Index to the Thailand Part of Ratanapañña's Chronicle* Jinakalamali (Oxford, 1994), p. 310.]

is much fuller and more detailed than the shorter section dealing with the early period; but there is still much on each: roughly one and one-half fascicles (or 'chapters') dealing with the earlier period, and two and one-half chapters dealing with the latter. Let us examine the periods separately.

The Earlier Period

On the whole, the fourteenth century is treated in a way not markedly different from the treatment accorded the preceding century, the era of Mangrai and Mangrai's father.[8] (Indeed, much of what applies here could be said as well of the succeeding reign.)

The world of the chronicles. Superficially, the *CMC* seems to be thoroughly imbued with a classical Buddhist view of the world with, of course, India at its center. I say 'superficially' because we need to remind ourselves that the chronicle was actually written only in the early nineteenth century, not in the fourteenth. Thus, although the chronicle as a whole is structured by Buddhist mythology,[9] and the text itself seems to be modeled in part on the *Mahavamsa* chronicle of Sri Lanka, one might dismiss these as later accretions. From what we have been able to see of the original sources on which the *CMC* might have been based, one notices that Buddhism—and specific Buddhist monks in particular—are very rare in the early fascicles of the *CMC*. The only consistent and frequent references to the Indic civilizational context have to do with Indic ideas of kingship, and to a world in which only a few kings have fully undergone Indic coronation. In chapter three, there is present the Indic conception (and rituals) of kingship, *and* the idea of legitimacy through royal descent: that is, the idea that only the descendants of kings could be 'real' kings.[10]

The best examples of this actually come from the reign of King Mangrai, although similar ideas undergird the succeeding period.

[8] *CMC*, fascicle 1. The same period is treated in, for example, *Tamnan Mangrai Chiang Mai, Chiang Tung [Chronicle of Mangrai, Chiang Mai, and Keng Tung, TMCMCT]*, ed. Thiu Wichaikhatthakha and Phaithun Dòkbuakaeo (Chiang Mai, 1993).

[9] Such a mythic base of the chronicle's argument forms the centerpiece of fascicle 8 (ff°. 8.17–8.26). See below.

[10] People are said to have come from Keng Tung to argue that 'As Phò Thao Nam Thuam was born from the flesh of King Cheyyasongkhram, who has great majesty, we should make him our lord,' and he thereupon became king of Keng Tung. *CMC*, f°. 3.14.1. (The third numeral is the line number.)

Sometime in the early 1270s, for example, King Mangrai is visited by a distant relative, *Thao* Kaen Phongsa, from the Tai polities of the Black Tai region of what is now northern Viet Nam. *Thao* Kaen Phongsa, stressing their common descent from a 'real,' consecrated king, administered the sacraments of coronation upon Mangrai, which then were maintained 'down to the present day.'[11] The twin themes of descent and coronation thereafter are repeatedly stressed in the *CMC*.

Similar sacrality is not attributed to places in the *CMC*, with the sole exception of places of ceremonial importance, such as the mountain upon which some early kings were consecrated. The regalia, however, especially the Royal Sword, not only follows the Indic formulas but even bears Sanskrit names, and has that enduring importance from earliest times down to the most recent.[12]

The earlier portion of the chronicle therefore defines kingship in terms both of the hereditary descent of rulers, and of the Indic (but not specifically Buddhist) rites of coronation. It is this latter aspect which distinguishes some kings from others. The chronicle makes it quite plain that there are numerous kings in 'the world'—that is, the world known to the people who are the subject of the chronicle (who are usually termed 'Lao' in earlier portions). This was a polycentric, or poly-royal, structure of authority, in which it was held to be natural that there should be innumerable rulers.

In a passage which I would take to be a later addition (that is, a bit of prose added by the nineteenth-century historian), the historian explains why the number of monarchs was reduced—and, incidentally, the importance of Indic coronation and regalia:

After King Mangrai had been consecrated king, he learned that rulers of the countries adjoining his own were fighting over manpower and land, each claiming that they belonged to him, which was a source of great suffering to the people of the domain. The lord [Mangrai] thought, 'Any land with multiple rulers is a source of great suffering to its people. Furthermore, much anxiety arises [from such situations]. All these [contending] rulers,

[11] *CMC*, f°. 1.32. I have not found the inscriptions of the period to be of much use in this current enterprise.

[12] Curiously, the first such coronation mentioned in the *CMC*—that of King Cüang—is given with a careful description of the ceremony, but no mention of the specific royal regalia (f°. 1.16), which begin to be mentioned only in connection with the reign of King Mangrai: the Sri Kañjeyya Sword then is mentioned (f°. 2.30) as having been 'a very ancient sword of [King] Lawacangkarat,' a distant ancestor of King Cüang. The sword is twice subsequently mentioned by name (ff°. 7.37 and 8.28), but only in the last portion of the *CMC*.

even though they be of the same lineage [as I]—the line of King Lawacangkarat, descendants of Lao Kòp and Lao Chang—not a single one of them has been duly consecrated a king. Only my paternal grandfather, King Lao Kao, who was the younger sibling of Cao Lao Khòp and Lao Chang, was consecrated a king, continuing the lineage down to me today. Furthermore, the regalia of coronation—for example, the Sword of Victory, the Spear, the Srikañjayya Dagger, and the Auspicious Gems—are things that have come down to me from Grandfather Lao Cong [Cangkaracha], and I have maintained them down to the present day, every one of them. All of those who are my neighbor kings have not undergone coronation like me, not one of them, and they [therefore] cannot withstand me. I should attack and take those domains.'[13]

Which, of course, he then proceeded to do, his efforts culminating in the capture of Hariphunchai (old Lamphun) and the subsequent foundation of Chiang Mai in 1296.

My inclination to take this passage as a later insertion, or interpretation, is strengthened by two considerations. First, the section of the *CMC* dealing with the period following the death of King Mangrai (1317?) shows us little of what we might call 'empire-building.' That is, that section of the *CMC* is little concerned with justifying rulers' expeditions to subdue their neighbors or even with their place in a wider world. Second, a chronicle text recently has come to light which deals exclusively with the reign of King Mangrai; and it justifies Mangrai's conquest of his neighbors only in the following words, which form the first sentences of the first page:

> Here we shall tell of Lan Na. King Mangrai ruled just Chiang Rai, Fang, Hang, Sat, Ngoen Yang, and Chiang Rüa, in succession to his father. Ruling these, he took troops to capture Phayao, Phan, Thoeng, Lamphun, Chiang Khòng, M. Luang, and M. Nan. Some he conquered and some he did not, taking one domain in some years and none in others; sometimes taking two or three years for one; sometimes taking one without a battle. Those he took, he ruled, killing the rulers he conquered. When he killed the rulers, he would have one of his officers govern there, and sometimes he would maintain [the previous ruler] in charge.[14]

I would judge this text to be representative of the sorts of evidence upon which the anonymous author of the 1827 *CMC* based his history.

This makes sense when we consider the world in which Mangrai's successors lived and reigned. To begin with, Mangrai's son and suc-

[13] *CMC*, f°. 1.22.1–4.

[14] *TMCMCT*, p. 1. It is clear that this text is in fact two separate chronicles, joined on f°. 22.

cessor Chaiyasongkhram did not even remain in Chiang Mai: he parceled his kingdom out among his sons, probably awarding the richest to his eldest son and progressively less-rich principalities (or 'domains') to his second and third sons: they were given Chiang Mai, Fang, and Chiang Khòng, while Chaiyasongkhram himself went to rule in Chiang Rai.[15] This pattern persisted for a long time thereafter. Mangrai's descendants controlled a few of the most important places, while other domains were controlled by local rulers who only gradually were displaced by Mangrai's line. For example, when Chaiyasongkhram fell out with his son Nam Thuam in 1324, that son was sent to become the first ruler of Keng Tung (Chiang Tung in the Lan Na sources).[16] What was to become the Kingdom of Lan Na was gradually expanded, sometimes by founding new domains and cities (as Chiang Saen in 1329),[17] sometimes by conquest, and sometimes by replacing local rulers with members of Mangrai's lineage. For a long time, the royal city was to the north, often at Chiang Saen; and it was not until the reign of Phayu (r. 1345/46–1367/68) that the paramount rulers reigned from Chiang Mai.

The querulousness of this 'bedlam of snarling states' (to borrow Harvey's memorable phrase) is suggested by a passage that indicates what happened when King Saen Phu fell ill around 1336:

> Cao Saen Phu had ruled for seven years when he fell ill, and a physician was fetched to a secluded place. The physician said that the prince's age was advanced, and would reach its end within that very year. All the councilors devised a strategy to have two very large rafts carry [a royal] dwelling to show that he was still healthy, and float it in the middle of the Mekong, thus not revealing to anyone that the ruler was ill, for if people knew, then rulers of other countries would find out, and would invade the country.[18]

By implication, the 'rulers of other countries' were other Tai rulers in the immediate vicinity of Chiang Saen.

Throughout the period from the death of Mangrai until about 1400, the *CMC* gives little indication of any concern with the areas beyond what is now the provinces of Chiang Rai and (the eastern half of) Chiang Mai. To be sure, there were occasional skirmishes with Phrae and Nan but these seem to have been inconsequential.[19]

[15] That the father was in Chiang Rai is indicated at *CMC* f°. 3.10.5. There is an explicit statement to this effect at *CMC* f°. 3.15.1.

[16] *CMC*, ff°. 3.13.4–3.14.2.

[17] *CMC*, ff°. 3.15–3.17.

[18] *CMC*, f°. 3.18.1–3.

[19] *CMC*, ff°. 3.19–3.21 mentions warfare with Nan and Phrae.

Early in the fifteenth century, however, within just a few years there was a dramatic and sudden widening of the horizons of the Lan Na polity. In quick succession, Lan Na first became embroiled in conflict with Siam, and then with the Hò—that is, with the Ming Chinese moving into Yunnan.

Actually, the *CMC* (and many related texts) does *not* say anything about Ayudhya, Siam, Lan Na, or China and the Chinese: the conflicts are described entirely in terms of the ambitions, greed, or personalities of the various rulers involved. The conflicts with Siam centered around dissension within both the Chiang Mai and the Ayudhya ruling houses; and the conflict with the Hò seems to be accounted for in the *CMC* partly by Chinese opportunism (taking advantage of Chiang Mai's involvement with Ayudhya) and partly by Chinese greed for more tribute. Even reading between the lines, the most one might say about this particular period is that the Chiang Mai people seem to have become increasingly aware of the existence of new major powers to the north and south. One is left with the impression that this inland principality was essentially still very parochial; still concerned primarily with its immediate neighborhood in the small mountain valleys of the interior of mainland Southeast Asia. In this early period, neither the Lan Sang Lao to the east nor the Shans to the west, not to mention the Burmese further west, figured very prominently in that world which was relevant to the lives of the Lan Na people.

The outcomes of the large-scale wars of this period for the most part were determined by personal martial qualities, or by superior tactics (or by trickery), rather than by such considerations as the relative balance of forces on the two sides, or the economic strength of one side or another, or by considerations of morale and leadership save as these were exemplified in the personal qualities of rulers.

Social organization. Nor do the sources tell us much of the social and political organization of this period, save in passing. What little the sources tell us suggests that social organization was relatively simple. The range of rank-prefixes associated with men's names in this period is very small; and such rank designators usually are attached to, or combined with, name-elements that indicate birth-order and/or place of origin. The *CMC* almost never indicates ethnicity, but it often mentions descent ('son of so-and-so,' for example). This social picture of a simple Lan Na society is consistent with the political picture we have already seen. A single passage suggests a social complexity that is otherwise missing in the text; a passage that occurs in connection with the foundation of Chiang Saen in 1329:

As for the allocation of territories dedicated to the Religion, those persons dedicated were to perform [their services] to the religious institutions, as specified in the instruments of dedication written on stone. As for the freemen of Chiang Saen, they were organized in levies, in *buak*, *kò*, *khum*, and *tò*.[20] As for those skilled with gold and silver, and drum smiths, they were to present [the fruits of their labors] to whoever ruled the domain. Similarly for ivory lost when elephants died, elephants, horses, laborers, cattle, beehives and wax, iron forges, distilleries, sweets manufactories, charcoal-burners, everything hanging from trees, lacquers, the produce of wet and dry rice fields and from orchards, and fish and game, all produced in the territory of the ruler were to be presented to the ruler.[21]

The phrase 'As for the freemen' implies that the people in the preceding phrase were not freemen: they were 'dedicated,' or indentured, or attached, to religious foundations. 'Freemen' (or *phrai*), by contrast, were organized (presumably in decimally-sized groups) to render labor service to otherwise unspecified officers. The fact that there seem to have been four different types of such labor groups suggests a fairly complex system of manpower organization, but only at the local (*müang*, 'domain') level. Only specialists, and especially craftsmen, were attached directly to 'the ruler,' but 'the ruler' in this case seems to indicate the local ruler (in this case, of Chiang Saen) rather than the king in far-away Chiang Mai.

Religion. If we were to base our view of this period primarily upon the well-known religious chronicles of the region, written in the early sixteenth century,[22] we would expect to find the *CMC*'s coverage of this period suffused through with Buddhist piety, for much of the fourteenth century apparently was characterized by great religious change as a new wave of Buddhism swept through the region from

[20] Manpower levies of some sort. Clearly, Notton had no clearer idea of what these might have been than we do, for he also had difficulty translating them (p. 79).

[21] *CMC*, f°. 3.17. The paragraph immediately preceding this one also outlines the structure and staffing of the administration of the domain of Chiang Saen.

[22] The most important of these is the famous *The Sheaf of Garlands of the Epochs of the Conqueror, Being a Translation of Jinakalamalipakaranam of Ratanapañña Thera of Thailand*, tr. N.A. Jayawickrama (London, 1968). See also Sommai Premchit and Donald K. Swearer, 'A Translation of "Tamnan Mulasasana Wat Pa Daeng": The Chronicle of the Founding of Buddhism of the Wat Pa Daeng Tradition,' *Journal of the Siam Society* 65:2 (July 1977), 73–110; and *Tamnan Mulasasana Chiang Mai lae Chiang Tung*, [The *Mulasasana* Chronicle of Chiang Mai and Keng Tung] ed. Prasert na Nagara and Puangkam Tuikeeo (Bangkok, 1994), a new and very important edition of the *Mulasasana* text.

Sri Lanka. The nineteenth-century author of the *CMC* was little interested in religion,[23] but he seems to have attempted scrupulously to follow his evidence, and we might expect him to have included far more on Buddhist developments here than he does (and does in later portions of his history). One of the striking things abut the *CMC*, however, is how much non-Buddhist religious practice is reflected in the earlier portions of the Chronicle. Two aspects of this practice are particularly important here. First, there are repeated references to divination employing chickens or chicken-bones.[24] Second, there are also many references to guardian spirits protecting the various domains of the region; spirits, for example, which helped defend Chiang Saen against the Hò attacks, especially in 1405/06.[25] This latter reference is particularly interesting because the author of the *CMC* explicitly indicates that his source was a certain 'History of the Hò Attack.' An identical cross-reference appears in a chronicle written in Nan in 1821, just a few years before the *CMC* was written.[26] This is not to say that Buddhism is not present in the accounts of the fourteenth and early fifteenth centuries, but only to say that such references to Buddhism are incidental and peripheral: Buddhism moved to the center of the ideological stage only later, during and after the reign of King Tilokarat.

Ideologically and intellectually, then, the world of Lan Na between the times of Mangrai and Tilokarat was predominantly local. Spirits were attached to, and protective of, specific places and people, and they were not transferable to other places and people. There was a congruence between this religious sphere and the political sphere: in both respects the Lan Na world was local, particularistic, and even parochial.[27]

[23] Cf. *CMC*, f°. 3.30.1, where he refers the reader to the Chronicle of the Sihinga Buddha.

[24] Cf. *CMC*, ff°. 3.20.1 (which also refers back to such divination in the time of King Mangrai), and 3.27.5. On chicken divination, see Renu Wichasin, 'Kanthamnai kraduk kai khòng khon Thai bang klum,' in *Ekkasan prakòp kansammana rüang khon Thai nòk prathet: phromdaen khwamru* [Documents for the Seminar on Tai Peoples Outside Thailand: Frontiers of Knowledge] (Bangkok, 1989), pp. 87–117. Dr Renu mistakenly writes that such divination is found among other Tai groups but not among the Tai Yuan of Lan Na. Her attention had not been drawn to the *CMC*.

[25] *CMC*, ff°. 4.03–4.05. Similar references figure prominently in the *Tamnan müang Nan* [The Nan Chronicle] (unpubl. ms., *Lanna Thai Manuscripts from the Richard Davis Collection, Australian National University*, no. fl–47).

[26] *PTMN*, ff°. 90–100.

[27] A similar argument is made in my 'Three Sukhothai Oaths of Allegiance,' *Studies in Thai History*, pp. 60–9.

The Later Period

The Lan Na world of the late eighteenth and early nineteenth centuries was very different from the same world four hundred years earlier. The circumstances, of course, were very different; and since the author of the *CMC* could write of these from personal experience and memory, the chronicle is much fuller on this period. We need to remind ourselves, however, that the differences between the earlier and the later period are by no means incidental: they reflect real changes that had occurred in the intervening centuries.

The world of the chronicles. There is even a sharp linguistic change between the earlier and the later portions of the *CMC*. The seventh and eighth chapters of the chronicle include many more 'Bangkok Thai' words than the preceding chapters, and include fewer local Chiang-Mai words. This does not indicate that the author was a Bangkok man: quite the contrary. The author clearly was a local, Chiang Mai person (probably male); and he is sufficiently critical of both the Siamese and the local Chiang Mai ruling elite for him to have been a member of neither group. The difference between the two different periods is attributable to, first, the fact that, while the author was hewing closely to older written sources to write about the earlier periods, he was writing of recent history from his own experience; if you will, in his own 'voice.' Second, the point is that it is the world-view, the experience, the values, and the orientation of the nineteenth-century world that is reflected in, or expressed in, the last two chapters of the *CMC*.

In the last two-and-one-half chapters of the *CMC*, Chiang Mai and Lan Na are but small parts of a much larger and broader world; a world that is dominated by the 'great powers' of the day: Burma and Siam. In this world, Lan Na (and Lan Sang) were but subordinate players. However, Lan Na remained not at the bottom of a hierarchical world, but rather somewhere in the middle. Chiang Mai was rapidly establishing its primacy in the world of the northern hills—including adjacent portions of Burma and Laos, or, more accurately, the adjacent Shan, Khoen, Lü, and Lao uplands: that is, Chiang Mai was in the process of establishing its hegemony over all of (what is now) Burma east of the Salween, the Sipsong Panna of southern Yunnan (China), and northwestern (now) Laos west of the U River valley.

The tokens of this hierarchy were, purely and simply, physical (especially military) power. There are two places in the final portions of the chronicle where two successive Chiang Mai rulers advised their relatives, which we now know as the founders of King Kavila's line, how they must behave as rulers.

The first speech of fatherly advice was given by Prince Chai Kaeo, father of Kavila and his brothers, on 5 January 1789. He was concerned primarily with internal matters, but noted:

> 'The past calamities of Lamphun, Chiang Mai, Keng Tung, M. Yòng, and Nan, all of them occurred because of discord among siblings and from failure to heed their parents' good advice, and because they vied for the royal wealth of the country, and oppressed and harmed each other. Disaster then followed, and they could no longer be countries as in days of yore. Thus you should carefully consider the fate of those domains and understand. Hear this advice: the swan with a single body and seven heads will know only discord. Though you have the great good fortune to rule in various domains, you must consider them to be a single domain.'[28]

His main concern, thus, was with unity and the management of discord; that is, in maintaining and fostering a hierarchy in which the ruler of Lan Na lorded it over the northern hills.

By the time his son Kavila had been reigning for three decades under the close patronage and supervision of Siam, his focus had shifted to the broader world of which his polity had become an integral part. When he assembled his younger siblings to hear his royal advice on 22 November 1806, they listened in the knowledge that the immediate dangers of warfare now were ended (with the capture of Chiang Saen, the last main Burmese outpost, in 1804, two years earlier). His speech is worth quoting in full.

> 'As from yore and since the time of their royal grandfather and father, when they were subjects of the Burmese and they were vassal domains of the Burmese who oppressed them for a period, happiness was unattainable. Then came the generation of all of us their descendants, and I became thy king. Facing such distress and sadness, we rebelled against the Burmese and led our younger siblings down to become the subjects of the Great King in Krung Sri Ayutthiya. We all, rulers and ruled, then could live happily. We could then eat and move freely, as the Great King nourished us and raised us up as king with the silver and gold insignia of rulership as king of the free Tai country in the fifty-seven domains of the Lan Na country.
>
> 'From this our own time, forever for ten generations, through our children and grandchildren and their children and grandchildren and great grandchildren until the very end of our royal lineage, whoever of our descendants might revolt against the Great King of Ayutthiya, they will become slaves of the Burmese, Hò, Gulawa,[29] Phasi,[30] and Vietnamese, who-

[28] *CMC*, ff°. 7.11.5–7.12.2.
[29] Perhaps the *kula* (Indians) and the Lawa?
[30] I think this refers to the 'White Turbans' of Yunnan.

ever; any such person, whatever they do, however successful they may be, may they be destroyed utterly and die, like the banana tree dies when its fruit are picked or the reeds wilt when cut, and fall into Hell for a hundred-thousand eons, never to be reborn or arise again. As for you lords, all my younger siblings, you must love one another and live in concord like the strands of a rope. Do not quarrel. Help one another. Don't criticize each other. When the elder knows, he helps; and when the younger knows, he helps. When the enemy invades, help one another. Don't betray the Great King of ours. Whoever lives in accordance with these [words of] advice from me, your elder, may you age and prosper and wisely rule, and may you be blessed with majesty and power and extinguish your enemies; may you have long age and long lives. Whoever does not follow these your elder's [words of] advice, may he be destroyed and perish.'

His Majesty the Elder Brother gave these royal [words of] advice to his six younger siblings and children and grandchildren, his civil and military officials in the three domains, in front of the Great Reliquary of Lampang in s. 1168, a *rwai yi* year, on the full-moon day of the second month, a Mon Thursday (Tuesday 13 November 1806).[31]

Virtually every sentence of this speech betrays the sort of world-view to which I have been alluding. There is a new consciousness of ethnic or cultural identity (Tai versus Burmese, Vietnamese, etc.) which does *not* extend to distinctions between various Tai groups (Shan, Lü, Khoen, Kao [of Nan], Lao, etc.). Kavila clearly prescribes a hierarchy in which the 'Great King' (i.e., the kings of Siam) are above Lan Na, and various other Tai groups *and* non-Tai groups (Lawa, Wa, Karen, etc.) are below them, but are part of the same structure as Chiang Mai, and all are opposed together to the Burmese, Vietnamese, and others.

There is one apparently glaring omission in Kavila's depiction of the world: not once does he even allude to the West. For that matter, the West is still completely absent from the *CMC* right down to its composition in 1827. I find it impossible to believe that the Chiang Mai people were unaware of the defeat of the Burmese by the English East India Company, and the Treaty of Yandabo, in early 1826.[32] I suspect that, in at least one important sense, the Burmese defeat is present throughout the *CMC*, and that in fact it is one of the reasons why the *CMC* was written. In fact, I think there are two events which motivate the composition of the *CMC* in 1827: the

[31] *CMC*, ff°. 8.03.5–8.05.4. This date is mentioned earlier in the text as being a Tuesday. I have retained that weekday here.

[32] We know, for example, that the Siamese learned of Yandabo within a few weeks of the event: see *The Burney Papers*, vol. I, pt 2 (Bangkok, 1910; reprinted Farnborough, Hants., 1971), p. 200.

Burmese defeat, and the defeat of Cao Anu of Vientiane at the hands of Siam (and a small Lan Na contingent). The former marks the end to an era in Lan Na's history, while the latter underlines King Kavila's comments about the 'Great King' quoted earlier—'whoever of our descendants might revolt against the Great King of Ayutthiya, they will become slaves of the Burmese . . . Vietnamese . . .'. Here we have, then, a new definition of international order; a hierarchy that is hardly present in the immediate post-Mangrai period of the fourteenth and fifteenth centuries. It is a hierarchy that is based, in the first instance, upon sheer physical power.

But what of the internal hierarchy of Lan Na—what the Chronicle calls the 'fifty-seven domains' of Lan Na? (The phrase comes from Burmese usage, a relic of the long, two-hundred-year period of Burmese domination of Lan Na.) The Burmese had encouraged a division of Lan Na into two halves, centered on Chiang Mai and Chiang Saen; but particularly in the chaos of the last half of the eighteenth century, Lan Na's integration had completely fallen apart. By the 1770s the region was very badly depopulated, to the point where even Chiang Mai itself was abandoned for more than twenty years; and when Lan Na was reconstituted, Kavila and his brothers did so on the basis of the manpower and resources of Lampang and, to a certain extent, Lamphun. Lan Na was reconstituted under the hegemony of Chiang Mai by physical power: early by, especially, Kavila's ability to enlist Siamese military support, and later by Chiang Mai's long, systematic effort to repopulate the region with manpower snagged from, especially, the Shan and Khoen and Lü regions to the west, northwest, and north. This means that not only was the new Tai population of Lan Na firmly under Chiang Mai's control, but also that local and even village power structures were under Chiang Mai's control. Thus, the warfare and repopulation efforts had given Chiang Mai an opportunity to reconstitute a new hierarchy of power in Lan Na.

Social organization. The social organization of the Kavila period of Lan Na history was considerably more complex than it had been in the post-Mangrai period. One indication of this fact is that there are so many more names mentioned in the *CMC* than in earlier periods, and that those names are prefixed by a bewildering array of designations of social and political/bureaucratic rank, as well as of function.

Although the countryside now, as earlier, was considerably atomized, village-by-village, those villages now were linked directly to the royal capital in Chiang Mai much more strongly than they had been a few centuries earlier. Their discrete atomization stemmed from the fact that the region now was composed largely of 'immigrant' villages forcibly captured and resettled in Lan Na, signaled by the fact that they often brought the old names of their villages with them to their new location.

The *CMC* of this later period seems not to mention slaves, nor traders; but it often mentions villagers. One curious reference even mentions lesbians, and the power of rumor as a means of social communication.[33] When the Kavila portion of the *CMC* mentions 'court' society, it does so in a more extended and more complex fashion. (For example, a prince, 'the royalty, rulers, civil and military officials, ministers, priests, and teachers' all are mentioned among those who participated in the raising of a new royal palace in 1827.)[34]

Two new groups are now prominent, though in very different ways. Individual Buddhist monks and ecclesiastical dignitaries often are named, together with the names of the monasteries with which they are associated; usually but not always in Chiang Mai city itself. The second new group is composed of non-Tai peoples, especially the Lawa but also including Karen and Wa. The Lawa in particular are given special ceremonial roles surrounding the installation of new rulers of Chiang Mai.[35]

There are no mentions of traders or merchants in the Kavila period.[36]

Religion. Although animism and elements of Brahmanical ritual appear frequently in the last section of the *CMC*, the dominant religious expression here is of Theravada Buddhism. Buddhism is voiced here in two ways.

First, in the eighth and final chapter of the *CMC* there is a long passage (ff. 8.17–8.25) which amounts to an insertion of an entire text, the 'Chronicle of the Reclining Buddha.' This is the tale of a particular Buddha image located just north of the present city of Chiang Mai, which, the story tells us, was erected on a site where the Buddha himself (and one of his predecessor buddhas) once visited and prophesied the future of Lan Na and Chiang Mai.[37] This

[33] *CMC*, f°. 8.27.3–4.

[34] *CMC*, f°. 8.50.3.

[35] *CMC*, f°. 8.38.5.

[36] One tantalizing view of the nineteenth-century economic environment of the area is Katherine A. Bowie, 'Unraveling the Myth of the Subsistence Economy: Textile Production in Nineteenth-Century Northern Thailand,' *Journal of Asian Studies* 51 (1992), 797–823.

[37] This passage inexplicably is omitted in Sanguan's 1971 edition of the *CMC*.

might seem to be a gratuitous insertion; but its purpose is indicated by the fact that the sentence immediately following the 'Chronicle of the Reclining Buddha' ties the chronicle to the whole eight-chapter text, explaining that King Kavila—who is the real subject of chapters seven and eight—had arisen in Chiang Mai to fulfill the Buddha's prophecy.[38] Without this 'sub-chronicle,' the *CMC* still makes narrative sense; but the *CMC* makes new sense when the sub-chronicle is considered. With it, not only does Lan Na's history seen from 1827 affirm retrospectively a Buddhist view of human history, but by implication (from the traditional Buddhist idea that Buddhism would endure for five thousand years) it links 2,340 years of a Buddhist past to 2,660 years of a Buddhist future still to come. That is, the historian who wrote the *CMC* tells us that the recent past and the present were foretold long ago by the Buddha himself, so that therefore what the Buddha said and did several thousand years ago remains relevant to the people of today and tomorrow.

Second, in editing the new translation of the *CMC* I frequently inserted italicized sub-headings in order to make the text more readable (and in order to make it easier to find things in the table of contents); and I find that I used the sub-heading 'Pious Works' (or similar phrases) no fewer than ten times in the final two chapters. In addition, there are numerous other episodes dealing with individual Buddhist monasteries, or ordinations, or alms-givings. This means that there are about as many references to Buddhist activities in the final two chapters as in all six of the chapters that precede them. All of these, of course, refer to royal religiosity: there is no mention of religious life in which the king was not directly involved. I suspect that we are dealing here at least in part with an author who was essentially secular, little interested in religion for its own sake, at least where history-writing was concerned. I believe that the 1827 author was himself responsible for all the eighteenth- and nineteenth-century portions of his work, and did not base them on previous chronicles. His copious references to the religious activities of recent kings do not mean that he was eager to privilege the Buddhist aspects of Lan Na life. He simply is pointing out that the then-current dynasty of rulers was attentive, where their predecessors had not been, to the primacy of Buddhist piety and its necessity for the proper functioning of the state. He was, therefore, very much like the King Rama I about whom I have written at length elsewhere,

[38] *CMC*, f°. 8.26.1.

whom one would not call a 'religious' man, but rather a 'moral' one, at least where state or public morality was concerned.[39] Buddhism had provided for these men a moral order—a moral order which accounted for the terrible times through which they recently had lived—but, while they were surely Buddhists, they were also Tai (or Siamese or Tai Yuan) and human beings, and none of those labels would suffice alone to describe them.

There is a very strange episode that took place in Chiang Mai in 1823 that serves in many ways to underline the contrasts we have seen between the age of Mangrai's successors and the age of Kavila.[40]

In 1822, the penultimate king of Kavila's generation died and was succeeded by his brother, who was confirmed as king in January of 1823. Royal dissension almost immediately broke out in Chiang Mai, led by the new king's nephew, even to the point where, in February, troops came up from Lampang and Lamphun to encamp by the bridge crossing the river in order 'to forbid quarrels between the two princes' (that is, the king and his Bangkok-named heir presumptive [*uparaja*] nephew). Following a royal convocation, two months later the king abdicated and was ordained as a Buddhist monk.

The historian of 1827—for whom these events must have been fresh in his mind—describes the crisis that ensued and how it was resolved:

> At that time, a misfortune arose to portend the calamity of a Kali Age. The two princes, namely the king Maha Suphathra and the Ratchawong Suwanna Kham Mun, quarreled, and threatened to fight each other. The civil and military officers of our country wanted a prince who lived by the eight royal precepts to rule the country to be the lord and master of all of us, and worthy of all our respect and obedience, past and future. So the Cao Hò Kham was pleased to say that we should sacrifice to the city spirits and [other] spirits, and to Indra and Brahma and take an oath and release a royal chariot to seek a lord who had merit and mercy.[41]

Animism and Brahmanism were pressed into service.[42] After extensive and lavish preparations, a special horse-drawn chariot was led

[39] See my 'The "Subtle Revolution" of King Rama I of Siam,' in *Moral Order and the Question of Change*, ed. D.K. Wyatt and A.B. Woodside (New Haven, 1982), pp. 9–53; reprinted in *Studies in Thai History*, pp. 131–73.

[40] *CMC*, ff°. 8.33–8.41. This episode also is confirmed independently in *TMCMCT*.

[41] *CMC*, ff°. 8.37–8.38.

[42] Why should they have turned to animism and brahmanism in an age which was supposedly piously Buddhist? Because, as Kirsch explains (A. Thomas Kirsch,

around the city and then turned loose to seek a 'lord who had merit and mercy' to be the new king. The horse 'chose' none other but the abdicated monk-king, Suphathra, who re-ascended the throne and reigned until his death in February 1825 at the age of seventy-one years.

There is little explicitly Buddhist about this episode (the 'eight royal precepts' would have been defined in Buddhist terms); but the whole is framed in an Indic context (signaled by the 'Kali Age') mediated and maintained through Buddhist institutions. The Hindu gods Indra and Brahma are invoked on the same level with the local guardian spirits. One of the functions of this paragraph is to identify for us the supramundane powers that upheld the moral order. The paragraph is almost telling us that Lan Na or Chiang Mai was not a 'barbarian' polity: it was subordinate to greater, eternal forces.

But there is one aspect of this paragraph that lies almost unnoticed in the narrative. It arises when we ask, ' "Our country"? Whose country? Which "country"?' and again when we ask 'Who are the "us" who seek a "lord and Master"?' and 'Why must "we" have a king "worthy of all our respect and obedience"?'

These are powerful questions because they bring us directly to the question of the differences between 1317 and 1827.

There is no question that Chiang Mai is the 'capital' of Lan Na in the seventh and eighth chapters of the *CMC*. In the first century after King Mangrai that issue was still unresolved; but in the seventh and eighth chapters, even when King Kavila had his 'temporary capital' at Pa Sang, south of Lamphun, he was just waiting for the right time to re-establish the capital at Chiang Mai. Chiang Mai's centrality had been established, and only in part by physical force.

It was Lan Na of which Chiang Mai was the center. In contradistinction to the usual stereotypes,[43] the Lan Na of the last portion of the *CMC* did *not* include Nan and Phrae, who had their own kings.[44] On the other hand, it *did* include, at least in 1827, portions of Burma and the Sipsong Panna. Not least because the Chiang Mai region by

'Complexity in the Thai Religious System,' *Journal of Asian Studies* 36 (1977), 241–66), Buddhism can provide no certainties in crisis situations, and these must be sought in the surviving syncretic elements of pre-Buddhist Thai religion.

[43] A mistake which my *Thailand: A Short History* (New Haven, 1984) is not alone in having committed.

[44] On which see my 'Five Voices from Southeast Asia's Past,' *Journal of Asian Studies* 53, no. 4 (Nov. 1994), 1076–91; and *The Nan Chronicle* (Ithaca, 1994), which is not to be confused with my 1966 book by the same title.

1827 included many thousands of settlers from those regions, the 'us' of the quoted paragraph included this broad range of people. Chiang Mai and Lan Na were hardly homogeneous! And yet it was a single 'country,' peopled by a single 'us.'

This was a profound change over these several centuries, yet it was one that occurred almost imperceptibly, without the slightest explicit notice. We notice it here only by comparing widely-separated times (and, implicitly, widely disparate texts, though those latter are for the most part incorporated into a single *CMC*). We have noted already the considerable social (and political and economic) change over the period, and the intellectual change and religious change upon which the latter is partly based. What we have failed so far to do is to account for how and why those changes occurred, and it is to those changes that we must now turn.

Part of the difficulty in unraveling the change of this 'middle' period stems from an essential philosophical issue. It is not in the essential nature of things that changes inherently and necessarily are 'political' or 'economic' or 'cultural' or whatever. Those particular names are labels that the later historian attaches to what he or she thinks he sees. Just as a king making a pious donation to Buddhist monks, for example, might conceive his action as having been 'religious' and the later historian might deem that action to have been 'political' or 'economic,' so too are the analytical labels which we place on past events necessarily arbitrary constructions.

Lieberman rightly has forewarned the reader about some of the dangers which his approach entails, as when he (under 'Criticisms') worries that 'this approach reads history backwards as prelude to an inevitable culmination' in 'reifying and eternalizing "nations".' Similarly, he adds that 'the preoccupation with centralization privileges the views of capital elites and victorious cultures'.

But the problem is deeper than this: The problem is not just that nations have been reified or eternalized, or that centralization privileges the position of one group versus that of another. The problem is that all the various units of analysis have tended to become tautological. That is, when we apply labels like 'political' and 'economic' to the past, we tend thereby to *create* 'political' and 'economic' phenomena. What we need to be doing is not to identify, to categorize, or to analyze the past in terms of these very handy and powerful categories, but rather to devise means to think about the past in ways that do not, in spite of ourselves, create in the past those items at which we are interested in looking. We need, if you will, a more supple and abstract way of looking at the past in a way which will preserve and defend the reality of the Past *as it really was* to those who lived *in* that past.

All of this is very abstract. Let me get rather more concrete by using some hypothetical examples from the phenomena at which I have been looking.[45] Those who were involved in the curious 1823 episode involving the 'chariot' to choose a new king carried with them 'in their heads' a certain vocabulary—a set of words, concepts, sounds—which they would have employed in that situation. That set of symbols was, in turn, based both upon their own personal experience within their own lifetimes, and upon the collective historical experience of the society in which they had been born and lived. It is important to remember that the 'vocabulary' they carried around was not something that at any time was complete, but rather it was something that had developed and changed over the generations. The symbol-set which that 1823 generation employed, however, probably had undergone significant changes in the previous half-century of chaos. In particular, the limits of what they could and could not accept as 'acceptable' behavior by a king or other royals had been transformed. I find it doubtful, for example, that an earlier generation would have been as critical of the grasping greed of Kavila's descendants as the *CMC* is.[46]

In her summary of the proceedings of the Eurasian history workshop, Mary Elizabeth Berry identified five general changes that are characteristic of this premodern period:

- the development of mercantile groups within societies;
- the refashioning of the status order of societies to include new groups;
- the movement towards bureaucratic regimes and away from personally-based systems;
- the redefinition of the spaces which societies deemed to be 'theirs' or relevant to them; and
- the increasing circulation of ideas.

These qualities all are characteristic of Japan, and of the countries on which Lieberman concentrates most fully; but they are also characteristic even of the upland interstices between such major polities

[45] In writing what follows, I have been particularly stimulated by David Carr, *Time, Narrative, and History* (Bloomington, Ind., 1986).

[46] *CMC*, f°. 8.42.1.

as Burma and Siam in the period between the thirteenth century and the nineteenth, as we can see in the case of Chiang Mai and Lan Na. Such changes are best thought of as processes, rather than as the final accomplishment of particular transformations; and in these terms we can think even of Lan Na as having been involved in the same sorts of global transformations as the major empires that surrounded it. All these changes ultimately involved 'subjective' transformations—changes in the ways in which people thought. Certainly Lieberman is investigating a profoundly important set of developments that involve the world in his period; but it would be useful to conceive of those changes in ways that go to the intellectual 'heart' of developments, rather than to stop short at the 'objective' changes which are but symptoms of the transformations that undergird them.

Civilization on Loan: The Making of an Upstart Polity: Mataram and Its Successors, 1600–1830

PETER CAREY

Introduction

This paper focuses on the south-central Javanese state of Mataram and its late seventeenth- and mid-eighteenth-century successors—Kartasura (1680–1746), and Surakarta (founded 1746) and Yogyakarta (founded 1749). It concentrates principally on the administrative, military and cultural trends of the period, looking at the ways in which Mataram and its heirs imported their cultural styles from the defeated east Javanese and *pasisir* (north-east coast) kingdoms, while developing a Spartan polity dominated by the exigencies of war and military expansion. The disastrous reign of Sultan Agung's successor, Sunan Amangkurat I (r. 1646–77), and the emergence of the Dutch East India Company (VOC) as a major political force in Java led to the rapid eclipse of Mataram/Kartasura's military influence during Java's 'Eighty Years War' (1675–1755) when the heritage of the great early Mataram rulers was squandered. This period of turmoil ended in the permanent division (*paliyan*) of south-central Java between the courts of Surakarta (Kasunanan, founded 1746, and Mangkunegaran, founded 1757) and Sultan Mangkubumi's new kingdom of Yogyakarta, which, in terms of its martial traditions, was the principal inheritor of the early Mataram polity. At the same time, the political authority of the courts continued to face challenges from regional power centres, not least the powerful administrators of Yogyakarta's eastern outlying provinces (*mancanagara*) based in Madiun and Maospati, and the networks of Islamic schools (*pesantrèn*) and tax-free religious villages (*perdikan*), which drew their strength both from court patronage and the piety of local communities.

The inability of the central Javanese courts to develop an effective fiscal system to tap the burgeoning wealth of the countryside, and the commercial development of the pasisir under the aegis of the post-1677 VOC administration (with its trading monopoly in imported textiles and opium), all contributed to the erosion of political authority in the Javanese centre, an erosion seen most clearly in the Java War (1825–30), when a series of locally based provincial revolts, loosely coordinated by the Yogyakarta prince, Pangéran Dipanagara (1785–1855), challenged the very survival of both the post-1816 colonial Dutch regime and their allies in the now terminally weakened south-central Javanese courts. The paper sees no evidence of any trends towards territorial consolidation, administrative centralization, cultural homogenization and the imposition of linguistic, ethnic and religious norms at the expense of once vibrant local traditions, unless one considers the Dutch East India Company to have been a form of Southeast Asian polity during this period.

Contemporary Contemplations

Students of contemporary Java tend to accept the view that the cultures of the erstwhile princely states of south-central Java (i.e. the Sultanate of Yogyakarta, the Kraton [Kasunanan] of Surakarta and the two minor principalities of the Mangkunegaran [Surakarta] and Pakualaman [Yogyakarta]) represent all that is most refined and developed in Javanese civilization. As John Pemberton has recently pointed out in his study of Javanese culture in the 'New Order' period (1966 to present [1999]), it is this central Javanese, particularly Solonese, style which was favoured by the first family of former President Suharto and his wife, the late Ibu Tien (1924–96), herself a junior member of the Mangkunegaran royal house, as the epitome of *adiluhung* (esteemed/outstanding) taste.[1] Nowhere is this more evident than in the New Order's state monuments: hence, the main audience hall and meeting pavilion which dominated the late Mrs. Suharto's kitsch Disneyland theme park, Taman Mini Indonesia Indah ('Beautiful Indonesia-in-Miniature Park'). Its twenty-seven 'Regional Customary Exhibition Houses', one for each of the provinces of Indonesia (including the illegally occupied former Portuguese territory of East Timor), were clearly in-

[1] Pemberton, *On the Subject of 'Java'* (Ithaca: Cornell University Press, 1994).

spired by central Javanese aristocratic architecture.[2] Even amongst non-Javanese, the highly abstracted motifs of central Javanese *batik* (waxed dyed cloth), in particular the *parang rusak, kawung and sido mukti batik,* once the preserve of royalty, are now regarded as *de rigueur* for society wedding ceremonies and public occasions, where the *upacara mantén* (wedding ceremonial) of the central Javanese courts is taken as the benchmark of everything that is most opulent and original (*asli*).[3]

At the same time, dances and musical compositions, evolved in the rarefied atmosphere of the central Javanese courts, are today taught to schoolchildren throughout the land as models of 'classical' music. The national language, *Bahasa Indonesia*, once a powerful vehicle for republican egalitarianism during the period of the nationalist 'awakening' (*jaman kebangkitan nasional*) from 1908, and during the physical struggle against the Dutch 1945–49), has been fundamentally affected by Javanese notions of hierarchy and deference. Ineluctably, it seems, Indonesian culture is being Javanized. Everywhere, the ubiquitous influence of the central Javanese courts, or, more accurately, a pastiche modern version of that court influence, holds sway.

It is not my intention here to present an analysis of the post-1965 'modernization of tradition' in Indonesia when so much fine work is currently being produced on this subject by scholars of present-day Indonesia. Instead, I will look at the historical origins of the myth of central Javanese superiority in terms of cultural and social standards, and the ways in which the central Javanese state of Mataram and its successors relied on the cultural achievements of the older established court centres on the north-east coast (pasisir) and east Java. In so doing, I will look at the process whereby Mataram gradually incorporated these areas into its so-called mancanagara (outlying) provinces from the early seventeenth century onwards, and the ways in which these provinces continued to exercise a decisive influence on the court cultures of central Java until well into the nineteenth century (i.e. until their eventual annexation by successive British and Dutch administrations between 1811 and 1830/31). For present purposes, the term 'pasisir' (lit.: 'coastal regions') will be used to cover both the traditional areas of Java's north-east coast, and the lands to the east of Mt.

[2] *Ibid.*, 152–61.

[3] *Ibid.*, 216–35; Philip Kitley, 'Batik dan Kebudayaan Populer', *Prisma*, 16.5 (May 1987): 54–70.

Lawu, which would eventually become the province of East Java in the post-1830 Dutch colonial state.

The Cultural Legacy of Majapahit

At the dawn of the sixteenth century, the political influence of the once mighty east Javanese Majapahit empire (*c.* 1290–*c.* 1527) was eclipsed by the rise of the new city-states of Java's north-east coast and the northern littoral of the Oosthoek (eastern Salient). Deeply imbued by the values of Islam, the religion of the mixed blood *peranakan* Chinese and foreign (Arab and Indian [Gujerati]) merchants, who assisted at their birth, these thalassic states continued to look to Hindu–Buddhist Majapahit for much of their institutional and artistic inspiration. Thus, late fifteenth- and early sixteenth-century Demak and successor pasisir polities adopted many of the courtly traditions of Majapahit, with master craftsmen brought over from east Java to work on court buildings and mosques, such as the famous mosque and minaret of Kudus, where traces of Hindu–Javanese architecture are visible to this day.[4] Although Islamic law (*fiqh*) was used extensively, it appears to have existed alongside older Hindu–Javanese *adat* (customary) law, which frequently took precedence over it.[5] In terms of the military organization of the pasisir kingdoms, many of the elite bodyguard regiments of the rulers had Majapahit precedents, with Islamic traditions now being more evident in the armed religious corps, for example, the Suranatan and Suryagama recruited from *santri* (students of religion) and *ulama* (Islamic divines). The same influences can be discerned in the style of urban fortifications.[6] In cultural matters, the old east Javanese shadow-play (*wayang*) theatre, *gamelan* orchestras and *kris* (Javanese daggers with intricate meteorite inlay) were all taken over and developed by the pasisir rulers and the locally revered 'apostles of Islam' (*wali*), who often combined temporal and sacral authority.[7]

This east Javanese influence on the cultural and religious world of the post-Majapahit successor states persisted when the centre of

[4] H. J. De Graaf and Theodore G. Th. Pigeaud, *De Eerste Moslimse Vorstendommen op Java. Studiën over de Staatkundige Geschiedenis van den 15de en 16de Eeuw* ('s-Gravenhage: Nijhoff, 1974), 68–71.

[5] *Ibid.*, 67.

[6] *Ibid.*, 68.

[7] *Ibid.*, 258, n. 68.

royal authority began to shift from the north-east coast to the interior during the course of the late sixteenth century. South of the limestone hills (Gunung Kapur) and the heavily afforested region between Grobogan in the west and Lamongan in the east, newly established Islamicized polities such as Pengging and Pajang held sway for a time over what had once been the westerly outlying regions (mancanagara) of the Majapahit empire. Pajang, in particular, maintained close links with the east Javanese heartland via the Bengawan, the great Sala River, which served as the principal commercial artery between central and east Java until the construction of railways and all-weather roads in the mid- to late nineteenth century. Jaka Tingkir, Pajang's most famous ruler (died 1587), is thought to have been related to some of the principal ruling families of Madura and east Java. Indeed, according to tradition, both his regnal authority and Islamic title of Sultan Adiwijaya were recognized by a gathering of east Javanese rulers convened by the ageing Sunan Prapèn of Giri in 1581.[8] The few architectural and archaeological remains from this period—for example, the celebrated gravesite of Sunan Tambayat to the south of Klathèn—indicate that the styles adopted by the Pajang rulers were deeply influenced by east Javanese models (e.g. the temple at Sendhang Dhuwur) and the Hindu Majapahit-style architecture of north coast states like Demak, Kudus and Jepara (Kali Nyamat).[9]

Mataram, Surabaya and East Java in the Seventeenth Century

Mataram's rise to power in the late sixteenth and early seventeenth centuries appears to have marked a change in the hitherto cordial relations between the Majapahit successor states in east Java and the pasisir, and south-central Java. Unlike Jaka Tingkir's Pajang and the north coast kingdoms, Mataram was geographically isolated—no sea lanes or navigable rivers linked it to the bustling trade marts of east Java and the Oosthoek. The only navigable stretch of the Sala River (Bengawan) below the later (post-1746) court city of Surakarta was two to three days' journey time away, accessible only by exec-

[8] *Ibid.*, 215.

[9] *Ibid.*, 216; Uka Tjandrasasmita, *The Islamic Antiquities of Sendang Duwur*, trans. Satyawati Suleiman (Jakarta: Archeological Foundation, 1975).

rable dirt highways which turned to mud in the rainy season.[10] Mataram's initial political orientation was thus towards the west, across the Bagawanta river to the future western mancanagara provinces of Bagelèn and Banyumas, and up through the agriculturally rich region of Kedhu, to Pekalongan, Tegal and Cirebon on the north-east coast, territories which it brought peacefully under its sway by treaty arrangements and marriage diplomacy in the late sixteenth and early seventeenth centuries.[11]

The political fulcrum of power in Java at this time, however, lay east of the Merapi–Merbabu watershed, in the lands between the Bengawan and the Brantas river basins. It was here that the initial energies of the Mataram rulers were expended in a series of bloody campaigns which culminated in the 1625 capture of Surabaya, the subjection of the priest-kings (*sunan*) of Giri (1636) and the vassalage of the potentates of Madura and the Oosthoek (1625–35).[12]

Despite her military successes, however, Mataram was no match for east Java when it came to matters of art and culture. Indeed, the gap which separated the boorish landlocked south-central Javanese kingdom from Pangéran Pekik's Surabaya was as vast and deep as that which separated the upstart Prussia of the late seventeenth and eighteenth centuries from Habsburg Austria and the internationally oriented Hanse cities of Germany's north coast. In the early seventeenth century, shortly before it fell to Mataram, Surabaya was at the height of its power, a great walled city with fortifications spanning an area 37 kilometres in circumference, with its political influence stretching as far afield as Pasuruan and Blambangan in the Oosthoek, the upper Brantas valley (Kedhiri, Blitar) and Sukadana in west Kalimantan (Borneo).[13]

Such political prestige was accompanied by a great cultural efflorescence which reached its peak in the reign of Pangéran Pekik's father, Panembahan Ratu Jaya (died 1630), a lineal descendant of the famous late fifteenth-century Islamic apostle, Sunan Ngampèl-Dhentha of Surabaya. It was at this time, for example, that the east Javanese 'Damar Wulan' romances, dealing with the fictional history

[10] P. W. van Milaan, 'Beschouwingen over het 17e Eeuwse Mataramse Weggenet', *Sociaal Geographische Mededeelingen*, 4 (1942): 205–39; B. J. O. Schrieke, *Indonesian Sociological Studies. Part Two: Ruler and Realm in Early Java* (The Hague and Bandung: W. van Hoeve, 1957), 105–11.

[11] De Graaf and Pigeaud, *Moslimse Vorstendommen*, 116.

[12] H. J. De Graaf, *De Regering van Sultan Agung Vorst van Mataram, 1613–1645, en die van zijn Voorganger, Panembahan Séda-ing-Krapyak, 1601–1613* ('s-Gravenhage: Nijhoff, 1958), 77–98, 205–22.

[13] De Graaf and Pigeaud, *Moslimse Vorstendommen*, 165–8.

of Majapahit (particularly its wars with Blambangan), and the Panji tales relating the adventures of Radèn Panji Ino Kertapati and a Kedhiri princess, became popular in the wayang shows and masked dance (*wayang topèng*) performances along the north-east coast of Java.[14]

Cultural attainments of this magnitude were naturally coveted by Mataram which now sought to emulate the cultural style of its defeated east Javanese rivals. In much the same way as Demak and its sister principalities on the north-east coast a century earlier had brought over craftsmen and artisans from Majapahit to build the mosques and compounds of the new pasisir kingdoms, Surabayan and east Javanese artificers were now pressed into Sultan Agung's (r. 1613–46) service as architects and builders for his new court at Karta on the Opak river. Amongst these craftsmen were a group of part-Balinese, part-Javanese carpenters and metalworkers known as the Kalang, who continue to maintain a separate identity in Kutha Gedhé and other south-central Javanese court towns until this day.[15] There were also the *wong pinggir* (lit: 'the people of the [outer] rim'), a special category of royal bondsmen who hailed from Blambangan in the Oosthoek. Originally brought to the Mataram capital as prisoners-of-war, these served as personal retainers of the rulers, the women often being taken as secondary wives (*selir*, *garwa ampéyan*)—and, when not so taken, being allowed to marry only with their permission—and the men working as skilled artisans on court building projects.[16]

[14] Raden Mas Oetaja, 'Beantwoording der Vragen gesteld door Mr L. Serrurier, over de Verschillende Soorten Wajangen in de Afdfeeling Batang, Res. Pekalongan', *Tijdschrift voor het Binnenlandsch Bestuur*, 10 (1894), 361–406; Theodore G. Th. Pigeaud, *Javaanse Volksvertoningen. Bijdrage tot de Beschrijving van Land en Volk* (Batavia: Volkslectuur, 1938), 106–8, 130, 403–7; De Graaf and Pigeaud, *Moslimse Vorstendommen*, 165.

[15] Thomas Stamford Raffles, *The History of Java*, 2 vols (London: Black, Parbury & Allen, and John Murray, 1816), II, 327–9; Theodore G. Th. Pigeaud, *Literature of Java. Catalogue Raisonné of Javanese Manuscripts in the Library of the University of Leiden and Other Public Collections in the Netherlands* (The Hague: Martinus Nijhoff, 1970), 267; Mitsuo Nakamura, *The Crescent Arises over the Banyan Tree. A Study of the Muhammadiyah Movement in a Central Javanese Town* (Yogyakarta: Gadjah Mada University Press, 1984), ch. 2.

[16] Johan Friedrich Karl Gericke and Taco Roorda, *Javaanse-Nederlandsch Handwoordenboek*, ed. A. C. Vreede and J. G. H. Gunning, 2 vols (Leiden: E. J. Brill, 1901), II, 342 [sub: 'pinggir']; Peter Carey, *The British in Java, 1811–1816: A Javanese Account* (London: Oxford University Press, 1992), 400, n. 6a; Geoffrey Forrester, 'The Java War 1825–30: Some Javanese Aspects', unpublished MA Thesis, Australian National University, 1971, 285.

That the dance, drama and music of east Java made such a deep mark on Agung's court is evident in the tradition that the celebrated Kyai Lokananta ('Sir Heavenly Music') gamelan orchestra with its specifically east Javanese *sléndro miring* (low *sléndro*) tuning (created to accompany *wayang klithik* or Damar Wulan performances) was brought to Karta by Pangéran Pekik when he was forced to take up residence in Mataram following the fall of his Surabayan kingdom in 1625.[17] Indeed, the prevalence of these east Javanese sléndro miring tunings in some of the most famous Javanese orchestras of the present-day Central Javanese courts—such as the Mangkunegaran's peerless Kyai Kanyut Mèsem ('Sir Swept Away by a Smile') and Kyai Udan Riris ('Sir Gentle Rain')—would seem to lend credence to this tradition.[18]

The same east Javanese influence is also apparent in the Gamelan Carabalèn[19] of the post-1757 Surakarta courts, which was used to accompany the Saturday and Monday tournaments (*Setonan*, *Senènan*) on the great northern square (*alun-alun*) to the north of the kraton, as well as the tiger and buffalo fights to the south.[20] Derived from an east Javanese adaptation of the Balinese war gamelan (*gamelan bebonangan*), which had been brought to the Oosthoek by Balinese armies fighting in the service of Blambangan rulers in the late seventeenth and early eighteenth centuries,[21] it may have been the inspiration for such sacred gamelan as the Gamelan Monggang (aka Kyai Guntur Laut, 'Sir Thunder of the Ocean'), which was played at the Yogyakarta court at Javanese Islamic ceremonies such as the

[17] Raden Mas Koesoemadilaga, *Pakem Sastramiroeda I* (Soerakarta: De Bliksem, 1930 [published from a MS written in *c.* 1850]).

[18] Jaap Kunst, *Music in Java*, ed. E. L. Heins, 2 vols (The Hague: Nijhoff, 1973), I, 245, nn. 1–4. The destruction by fire on 31 January 1985 of the Kraton Surakarta copy of Kyai Lokananta and its *pélog* counterpart, Kyai Semar Ngigel ('Sir Dancing Semar'), may mean that the research which might prove this east Javanese origin will be difficult to accomplish. I would like to thank Mr Amrit Gomperts of Amsterdam, a great connoisseur of Javanese gamelan, for his help with these musicological references.

[19] Kunst, *Music*, I, 265, n. 1 surmised that the term '*carabalèn*' may be a reference to the 'Balinese style' (*cara* = 'manner'; *balèn* = 'à la Bali'), a reference seemingly borne out by the harsh, almost fiery, fashion of playing the drums, as well as by the fact that, as in Bali, two drums are played, not one.

[20] Hence, the term '*gangsa Setu*' ('Saturday gamelan') in distinction to the '*gangsa Senèn* ('Monday gamelan') of the ruler's vassals—i.e. Bupatis and apanage holders from the mancanagara and pasisir districts—who were only allowed to hold their tourneys and gamelan accompaniments on Mondays. See further, Kunst, *Music*, I, 259.

[21] Kunst, *Music*, I, 245, nn. 3–4, 265; II, 455.

Garebeg Mulud (the Prophet's Birthday).[22] Certainly, the gamelan and gun foundry skills of the craftsmen of the Gresik area were well known in the eighteenth- and early nineteenth-century central Javanese courts, and regular journeys were made down the Bengawan by royal—customs' free—lighters (*prau pengluput*) to collect the products of the east Javanese port's metallurgical and armaments industries.[23]

Traditions relating to the life of the great central Javenese apostle of Islam (wali), Sunan Kalijaga, are pertinent here. Said to have been a son of a senior Majapahit official of mixed Javanese and Arab ancestry, Kalijaga is credited with the Islamicization of south-central Java in the sixteenth century.[24] To assist him in this task, he is supposed to have introduced the more refined artistic forms of the pasisir (specifically Surabaya, Giri and Pathi) to the Mataram area. Amongst these were *wayang gedhog* (Panji cycle) and wayang topèng (masked dance) performances, the first professional dancers being said to have been brought down by Kalijaga from the Seséla region near Grobogan to settle in the village of Palar near Tembayat. According to local folklore, their masks and costumes were based on the Panji cycle (gedhog) puppets of east Java, with the skill of topèng mask carving being taught later in south-central Java by a craftsman from Japara, a pasisir region renowned for its teakwood carvers. (Before that time the wayang gedhog features had apparently been painted on flat wooden boards.)[25]

Even though Agung's newly established court at Karta had much to learn in terms of art and aesthetics from the vanquished pasisir and the eastern outlying regions, the relationship was never a one-sided one. Mataram, with its strong western pasisir links, forged

[22] The older more archaic central Javanese *gamelan*, such as *gamelan monggang*, with their low-pitch three-toned *bonang panembung*, and large flat-shaped *kenong* (known appropriately as the *kenong Japan*, i.e. Japan/Majakerta-style *kenong*), may have derived originally from the Balinese-influenced *gamelan bonang-rètèng* and *gamelan ponggang* (*gamelan talu*) of east Java and the Oosthoek. See Kunst, *Music*, I, 155–6, 267–95; and II, 437 (illustration 114) and 445 (illustration 163), which reproduces the Woodbury and Page photographs of an east Javanese (?Malang) *gamelan ponggang* (*gamelan talu*), and the Bupati of Kedhiri's *gamelan bonang-rènthèng* in *c.* 1875 (this last is wrongly described by Kunst as a 'Sundanese regent's *gamelan*').

[23] Gomperts and Carey, 'Campanological Conundrums: A History of Three Javanese Bells', *Archipel*, 48 (1994): 13–31, esp. 26, no. 10.

[24] Solichin Salam, *Sekitar Wali Sanga* (Kudus: Menara, 1963); Theodore G. Th. Pigeaud and H. J. De Graaf, *Islamic States in Java, 1500–1700: A Summary, Bibliography and Index* (The Hague: Nijhoff, 1976), 157 index sub: 'Kali Jaga [sunan]').

[25] Pigeaud, *Javaanse Volksvertoningen*, 44, 51–3, 411.

through innumerable marriage alliances, had access to other cultural traditions besides those of east Java. One thinks here of the vital *wayang purwa* (Ramayana and Mahabharata shadow-play) culture of west Java, which had a deep influence on the wayang performance traditions of the south-central Javanese heartland. Indeed, this heartland became something of a transition zone at this time in terms of shadow-play practice (*kawruh dhalang*), with the clown-retainer Pétruk plots (*lakon*) of the 'senior' (*kasepuhan*; i.e. Kyai Anjasmara) west Javanese line mingling with the Bagong lakon of the 'junior' (*kanoman*; i.e. Nyai Anjasmara) line of east Java.[26] This cultural intermingling can be seen to this day in Yogyakarta, where shadow-play performances regularly feature all four clown-retainers (*panakawan*)—i.e. Semar, Garèng, Pétruk and Bagong.[27] Much the same cultural symbiosis occurred in nineteenth-century Yogyakarta, where the dance drama (*wayang wong*) performances of Sultan Hamengkubuwana V (r. 1822–26/1828–55) successfully blended west Javanese wayang purwa plots with the masked dance (wayang topèng) traditions of east Java.[28]

As Mataram's power grew in the seventeenth century so the cultural boundary dividing central from east Java also began to shift. The steady eastwards expansion of the kasepuhan shadow-play tradition illustrates this very clearly: whereas in the seventeenth century everything to the east of the Merapi–Merbabu watershed had been kanoman territory (even as late as the early 1800s, the then Senior Yogya Administrator [Bupati Wedana] of Madiun was still patronizing east Javanese wayang forms),[29] by the time Pigeaud was researching his *Javaanse Volksvertoningen* (Javanese folk performances) in the 1930s, the line between the kasepuhan and the kanoman (and also between central and east Javanese dialect) was deemed to lie along the watershed dividing Kedhiri and Blitar from Malang.[30]

In fact, throughout the two centuries following Agung's reduction of

[26] *Ibid.*, 61.
[27] *Ibid.*
[28] *Ibid.*, 78; Peter Carey, *Babad Dipanagara: An Account of the Outbreak of the Java War (1825–30)* (Kuala Lumpur: Art Printers, 1981), LXII, n. 51; Jennifer Lindsay, 'Klasik Kitsch or Contemporary: A Study of the Javanese Performing Arts', unpublished PhD Thesis, University of Sydney, 1985, 94ff.
[29] Carey, *British in Java*, 59, n. 79.
[30] Pigeaud, *Javaanse Volksvertoningen*, 131–2.

Surabaya in 1625, relations between central and east Java also remained highly dynamic: occasionally, as during the 1675–79 revolt of the Madurese adventurer, Radèn Trunajaya (*c.* 1649–80), the 1717 Surabaya uprising, and the 1810 revolt of the Yogya Bupati Wedana of the eastern mancanagara provinces, Radèn Rongga Prawiradlrja (in office, 1796–1810), the old political rivalry between the two regions seemed to be reasserting itself.[31] But, with the passage of time, the family links that bound the east Javanese, Madurese and central Javanese elites (which began with Pekik's own marriage to a sister of Agung) became ever closer, facilitating a process of social and cultural interaction which defused political rivalries. Equally important was the functioning of the central Javanese administrative system which brought the eastern mancanagara Bupatis, their families and retainers to the courts twice a year for the celebration of the Prophet's birthday *(Garebeg Mulud)* and the festival to mark the end of the fasting month *(Garebeg Puwasa)*. It is to this process of interaction which we must now turn to understand the development of central Javanese-pasisir relations and the nature of the Javanese state in the post-Giyanti (1755) period.

Core and Periphery, 1755–1830: The Central Javanese Courts and the Eastern Mancanagara Provinces

The eighty years of intermittent warfare in central and east Java between the outbreak of the Trunajaya Revolt in 1675 and the 1755 Giyanti treaty, which divided what was left of Agung's Mataram between Surakarta, Yogyakarta and (post-1757) the Mangkunegaran, had a profound effect on Javanese society. In material terms, east Java, the Oosthoek in particular, suffered much more severely than the Mataram heartlands south and west of the Merapi–Merbabu watershed. In some areas, such as the Malang highlands, scene of many bloody encounters between the armies of the Balinese adventurer Untung Surapati (*c.* 1650–1706) and various VOC, Javanese, Madurese and Balinese armies, death and flight occurred on a dramatic scale.[32] Elsewhere in east Java, there was a shift in eco-

[31] M. C. Ricklefs, *A History of Modern Indonesia c. 1300 to the Present* (London and Basingstoke: Macmillan, 1981), 69–84, 108; *idem*, *War, Culture and Economy in Java, 1677–1726: Asian and European Imperialism in the Early Kartasura Period* (Sydney: Allen & Unwin, 1993), 30–57.

[32] M. C. Ricklefs, 'The Missing Pusakas of Kartasura, 1705–37', in Sulastin Sutrisno, Darusuprapta and Sudaryanto (eds), *Bahasa, Sastra, Budaya. Ratna Manikam Untaian Persembahan kepada Professor Dr P. J. Zoetmulder* (Yogyakarta: Gadjah Mada University Press, 1986), 28.

nomic strength away from the upper Brantas valley (Kedhiri, Sarèngat, Blitar) to the more westerly Madiun valley (Panaraga, Magetan, Kadhuwang) and the fertile plain of the Bengawan (Sala River), where regions such as Jipang and Jagaraga began to come into their own as important commercial centres.[33] On the northeast coast, the destruction of much of Surabaya and Gresik's carrying trade, first by the 1677 VOC commercial monopoly and then by the depredations of Bugis and Madurese 'pirate' flotillas, dealt a death blow to the once mighty east Javanese entrepôt ports. According to Pigeaud, it was from this time that the cultural ascendancy of central over cast Java became more marked, an ascendancy, which, in his view, grew increasingly pronounced once the 1755 political settlement brought a measure of peace to the central Javanese heartlands.[34]

Yet Pigeaud's conclusions may be too hasty when we consider both what little is known about the cultural relations between the central Javanese courts and their eastern provinces in the post-Giyanti period, and the administrative methods of the post-1755 Javanese state. Ricklefs, for example, has pointed out that many of the sacred heirlooms (*pusaka*) of the Kartasura court (fl. 1680–1742) were lost during these decades and it is likely that those few items which still passed as pusakas at the time of the 1755 division of the realm between Pakubuwana III (r. 1749–88) and Hamengkubuwana I (r. 1749–92) were at best copies (*putra*) of the originals.[35] Amongst these lost or dispersed heirlooms were the revered gamelan of the Kartasura court, few of which appear to have survived its sack by the Chinese forces of Radèn Mas Garendi (Sunan Kuning) in June 1742.

The contribution of the east Javanese provinces (*kabupatèn*) to the cultural development of the central Javanese courts in the post-1755 period remained important, however. There are interesting references in the Javanese sources to gamelan being brought to the courts by visiting eastern mancanagara Bupati, although whether these were specifically east Javanese orchestras or remnants of older Kartasura court collections is unclear.[36] An insight into the way in which

[33] *Ibid.*, 27–8.

[34] Pigeaud, *Javaanse Volksvertoningen*, 348.

[35] Ricklefs, 'The Missing Pusakas', 601–30; *idem*, *War, Culture and Economy*, index sub: '*pusakas* [holy regalia]'.

[36] Peter Carey, 'Core and Periphery, 1600–1830: The Pasisir Origins of Central Javanese "High Court" Culture'. in Bernhard Dahm, (ed.), *Regions and Regional Developments in the Malay–Indonesian World* (Wiesbaden: Otto Harrassowitz, 1992), 99, n. 42.

the culture of east Java continued to influence central Javanese court styles during the 1755–1825 (i.e. Giyanti to Java War) period can be seen in a recent study of the *Beksan Wirèng Bandabaya* dance drama of the Pakualaman, the minor Yogyakarta court, after June 1812.[37] This dance, which derives from the east Javanese *beksan gebug* fighting dance, became the most practised warrior dance of the Pakualaman and was always performed at the time of the installation of a new Pangéran Adipati (ruling prince). It was apparently choreographed by the second Pakualam (r. 1830–58) after he had seen a troupe of dancers brought to Yogya by his kinsman, the Bupati Wedana of Madiun, during one of his periodic visits to the Sultan's capital to provide tigers for the royal tiger–buffalo contests.[38]

Until June 1812, when the obligation of the eastern mancanagara Bupati to provide corvée labour services for the rulers was abolished, large numbers of east Javanese workers and officials sojourned for two to three months in the royal capitals.[39] So it is scarcely surprising that they left their mark on the cultural life of the courts. We know, for example, that during the third sultan's reign (1812–14), gamelan orchestras belonging to the Yogya Bupati were played during construction projects to boost the morale of the workers, and that dance performances, including the *Beksan Lawung* ('lance' dances), were held in the court for officials and royal relatives overseeing the work teams.[40] Both the Rongga Prawiradirjan and Sumadipuran families, which provided senior officials for the Yogyakarta court in the period 1755–1859—the first as chief administrators (Bupati Wedana) of Madiun (in office, with only brief intermissions, between 1755 and 1859)," and the second as prime minister *(patih)* of the sultanate (in office, 1813–47)—hailed from the east Javanese provinces of Sokawati and Japan (Mojokerto), respectively. Both retained their east Javanese style of speech long after their appointment to high office,[42] and achieved renown as patrons of the arts, Radèn

[37] Mardjijo, 'Beksan Bandabaya di Pura Paku Alaman', unpublished BA Thesis, Akademi Seni Tari Indonesia (ASTI), Yogyakarta, 1976; Lindsay, 'Klasik Kitsch or Contemporary', 70–1.

[38] Carey, *The British in Java*, 26, 461, n. 297.

[39] Peter Carey, 'Waiting for the "Just King": The Agrarian World of South-Central Java from Giyanti (1755) to the Java War (1825–30)', *Modern Asian Studies*, 20, 1 (1986): 71, n. 43.

[40] Carey, *The British in Java*, 181, 376.

[41] Peter Carey, *The Archive of Yogyakarta. Volume I. Documents Relating to Politics and Internal Court Affairs* (London: Oxford University Press, 1980), 194.

[42] Carey, *The British in Java*, 173, 368, 500, n. 492.

Rongga Prawiradirja III (in office, 1796–1810) gaining recognition as a *littérateur* in his own right through his composition of new plots for the east Javanese Damar Wulan cycle, and Sumadipura (Danureja IV) becoming known for his keen interest in sartorial styles (including topèng dance dress, which was apparently sold at his official residence).[43] In this context of continuing east Javanese cultural and linguistic influence at the early nineteenth-century central Javanese courts, it is significant how many archaic east Javanese dialect words can be found in the *Serat Centhini*, that great encyclopaedia of Javanese life and manners compiled in Surakarta between 1815 and 1820, which tells the tale of a group of well-born fugitives from the defeated Majapahit court in the fifteenth century who, in disguise, toured Java, undergoing many remarkable experiences of a mystical, cultural, religious, and even pornographic, nature.[44]

These cultural and linguistic influences were reinforced by a series of marriage alliances entered into by the rulers with the daughters of eastern mancanagara Bupati in order to try to ensure themselves the loyalty of these far-flung provinces. These included the families of powerful religious teachers (*Kyai*) from *désa perdikan* (tax-free villages set aside for the upkeep of religious communities (*mutihan*), who maintained religious schools (*pesantrèn*) or were guardians (*jurukunci*) of gravesites and holy places (*kramat*). One famous example was Pangéran Dipanagara (1785–1855), the Javanese prince who later became the chief protagonist of the Java War (1825–30). The eldest son of the third sultan of Yogyakarta, he was from an unofficial wife (*selir*), who hailed from the religious centre of Tembayat (Bayat) to the east of Yogya. He was thus linked with Sunan Bayat (died 1512), the supposed tenth wali (apostle of Islam), a once wealthy pasisir ruler in the Semarang area, whose gravesite still attracts pilgrims from all over Java,[45] especially those anxious to

[43] Carey, *The Archive of Yogyakarta*, 190; Raden Prawirawinarsa and Raden Djajengpranata, *I: Babad Alit, mawi rinengga ing Gambar sarta Kar. II: Jumenengipun Cungkup ing Pasaréyan Kutha Gedhé* (Weltevreden: Volkslectuur, 1921), pt 21; Raden Adipati Aria Djaja-adiningrat, 'Schetsen over den Oorlog van Java 1825–30 opgesteld door den Bopatti van Karang Anjar Raden Adipatti Ario Djaja-adiningrat, 1855–1857', ed. J. Hageman Jcz. Malay manuscript no. ML 57, Musium Nasional, Jakarta, 1857, 7; Carey, *The British in Java*, 174, 498, n. 486, 500, n. 493.

[44] Theodore G. Th. Pigeaud, 'De Serat Tjabolang en de Serat Tjentini. Inhoudsopgave bewerkt door Dr. Th. Pigeaud', *Verhandelingen van het Bataviaasch Genootschap van Kunsten en Wetenschappen* (Jakarta), 72, 2 (1933): 1–89; *idem*, *Javaanse Volksvertoningen*, 129.

[45] Pemberton, *Subject of Java*, 279–88.

improve their material status. His mother's ancestry could also be traced back to Sunan Ngampèl-Dhentha of Gresik, whom we have met above as one of the first walis in Java and founder of an important Islamic community in east Java before the fall of Majapahit (*c.* 1527).

Dipanagara's great-grandmother, Ratu Ageng (Tegalreja) (died 1803), a consort of the first sultan (r. 1749–92), who acted as his guardian and mentor during his youth at her Tegalreja estate just to the west of Yogya, had an equally eminent family background, being the daughter of a prominent religious teacher (Ki Ageng Prampèlan) in the Sragèn area of Surakarta by a woman who was descended in the third generation from the Sultan of Bima, a staunchly Islamic principality in eastern Indonesia.[46] Ratu Ageng's sister was married first to the chief religious functionary (*Pengulu*) of Yogyakarta, Pekih Ibrahim (died 1798), and then to an *ulama* (religious scholar), Haji Ibrahim, who carried secret messages between the central Javanese rulers in 1811–12 after the British invasion (August 1811), and was later reported to have travelled to Sumbawa and engaged in the slave trade.[47]

These relationships with members of the Indonesia-wide religious communities were crucial for Dipanagara at the time of the outbreak of the Java War (July 1825), when he was able to call on a far-flung network of santri support to assist him in his resistance to the Dutch and their central Javanese allies. His marriage in 1807 and 1813 to daughters of eastern mancanagara regents, the latter the offspring of the recently deceased Radèn Rongga Prawiradirja III of Madiun, further enhanced his links with east Java, links which had already been forged by his father, the third sultan whose matrimonial alliances with eastern mancanagara Bupati families and reliance on east Javanese officials during his time as Yogya Crown Prince was noted by contemporary chroniclers.[48]

The importance of these links between the Yogya court and the families of prominent local gentry was amply illustrated at the time of the British attack on the sultanate in June 1812, when many

[46] Salasilah Kadanoerejan ('Genealogical History of the Danurejan Family [Yogyakarta]'). Panti Budaya (Sana Budaya Museum, Yogyakarta) MS B.29. Copied in Yogyakarta in 1932 from a MS bought by Ir J. L. Moens for the Koninklijk Bataviaasch Genootschap in 1930, p. 127.

[47] *Ibid.*, 127; *Besluit van den Gouverneur-Generaal in rade*, 19 October 1818, no. 3 (Arsip Nasional RI, Jakarta).

[48] Carey, *The British in Java*, 478, n. 369.

Yogya princes fled from the court to take shelter with their female relatives in the countryside;[49] and, again, during the Java War (1825–30), when Dipanagara's uprising in Yogya was the signal for a whole spate of local revolts, particularly in east Java (Madiun [August–December 1825] and Rembang and Rajegwesi [December 1827–March 1828]) and the north-east coast and western mancanagara (Semarang, Pekalongan, Ledhok and Banyumas [August 1825–January 1826]), which owed only loose allegiance to Dipanagara at the centre.[50]

A glance at the nature of the pre-1825 Javanese apanage system bears out the continuing importance of these provincial networks in the decades before the Java War, and helps to explain the strength of local loyalties, especially at times of crisis and war.

The Javanese Apanage System and the Village Community, 1755–1825

The inefficiencies of the Javanese apanage system and the inability of rulers to tap the new sources of wealth being generated at the village level by the generation of 'landowning' (*sikep*) peasants and their dependants who lived in the more peaceful post-1755 era, meant that the courts were always at the mercy of powerful vested interests in the localities for the payment of tribute. Unlike the experience of some mainland Southeast Asian states during this period, where clearly discernible trends towards territorial consolidation, administrative centralization and cultural homogenization seem to have taken place,[51] the example of central Java underscores the rather different situation of the island world.

Here, despite the seemingly impressive power structure and organization of the courts, the rulers simply did not have the administrative sources at their disposal to lay claim to newly developed lands (*tanah yasa*) at the village level or even impose new tribute burdens on them.[52] No revised cadastral registers of cultivated land

[49] *Ibid.*, 27, 75–6.

[50] P. J. F. Louw, *De Java-Oorlog van 1825–30*, Volume I (Batavia: Landsdrukkerij & 's-Hage: Nijhoff, 1894), chs 12, 14 and 18–19; *Idem*, *De Java-Oorlog van 1825–30*, Volume III (Batavia: Landsdrukkerij & 's-Hage: Nijhoff, 1904), chs 6–9.

[51] Victor Lieberman, 'Local Integration and Eurasian Analogies: Structuring Southeast Asian History, *c.* 1350–*c.* 1830', *Modern Asian Studies*, 27, 3 (1993): 475–521, 569–72.

[52] Carey, 'Waiting for the "Just King" ', 109ff.

were drawn up after the 1773 'New Book' *(Serat Ebuk Anyar),* and even that was heavily based on a late seventeenth-century model. Indeed, both the principal central Javanese rulers in the late eighteenth and early nineteenth century feared that if the cadastral surveys were revised anew, the Dutch would either seek to even out the landholdings between the courts (which would disadvantage Yogyakarta), or annex to themselves all the lands opened out since the 1773 census. Subsequent attempts by the British (1811–16) and post-1816 Dutch colonial administrations to compile accurate statistical accounts of the landholdings and population in the princely territories were only partially successful, with the main surveys being conducted in certain enclave areas (Pacitan, Lowanu, Nanggulon [Kulon Progo]), where they were directly involved in cash-crop production (pepper and indigo) or in local administration.[53]

Torn between their desire to see the great increase in post-1755 agricultural productivity in south-central Java reflected in steadily rising tribute (*pajeg*) returns, and their constant fear of Dutch annexation, the Javanese rulers were forced to rely on a series of haphazard and highly arbitrary administrative expedients, which spoke more of desperation than administration competence. Such desperation found voice in threatening (and singularly ineffective) royal decrees enacted against officials found holding land in excess of the amounts allocated to them by their adminsitrative *piagem* (letters of appointment). A series of punishments involving chaining, beating and imprisonment were enacted, but the numbers of officials who were actually disciplined for the crime of 'concealing ricefields' (*angumpet sabin*) seems to have been pitifully small. Although the Yogya ruler threatened his officials with the visitation of his village 'surveyors' (*abdi-Dalem priksa dhusun*; *Mantri papriksan negara*), he must have known full well that such threats were almost impossible to carry out, given the complex and far-flung nature of his territories (the Giyanti treaty had intentionally mixed Yogyakarta and Surakarta lands together in the central apanage regions to meet the demands of local landholders),[54] and the extremely limited number of surveyors available to him.[55]

[53] *Ibid.*, 109–10.

[54] *Ibid.*, 72–4.

[55] Louw, *De Java-Oorlog*, I, 594, for example, mentions seven *Lurah priksa negara* in the Sultan's administrative establishment in *c.* 1820.

A clause was often inserted in the official apanage grants demanding notification from officials about the extent and populousness of the lands under their charge, a clause which led to numerous notifications regarding land units (*cacah*) that had become depopulated or uncultivated, something which occurred with particular frequency in the more sparsely populated eastern mancanagara where a special distinction began to be made between 'living' (i.e. cultivated) cacah (*cacah gesang/urip*) and 'dead' (i.e. uncultivated, abandoned) cacah (*cacah pejah/mati*). But there were naturally few admissions regarding increased productivity on older established ricefields, or the existence of newly developed lands (tanah yasa) which had not appeared in the 1773 cadaster.

The degree of administrative confusion and blatant concealment which took place can be seen in the reports on the areas of the princely states (*vorstenlanden*) annexed both by the British in August 1812 and the Dutch in 1830–31 after the end of the Java War. With reference to Pacitan, a south coast district where European-administered pepper estates had been in existence since the late eighteenth century, a Dutch official reported bluntly in 1793 that 'the survey of ricefields shows that since the Peace of 1755 [i.e. Giyanti], [these] have been greatly expanded in area, but that this increase has been hidden from the courts so that local farmers can appropriate the newly developed lands for themselves'.[56] Just over a quarter of a century later, when a more accurate assessment of population and landholdings was completed, the number of 'landowning peasants' was put at 3,757, and this in a district where the officially declared taxable population was just four hundred cacah (i.e. productive family units) divided equally between the two main courts![57]

The Javanese rulers tried to circumvent the shortcomings of their own fiscal regimes by resorting to extraordinary administrative expedients. In Yogyakarta, for example, the first sultan set in train a massive attempt to resurvey the landholdings of the court shortly before his death in March 1792, when the old agrarian unit of the Majapahit rood was reintroduced into the central districts. His suc-

[56] Carey, 'Waiting for the "Just King"', 111–12, quoting Wouter Hendrik Van IJsseldijk, 'Eerbiedige Bericht aangaande de Landen van Z. H. den Sulthan van Djocjocarta', unpublished report on the Dutch-leased indigo estates in Lowanu and Genthan in north-eastern Bagelèn, and pepper gardens in Pacitan on the south coast, contained in Arsip Nasional (Jakarta) 'Bundel Djokjo Brieven', no. 45, Van IJsseldijk (Yogyakarta) to P. G. van Overstraten (Semarang), 15 Jan. 1793.

[57] Carey, 'Waiting for the "Just King"', 112.

cessor, Hamengkubuwana II (1792–1810/1811–12/1826–28), went a stage further by attempting to measure his lands with a cadastral gauge (Jav. *cengkal* or *tumbak*, lit: 'lance length') which had been deliberately shortened for the purpose. This stratagem, known as '*pancas*' (lit: 'cutting') was attempted twice in the early part of his reign, and together were supposed to have contracted the average size of the Yogya cacah by 20% when compared to its Surakarta equivalent.

As a solution to the problem of the under-reporting of land, however, it had only a limited impact. In fact, the pancas revisions sharpened all the inherent imbalances in the level of tribute demands on individual cacah, demands that already had been fixed in the most haphazard fashion by the apanage holders and the central Javanese rulers after 1755.[58] The pancas were, therefore, equivalent to a major currency devaluation with land being used instead of coin, and it fuelled inflation in the countryside, a situation compounded by poor harvests in the 1790–1810 period and reflected in record rice prices in May–June 1804. In retrospect, it can be seen that the pancas helped to prepare the ground for the widespread agrarian uprising in south-central Java in July–August 1825 when Dipanagara's leadership seemed to many Javanese peasants to hold out their only promise of an end to intolerable fiscal oppression.

The iniquities of the Javanese fiscal regime and the inability of the rulers to wring out at source the wealth being generated by the 'landholding' (sikep) peasantry were further underscored by two related developments: tax-farming (particularly by Chinese) and the increased use of tollgates (to raise money from the transport of goods and agricultural produce to local markets). The latter, in particular, highlights once again the dependence of the Javanese rulers on indirect rather than direct taxes. In so far as they necessitated the imposition of a 'comb' on the countryside, with all the harmful effects that inevitably had on the free passage of goods and services, these taxes were a sign of administrative weakness. Much more efficient and ultimately productive would have been some method of extracting the agrarian surplus at source through a properly calibrated land-tax, such as was found in some contemporary mainland Southeast Asian states.

The provincial tax-farmers to whom royal apanage holders delegated authority were known as Demang or Mantri-désa. They gathered the land-rent (pajeg) payments from between ten and

[58] *Ibid.*, 115.

thirty village tax-collectors, according to the size of the apanage, and, in return, were permitted to retain one-fifth of the rents as their own remuneration. The spread of this tax-farming system in the early nineteenth century went hand in hand with two further developments. First, the tendency for a multitude of village taxes and labour services (except for the royal corvée or *kerigaji*) to be replaced by a fixed cash sum, which was paid annually and known as *pajeg mati* (lit: 'fixed tribute'). The second was the great spread in the princely states, after the turn of the nineteenth century, of Chinese (and to a lesser extent, Europeans and Eurasians), whose 'skill and frugality', in the words of John Crawfurd, enabled them to pay higher tax-farm rents than their Javanese rivals.[59] Indeed, it is clear that, after 1812, with the increasing change to money taxes in the core apanage areas and the pressures on available land (due to British annexations), the Chinese were propelled into an ever more prominent position as tax-farmers, agricultural entrepreneurs and moneylenders in the principalities. A senior Dutch official who gave evidence to the commission charged with the incorporation of the annexed central Javanese territories in 1830–31, reported that one-third of the Surakarta eastern mancanagara province of Kedhiri and the whole of Saréngat-Wétan had been farmed out by local Bupati to the Chinese. Elsewhere, in the adjacent Yogya regency of Madiun, the Chinese had apparently played a key role in the collection of land-rent (pajeg) from the local population under the supervision of the Bupati Wedana and his subordinates.[60]

The institution of pajeg mati (fixed tribute) and the tax-farming methods of the Chinese were just two of the ways in which the hard-pressed apanage holders reacted to the colonial land annexations of 1812. Another tactic was that used by the Surakarta ruler Sunan Pakubuwana IV (r. 1788–1820), who attempted to solve the problem of limited apanage lands by allocating new apanages in the outlying provinces, areas hitherto administered as 'tribute' (pajeg) for the ruler by the mancanagara Bupati. Instead of remaining under the direct rule of these Bupati as in the rest of the mancanagara, the new apanage areas were farmed out to Demang (provincial tax-farmers), most of whom were non-Javanese. This led to a more ruthless fiscal exploitation of the local population, a situation which

[59] *Ibid.*, 78, quoting Crawfurd, 'Report upon the District of Cadoe [Kedhu] by Mr [John] Crawfurd', 15 November 1812, in India Office Library (now British Library), Mackenzie Collection: Private, pp. 271–310.

[60] Carey, 'Waiting for the "Just King" ', 78–9.

paralleled developments in the traditional core apanage regions (*nagara agung*) where Chinese Demang had been active since the late eighteenth century.[61]

Conclusions

It is clear from the available evidence that the Javanese fiscal system was in crisis in the first quarter of the nineteenth century, and this crisis explains much about the widespread scale and depth of popular unrest unleashed in the countryside by the outbreak of the Java War (1825–30). South-central Java may not have been so unusual in terms of contemporary developments in the island world of Southeast Asia in the period *c.* 1670–*c.* 1830, which Lieberman, for one, has characterized as an era of 'fragmentation'.[62] But, if we compare the area with Konbaung Burma, Chakri Siam and post-1802 Nguyen Vietnam, the differences are stark. Javanese rulers, like Yogyakarta's dynamic first sultan, Mangkubumi (r. 1749–92), may have wished to emulate their mainland Southeast Asian counterparts in terms of the territorial consolidation, administrative centralization and cultural integration, but their achievements were heavily circumscribed by the fissiparous nature of their polities and the continuing vitality of local traditions. If we add here the political influence of the post-1677 Dutch East India Company, and the overwhelming military superiority of the post-1811 British and post-1816 Dutch colonial regimes, then it is easy to see how different was the experience of south-central Java from mainland Southeast Asia.

In the cultural sphere alone, it is striking how, right up to the Java War, south-central Java, regarded today as the epitome of all that is most refined in Javanese culture, remained deeply influenced by the civilization of the pasisir, especially that of east Java. Although this influence may have begun to weaken somewhat with the decline of the great east Javanese emporia like Surabaya and Gresik in the late seventeenth and early eighteenth century, it nevertheless remained a dynamic force until the artificial severance of the core apanage regions (nagara agung) from the mancanagara provinces in 1830–31 following Dipanagara's defeat in the Java War. This partition led, over time, to south-central Java coming to be seen as a sort of 'island'

61 *Ibid.*, 118.

62 Lieberman, 'Local Integration', 553ff.

of 'authentic' Javanese culture, the *tanah Kejawèn* of Dutch colonial myth, inward-looking and largely untouched by 'foreign' influences—the place, where, in J. Petrus Blumberger's famous phrase, 'the heart of Java beats'.[63] This static view of Javanese culture, which is found in so much Dutch colonial literature on the princely territories and in the Geertzian paradigm of Javanese 'involution', owes much to this deeply distorted vision of Javanese society. Only now, with the coming of age of a new generation of scholarship on colonial and post-colonial Java, especially the post-modernist analysis of Suharto's 'New Order', is this vision at last being challenged.

[63] J. Th. P. Blumberger, *De Nationalistische Beweging in Nederlandsch Indië* (The Hague: Nijhoff, 1931), 55.

Connected Histories: Notes towards a Reconfiguration of Early Modern Eurasia[1]

SANJAY SUBRAHMANYAM

The majority of Japanese even today believe that the politico-cultural universe of the Edo period was fundamentally determined by the closure of the country. They also think that the opening of Japan can be reduced to the development of exchanges with the West, following the birth of the Meiji regime. It is hard for them to imagine that Japan developed in relation with other Asian countries, since they are hardly used to appreciating Asian cultures.

—Yuko Tanaka (1995).[2]

I

The paper is a somewhat indirect response to the 'theme essay' around which the present volume is organized. Victor Lieberman's exercise seeks to compare six countries, Burma, Siam, Vietnam, France, Russia and Japan, and sets out twelve factors on the basis of which a 'calculus of integration' can be notionally set out for them. In an earlier version of the essay, he had proposed strong parallels between the experiences of these countries based on a neo-Gerschenkronian formulation of rimlands and cores, with the rimlands having the 'advantage of relative backwardness'. Abstracting from the details, we see that this represents a neo-cyclical theory, since the cores eventually must become rimlands, as the rimlands develop 'advanced' features at a rapid rate.

[1] This paper was originally prepared for the seminar, 'The Eurasian context of the early modern history of mainland South East Asia, c. 1400–1800', at the Centre of South East Asian Studies, SOAS, 22–4 June 1995. A preliminary version was presented to a seminar at Leiden University in May 1995. I am grateful to Peter Carey, W. G. Clarence-Smith, Jos Gommans and David Wyatt for comments or helpful reflections.

[2] Tanaka Yuko, 'Le monde comme représentation symbolique: Le Japon de l'époque d'Edo et l'univers du *mitate*', *Annales, Histoire, Sciences Sociales* 50, 2 (1995), 281.

Various responses are possible to this large, highly ambitious and wide-ranging project. Let us begin by noting that in his paper in this volume at least (in contrast to another published by him a few years ago in the pages of this journal), Lieberman pays relatively little attention to South Asia (one of the ostensible areas of my own expertise), and—as in the other paper—none at all to Iberia, my other major area of interest.[3] In closing the paper, he presents us with a rather sketchy discussion of India, partly juxtaposed to his earlier discussion of China.[4] Given Lieberman's limited foray into early modern South Asia, one might think that the task for the South Asianist in this context has been cut out in simple terms: to make those comparisons which elude Lieberman, and locate South Asia (either in whole, or in bits and pieces) in his rank-order scheme. But in view of the notorious recalcitrance of South Asianists, and their well-known lack of desire to be cannon-fodder for other people's model building, it might be optimistic to expect such an exercise. What I shall attempt to bring to the table here are therefore not the missing South Asian pieces in Lieberman's puzzle, but a rather different view of the problem of early modern comparison, a set of reflections that I hope to develop and carry in part into two works-in-progress.[5]

My concern in general (as implicitly that of Lieberman) is with a period that specialists of many different regions (and not only western Europe) have begun to call, with growing comfort and confidence, the 'early modern' epoch. The chronological coverage of this period obviously needs some definition. I would provisionally propose a rather more generous definition than the usual one, arguing that the 'early modern' in Eurasia and Africa at least (pre-Columbian America being a more complex problem) would extend from the middle of the fourteenth to the middle of the eighteenth century, with a relatively great emphasis on the period after about 1450. For those who like political demarcations, it might be suggested per-

[3] See Victor Lieberman, 'Secular Trends in Burmese Economic History, c. 1350–1830, and their Implications for State Formation', *Modern Asian Studies* 25, 1 (1991), 1–31.

[4] Nevertheless, the present project by Lieberman represents, in my view at least, a considerable advance on his earlier conceptual framework of the 'administrative cycle'; for which see his *Burmese Administrative Cycles: Anarchy and Conquest, c. 1580–1760* (Princeton, 1984).

[5] Sanjay Subrahmanyam, *The Making of Early Modern Asia* (Boulder: Westview Press, forthcoming); Subrahmanyam, *The Early Modern World* (Oxford: Basil Blackwell, forthcoming).

versely that the reformulation of Eurasian polities in the context of the great enterprise of Amir Timur Gurgan (d. 1405) could serve as the convenient, obviously somewhat symbolic, point of departure.[6] Of course, an earlier date could be chosen—say the late twelfth century, in the sense of marking the Great Mongol Moment. But there are reasons to feel, all in all, that this would be really be an abuse of the notion of 'early modern', drawing protests from medievalists the world over! At the same time, it is of some importance (and here I part company with Lieberman in some respects) to delink the notion of 'modernity' from a particular European trajectory (Greece, classical Rome, the Middle Ages, the Renaissance and thus 'modernity' . . .), and to argue that it represents a more-or-less global shift, with many different sources and roots, and—inevitably—many different forms and meanings depending on which society we look at it from.

Nevertheless, some obvious unifying features are present. To begin with, the early modern period defines a new sense of the limits of inhabited world, in good measure because it is in a fundamental way an age of travel and discovery, of geographical redefinition. There were thus various attempts, often from conflicting perspectives and points of departure, to push back the limits of the world, as they were known to different peoples in about 1350. Rather than treat the European voyages of exploration as the sole or even the single most important focus, we need to bear in mind that the period witnesses the expansion in a number of cultures of travel, as well as the concomitant development of travel-literature as a literary genre, whether the routes explored are overland (trans-Saharan, trans-Central Asian) or maritime.[7] The notion of 'discovery' thus applies as much to Zheng He's Indian Ocean voyages in the early fifteenth century as those of Cabral or Magellan a century later. These voyages were accompanied by often momentous changes in conceptions of space and thus cartography; significant new empirical 'ethnographies' also emerged from them.[8]

[6] Cf. the relatively recent, important, work on Timur by Beatrice Forbes Manz, *The Rise and Rule of Tamerlane* (Cambridge, 1989).

[7] See, in this context, the essays collected in Claudine Salmon (ed.), *Récits de voyage des asiatiques: Genres, mentalités et conception de l'espace* (Paris, 1996); and more particularly on (semi-fictional works for) Japan, Kosugi Keiko, Satake Akihiro and Jacqueline Pigeot, *Voyages en d'autres mondes: Récits japonais du XVIe siècle* (Paris, 1993).

[8] The history of 'early anthropology' is obviously in need of revision, as are the implicit presuppositions of such pioneering but dated works as Margaret T. Hodgen, *Early Anthropology in the Sixteenth and Seventeenth Century* (Philadelphia, 1964). The

But the early modern period also sees other shifts. Among these is a heightening of the long-term structural conflict that inhered in relations between settled agricultural and urban societies on the one hand, and nomadic groups (hunter gatherers, pastoralists, etc.) on the other.[9] This tension, to which ecologically minded historians have drawn our attention in recent times, represents a paradigm within which to address questions relating to the agricultural frontier and agricultural innovation, demography, urbanization and patterns of urban settlement, and the issue of travel, discovery and colonization as leading to an ecological shift of global dimensions.[10] Obviously, the balance between settlers and wanderers differed, too, from continent to continent and region to region. However, rather than pose the issue in terms simply of the ostensible conflict between non-European societies, which had achieved some form of ideal, Golden Age, equilibrium between settlers and wanderers, and an expanding Europe which had somehow broken out of this (on account of its unfortunate 'modernity'), it may be more useful to argue for certain broadly universal conflicts during the period in life-styles, and modes of resource-use. In turn, it is of obvious interest to link up these questions with the issue of global trade flows (commodities, bullion), their dimensions and their implications both backwards and forwards, for producers and consumers. Amongst other matters, the early modern period sees the rise of a slave trade of unprecendented dimensions (both in the Atlantic and elsewhere), as also the emergence of new cash crops with powerful social consequences for both producers and consumers, notably tea and coffee, but also opium, the production of which expands considerably, even if it was already traded in an earlier period.

These shifts are equally accompanied by complex changes in political theology (to borrow a phrase from Ernst Kantorowicz), which the exclusive focus on the emergence of the nation-state and the ideologies that go under the name of 'nationalism' has served to

important work of Anthony Pagden, *The Fall of Natural Man: The American Indian and the Origins of Comparative Ethnology* (Cambridge, 1982), adds depth to the analysis, but does not shift the perspective.

[9] For a sense of some of the complexities of this relationship through a careful case-study, see Joseph Fletcher, 'The Mongols: Ecological and Social Perspectives', *Harvard Journal of Asiatic Studies* 46, 1 (1986), 11–50.

[10] Besides the oft-cited (and oft-criticized) works of Alfred Crosby (*The Columbian Exchange*, and *Ecological Imperialism*), see the recent and ambitious synthesis by Richard Grove, *Green Imperialism* (Cambridge/Delhi, 1994), which pays far greater attention to Asia than does Crosby.

obscure. The early modern construct of the Universal Empire obviously had classical (and even mythological) roots, but was considerably reworked in the new geographical and political settings of the period. Thus, on the one hand, we have the Chinggis Khanid–Timurid tradition, that informs a great deal of what occurs in West Asia, the Ottoman Empire, Iran, North India and Central Asia; one part of this legacy is also present in China. In pre-Columbian America and Southern and Central Africa, equally, notions of universal empire existed, related to indigenous cosmologies (as in South Asia, or the 'galactic polities' of Southeast Asia).[11] The great projects of universal empire embodied by the Spanish Habsburgs (who looked back to classical roots—especially the Holy Roman Empire), and later even by the major trading Companies, and eventually by Great Britain, need to be related to these other, at times pre-existent and autonomous, notions of empire. A number of authors in recent times have addressed both the technology and insitutional bases of empire-building (warfare, the 'military revolution', financial markets, accounting, record-keeping on paper, etc.), but have paid far less attention to the symbolic and ideological constructs (in particular, millenarian visions of empire) that underlie these.[12] This may be the result of embarrassment in the face of this seeming contradiction, or a residue of naive Enlightenment teleologies. But one of the points to be developed (and which is touched on briefly by Lieberman, albeit in a rather different context) is the coexistence of such seemingly archaic forms of political articulation as empires and the notion of an emerging 'modernity'—thus a return in a manner of speaking to the issue addressed (albeit not wholly satisfactorily) by Joseph Schumpeter in his classic work on imperialism.

The early modern period also raises a number of key issues that may be addressed under the broad head of 'historical anthropology'. Thus, it is of obvious interest to examine how notions of universalism and humanism emerge in various vocabularies, and yet how these terms do not in fact unite the early modern world, but instead lead to new or intensified forms of hierarchy, domination and separation.

[11] Cf. Serge Gruzinski, *Les Hommes-dieux du Mexique: Pouvoir indien et société coloniale, XVIe–XVIIe siècle* (Paris, 1985); also the very widely cited work by the same author, *La colonisation de l'imaginaire: Sociétés indigènes et occidentalisation dans le Mexique espagnol, XVIe–XVIIIe siècle* (Paris, 1988).

[12] An exception is Geoffrey Parker, 'David or Goliath? Philip II and his World in the 1580s', in Richard L. Kagan and Geoffrey Parker (eds), *Spain, Europe and the Atlantic World: Essays in Honour of John H. Elliott* (Cambridge, 1995), 245–66.

This may be seen in a certain sense as the 'paradox of enlightenment' revisited (with or without the capital E, to be sure). A subsidiary question is to re-examine what remains (after a half-century and more of debate) of the well-known Burckhardt hypothesis, concering the new notion of the individual that emerges with modernity.[13] This would require *inter alia* an exploration of literature, and literary forms, as they are established in the period, not just in Renaissance and post-Renaissance Europe, but elsewhere in the world. Some links with the 'social history of medicine' literature are also indicated, since there are some obvious links to be made between medical and biological knowledge, and conceptions of the individual.[14]

Taking all these questions together, it is obvious that we are faced with a very much larger agenda than even that of Lieberman, and what is worse, it is still not a comprehensive one. But what is also significant for our purposes is that it is more or less orthogonal to the approach proposed by Lieberman, who really seeks to downplay the global and connected character of the early modern period, in order to reify certain chosen national entities. However, this critique has been partly acknowledged by him, and indeed in response to it, he has sought to dilute his hypotheses to the point at times of having more exceptions and qualifications than clear hypotheses. In this context, a brief retrospective may be in order here. Roughly a decade ago, the present author found himself embarked, willy-nilly, on a comparative exercise that sought to link and compare the histories of India and Indonesia between roughly 1500 and the present, as part of the so-called Cambridge–Delhi–Leiden–Yogyakarta project.[15] Seeking out buoys in those relatively little-charted comparative waters, the most striking fact at that time was their very absence: the great lack of serious comparative work that linked even the two adjacent regions of South and Southeast Asia, apart from a few grand

[13] In this context, see the useful essay by Cemal Kafadar, 'Self and Others: The Diary of a Dervish in Seventeenth Century Istanbul and First-person Narratives in Ottoman Literature', *Studia Islamica* 69 (1989), 121–50, which draws in turn on Natalie Zemon Davis, 'Boundaries and the Sense of Self in Sixteenth-Century France', in T. C. Heller, M. Sosna and D. E. Wellbery (eds), *Reconstructing Individualism: Autonomy, Individuality and the Self in Western Thought* (Stanford, 1986), 53–63.

[14] This point was made forcefully by Frank Dikötter, 'Parallel Modernities: Normalization, Individuation and the Biologizing Process in China', presented to the seminar, 'The Eurasian context of the early modern history of mainland South East Asia, c. 1400–1800', at the Centre of South East Asian Studies, SOAS, 22–4 June 1995.

[15] For selected papers of that conference, see P. J. Marshall, R. van Niel *et al.*, *The Ancien Régime in India and Indonesia* (Leiden, 1988).

and fast-aging overarching syntheses, notably those of J. C. van Leur, and to a lesser extent J. S. Furnivall. The project was not a great success, to put it bluntly, but some of the participants in the third of the C.D.L.Y. conferences ('The Ancien Régime in India and Indonesia'), went on themselves to produce some grand syntheses, usually in a spirit informed by the notion of 'world-systems': one need only refer to K. N. Chaudhuri's *Asia Before Europe* (Cambridge University Press, 1990), or André Wink's *Al-Hind* Vol. I (Leiden: E. G. Brill, 1990), to have a sense of these. Even others, more cautious, and more solidly anchored in Anglo-Saxon empiricism, like C. A. Bayly, produced such works of global ambition as *Imperial Meridian* (London: Longman, 1989) in the same context.

A brief comparison between these three works—Chaudhuri, Wink and Bayly—may be instructive, as alternate ways of approaching the problems that the present collection of essays seeks to address. All three are works of considerable erudition, but framed in very different ways. Wink seeks to examine a space that he defines as the 'Indo-Islamic world', and which includes a good part of Southeast, South and West Asia. In his view, the defining notion is that of 'Islam', a glue that holds his 'world-system' together (and in this Wink follows Marshall Hodgson, and to a lesser extent Maurice Lombard and D. S. Richards). The treatment is largely monocausal, and materialist, in the sense that the growth of trade (which is actually asserted rather than demonstrated) is portrayed as the sole motor of change in the system.

In evident contrast to Wink's linear vision of the inexorable march of Islam, and trade-oriented perspective, is Chaudhuri's massive, primarily structural comparison of various civilizational entities in Asia before 1750. The overt theoretical apparatus here is highly eclectic, but what underlies it is an approach that uses anecdotal evidence to present a surprisingly static vision of Asia before the 'European impact'. More than Wink, Chaudhuri takes as given the traditional division of Asia into areas, and posits structural characteristics for each, even going so far in some draft versions of the chapters to 'plot' the characteristics using elementary Cantorian set theory. The work has had a rather mixed reception, but even its admirers would find it difficult to find clear threads of historical (as opposed to structural, essentialist) argument running through it.

Finally, Bayly's *Imperial Meridian* is ostensibly the least ambitious of the three, certainly the most traditional in its overall construction and coverage, but in many respects the most subtly argued. Despite a number of minor errors, the argument is of change on a global scale, with many different impulses to change that interact, to produce *inter alia*, the British Empire of the late eighteenth and early nineteenth centuries. To be sure, this is still macro-history, painted in bold brush strokes, but there is plenty to argue with or even against, and a series of positions that are staked out, both on the political economy of the metropolis, and the multilateral nature of causality.[16]

Taking one thing with another, and considering the works discussed above with a whole host of others, it would appear obvious that we are today in a far better situation with respect to placing early modern Southeast Asian history in a larger comparative context than we were a decade ago. One noteworthy reason for this is that specialists working on Southeast Asia, such as Anthony Reid, Lieberman himself and Denys Lombard, have taken it upon themselves to open up the doors of comparison, and to project early modern Southeast Asia, as it were, on a world stage. This is a significant fact, even if the Anglo-Saxon and Gallic traditions approach the problem rather differently (despite Reid's genuflection in the direction of Braudel). Generalizations are, to my mind, obviously too important to be left to specialized generalists anyway. Yet it is the generalists who, in this century, have all too often generated the 'big' hypotheses in early modern history, be it the great project of the study of comparative civilization proposed and implemented by Max Weber early in this century, or the latter-day historical sociology of Barrington Moore, Perry Anderson, Immanuel Wallerstein or Jack Goldstone.

There is thus a warning to be sounded at the very outset. Area studies can very rapidly become parochialism, and we often see an insistence, taken to the limits of the absurd, concerning the unity of 'Southeast Asia', 'South Asia' or whatever one happens to study. In the case of South Asia, appeals are made to 'caste' and other multi-millennial 'civilization constants' as defining foci. It is as if these conventional geographical units of analysis, fortuitously defined as givens for the intellectually slothful, and the result of complex (even murky) processes of academic and non-academic engagement, somehow become real and overwhelming. Having helped create these Frankenstein's monsters, we are obliged to praise them for their beauty, rather than grudgingly acknowledge their limited functional

[16] My own book, *The Portuguese Empire in Asia, 1500–1700: A Political and Economic History* (London, 1993), drew inspiration in part from Bayly's work. There are, of course, a number of points of divergence, both stylistic and substantive.

utility.[17] Thus, when Anthony Reid at the outset of his *Southeast Asia in the Age of Commerce*, Vol. I, argues (taking half a leaf out of John Smail's book) that Southeast Asia is a well-defined region, has a series of long-standing physical, ethnic, cultural and linguistic characteristics of its own, and thus has a right to an 'autonomous history', the sceptical reader still remains unconvinced. One wonders whether such an argument, made resoundingly in terms of objective absolutes, is at all necessary to justify the choice of a particular geographical canvas, which is after all a mere contingent device. And it is salutary to bear in mind that any Vietnamese voyager who found himself in Arakan in the late seventeenth century would have been as much at a loss as he would in Hughli, whereas many a Bengali notable found a comfortable living in the Magh court.

A collective reflection such as this one may thus seem at first a useful occasion to break out of our specializations and compare notes, perhaps even to reorient our research agendas and 'tune our violins' (as the French put it). The obvious device that presents itself, if we wish to free ourselves from our self-imposed straitjackets and embark on a Roman Holiday, is surely that proposed in Victor Lieberman's theme paper: namely to take the geographical units as given from the conventional wisdom, and then proceed to a higher level of comparison using these very units as building-blocks. This recalls earlier exercises in a similar vein by Perry Anderson, Barrington Moore, Eric Jones and even Braudel (notably in his *Capitalism and Civilisation*). Thus, Lieberman proposes that we accept as appropriate such units as the ones Area Studies provide, or even more conventionally, the borders of modern-day nation-states. Then, working outwards from such units as 'Burma', 'Siam', 'Vietnam', 'Russia', 'France' and 'Japan', we should attempt to generate a series of general propositions. Lieberman periodically argues besides that all of Eurasia can be divided into two blocs: the 'heartlands' or 'cores', and the 'rimlands' that he himself surveys. This very process of arrangement is seen as advancing the argument, even if scholars of France will be somewhat dismayed by his view that the Great Hexagon was a 'rimland', of lesser centrality than, say, Kurdistan.

However, the exercise as it is carried out gives reason for pause. It is striking from my own perspective that the strategic momentum

[17] From a rather different perspective, this parallels observations made on the study of systems of medicine by Francis Zimmermann, *Généalogie des médecines douces: De l'Inde à l'Occident* (Paris, 1995).

of Lieberman's formulation is not a revisionist, but rather a *conservative*, one, namely to compare Southeast Asia with what are today seen as the really 'big players' in early modern history, Japan and western Europe (the case of Russia being admittedly more complex), to the neglect and detriment of other intra-Asian comparisons. As he himself notes disarmingly, it may seem that the purpose of this exercise is to say that Burma or Laos are as important for early modern world history as the countries of north-western Europe, that is to valorize these areas (today seen as 'marginal') by comparing them with the areas of 'serious' research. From his comparison of the 'rimlands' as he defines them, four general propositions are produced:

1. That the early modern period in these lands is characterized by a sustained movement from local fragmentation to political consolidation.
2. That a drive towards centralization and the growth of coercive state apparatuses accompanies this process.
3. That the standardization of culture and ethnicity within each domain is a concomitant.
4. That commercialization and a 'military revolution' also go hand in hand to interact with the features noted above.

Two objections can be raised directly. Are these four characteristic processes equally true of the areas surveyed by Lieberman? Clearly not, despite the fact that the dice is already loaded in Lieberman's favour, in the sense that he has chosen the examples most congenial to his argument. And are they more true of these areas taken together than of the areas left out? Could they not be equally applied to Spain and Portugal, to the Netherlands, or to Iran under the Safavids and Qajars? Even the case of India appears to be closer to some of these propositions than Lieberman posits.[18]

There is also something to be said for methodological scepticism concerning comparative exercises that are based on an acceptance of what appears to be the broadest conventional wisdom in each of the area-based historiographies under consideration. These area specialists will merely find themselves either 'fitted in' to a big picture, or 'left out'; and no true dialectic engagement will be really possible here between the area specialists and the (even temporary) generalist. Is there a realistic methodological alternative, one that

[18] For a discussion, see Muzaffar Alam and Sanjay Subrahmanyam, 'L'Etat Moghol et sa fiscalité', *Annales HSS* 49, 1 (1994), 189–217.

does not require one to become a specialist on everything? There are probably several, and in what remains of this paper, I shall concentrate on one broad possibility, namely that of 'connected histories' as opposed to 'comparative histories'. What I shall summarize here are arguments that are developed at greater length elsewhere, and emerge from a series of engagements with specialists on Central Asian and West Asian history, as well as a long period of reflection on the Bay of Bengal as a locus of early modern interaction. To do so, however, we must abandon the developmental perspective that comes down to us with two fathers (Marx and W. W. Rostow), and which believes that the only question worth asking is that of Who Succeeded and Who Failed on the long road to modern industrial capitalism, from a list of modern nation-states.

II

Contrary to what 'area studies' implicitly presumes, a good part of the dynamic in early modern history was provided by the interface between the local and regional (which we may call the 'micro'-level), and the supra-regional, at times even global (what we may term the 'macro'-level). For the historian who is willing to scratch below the surface of his sources, nothing turns out to be quite what it seems to be in terms of fixity and local rootedness. Methodologically, this poses a problem not only to local patriotism, but to the methodological fragmentationism (*émiettement*, if one likes) proclaimed from the rooftops by some of our post-modernist colleagues to be the only alternative to the Grand Narrative of Modernization. Alas, these post-modernists have conveniently forgotten here that *their* entire theoretical charge is based on the universalization of certain rather limited and specific interventions by philosophers of one particular tradition in relation to others of the same tradition, and—even worse—that it is based on the assumption that certain arbitrarily chosen (and usually evil!) Great Historical Processes (the Enlightenment, Colonialism) have an objective basis that is inexplicably denied to others.

How might the local and specific have interacted with the supra-local in our terms? Consider the Bay of Bengal in the sixteenth and seventeenth centuries. Although not a closed sea, the littoral areas of the Bay are a far more tightly knit unit of interaction in this period than the Indian Ocean taken as a whole. Within this zone, we can witness on the one hand the development of networks of commercial exchange (trade between the Coromandel coast of south-eastern India and Bengal, and Burma, Mergui and the Malay coast), and on the other hand a significant nexus by which military elites, courtiers and religious specialists crossed the Bay on a regular basis. Yet, reading Lieberman's account of Siam, one is left with little or no sense of how this Bay of Bengal nexus mattered for polities like Ayutthaya or Arakan.[19] After all, even Shah Sulaiman's ambassador, Muhammad Rabi', makes it clear in his *Safīna-yi Sulaimânî*, written in the 1680s, that the Persian influence in Ayutthaya was played out through the commercial networks of the Bay of Bengal. We have little sense for that matter, from the standard accounts, that the Arakan ruler Thirithudhamma (r. 1622–38) routinely conducted his diplomatic correspondence in Persian, and that he boasted in his letters that his power came not only from Firangis (Franks, here Portuguese and Luso-Asians), but also Telangas (viz. troops from the Deccan).[20] It is almost as if a set of blinkers oblige the historian of Southeast Asia to write, on the one hand, of agriculture, and on the other hand of European trade, as if all external contact in the early modern world was limited to dealings with Europeans. Yuko Tanaka's comments, cited in epigraph at the outset of this paper, are obviously of relevance to more than Japan alone. It makes little sense, to my mind, to talk of mainland Southeast Asia in this period as if it were isolated from the Indian world, even though Southeast Asianists may fear for their part that this is the thin end of the wedge of a revamped 'Greater India' formulation.

Let us continue with a simple example that takes us further west. During the course of a campaign in Afghanistan in mid-1581—that is in the year 989 of the Hegiran calendar which is followed by most Muslims the world over—the Mughal ruler Jalal al-Din Muhammad Akbar began quizzing the Portuguese Jesuit António Monserrate (then on a mission to his court) on matters pertaining to the millennium, that is about 'the Last Judgement, whether Christ would be the Judge, and when it would occur'. The underlying purpose was

[19] For an earlier, more empirically substantiated, statement, see Sanjay Subrahmanyam, *The Political Economy of Commerce: Southern India, 1500–1650* (Cambridge, 1990), ch. 4.

[20] I develop these themes at greater length in my paper, 'Persianisation and Mercantilism: Two Themes in Bay of Bengal History, 1400–1750', in Denys Lombard and Om Prakash (eds), *Trade and Cultural Contacts in the Bay of Bengal, 1400–1800* (Delhi: Manohar, forthcoming).

complex, and surely lay in part in Akbar's desire to tease out both the theological differences and the commonalities between his own heterodox brand of Islam and the Jesuit version of Christianity. Monserrate, himself a strong believer in portents like some other influential members of his order, reports in his *Mongoliecae Legationis Commentarius* that he stated that the Day of Judgement was a divine mystery, which would, however, be known by certain signs, namely 'wars and rebellions, the fall of kingdoms and nations, the invasion, devastation and conquest of nation by nation and kingdom by kingdom: and these things we see happening very frequently in our time'.[21] The hint in the last phrase was rather broad, and must have found an echo in a court where millenarian verses attributed to Nasir-i Khusrau and others, enjoyed wide circulation. Later, Akbar is reported to have asked if Muhammad was mentioned in the Gospel, to which Monserrate responded by insisting that he was not, being a false prophet. Monserrate now writes that Akbar wondered aloud, somewhat disingenuously, 'Surely Muhammad cannot be he who is to appear at the end of the world as the adversary of all mankind (that is he whom the Musalmans calls Dijal)', the reference being to the idea of the *masîh al-dajjâl*, the Anti-Christ who appears in some Islamic legends as riding on an ass at the end of time.

This incident, a trivial one, begins to assume significance when set in its wider regional and supra-regional context. For a millenarian conjuncture operated over a good part of the Old World in the sixteenth century and was the backdrop to such discussions as that between Akbar and Monserrate, which took place just eleven years before the year 1000 A.H (1591–92). This was a time when many Muslims in southern and western Asia, as well as North Africa anxiously awaited signs that the end of the world was nigh, and when the Most Catholic Monarch, Philip II of Spain, equally wrote gloomily: 'If this is not the end of the world, I think we must be very close to it; and, please God, let it be the end of the whole world, and not just the end of Christendom'.[22] Speaking of supra-local connections in the early modern world, we tend to focus on such phenomena as world bullion flows and their impact, firearms and the so-called

[21] H. Hosten (ed.), 'Mongoliecae Legationis Commentarius', in *Memoirs of the Asiatic Society of Bengal* 3 (1914), 513–704; S. N. Banerjee and John S. Hoyland (tr.), *The Commentary of Father Monserrate S.J. on his Journey to the Court of Akbar* (London, 1922).

[22] Cited in Geoffrey Parker, *Philip II*, 3rd ed. (Chicago, 1995), xvi. The letter is dated December 1574.

'Military Revolution', or the circulation of renegades and mercenaries. But ideas and mental contructs, too, flowed across political boundaries in that world, and—even if they found specific local expression—enable us to see that what we are dealing with are not separate and comparable, but connected histories. The fact that Akbar and Monserrate could and did converse on the impending End of the World (or *qiyâmat*, from an Indo-Persian viewpoint) obviously reflects several facts. First, it points to the conspicuous presence of European Catholic missionary orders, who—partly propelled by the Counter-Reformation—made their way to Asian and African courts, and thus were an element of circulation in early modern Eurasia, together with mercenaries, renegades, diplomats, Buddhist monks and Sufis. Indeed, Augustinians and Jesuits are to be found in both Burma and Cambodia at the turn of the seventeenth century, and provide valuable insights into local histories (especially elite politics) at the time. Any consideration of early modern state-building activity that neglects this element of elite circulation misses out on one of the key themes that characterizes the period: namely a change in the nature and scale of elite movement across political boundaries. Besides, the Akbar–Monserrate conversation points to the permeability of what are often assumed to be closed 'cultural zones', and the existence of vocabularies that cut across local religious traditions, here the heterodox Sunni-inflected Islam represented by Akbar, and Monserrate's zealous Counter-Reformation Christianity. These vocabularies were partly 'secular' (in the sense, at least, of spilling across sectarian boundaries), and also drew on a body of lore and myth that went back to medieval times. And, finally, the locus of the conversation itself is not without interest, for it took place as Akbar was on an expedition to suppress the ambitions of his half-brother Mirza Muhammad Hakim, ruler of Kabul, and a rival claimant in the Indian sub-continent to the legacy of the 'world-conquerors' Chinggis Khan and Timur. Akbar's eventual triumph, and the death of Mirza Hakim in 1585, signalled the victory of a Timurid order that was less oriented towards Central Asia, less prone to appanaging and which sought to adumbrate a theory of sovereignty with a far wider social basis than any that had existed in the domain of the Indo-Islamic states.[23] The conversation on Messianism thus represents one

[23] For a further discussion, see Sanjay Subrahmanyam, 'A Note on the Kabul Kingdom under Muhammad Hakim Mirza (1554–1585)', *La Transmission du savoir dans le monde musulman périphérique, Lettre d'information No. 14* (1994), 89–101.

of the many ideological currents that were present in Akbar's court at this crucial moment of transition.[24]

The notion of the 'early modern' is hence linked, if not directly, then in some important indirect respects to a changed domain of global interaction that has to do with such diverse matters as the legacy of Chinggis Khan and Timur, the Counter-Reformation and its overseas drive to proselytize, as well as the so-called Voyages of Discovery. Indeed, researches in recent years have shown that millenarian aspirations helped drive Columbus on his westward voyage, and that there may even have been a curious—and ironical—parallel between that millenarianism and the apocalyptic vision of some of the indigenous American peoples that the Spaniards encountered in the aftermath of 1492. Columbus, it now appears, was heavily influenced by Franciscan apocalyptic thought on the coming of the millennium, so much so that he asked to be buried in the habit of that religious order.[25] Thus, the Great Discoveries to the west, for long regarded as signalling the Birth of Modernity and the beginnings of a truly universal sensibility, now appear to historians to have been the product not only of advances in navigational techniques and geographical knowledge, or of the materialist drive to acquire riches (as Vitorino Magalhães Godinho argued so forcefully in the Portuguese case), but equally of an embarrassingly 'medieval' view of the world, which had as much in common with Joachim of Fiore as with Copernicus.[26] Not only Columbus, but the Portuguese monarch Dom Manuel (r. 1495–1521) and some of his chief ideologues and agents such as Duarte Galvão and Afonso de Albuquerque inhabited this altogether curious collective mental world.

In fact, as the fifteenth century of the Christian calendar drew to a close, the power of signs and portents concerning the millennium did not diminish; they were merely modified, and appeared in unprecedented forms. The sixteenth century thus saw the emergence of a new set of material conditions within which millenarianism could

[24] In this context, we may note that the social, ideological and political ramifications of the important Mahdawi movement in sixteenth-century northern India will be discussed in the forthcoming work of Derryl Maclean, *Waiting for the End of the World*.

[25] Abbas Hamdani, 'Columbus and the Recovery of Jerusalem', *Journal of the American Oriental Society* 99, 1 (1979), 39–48; also John L. Phelan, *The Millennial Kingdom of the Franciscans in the New World* (Berkeley, 1970).

[26] Cf. Vitorino Magalhães Godinho, *Mito e mercadoria, utopia e prática de navegar, séculos XIII–XVIII* (Lisbon, 1990); and in contrast, the important new interpretation in Luís Filipe F. R. Thomaz, *De Ceuta a Timor* (Lisbon, 1994).

arise, and propagate itself both as a current that embraced a large geographical space, and as a phenomenon that had specific, and even unique, local manifestations. The metaphor of monetary circulation, although inevitably flawed, may be useful here, for the sixteenth century saw dramatic transformations in world bullion flows as well, as a vast interpenetrating network of silver girdled the globe. And yet, the consequences of this phenomenon were different for different societies. The inflation and accompanying social unquiet witnessed in the Iberian peninsula found only a pale reflection in the Ottoman domains, and India seems to have witnessed practically no inflation at all. Millenarianism, like money, allows us to approach a problem of global dimensions, but with quite different local manifestations.[27] This means in turn that we cannot attempt a 'macro-history' of the problem without muddying our boots in the bogs of 'micro-history'.

As has been pointed out by the Ottomanist historian Cornell Fleischer, in his forthcoming work *A Mediterranean Apocalypse*, one can show, using the notion of a millenarian conjuncture, that the historical rhythms of the northern and southern shores of the early modern Mediterranean were linked together not only by climate and geography, economic forces and political rivalries (as argued by Fernand Braudel), but by certain common cultural traits, including a shared sense of millenarian expectation in the century after Columbus. Drawing on primary materials from the Ottoman domains, and linking them to an array of secondary millenarian materials from the European Mediterranean, ranging from writings on Savonarola in Florence, to Carlo Ginzburg's celebrated miller, to the millenarian expectations at the court of Philip II of Spain set out by Richard Kagan and others, Fleischer skilfully suggests that the entire Mediterranean was the space over which a millenarian conjuncture operated in the Age of Charles V and Philip II.[28] While this is undoubtedly valid, I shall argue that it may be equally fruitful to see Ottoman millenarianism in relation to similar processes further east (notably in Safavid Iran, Mughal India and the Deccan), while at the same time suggesting that, in the far west of Eurasia, Portugal, too,

[27] See the important paper by Cemal Kafadar, 'Les troubles monétaires de la fin du XVIe siècle et la prise de conscience ottomane du déclin', *Annales ESC* 46, 2 (1991), 381–400.

[28] See, for example, Richard L. Kagan, *Lucrecia's Dreams: Politics and Prophecy in Sixteenth-Century Spain* (Berkeley, 1990); and earlier, Donald Weinstein, *Savonarola and Florence: Prophecy and Patriotism in the Renaissance* (Princeton, 1970).

should be brought into the picture for a rounded understanding of the Mediterranean.

Taking a broad view of the Ottoman Empire, Iran and North Africa, we see that in the context of the year 1000 A.H., expectations in these areas were not uniformly apocalyptic. Rather, they also hovered optimistically around the possibility of a re-ordering of the known world, through the intercession of a *mujaddid* (or 'Renewer'); thus, at least one celebrated religious reformer of the late sixteenth and early seventeenth centuries in India, Shaikh Ahmad Sirhindi of the Naqshbandi Sufi order, assumed the title of *mujaddid-i alf-i s̱ânî* ('Renewer of the Second Millennium'). The idea of the *mujaddid* paralleled, but did not replace, another idea with deep roots in Islamic history, namely the notion of the Imam Mahdi, the Concealed or Expected One, who would emerge to reform the world in a radical fashion. Canonical texts describe the Imam Mahdi thus: that he would be a descendant of the Prophet and hence a member of the Quraishi clan, that he would be a certain Muhammad Mahdi and that when he appeared Christ (Isa Masih), too, would appear. After all men had been led to Islam by the Mahdi's intervention, the Day of Judgement would commence.

It has sometimes been asserted, somewhat erroneously, that it is the Shiʿas alone who believe in the Mahdi. This appears to be incorrect, even if some orthodox Sunnis have argued in a similar fashion at various points in time. We may consider the example of Morocco in the middle years of the sixteenth century, where the ruler Muhammad al-Shaikh, second of the Saʿdi dynasty of Sayyids from the southern Atlas, took to titling himself 'al-Mahdi'. Of Al-Mahdi's older brother, Ahmad al-Aʿraj, it had already been said by his admirers that he was the one who had been promised by the Prophet and Law-Giver (*sâhib al-shariʿa*) as 'the one who would appear at the end of time'. It is noteworthy that their opponents, the Wattasids, reacted to their challenge by accusing them of being Shiʿas, whereas it appears far more probable that these millenarian ideas were brought to their court by Andalusian Muslims.

Indeed, as Cornell Fleischer has demonstrated, that most Sunni of states, the Ottoman Empire, had a long-drawn-out flirtation with Mahdism in the mid-sixteenth century, particularly during the reigns of Yavuz Sultan Selim (r. 1512–20) and his son Sultan Süleyman (r. 1520–66). He cites a text composed after Selim's conquest of eastern Anatolia, Syria and Egypt, in 1517, which uses a series of grandiose epithets to describe him, ranging from 'Succoured by God', to 'The

Master of the Conjunction', to the 'Shadow of God' (*zill Allâh*). A later retrospective account from the 1550s went much further: in this text by Lutfi Pasha, titled *Tawârîkh-i Âl-i ʿOsmân*, Selim is described as the *mujaddid* of the age, and as a World Conqueror. Lutfi Pasha cites with evident approval two letters addressed to Selim, ostensibly written by Sunni *'ulama* from Transoxania, which refer to him quite unambiguously as *mahdi-yi âkhir-i zamân* ('Last Messiah of the Age'), and as *qudrat-i ilâhî* ('Divine Force'). Fleischer argues in some detail that the nature of Süleyman's ambitions and self-perception changed rather extensively between the 1520s, when he first came to the throne, and the 1560s. In the first half of his reign, the Ottoman Sultan appears to have been strongly influenced by the millenarian currents that had been inherited from the previous reign, and had taken to designating himself *Sâhib-Qirân*, 'Master of the Conjunction' (a title derived paradoxically, from the Ottomans' erstwhile enemy, Timur), as also *Mujaddid*.

At the same time, the particular vocabulary utilized in the entourages of Selim and Süleyman must be seen in the context of developments immediately to their east, notably their long-standing rivalry with the Safavids, a dynasty with fairly overt messianistic pretensions. The founder of the dynasty, Shah Ismaʿil, on his assuming royal titles in 1501, emerged rapidly as a figure with an eschatological aura surrounding him.[29] Identified by himself and by his followers variously with the prestigious figures of ʿAli and Alexander, and at times even with God himself, Shah Ismaʿil's appearance on the scene of Iranian politics caused ripples as far as Venice and Lisbon. Surrounded by his *qizilbâsh* followers, who saw in him a Sufi master of whom they were the disciples, Shah Ismaʿil elaborated a set of rituals, drawing elements from the practices of both earlier Sufi orders, and shamanistic ritual. The contemporary Italian traveller, Francesco Romano, wrote of him: 'Some say that he is God, others that he is a Prophet. All of them, and in particular his soldiers, say that he will not die, and will live eternally'; another Italian reporter, Giovanni Morosini, wrote to his principals from Damascus in 1507 that the Shah was 'adored in place of one Ali, a relative and apostle of Muhammad'. There was a certain element of simplification inherent

[29] For the best discussion to date of early sixteenth-century Iran, see Jean Aubin, 'L'avènement des Safavides réconsideré', *Moyen Orient et Océan Indien* 5 (1988), 1–130. My discussion of Shah Ismaʿil draws liberally on this extensive, and very well-documented, essay. But, see also several of the essays in Jean Calmard (ed.), *Études safavides* (Paris–Teheran, 1993).

in this description, of course. Some of Shah Isma'il's own seals suggest that he took a more nuanced view of his own position, as we see from the epithet 'Sovereign whom God has in His Grace accompanied on the way' (*Shahanshâhi ke khudâ shud be lutf hamrâh ash*) used in one of them. Further, his own poetry, while judged to be not of the highest literary quality, is significant for its simultaneous identification with Alexander, God and 'Ali, and its use of the pen-name (*takhallus*) of Khatâ'i, which is to say 'The Sinner'.[30]

While the reign of Shah Isma'il's successor, Tahmasb (r. 1524–76), remains obscure in many respects, it appears more or less certain that he had begun by its middle years to retreat from the messianic pretensions that attended the dynasty's foundation. Ties with the *qizilbâsh* were gradually loosened, and the old Turkoman Sufi followers of Shah Isma'il kept at a distance from the reign. The contested and bloody interregnum that followed this reign, and especially the rule of Shah Isma'il II (1576–77) and its aftermath, saw the recrudescence of millenarian rumours and political forces.[31] However—and this is significant—such groups as adhered to millenarian ideologies were now largely ranged against the state, usually through the device of supporting pretenders claiming to be Shah Isma'il II, miraculously returned from the dead. The most important of these episodes dates to 1580–81 (988 A.H.), when a *qalandar* (or dervish) called Muzawwar emerged to challenge Safavid regional governors, claiming to be the dead Shah. This movement claimed at its height some 20,000 supporters, and was eventually brutally crushed through military force. Other similar movements appeared over the next few years, albeit with more limited popular support.[32]

With the accession in Iran of Shah 'Abbas in the late 1580s, the millenarian atmosphere there took on a decidedly different twist. The first decades of the reign are marked by conflicts between the Shah and a resurgent order of heterodox Sufis, the Nuqtavis. As recently analysed in some detail by Kathryn Babayan, the Nuqtavi challenge fructified precisely because the Safavids moved from their initial insistence on

[30] Cf. V. Minorsky, 'The Poetry of Shâh Ismâ'îl I', *Bulletin of the School of Oriental and African Studies* 10, 4 (1942), 1006a–53a; for other verses, see also Tourkhan Gandjei, *Il Canzoniere di Shâh Ismâ'îl* (Naples, 1959).

[31] For a brief overview of this reign, and an attempt to rehabilitate the reputation of this ruler, see Michel M. Mazzaoui, 'The Religious Policy of Shah Isma'il II', in M. M. Mazzaoui and Vera B. Moreen (eds), *Intellectual Studies on Islam: Essays Written in Honour of Martin B. Dickson* (Salt Lake City, 1990), 49–56.

[32] R. M. Savory, 'A Curious Episode in Safavid History', in C. E. Bosworth (ed.), *Iran and Islam: In Memory of the Late Vladimir Minorsky* (Edinburgh, 1971), 461–73.

ghuluww (which is to say heterodox beliefs of a chiliastic nature, in their case), to a form of Imamism which brought them far closer to the *sharî'a*.[33] This meant abandoning an attachment to certain legendary or semi-legendary characters in early Islamic history, such as Abu Muslim, and Muhammad ibn Hanafiyya, who had earlier played a significant role in the Safavid world-view. In turn, the Nuqtavis took to claiming by the 1580s that the Shahs had lost legitimacy, and that it was one of their number who would convert 'spiritual monarchy' into a form of real sovereignty (*pâdishâhî-yi sûrî*). A large number of *qizilbâsh*, who had in any case been drifting away from the Safavid dynasty, now attached themselves to the new order, leading to a most dramatic confrontation in the early 1590s.

In a first step to resolving the tensions with the Nuqtavis, Shah 'Abbas went so far as to declare himself a disciple of the powerful Nuqtavi, Darvish Khusrau. But this was not enough to appease the Nuqtavis, who began to claim that in Muharram 1002 (1593), one of their number would emerge as ruler and displace 'Abbas. Once the Safavid court astrologer, too, announced that the imminent conjunction of Saturn and Jupiter portended the death of the ruling sovereign, 'Abbas decided to resolve the affair in a novel manner. He imprisoned or executed the bulk of the Nuqtavis, but chose one from amongst them—a certain Yusufi Tarkishduz—to whom he abdicated the throne. Thus, the puppet Yusufi was the one who actually sat the throne during the unlucky conjunction, while Shah 'Abbas claimed merely to be the guardian of the harem gates for the interim. Once the conjunction had passed, after a four-day reign in which he was kept under strict guard, Yusufi was taken out, shot and his body hung on a scaffold for public view.[34] Thus, the prophecy was nominally fulfilled; a Sultan did indeed die, but it was not Shah 'Abbas! In other words, millenarianism was not a given to be accepted fatalistically, but a resource that a monarchy with centralizing tendencies of no mean dimensions could make use of creatively.

III

Millenarianism was thus a force to be reckoned with, and a potent and complex political strategy, in the sixteenth century not only in

[33] Indeed, my discussion here draws largely on Kathryn Babayan, 'The Waning of the Qizilbâsh: The Temporal and the Spiritual in Seventeenth-Century Iran' (Princeton University, Ph.D. dissertation, 1993).

[34] Babayan, 'The Waning of the Qizilbâsh', 48–64.

the Mediterranean but further east, indeed as far as Southeast Asia, as I shall argue below. If at times it was used to build a state, as with Shah Isma'il, or to consolidate a phase of rapid geographical expansion, as with Sultan Selim, it was at other moments used to challenge the state in significant ways. Before we extend our analysis further into India, it may be useful to pause a moment to set out some of the common salient elements of Islamic millenarianism as it extended in the sixteenth century from North Africa and the Balkans into South Asia. Central to the issue, we have seen, was the imminent arrival of the millennium. The expectation of a messianic figure was linked to dreams of a 'universal' kingdom, which in the Ottoman case was perhaps interpreted somewhat literally, but in other instances appears to have a more metaphorical content ('universal' being interpreted to signify the conquest of an enemy, who was at the same time a 'complementary' element). Such a quest for universal conquest led almost inevitably to a reinterpretation of the legend of Alexander, the quintessential World Conqueror for the Islamic world in the epoch.

The eastern recension of the Alexandrine legend, which passed from Syriac into Persian, and was raised to classical form by Nizami Ganjawi in his *Sikandar Nâma*, usually recognized Alexander not only as a World Conqueror but as a Prophet.[35] Certain elements in the legend were seen as key in nature. There is first the linking of him to Darius, in fact his Achaemenid opponent in history, who is now often seen as Alexander's half-brother. The war between the two is thus a fratricidal one, and is an important step in Alexander's (Sikandar's) claim to be a universal monarch and a world conqueror, uniting the Hellenic and Persian worlds. Darius is defeated by Alexander (hence the latter's epithet of *dârâ-shikan*), and in many versions two traitors among his own men stab him, hoping to win favour with Alexander (in fact, Darius was assassinated by a satrap at Hecatompylos, in 330 B.C.). Alexander kills the two traitors and visits a dying Darius, promising to restore him to his throne; but it is too late. This pairing appears not only in the *Sikandar Nâma*, but equally in the *Akhbâr-i Dârâb*, or *Dârâb Nâma*, a fantastic cycle of stories, which provided the basis for some fine paintings of the early Mughal period (*c.* 1580).[36]

[35] *The Sikandar Nâmah-i-Bahri by Nizâmî*, 2 vols, eds A. Sprenger, Agha Muhammad Shustari and Moulawi Ali Agha Ahmad Ali (Calcutta, 1852–69).

[36] The *Dârâb Nâma* in question is by Abu Tahir ibn Hasan Musa al-Tarsusi, British Museum, London, MSS. Or. 4615; two paintings representing the swallowing of Shah Ardashir by a dragon, and the island of Nigar are reproduced in Stuart Cary Welch, *Imperial Mughal Painting* (London, 1978), 48–51.

A second element in the legend concerns the science of signs, for Sikandar is shown not merely as conqueror but seer. There are thus a number of treatises in astrology (*Fâl-Nâma*) attributed to him. Alexander's association with Aristotle obviously did his reputation no harm in this respect. In terms of pictorial representation, this aspect of the legend often focuses on the so-called *waqwâq* tree, or he tree of Waqwaq island. Alexander, in his wanderings, is reputed to have arrived at this legendary island, in which monkeys had been taught to sweep houses and fetch wood, where gold was in such easy availability that the inhabitants made their utensils from it, and where a celebrated tree had fruits that resembled the heads of animals and men. In the legend, it is the *waqwâq* tree that informs Alexander of his own impending doom. It is the science of signs, and astrology, that also helps to establish the connection between the Alexandrine legend and another key piece in the textual fabric of sixteenth-century millenarianism. This is the Book of Daniel (or *Kitâb-i Dâniyâl*), which revolves around the apocalyptic myth concerning the interpretation of Nebuchadnezzar's dream.[37] Much used by court-astrologers in the sixteenth century, the Book of Daniel was often conflated, or read together with talismanic texts, and the *Fâl Nâma* texts attributed to Alexander. It also helped give currency to the equivalence between the Universal Kingdom to be established in the millennium, and the Fifth Empire of Daniel's interpretation.

A third element in the legend is Alexander's search for immortality and the Water of Life (*âb-i hayât*), to which end he receives instruction not merely from Aristotle. His guide in this search is none other than Khwaja Khizr, the immortal prophet of verdure, who takes him to the very end of the journey, where Alexander eventually fails. Khizr, on the other hand, drinks the elixir, hence his immortality. He thus represents a sort of initiator and guide-cum-prophet, who is also a sign of the coming of the Eternal Kingdom; in sixteenth-century North India and the Ottoman Empire, we can see him clearly linked to Islamic millenarian expectations.

Finally, an element of great significance in the eastern Alexandrine legend is his protection of 'civilization' against 'barbarian' forces. Concretely, this is the episode that recurs in most such texts, where Alexander (Sikandar) builds a copper wall at the edge of the

[37] Cf. in this context, Lucette Valensi, *Venise et la Sublime Porte: La naissance du despote* (Paris, 1987), 59–70.

world, to defend civilization against the depredations of Gog and Magog (*ŷajûj wa majûj*), again figures that can be used to trace links to the Old Testament. The crucial point underlying the legend must, however, not be forgotten. It is Alexander's destiny to establish not merely an universal kingdom, but a kingdom of *Islam*, and Gog and Magog are thus the enemies of Islam. Assimilated to the tenuous figure of the Zu'lqarnain (the 'Two-Horned') in the Qur'an, Alexander is thus to the Persian, Indo-Persian and Ottoman authors a paragon of Persianized Islam.[38]

We can briefly follow the Alexandrine legend in its career into Southeast Asia as well. In the case of Aceh, we see the production of the *Hikayat Iskandar Zulkarnain* in several Malay recensions, dating to the late sixteenth and early seventeenth centuries, and a fairly explicit attempt to assimilate the legend to the figure of the celebrated Sultan Iskandar Muda (r. 1607–36), whose title and grandiose patronage to texts (some based explicitly on Mughal models) tell their own tale. Elsewhere, Denys Lombard has analysed this text in some detail, and also placed it in a comparative perspective, by relating its world-conquering ambitions to those of the *Voyages of the San Bao Eunuch* (i.e. the Chinese admiral Zheng He), and Camões's *Lusíadas*.[39] He concludes that this text represents the beginnings of a rather different ordering of space in the Malay world, and argues in turn that this can be related to an emerging conception of the individual and of agency in the commercial cities of the *pasisir* and elsewhere. Later in the same century, a version of the *Sikandar Nâma* was written at the Arakan court by Sayyid Alaol, in Bengali; this version portrays Sikandar as a protagonist of a vigorous and altogether uncompromising Islam, who appears to be compared with Alaol's sometime patron, the Mughal prince Shah Shujaʿ. The Arakan court, wherein the court chronicles were written in Pali, but where Persian was used, and Bengali the major language of literary expression, has escaped scholarly attention for the most part,

[38] I have closely followed the summary in Mohammad Wahid Mirza, *The Life and Works of Amir Khusrau* (Delhi, 1935), 200–1; but, see also Peter Gaeffke, 'Alexander and the Bengali Sufis', in Alan W. Entwistle and Françoise Mallison (eds), *Studies in South Asian Devotional Literature, Research Papers, 1988–1991* (New Delhi, 1994), 275–84, basing himself on the text in Ahmad Sharif (ed.), *Alâûl viracita Sikandarnâma* (Dhaka, 1977).

[39] Denys Lombard, 'Les *Lusiades* comparées à deux autres "visions" de la fin du XVIe siècle: le *Xi Yang Ji* et le roman malais d'Alexandre', in Artur Teodoro de Matos and Luís Filipe F. Reis Thomaz (eds), *As Relações entre a Índia Portuguesa, a Ásia do Sueste e o Extremo Oriente* (Macau–Lisbon, 1993), 173–86.

because it falls in the cracks between defining Area Studies. Yet, it may very well be here, at the uncomfortable edges of our categories, that we may find important clues that help us to define the key elements of connectedness and transmission that characterize early modern history. After all, Arakan was in the sixteenth and seventeenth centuries also a player in the network of inter-state politics that concerned the control of Buddhist relics; in Arakan, as in Kandy or in lower Burma, such artefacts and their circulation were central to the definition of the state's legitimacy, and explain the frequent exchange of embassies, relics and learned Buddhist monks between Southeast Asia and Sri Lanka.[40]

How are we to read such materials in the context of a broader notion of what constitutes early modern history? Clearly, we have the possibility of posing such questions in the context of a comparative model, in which individual states are taken as building blocks. Thus, we may take, for example, the synthesis proposed by comparative sociologist Jack A. Goldstone (from which Lieberman explicitly draws sustenance), where we have a discussion of 'Ideology, Cultural Frameworks, Revolutionary Struggles, and State Reconstruction' (Chapter 5), in which the reader is presented with a model in which 'state breakdown', often accompanied by millenarian movements, is the result of a Malthusian population–resource imbalance in a series of autonomously modelled states. Thus, population pressure leads to a fiscal crisis, the fiscal crisis to intra-elite conflicts, and these interact with popular unrest (centring inevitably on food shortages) to produce ideologies of 'rectification and transformation'.[41]

Further, and rather more curiously, Goldstone's early modern world is divided neatly into two sub-sets, societies that work with 'eschatological' frameworks, and those that work with 'cyclical' frameworks. He concludes, moreover (pp. 447–8), that Iran alone from the Islamic world adhered to 'a uniquely eschatological strain of Islam', namely Shi'ism, and that otherwise the 'eschatological element was an innovation of Judeo-Christian culture'. Goldstone does

[40] Cf. in this context, H. L. Seneviratne, *Rituals of the Kandyan State* (Cambridge, 1978), for an exploration of Buddhist rituals around the sacred tooth relic at Kandy, and its relations to state-building. Also, C. E. Godakumbara, 'Relations between Burma and Ceylon', *Journal of the Burma Research Society* 44, 2 (1966), 145–62, and most recently, Catherine Raymond, 'Étude des relations religieuses entre le Sri Lanka et l'Arakan du XIIe au XVIIIe siècle: Documentation historique et évidences archéologiques', *Journal Asiatique* 283, 2 (1995), 469–501.

[41] Jack A. Goldstone, *Revolution and Rebellion in the Early Modern World* (Berkeley, 1991).

not draw any major conclusions from this for his model, which is after all constructed with a mechanistic materialism that makes Maurice Cornforth appear a cultural relativist. But, the characterization is, nevertheless, important in and of itself as a way of analysing early modern ideological frameworks. And, needless to add, the brunt of our argument has been to argue for the contamination of such neat categories: far from being a mere prisoner of the cyclical vision of Ibn Khaldun's *Muqaddimâh* (as Goldstone bluntly states), the Ottoman version of sixteenth-century millenarianism contained significant areas of commonality with both Iran, India and the Christian Mediterranean, to say nothing of some parts of mainland and insular Southeast Asia.

IV

To resume the argument thus far, it has been that several spheres of the circulation of powerful myths and ideological constructs relating to state formation existed in early modern Eurasia, and that these often transcended the boundaries defined for us retrospectively by nation-states or Area Studies. How were these myths and ideas carried, and did the channels by which they circulated also serve as the sluices for the convection of other 'technologies'? Before entering into this question, it is imperative to note that the brunt of our argument is not to negate the notion of difference, and to reduce the Eurasian landscape to a flat terrain. Even if we were to accept Frank Perlin's picturesque formulation of Eurasia as an 'unbroken landscape' before say, 1900, this would not require us to argue that continuity (thus, unbrokenness) and change (thus, difference) were antonyms.[42]

My purpose here is more complex. It is, first of all, to shift the grounds of discussion from Lieberman's highly materialist conception (wherein agricultural expansion, commercial exchange, firearms, fiscal methods and functional ideologies are all that count) to a rather broader-based conception of early modern history. This partly reflects my concern as a historian trained in economics at the rather cavalier use of materialism by colleagues, who are constantly dashing off to find Price Revolutions and Little Ice Ages, just because they

[42] Cf. Frank Perlin, *Unbroken Landscape: Commodity, Category, Sign and Identity: Their Production, Strengths and Knowledge from 1500* (Aldershot, 1994).

happened to be in vogue twenty years ago in the European historiography. The fact is, as the symposium on the 'seventeenth-century crisis' in Asia in this journal (Vol. XXIV, No. 4, 1990) some years ago shows, that the major evidence thrown up by W. S. Atwell, Anthony Reid and John Richards of such a 'crisis' is the traditional evidence of political crisis at the level of states.[43] The attempts to link these up to gigantic materialist motors puts one in mind of Rube Goldberg rather than any recognizable form of social science.

What underlies these materialisms? There is, first of all, the option of geographical determinism: some states are too small, others too large, others have mountains to their north, some to the south, still others are islands and so on. Since such arguments are used fitfully and opportunistically for the most part, once the outcome is known, there is obviously quite a lot of room for manoeuvre once geography has been disposed of. The second is residual cultural explanation, of the type favoured by Weber, and still the ghost in many machines. Here the 'failure' to be the same (as western Europe, naturally) is eventually laid at the door of 'culture' because no other reason exists. There is, of course, a profound circularity in this type of reasoning, since no two cultures are the same by definition.

Taking as our point of departure the notion of connectedness may conceivably lead us down a different path. After all, even within a 'society', however we choose to define it, the constituent sub-units fare differently over historical time, not only in the sense of better and worse, but in the sense of survival and elimination, or more simply difference. Thus, when inflation struck Spain in the latter part of the sixteenth century, not all parts of Spanish society were equally affected by its negative effects; some sections may even have been better off as a consequence. Regional and social differences are likely to have affected the response to, and the making of, this phenomenon.[44] At one level, the global phenomenon of bullion flows

[43] For the most thought-provoking piece in the collection, see brief essay by Niels Steensgaard, 'The Seventeenth Century Crisis and the Unity of Eurasian History', *Modern Asian Studies* 24, 4 (1990), 683–97. It is curious that what inspired this 'revisionist' wave in early modern Asian studies was the singularly inconclusive, and at times positively woolly-headed, debate on seventeenth-century Europe, for which see Geoffrey Parker and Lesley M. Smith (eds), *The General Crisis of the Seventeenth Century* (London, 1978).

[44] For one detailed case-study, see Carla Rahn Phillips, *Ciudad Real, 1500–1750: Growth, Crisis and Readjustment in the Spanish Economy* (Cambridge, Mass., 1979), 71–5, *passim.* The 'bureaucratic elite' of the area is shown to have invested in land, taking advantage of distress sales by small landholders.

both magnifies and renders complex what we can see in Iberia. The extent of regional and social variants becomes that much more complex, and the consequences in terms of the redistribution of wealth are also rendered so, without wholly altering the nature of the phenomenon.

Nationalism has blinded us to the possibility of connection, and historical ethnography, whether in one of its western variants of high Orientalism, or whether practised in the East, has aided and abetted this unfortunate process. The thrust of such ethnography has always been to emphasize difference, and more usually the positional superiority of the observer over the observed (save in particular situations where the 'colonized' observer had internalized someone else's values, and found himself and his own society wanting by those measures).[45] At the same time, this ethnography itself was the product of certain characteristically early modern phenomena, the intensification of travel, the desire to be able to map the world in its entirety and locate each human 'species' in its niche, and thus, to separate the civilized from the uncivilized, as well as to distinguish different degrees of civilization.

Contrary to what is sometimes argued, I do not see these phenomena as peculiar products of European expansion, although western Europeans were often in a better position, empirically speaking, to practise it than others. Nevertheless, almost any process of early modern empire building was also a process of classification, of identifying difference either in order to preserve it (as in the case of the Ottoman *millet* system), or in order to further a civilizing mission of acculturation. The post-modernist wave in social science persists in the error of identifying this urge to define, describe and classify (and eventually to differentiate) with the European Enlightenment, but in fact it exists outside of Europe, and earlier than the so-called Enlightenment. We find ourselves, in part, its victims even today, and it would be absurd to suggest that we could throw off this heavy heritage by a mere act of will. Given the fragmentary nature of access to knowledge, each of us is more or less condemned in greater or lesser measure to Area Studies. Let me end, therefore, with the plea, once more, that we not only compare from within our boxes, but spend some time and effort to transcend them, not by compar-

[45] For an excellent (albeit uneven) collection of papers on these questions, see Stuart Schwartz (ed.), *Implicit Understandings: Observing, Reporting, and Reflecting on the Encounters between Europeans and Other Peoples in the Early Modern Era* (New York, 1994).

ison alone but by seeking out the at times fragile threads that connected the globe, even as the globe came to be defined as such. This is not to deny voice to those who were somehow 'fixed' by physical, social and cultural coordinates, who inhabited 'localities' in the early modern period and nothing else, and whom we might seek out with our intrepid analytical machetes.[46] But if we ever get to 'them' by means other than archaeology, the chances are that it is because they are already plugged into some network, some process of circulation.

[46] Cf. in this context, the pertinent comments in David Ludden, 'History Outside Civilization and the Mobility of South Asia', *South Asia* (n.s.) 17, 1 (1994), 1–23.

Contributors

MARY ELIZABETH BERRY is Professor of History at the University of California, Berkeley.

PETER CAREY is Laithwaite Fellow and Tutor in Modern History at Trinity College, Oxford.

JAMES B. COLLINS is Professor of History at Georgetown University.

VALERIE KIVELSON is Associate Professor of History at the University of Michigan.

VICTOR LIEBERMAN is Professor of History at the University of Michigan.

R. I. MOORE is Professor of Medieval History at the University of Newcastle upon Tyne.

SANJAY SUBRAHMANYAM is Directeur d'etudes, Ecole des Hautes Etudes en Sciences Sociales, Paris.

JOHN K. WHITMORE is Adjunct Associate Professor of History at the University of Michigan.

DAVID K. WYATT is The John Stambaugh Professor of History at Cornell University.

Index